METALWORKING IN THE HOME SHOP

E.F. LINDSLEY

Drawings by Forrest J. Battles

Popular Science Books
New York

 Van Nostrand Reinhold Company
New York   Cincinnati   Toronto   London   Melbourne

Published by
Popular Science Books
Times Mirror Magazines, Inc.
380 Madison Avenue
New York, NY 10017

Distributed to the trade by
Van Nostrand Reinhold Company
135 West 50th Street
New York, NY 10020

Library of Congress Cataloging in Publication Data

Lindsley, E. F.
  Metalworking in the home shop

  Includes index.
  1. Metal-work—Amateurs' manuals. I. Title.
TT205.L57 1983   684'.09   83-15973
ISBN 0–442–25984–0

Manufactured in the United States of America

CONTENTS

METALWORKING IN THE HOME SHOP

INTRODUCTION TO METALWORKING

Metalworking is an extremely creative and satisfying craft. Once you've learned the basics, you can try your hand at a wide range of applications: making jewelry, wrought-iron decorations, or copper cookware; repairing appliances; restoring antique cars or airplanes; shaping tools and parts on a lathe; sculpting art objects. This book will get you started.

Nearly all the metalworking books I've seen are aimed at vocational education, to fit the student for a job in industry. There is no such intent here. This book is for the home-shop worker. It contains many skills taught me by my father, others learned as an aircraft mechanic, and still others acquired during countless happy hours in my own shop. There are practical reasons for learning these skills, not the least of which is the increasing difficulty of getting anyone to fix anything anymore. But the best reason I can think of is to experience the enjoyment of working with metal.

Try to picture our daily life without metal products and you'll realize that without metal we would all revert to the Stone Age. Until humans learned to work with metal, our tools, structures, weapons, and decorative objects were all made from mineral, animal, or vegetable materials. Although sometimes effective, even beautiful, they imposed formidable constraints on human activities.

Imagine, then, the excitement of the first worker in metal, this wonderfully strong, malleable stuff which could be shaped, formed, and sharpened. No longer was he forced to accept the forms supplied by nature in bone, stone, or wood. Now he could dream and create rather than merely adapt. You, too, will understand this joy of creating when you learn to shape and form metal.

METALWORKING TOOLS

Most metalworking tools are derived from tools originally used to work wood or stone. Like other materials, metal must be cut, shaved, and drilled. If you are even a fair amateur woodworker, you will soon come to recognize the common ground and the differences. For example, the wood saw, with its coarse teeth, has its counterpart in the hacksaw with its comparatively fine teeth. You simply don't have the muscle power to force coarse wood-saw teeth through metal. Put a wood auger bit in a brace, turn the handle, and great, clean, satisfying chips spiral out. You can also drill metal with a brace or breast drill, but the twist drill you use is slightly different from the wood auger. Although the chips will emerge much like wood chips, you must press much harder. Since muscles have only limited power, you'll probably switch to an electric drill.

1

The common woodworking lathe is matched by the metal-cutting lathe. But unlike the hand-held gouges and chisels of woodworking, the metal lathe tool is almost always fastened rigidly in a holder. The cutting edge of the tool must be forced into the metal with screw pressure and the chuck, the part that holds the work metal,

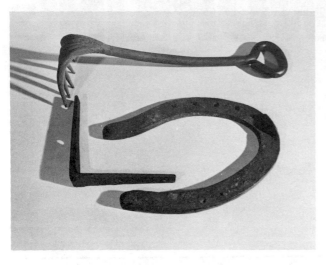

Historically, farmer, merchant, and householder depended on the blacksmith. The clawlike tool at top was used to remove nails from a keg at the general store; horseshoes were essential in the pre-motorized age; the shelf bracket was a home-convenience item. *Courtesy Lorleberg's Hardware Store, Oconomowoc, Wisconsin.*

must be ever so much firmer than the spur used for wood.

All of these rather self-evident observations deserve a bit more consideration since they contain two important points that will have a huge bearing on your future success in metalworking.

Most tools for working wood and other soft materials have thin, keen edges for severing or slicing fibers. Examine the end of an auger bit and you'll see two sharp, knifelike lips which cut the outer edges of the hole cleanly in the wood. Inside the circle cut by the edges you'll find two more sharp cutting lips which slice under and lift the waste wood out of the hole. Note that both pairs of cutting edges are quite thin. The fact that the steel of the auger bit is much stronger than the wood fibers makes this thinness possible.

Now, examine a common metal-cutting twist drill. An obvious difference is that the twist drill does not have a sharp, screwpointed center member to pull the drill into the work. Such a point would be destroyed immediately if you tried to feed it into a block of steel. Secondarily, if you think about it, this lack of a point also means that there is no real center to locate and hold the drill dead on your center mark. The metal-cutting twist drill cannot be centered easily and unless certain steps are taken it will wander off center when starting.

Observe, too, that the twist drill has no sharp

This modern blacksmith at the Kreissle Forge in Sarasota, Florida, is working wrought iron. Perhaps you'd rather build an intricately machined working model engine, below. Smithing and machining are only two of the metalworking arts you can pursue in your home shop.

Metalworking offers unlimited opportunities for creative art. This bronze bird in flight at the Tampa International Airport is part of several inspiring groups by Roy Butler.

The primitive worker in stone had to conform his finished tool to the shape of his raw material. Compare this prehistoric stone axe head, its handle mount broken away, with the skillfully shaped metal axe, below, from the Bronze Age. With metal, the worker could choose and plan his finished shape. This difference between stone and metal enormously expanded man's horizon. *Logan Museum of Anthropology, Beloit College.*

cutter lips to circumscribe the hole. Without these lips the auger would tend to splinter and break out the edges of the hole. Indeed, although wood can be, and often is, drilled with twist drills, the hole is never as clean as it would have been with an auger. Metal, lacking the splintery fibers of wood, can be drilled cleanly without the cutting lips. Finally, although the cutting edges of the twist drill are sharp, they are much less knifelike and are backed up by more metal. This is a fundamental of most metalworking. Most metal-cutting tools force or wedge aside the metal being cut rather than slicing it as do woodworking tools.

Further evidence of this is apparent if you examine the teeth of a crosscut wood saw. The teeth are actually a series of miniature knives,

each in turn "set," or bent out slightly from the main blade. They slice two slightly separated lines, or kerfs, in the wood. In soft wood you need scarcely more force than the weight of the saw. Compare this with the teeth of a hacksaw. Here, each tooth is like a tiny chisel. Each tooth must be driven into and under a fragment of metal to force it up and out of the cut.

In summary, metalworking tools are nearly always dependent on a fairly high level of force concentrated on a husky cutting edge. Depending upon the size of the tool, the hardness of the workpiece, and whether or not the tool is driven by an electric motor, human muscle force may or may not be adequate for effective cutting. An example is a ¼-inch electric drill. Even up to its full capacity, it is not difficult to force the drill point into ordinary mild steel if you can lean part of your body weight on it. Drilling may be quite tiring if you are in an awkward posture and unable to put your weight against the drill. The same hole could be drilled with a hand-powered breast drill, but that becomes even

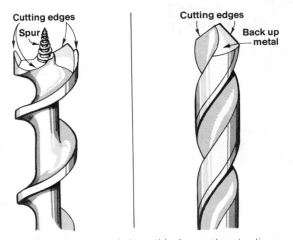

Woodworking tools commonly have thin, keen edges to slice or shave wood. Wood auger, left, has four such edges, plus a feed screw. Twist drill, right, has two cutting edges but they are not as thin because extra metal is needed to back up the cutting action. Also, there is no feed screw.

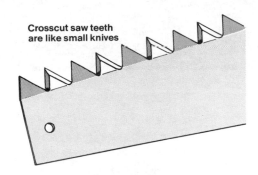

Look at the teeth of a crosscut wood saw and you'll find that they are much like two parallel rows of small knives.

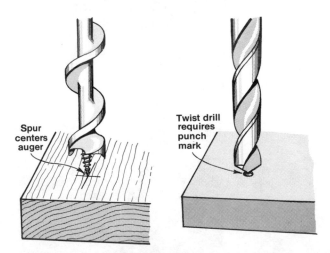

It's easy to center the feed screw of an auger bit exactly on the mark, but a twist drill will wander and start drilling off center unless you provide a center-punch dimple to locate it.

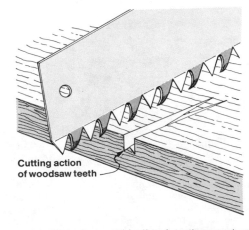

Each row of knives slices a thin line into the wood and the waste is easily forced out from between these lines.

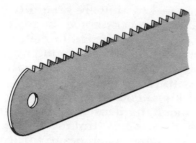

Although the teeth of a hacksaw blade are also "set" to make the cut slightly wider than the blade for easier sawing, they are more chisel-like than knife-like.

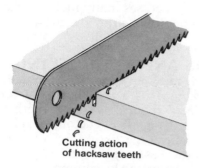

Cutting action of hacksaw teeth

Hacksaw teeth must bite underneath and force each chip out of the cut. The pressures on the teeth are higher than for wood; usually the work must be held firmly to resist this pressure.

more tiring. An enormous difference is apparent when you put the ¼-inch drill in a drill press and use the mechanical advantage of the feed lever. Now the drill seems to penetrate the steel almost effortlessly.

The powerful force needed to cut metal has two important consequences:

● The work metal usually must be firmly se-

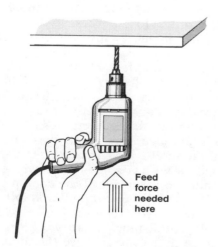

Overhead drilling might be fairly easy with a wood auger because of its feed screw, but it can quickly become hard work with a twist drill since you must supply the feed pressure.

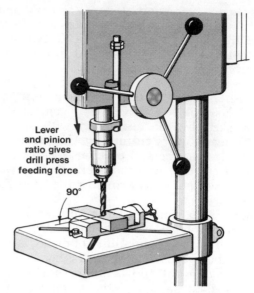

Lever and pinion ratio gives drill press feeding force

90°

Drill press not only aligns the drill squarely, but the rack-and-pinion feed and handle leverage give you a big mechanical advantage for applying pressure.

cured in some sort of gripping device to resist the pressure of the tool.

● Guides of some sort often are required to control the path of the tool since muscle power is not enough.

I've mentioned the common practice of whittling soft wood with the work gripped in one hand and the knife in the other. Or, consider the familiar wood-saw action where the board is secured on a sawhorse by the weight of your knee. Equivalent operations in metalworking might be sharpening a hoe or an axe with the tool held in one hand and a file in the other. Sometimes one sees an electrician or plumber hacksaw a piece of metal-clad BX cable or conduit while holding the work in his hand. Such techniques are limited. Both jobs are better done with the work solidly clamped in a vise.

THE MALLEABILITY OF METAL

So far I've stressed that metal is more resistant to cutting and drilling than wood and therefore demands specialized tools. But metal possesses another important property: malleability. All common metals can be shaped by forging, bending, pressing, and stretching. Whereas nearly all wooden shapes are formed by cutting away waste stock, metal can be hammered into the desired form.

The ferrous metals, iron and steel and their alloys, cannot be readily forged or shaped without heating them until they become plastic. Exceptions are various cold-forming operations in industry using enormous force. Car body and chassis parts shaped in huge presses are examples. So are a vast number of bolts, screws, and other small items formed under great pressure, often with a succession of blows.

But these are industrial, not home-shop, processes. Other, softer metals such as aluminum, copper, brass, pewter, silver, and gold are so easily worked by the craftsman with simple tools that nearly every culture, even in primitive times, created artifacts of precious metal peculiar to that culture. Enormous elaboration was possible, as with ancient armor or the King Tut treasures.

As might be expected, a large number of special techniques have evolved that make use of the malleability and bendability of metal. Later, we'll talk about those of use in the home shop, including laying out and bending sheet metal, forming steel strap and rods, forging simple tools, and spin shaping. Any one of these is a skill in its own right. Many hobbyists derive great satisfaction from such specialties as working in pewter, brass, or jewelry metals.

CASTING METAL

Another aspect of metalworking which has no equivalent in woodworking is casting molten metal into a mold. Casting was probably the first of the metalworking processes. Some may debate this since forgers of the bits and pieces of raw native metal were also common in primitive times. Historical arguments aside, it is not hard to imagine the delight of a tribesman who had managed to smelt an ore into metal and then allowed the molten metal to trickle into the form of his hand or foot pressed into the sand. From here one can only conjecture about the experiments and accidental discoveries that led to the magnificent bronze castings of early history.

Although we can only imagine the primitive hearth, the simple fact that metal can be melted and poured into a mold of a desired shape must have been one of mankind's greatest discoveries. No longer did he have to adapt his work to the shape of a stone or a bone.

Iron or steel casting are generally beyond the practical range of the home shop because of the heating equipment needed to melt ferrous metals. Many other metals, including aluminum, antimony, lead, and gold and silver can be melted with relative ease in simple gas-fired or charcoal kilns. Poured into suitable molds, the molten metal hardens into the desired form. Castings may range from working parts for small models and machines to intricate jewelry settings. The molds may be formed in a simple flask or box filled with sand, or in plaster by melting out wax patterns. The opportunities are almost endless, and after experimenting with the various processes many metalworkers settle on a technique they enjoy the most.

REPAIRS AND REMODELING

Although it may not exactly fit the definition of metalworking, it is a fact that most repairs on metal objects require taking something apart and putting it together. The object might be an appliance, plumbing fixture, or a small engine. As you gather experience you soon learn that there are certain fairly common and standard ways used to assemble most equipment. You also learn, the hard way, that there are some common pitfalls and booby traps.

In comparison to the limited ways wood pieces go together, normally with nails, screws, bolts, and glue, there are dozens of ways to assemble metal components. For example, parts may be drilled for bolts, tapped for threads, riveted, welded, brazed, soldered with soft or hard solder, pinned, staked, held by setscrews, held on a taper, keyed, shrunk in place, pressed in place, folded over in seams, locked with tabs, or even glued with special adhesives. Usually the first part of a repair job is to determine how to disassemble things to get access to the defective part without damage to the rest of the equipment.

Consider, for example, the following jobs: The door handle on your freezer is loose. Tightening the screws requires, first, determining if the screws are standard slotted heads, Phillips heads, or something else. If you then decide that the threads no longer hold tightly, you must determine if the screws are threaded into the door metal, such as with a sheet-metal screw, or if there are nuts on the inside of the door. Are they captive nuts or will they drop off and fall down inside the door if you remove the screws? The latter would entail much more work than you started out to do just to retrieve the nuts. Your decisions will govern your procedures.

Or, how about a garden spade with a broken handle? Should you file or grind off the old rivet to replace the handle? Might it be better to centerpunch and drill them out? Should you use slightly larger rivets because the old holes are worn? Whatever route you choose you're not likely to cause serious trouble.

Another typical job could be replacing a worn or broken pulley on a washing machine or a lawn tractor. Replacement may be no problem if you can remove the old pulley. But the pulley may be retained by a setscrew, taper pin, key and setscrew, or a retaining nut and a taper. The retaining nut may be right-hand or left-hand thread. These are things that only careful inspection can reveal. Even after removing the screw, pin, or other retainer, the old pulley may be rusted firmly on the shaft. What kind of puller is needed to remove it? Would it help to apply some heat with a propane torch? Would that be dangerous, perhaps because of a nearby gas tank, line, or electrical wiring? As you gain practice in metalworking, such thought processes will become habitual.

Equally important, if you take a little time for examination and analysis as you take things apart, you'll learn why they failed or don't work properly. You'll learn to spot wear, looseness, tight bearings, and corrosive damage. Such knowledge helps in diagnosing what's wrong when our complicated devices for living act up.

Even if mechanical repair is not your favorite activity, most householders become involved with plumbing and appliances. Even a garbage disposer or dishwasher requires drain and water-supply connections. Such connections are not difficult to make but you must know how to handle the wrenches needed for pipe, how to cut and flare tubing, perhaps how to solder copper fittings and how to recognize a tapered pipe thread compared to a straight thread. These skills are basic to metalworking. They also apply to running electrical conduits, replacing the exhaust muffler on your tractor, and dozens of other jobs which are expensive, bothersome, or sometimes poorly done if you call in a pro.

ARTS AND PROJECTS
If repairs and remodeling don't excite you, metalworking offers a multitude of other outlets. Admirers of wrought-iron railings, hand-forged pot hooks, and fancy hinges or personally designed fireplace tools can originate or reproduce such items at will. If you want to build playground swings or children's play cars, boat docks or trailers, they are all in the home shop range. On a more delicate scale, even apartment-size shops can be the birthplace of art objects, graceful decorative items, jewelry, or personal-

If you'd like to try ironwork, why not start with fireplace tools such as these homemade log tongs. Design your own.

Soft art metal taking form under the craftman's hammer can be shaped into either a decorative or useful object. This is one of the most satisfying skills in metalworking. *Courtesy Fine Arts Dept., University of Wisconsin.*

This partially finished silver tankard is a good example of fine-arts metalworking. Tool marks from the forming operations are still visible, and the roughly shaped handle must be finished and attached. *Courtesy Fine Arts Dept., University of Wisconsin.*

ized gifts from ashtrays to flowerbasket supports. For many metalworkers, making jewelry is a consuming interest, and some combine it with the lapidary arts. It's almost certain that somewhere in metalworking, from repairs to creative enterprises, you'll find personal enjoyment and perhaps a release from everyday pressures. You may even find that working with metal enhances your ability to think logically and examine alternate procedures fully.

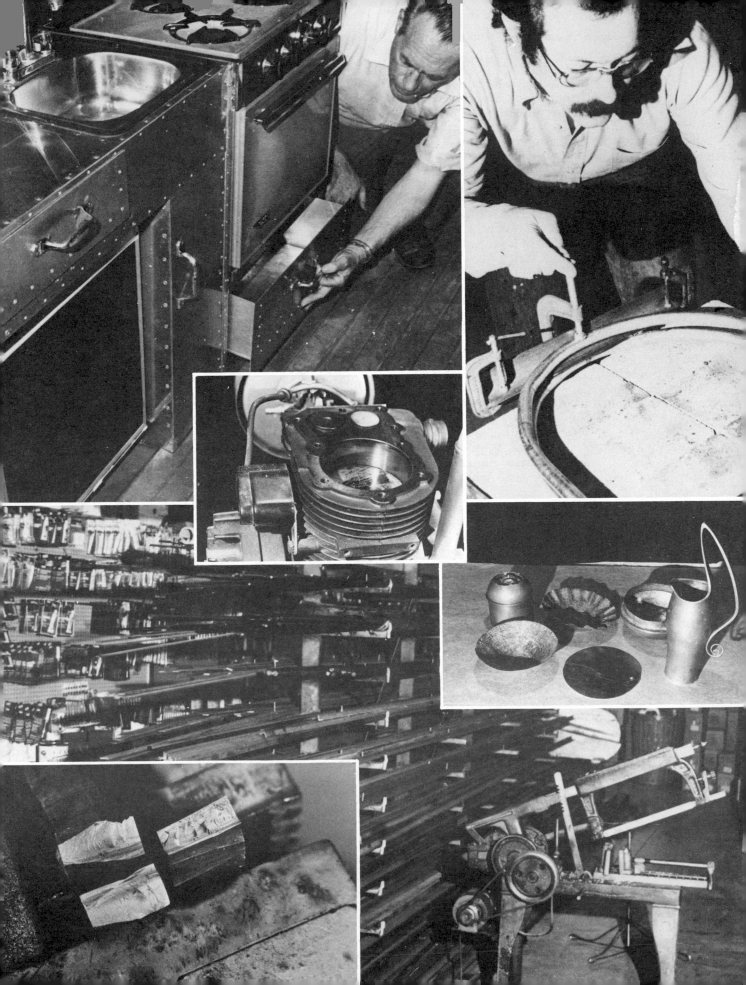

PART I
METALS FOR THE HOME SHOP

1. IRON AND STEEL

You don't have to do much woodworking to become familiar with the common home shop woods. Ordinary pine is easily distinguished from oak, and oak from maple, walnut, or mahogany. Much the same is true of metals used in the home shop. It's easy to tell steel from lead, brass, or copper. Few of us would confuse cast iron with silver, gold, or platinum. But aside from such obvious differences, metals are much more difficult to identify than woods. Their most important characteristics are not often visible as grain or color; more often they relate to how the metal performs when heated in a certain way to harden or soften them.

Cast iron, steel, copper, and aluminum are all products of complex extracting and refining processes. The basic metals are then treated, alloyed, worked, subjected to processing, and manipulated in thousands of ways to suit an infinite variety of industrial purposes.

In the home shop, however, it usually suffices to know that rigid copper pipe is different from soft copper tubing. Or that the hard steel in a knife blade is different from the soft steel used to form shapes for car bodies. The soft, easily dented aluminum in a kitchen pot may look like the high-strength alloy used in aircraft construction, but the former can be bent with finger pressure, the latter cannot. The working characteristics of a metal are much more important than its specific chemical makeup.

Most woodworkers soon recognize that a piece of wood suited for use as a 2×4 or a fence rail won't bend properly to the contours of a boat. Some woods accept a nail readily; others split frustratingly. By the same token, metalworkers have to know that ordinary mild steel is readily drilled and cut but stainless steel can be very hard to drill or cut; that brass, although it appears soft, will snag and break a drill or lathe bit that has been sharpened to handle steel with ease; that aluminum and copper bend and hammer-form very easily for a short while, but then harden and must be softened (annealed) before going on. The main things to know about your metals are the best ways to work them and how they will behave.

Only a few metals are occasionally found as actual, metallic substances. Among these are copper, gold, silver, platinum, and mercury—the last certainly not a home-shop metal. Such native metals are usually mixed with or bedded in rock, sand, and foreign substances which must be broken away.

With the above exceptions most common metals are encountered as ores. Such ores are sometimes complex chemical combinations of the metal with sulfur, carbon, silica, and oxygen. In the simplest chemical terms, some of the outer

Most woodworkers will quickly spot the woods above as, left to right, maple, oak, walnut, and mahogany; and such metals below as aluminum, brass, steel, and lead can be recognized in a broad sense. But who can tell what the alloy content of these metals might be? Fortunately, this is seldom really critical in the home shop.

Both of these pieces are steel, but the piece on the left is mild steel with a low carbon content. It bends and dents readily. High-carbon tool steel, right, is hard as glass and shattered when struck with a hammer.

ring electrons in the metal atom have been borrowed by the combining nonmetallic substance. Restoring the metal to a useable metallic state thus becomes a chemical or electrical process. Quite often it involves providing the ore with still another substance from which the electrons are more readily borrowed so that those belonging to the metal are returned. Producing iron and steel from ore is a classic example of such a process.

CAST IRON

One might think of iron ore as iron rust or oxidized iron. Its chemical formula is Fe_2O_3, which means that a molecule of iron ore is composed of two atoms of iron (Fe) and three of oxygen (O). The ore is heated in a furnace, and carbon (C) is added in the form of coke. The purpose of the carbon is to combine with the oxygen now sharing electrons with the iron. Carbon does this readily under the proper temperature conditions. The simplified chemical reaction is $2Fe_2O_3 + 3C = 4Fe + 3CO_2$. Since CO_2 (carbon dioxide) is a gas, it can be carried away as such.

Sand, or silicon dioxide, is also commonly present in ore, and for this reason limestone or calcium carbonate is also added. This ends up producing glassy calcium silicate as slag. The slag floats on the iron and may be drawn off as a liquid.

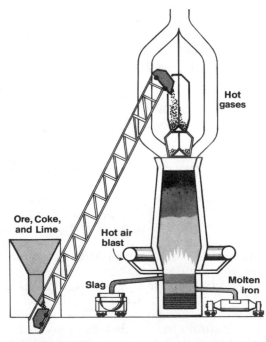

To convert crude iron ore to metal requires heat and carbon to combine with the oxygen that is part of the ore. Lime is also added to remove silicon, the other main impurity.

Low-grade cast iron, used for many common objects, fractures sharply when struck. It will also crack if heated unevenly.

High-quality cast iron is tough and provides an excellent wearing surface for this engine cylinder.

When iron is produced in a blast furnace as described, it is drawn off in a molten state and either passed along to the steel-making process or poured (cast) into molds where it cools to form pigs of cast iron. Such pig iron may later be melted and cast into molds for some useful object, but it is characteristically hard and brittle, and lacks strength. It is really only suited for cheap products or those of considerable mass and weight. For the home shop, low-grade cast iron is usually disappointing to work with since it cannot be annealed or hardened readily and tends to crack easily.

The most important thing to understand about cast iron is that most of its undesirable characteristics are caused by large amounts of carbon and other impurities. As might be guessed, some of the carbon used to remove the oxygen in the blast furnace ends up dissolved in the iron.

This concept of carbon content is a sort of jumping-off place for the metalworker. In due course you'll learn to think in terms of the amount of carbon present in the steel you'll work with. We'll discuss this shortly. Meanwhile, crude cast iron may have 2% to 7.5% carbon. This doesn't mean it can't be made into a useful material. There are many extremely useful varieties of cast iron, some developed only in recent years.

As a beginning improvement, white cast iron from the blast furnace may be changed in structure by careful heating and prolonged cooling to produce malleable iron, a stronger and tougher material. Such iron is commonly used for hardware items such as hooks and rough tools. An example might be an ordinary shop C-clamp.

Some of the cheapest, made of white iron, will crack suddenly if overtightened. Others, usually marked as "malleable iron," will bend or distort before breaking.

Gray iron is another form of iron of great usefulness in foundry casting because it flows with comparative ease into tortuous contours and passages. It also provides an extremely good wearing surface after machining and is the common material for cylinder blocks and pistons in engines. Still other casting irons are used for such highly stressed products as engine crankshafts. These are sometimes called nodular irons and ductile irons. Their characteristics depend on the pattern of their crystalline structures and the way their carbon is dispersed.

WROUGHT IRON

True wrought iron is not common today; most of the ornamental ironwork we see is actually mild steel. The old reverberatory furnaces produced a product called wrought iron containing 0.3% or less carbon. This iron could be hand forged, twisted, stretched, and drawn into a thousand shapes by the old-time blacksmith. One of its greatest advantages was that it could be welded simply by fluxing the two pieces with borax and hammering them together while the metal was hot and plastic. Remember, this preceded gas and electric welding by many years.

Some of wrought iron's characteristics stemmed from rolling or squeezing the soft iron as it came from the furnace. This distributed the remaining slag through the metal much like small fibers. In truth, wrought iron was not a closely controlled product in the days before metal analysis and it varied greatly from batch to batch. It is interesting to read the old memoirs of blacksmiths. Some irons were praised and others given salty damnation. An extra bit of sulfur, for example, made the iron extremely hard to weld. Lacking significant carbon, these dubious grades of iron were also short of another important property—they could not be hardened and tempered. Thus, their use was confined to rude agricultural tools and hardware that did not require either a keen edge or springiness.

STEEL FROM IRON

The usefulness of cast iron is limited by four impurities—carbon, silicon, sulfur, and phosphorus. To produce steel from raw iron these impurities must be removed or reduced in amount. A number of steel-making processes have evolved over the years starting with the reverberatory furnace and followed by the Bessemer converter, the open hearth, and the more modern basic-oxygen process. Still further refining may be done in electric furnaces and vacuum processors. The latter processes are primarily aimed at producing carefully formulated, high-grade, alloy steels after the basic conversion to steel from cast iron.

Without becoming too deeply involved in the complexities of making steel, we can note that the process consists of removing excess carbon by heating the metal to the molten state and exposing it to oxygen from either an air blast or by introducing pure oxygen. The carbon combines with the oxygen to produce either CO (carbon monoxide) or CO_2 (carbon dioxide). The process must be precisely controlled to consume the carbon without oxidizing the steel. The three remaining impurities are less easily removed. Their removal is accomplished by adding materials, or coating the vessel interior, with so-called basic chemicals such as calcium oxide and magnesium oxide, which combine with the impurities to form slag. Periodically the process must be checked by sampling and analyzing the batch of steel to be certain the final product will meet the specified carbon content.

Modern steels contain fewer impurities than the old wrought iron, but most important, their carbon content is closely controlled between less than 0.30% for very soft, nonhardenable, to 2.0%, the latter extremely hard after heat treatment. Although there are many finely divided grades of steel for commercial purposes, the home metalworker has no real way to identify the usual material he works with except in a general way. The ordinary carbon steels can be classified as: low carbon, easily worked and

METAL WEIGHTS

Material	Chemical Symbol	Weight, in Pounds Per Cubic Inch	Weight, in Pounds Per Cubic Foot
Aluminum	Al	.093	160
Antimony	Sb	.2422	418
Brass	—	.303	524
Bronze	—	.320	552
Chromium	Cr	.2348	406
Copper	Cu	.323	450
Gold	Au	.6975	1205
Iron (cast)	Fe	.260	450
Iron (wrought)	Fe	.2834	490
Lead	Pb	.4105	710
Manganese	Mn	.2679	463
Mercury	Hg	.491	849
Molybdenum	Mo	.309	534
Monel	—	.318	550
Platinum	Pt	.818	1413
Steel (mild)	Fe	.2816	490
Steel (stainless)	—	.277	484
Tin	Sn	.265	459
Titanium	Ti	.1278	221
Zinc	Zn	.258	446

Although metals differ widely in color and strength, they also have remarkable variations in weight. Surprisingly, aluminum, one of the lightest, and gold and lead, among the heaviest, are all soft metals.

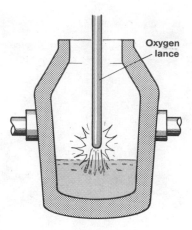

Making steel is basically a process of refining iron and bringing its chemical structure to a condition suited for the products to be made from it. The first step is to lower the carbon content and further eliminate impurities. Here, an oxygen jet is directed into the molten metal under high pressure.

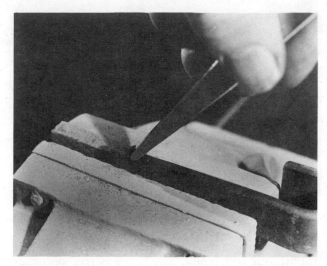

Hardened, high-carbon steel in this cold chisel cuts mild steel easily. The carbon content masks the difference.

welded but nonhardenable; medium carbon, a harder, tougher grade often used for tools and hardware; and high carbon for products such as cutting tools and precision parts which must be hardened after working.

There are simple spark tests made by touching a sample of steel to a grinding wheel that help establish the approximate carbon content. These classic spark tests are shown for your experimentation but you'll soon find out that such rule-of-thumb tests can be misleading, hard to judge, and confused by the addition of alloys to the basic carbon steels. One quick way to judge a steel sample is to heat a small area to cherry red and plunge it into water. If this makes no

difference and you can still file the steel easily afterwards, it's low-carbon steel. If it is definitely harder to file but you can still file it, it's probably a medium carbon. If it becomes glass hard to the file it's high-carbon or alloy steel.

The high-carbon steels make excellent cutting tools for woodworking and manual metalworking. Indeed, many metalworkers salvage such metals from old car springs and like parts for personalized chisels, screwdrivers, and the like. It should be noted that many modern alloy steels are better suited to mass production processes and are commonly used in the edge tools found today in hardware stores. Unfortunately, a few hours spent working with a 75-year-old Buck

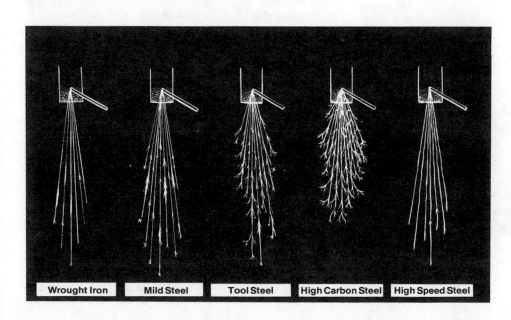

Wrought Iron   Mild Steel   Tool Steel   High Carbon Steel   High Speed Steel

No metalworking book would be complete without showing the classic spark tests to determine the nature of an unknown steel. Be warned, however, that few modern steels really produce the sparks the pictures show. The tests worked better years ago when steels were less complex.

Bros. chisel, for example, reveals with painful clarity that the old-timers knew what they were doing in spite of their lack of sophisticated metallurgical analysis.

HIGH-SPEED STEEL
High-carbon steels were, and are, great for hand tools such as chisels, knives, and manually powered drills. They do not, however, take kindly to overheating. If, while sharpening a high-carbon steel chisel, you accidentally hold it too long in one place on the grinding wheel, or press too hard, the edge instantly turns blue. The metal in the dark area is now ruined; it cannot be sharpened to a durable cutting edge. You must now grind it back slowly and carefully to clean metal and resharpen. The same is true of a carbon steel twist drill. Such a drill can easily be overheated and turn dull, soft, and blue at the tip when used with an ordinary electric drill. If you have inherited a collection of such old drills, confine their use to wood and soft materials or use them only with a hand drill. This vulnerability to heat is not acceptable with modern power tools.

About fifty years ago an alloy steel was developed called high-speed steel. Nearly all tools for drilling, lathework, and milling are today made of high-speed steel or an alloy with an equivalent ability to work at high temperatures and self-harden. When shopping for drills and cutters for your power tools always look for the words "High-Speed Steel" on the tool or package.

High-speed steel is just a broad term for a variety of alloy steels used for cutting tools. There are literally hundreds of alloy steels

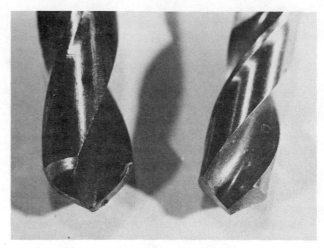

Carbon-steel twist drill, left, is badly burned by use in an electric drill. High-speed steel drill, right, is undamaged.

containing, among other things, chromium, manganese, molybdenum, nickle, vanadium, tungsten, and cobalt. Each adds certain characteristics such as toughness, shock resistance, corrosion resistance as in stainless steel, fine grain structure, and so on, singly or in combination. Again, unless you have access to a controlled source for such steels there is no way you can identify them.

TUNGSTEN CARBIDE
Even high-speed steel and alloy steels cannot withstand the speeds and temperatures of modern production machinery. A much harder and more resistant metal-like product is made by combining powdered tungsten and carbon in a heat and pressure process. You can usually recognize a tungsten-carbide cutting edge because it is dark in color and is brazed onto the base tool just at the cutting edge. If you're a woodworker you probably have a circular saw or two with individual carbide teeth brazed onto the main steel disc of the saw. Or, you may have carbide-tipped router bits. In each case, the tools stay sharp much longer than high-speed or carbon-steel tools. The only problem is that they are also much harder than the common aluminum-oxide grinding wheels of home-shop grinders. You cannot sharpen them by grinding or filing. Special diamond wheels are required and resharpening is essentially an industrial process.

IDENTIFYING STEELS
As suggested, there are so many grades and compositions of steel that trying to do more than be

Burned chisel edge from careless sharpening shows that overheating has destroyed hardness at the edge. Tool is useless until burned metal has been ground away without overheating.

aware of them becomes an academic exercise for the home-shop worker. If you wish to pursue the study of carbon steels, alloy steels, their hardenability characteristics, and so on, I suggest that you consult a Society of Automotive Engineers (SAE) handbook. You will find lengthy tabulations of various steels listed according to their SAE numbers.

The basic numbering system assigns numbers, starting with the number 1, to various steel groups. Thus, a carbon steel would carry the number 10xx, with numbers such as 11xx, 12xx, and so on indicating the various heat-treatment processes in manufacture. The last two digits, shown as "xx" above, show the carbon content in hundredths of one percent. In the interest of accuracy, the following brief quote directly from a recent SAE handbook summarizes the numbering system in a general way:

"A numeral index system is used to identify the compositions of the SAE steels, which system makes possible the use of numerals on shop drawings and blueprints to describe partially the composition of the material. The first digit indicates the type to which a steel belongs, that is, '1' indicates a carbon steel; '2' a nickel steel; and '3' a nickel-chromium steel. In the case of the simple alloy steels, the second digit generally indicates an alloy or alloy combination, and sometimes the approximate percentage of the predominant alloying element. Usually, the last three digits indicate the approximate carbon content in "points" or hundredths of one percent. Thus, "SAE 5135" indicates a chromium steel of approximately 1% chromium (.80 to 1.05%) and 0.35% carbon (0.33 to 0.38%)."

HOME-SHOP STEEL

Few home-shop metalworkers need to worry about such exotic metallurgy. Unless your work is more advanced than is expected of readers of this book, you will more often than not be using salvaged scrap metal and metal bought over the counter at your hardware store. Your tool bits, drills, and reamers will be purchased and will have the proper alloy content.

Probably 90% of your projects will be built with ordinary mild steel. If you go to the hardware store and want a rod or a bar it will normally be offered in fractional dimensions of ¼", ⅜", ½", and perhaps ¾" or 1". Usually this product will be labeled CRS, meaning "cold-rolled steel." Such steel is low in carbon and cannot be hardened or tempered, but it is well suited to bending, twisting, turning in a lathe, or even heating and hammering into a shape.

Do not expect cold-rolled steel to carry heavy loads. You might, for example, use it without question for the axles of a child's kiddy-kar or small wagon. Typically, you'd use ½" or 9⁄16" diameter rods and mount the wheels on ball bearings or bushings. But if you intended to use the axle for something heavier, such as a lawn roller

Storage rack at the author's local hardware store holds a wealth of sizes and shapes of mild steel stock. If you plan metal purchases carefully, you can often get pieces cut to proper length at the store. Even if they charge for it you can save a lot of sawing if you lack power metal-cutting equipment. They use a power hacksaw, foreground.

or a high-speed racing go-kart, it would be better to buy drill rod. You'll notice that CRS is not finished to great smoothness, but drill rod has a polished and ground surface, being more accurately controlled in its finished dimensions. You pay, of course, for this extra quality. Drill rod is also much stiffer. If you clamp a piece of CRS in a vise by one end and tug it a little, you'll find that you have imparted a little bend. The same force will not bend drill rod.

You will also find that if you heat drill rod to blood red and quickly quench it in water it will resist a file more than in its original state. Hardware-store drill rod is not fine tool steel and has its limitations, but it does provide a fairly inexpensive metal for projects.

STRIPS, RODS, AND TUBES

Flat mild steel is available at hardware stores in strips ranging from ½" to sometimes 2" wide, and from about ¹⁄₁₆" to ¼" thick. The clerk will shear or saw off almost any length you want. Sometimes you can buy it with a bright, clean surface but it usually comes with a dull black surface from the rolling and pickling process. Such steel is enormously handy for homebuilt hardware, wrought decorative gates and grills, reinforcing household structures, and most routine jobs.

Your local hardware store will also have a variety of angle and channel shapes. Angle iron, with two faces forming a right angle, is usually available in dimensions from about ½" to 2" or even larger. Channel iron, with two upright legs like a shallow U is also a common item. Together, they can be used for almost anything from a boat trailer to a pier, supports for a carport, or playground equipment. Remember, this is all mild steel, which can be welded with home-shop equipment, is easily drilled, sawed, bent hot or cold, and is strong enough for most home purposes.

Steel tubing is less easily found. In many cases you might build a light structure from electrical conduit, but it was never intended to support heavy loads. Even black iron or galvanized pipe is often useful; so is well casing and well pipe. Heavy pipe for such industrial uses, sometimes referred to as "schedule 40" is especially good for strong structures, such as children's swing sets, cantilevered deck and patio structures, and anything where strength and rigidity are vital. Usually, you will have to buy such metal from a commercial user such as a well driller, industrial plumber, or blacksmith. For square tubing and special shapes such as bannister rail your first step is probably the Yellow Pages for a nearby vendor of commercial metal.

Be inventive with materials you can obtain. Here, electrical conduit, not intended for structural use, shapes up just fine for the legs of a sewing table.

My review of what's available at the local hardware store may sound hollow if your hardware store is primarily a vendor of appliances, pots and pans, and small tools in a flossy shopping center. Hardware stores which have angle iron and the like must first of all have room to store such heavy material in racks and the saws, shears, and manpower to cut it. Most important, they must have customers who buy it. If you draw a blank look at the store in the shopping mall, try the barnlike, rural hardware store with flyspecked windows and clerks in bib overalls.

It's quite possible that your metalworking may not require this type of structural material. You may want small scraps from stampings or cut-offs from machine tool production. Although tons of such stuff are hauled away from large industrial plants each day, officially, and in lunch boxes and pockets unofficially, such plants are simply not organized to sell to buyers who want to paw through scrap bins and who might get cut doing so. A better choice is to locate small metalworking shops of the less-than-six-employee variety. The owner may even take an interest in your projects, offer good suggestions, or dig out just the metal you're looking for.

At the same time, it's worthwhile to ask about acquiring old reamers, drills, counterbore tools, and milling cutters. Often such tools become worn, too short, or a thousandth or two undersize and unsuited for commercial production use. Many, with a little touching up on the grinder, serve well in the home shop. Another good source of such tools is the small, independent grinding shops that resharpen industrial tools. They, too, have scrap or reject tools well worth having.

SHEET STEEL

Aside from galvanized iron, used in roof and gutter work, you may find it difficult to buy sheet steel. This is especially true if you need large sheets since the main users are industrial plants and it's seldom sold at retail. The same is true of flat plate stock in the heavier thicknesses. Your best choice here is to check the phone book for a commercial steel dealer. Although he may not encourage your trade he usually has cut-offs and trimmings that may be useful. Moreover, he has large shears and cutting equipment to bring such stock to haulable size and weight. When you visit such a source it pays to know what you want and have a little sketch with dimensions on it. Buying to size costs a little more, but it can save a lot of very hard work.

2.
ALUMINUM: A HOME SHOP FAVORITE

If I had a choice of metals for any given project, I'd choose to work with aluminum. This is purely a personal feeling, just as some woodworkers prefer maple, or walnut, or pine. Others might prefer to work with brass, or even copper, gold, or silver. Perhaps my preference goes back to experience as an aircraft mechanic in the days when the so-called streamline cowlings, wheel pants, and flowing fillets were crafted from flat sheets. I like the clean, neat silver of aluminum, but someone else may prefer the glowing warmth of brass or the robust gleam of copper. Metals, like woods, have a character both in the way they work and the way they look as a finished product.

Aluminum is a soft metal in the sense that in its mostly pure state it can be bent, hammered, and impressed into forms without heating. Aluminum is also well suited to spin forming without extreme force. Also, aluminum melts at a fairly low temperature, about 1220°F, and this makes it an easy metal to cast in the home-shop foundry.

Some aluminum alloys can be brought to a fairly hard state by adding other materials, and by work hardening, but they are still easily drilled and filed. Aluminum cannot be brought to the glass hardness of quenched tool steel. Best of all, aluminum is fun to work with and that's the main reason it is so popular with home metalworkers.

PRODUCING ALUMINUM

Unlike the early processes for recovering other metals, practical recovery of aluminum was not achieved until 1886 when the genius of Charles Martin Hall found a way to produce aluminum by electrolysis. This is an odd fact since one-twelfth of the earth's crust is estimated to contain aluminum, and it is one of the most common substances in nature. Bauxite ore, containing aluminum hydroxide, cannot be smelted like iron ore since aluminum is a very active lender of electrons and the exchange process with carbon used for iron ore will not work.

It long seemed apparent that bauxite could be returned to its metallic aluminum state if some way could be found to replace the electrons the aluminum had loaned to form aluminum oxide. Hall found that a white mineral, cryolite, when heated and melted, acts as a solvent for the alumina and provides an electrolyte. By immersing large carbon electrodes in a boxlike cell, also lined with carbon, and passing a heavy current through the contents, the necessary melting takes place, the electrons needed are added to

Aluminum, with its no-rust, no-rot features, proved an easily worked material for the sink and cabinet in this camper.

the aluminum oxide, and the metal collects at the bottom of the cell.

Recent technology has developed other solvent materials, but the process still depends on high levels of electrical power. Some texts say it takes 12KwHrs of electrical energy to produce 1 pound of aluminum. This is the reason that aluminum can be recycled economically.

ALUMINUM FOR SPECIAL JOBS

Each of the soft metals has certain special features which make it the best choice for a given job. Aluminum has the obvious advantage of lightness. It's easy to handle in the shop and the finished product is easily moved, carried, or towed behind a car.

But aluminum has one notable disadvantage. It is difficult to weld without special equipment. It is also difficult to solder. The problem is an oxide coating which intrudes and prevents adhesion. You can see evidence of this when you scrape or sandpaper aluminum so it is bright and shiny. Almost immediately the exposed aluminum combines with the oxygen in the air to form an oxide coating on the surface.

Even so, because of its automatic protective coating, aluminum may be exposed, unpainted, for years, to the sun, wind, and rain without significant harm. Boat masts, flagpoles, and lawn furniture prove this. But aluminum does not take kindly to some corrosive agents such as road or sea salts, and it behaves even worse when it is part of a structure containing other

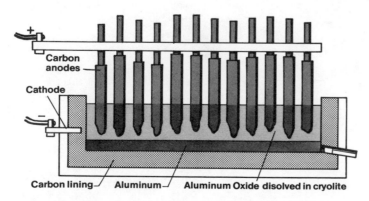

Carbon anodes

Cathode

Carbon lining   Aluminum   Aluminum Oxide disolved in cryolite

To convert aluminum ore to metal it is necessary to supply electrons from an outside source. This is done by dissolving the ore and passing a heavy electrical current through it. Recycling scrap aluminum is easier.

active metals such as copper. Even steel rivets or bolts are trouble sources. This results from a galvanic action because the atomic structure of aluminum places it as one of the very active metals.

SHAPES AND SIZES

One of the great features of aluminum is the ease with which manufacturers can extrude useful shapes in broad variety. The extrusion process resembles squeeezing toothpaste from a tube except that enormous pressure is needed. The outlet from the press is shaped to produce the desired form. From the metalworker's standpoint this wonderful selection of shapes and sizes presents a mouthwatering array of possibilities. Thumb through the pages of an aluminum manufacturer's catalog and you'll find a surprising number of shapes.

Another advantage of aluminum is that the most common shapes—rods, angles, tubing, and channels—are usually stocked at nearly all hardware stores. As supplied, this aluminum is soft enough to cut with a hacksaw, even a fine-tooth woodsaw, or a carbide-toothed bench saw. There are tricks and hazards to all of these operations and we'll talk about them later. For example, soft as it is, aluminum extrusions are somewhat work-hardened and a little known process of shop annealing can make them much easier to form.

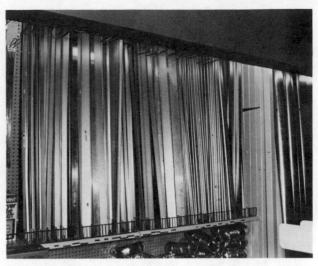

Aluminum rack at the hardware store offers a remarkable variety of forms and sizes. Other racks have prefab screen and window stock, moldings, and other shapes suited to adaptation.

Sheet aluminum in larger sizes is not easily purchased. You can buy a variety of punched out and embossed panels for screening and decorative use, but few stores carry wide sheets. They do, however, carry sheets or rolls about 24" wide and 1/32" thick for use as roof valleys and flashings. These will often serve, but if you need sheets wider and thicker you'll have to go to your local commercial warehouse.

3.
COPPER, BRASS AND PRECIOUS METALS

Ask the purely practical home-shop craftsman about copper and he'll probably talk about copper tubing for water pipes, fuel lines, and wire for electrical hookups. The same question directed to a metalworking artisan may bring a long discussion on handworking copper into artifacts, vessels, pots, trays, and representations of things real and imagined. Anyone who has ever passed through Tampa, Florida's airport has seen the magnificently crafted, suspended copper creations of birds in flight. They are the work of Roy R. Butler, a truly skilled and imaginative artist/craftsman.

Or, ask an archeologist, and you'll be rewarded with a discussion of ancient weapons, art objects, fishing and hunting implements, and exotic ceremonial equipment. Moreover, almost any museum has a number of man-made copper objects which have survived through the ages.

Each of the above viewpoints tells you something about copper. Its use by the ancients was probably the result of virgin metal being found in a soft and workable state and ready for use after crushing and breaking away the rocks containing it. The very fact that this metal survived over geological ages testifies to copper's remarkable durability and resistance to weathering. Thus, workability and durability add up to all the other uses I've mentioned. Copper outlasts

other metals in plumbing pipes, roof coverings, and gutters. And since copper is not only workable, but also ductile, it can be drawn (stretched) into wire and formed into vessels or art objects by hand.

Today, of course, native copper is not commercially produced as such. Most copper is found in complex chemical combinations, and the extractive processes from these ores are too involved to detail here. But copper still retains all its old virtues, not the least of which is the ability to develop a surface patina which is both attractive and protective.

HARD AND SOFT COPPER
Like aluminum, copper work hardens. This means that any method of mechanical manipulation—hammering, drawing, stretching, or bending—causes it to become progressively harder and more resistant to the craftsman's touch. However, the addition of small amounts of alloys will produce a stiffer and stronger material such as rigid copper pipe. Installing this type of pipe in a new house speeds the work, but if you are faced with snaking in water lines to a dishwasher or other appliance you may find it much easier to use soft tubing which is readily bent and directed as needed.

Even so, if you do enough trial-and-error

Another example of Roy Butler's work in metal sculpture, this bird, as well as the pilings and rest of setting, are all formed from copper. On display at Tampa International Airport.

bending you'll find the soft tubing getting more obstinate and maybe kinking or cracking. The same would be true if you were hammering out a tray or vessel. The answer is a process called annealing. Simply heat the copper to a cherry red and quench it or let it cool and it will regain its ductility. There is a myth that the Indians discovered a secret way to harden copper. Actually, about all they discovered was that the more you hammered the stuff the harder it got. Whether they found out how to anneal it is unknown.

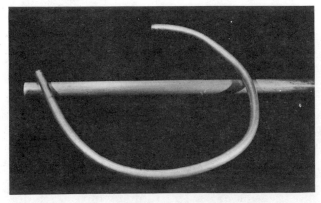

Soft copper tubing, curved piece, is usually sold in coils and can be bent to suit piping space needs. Rigid pipe is much harder and lacks flexibility. It's ideal for straight runs.

If all you ever do with copper is install pipes, it's enough to know the difference between soft tubing and rigid pipe. But, if you want to shape and form sheet copper into useful objects or art forms you will need to recognize that copper is sold commercially in nearly 100 different alloys with recognized SAE or ASTM designation numbers, plus trade and specialty products beyond count.

These metals range from the familiar soft copper we've discussed to various grades of brass, aluminum bronzes, and other bronze alloys, each with characteristics suited to such diverse products as automobile radiators, thermostat bellows, springs, bearings, and electrical parts. It follows that if you obtain your work materials from shop scrap there's always the possibility of expending considerable labor on an alloy unsuited to hand working. One good rule is to try your most difficult forming operation on a scrap piece to see if it tends to crack, become brittle, or simply refuses to form. Your best choice is to buy so-called art metal, which is at least claimed to be fully suited to handcrafting.

Note also that some projects require several different forming methods. The copper or brass which hammers well into a teapot shape, for example, may be a poor choice for lathe turning the little decorative knob on top of the pot. Some coppers and brasses are absolute nightmares to turn, drill, or tap. Soft copper can be one of the worst and some bronzes will scream, chip, and almost refuse to cut in a lathe.

JOINING COPPER

Copper and its alloys melt at temperatures ranging from 1650–2200°F. Copper is also an excellent heat conductor. This means that although copper is an excellent material for cooking vessels, it is difficult to solder or braze. Soft solder adheres to and flows well on copper but makes a poor color match for fine work. It is also totally unsuitable for anything likely to contain a food or drink since solder contains lead. Moreover, the rapid heat conduction of copper may let unwanted heat spread to a completed joint while you're soldering another. Later, we'll discuss the techniques of working with copper and other soft metals.

PRECIOUS METALS

Metalworking in precious metals such as silver may range from tableware and ornate vessels to tiny jewelry devices wrought under a magnifying lens. Such crafts are a specialized form of metalworking and anyone seriously considering

All art-metal pieces here are copper except for pewter goblet at right. Metalworker starts with a copper blank such as that at front center. He works metal by hammering, anneals it to keep it soft.

them should arrange to attend a class in such arts. Also, excellent books are available.

At the slightly less serious level the home shop can be the site of many jewelry repairs and there's no reason not to try one's hand for the fun of it. For one thing, the tools are small and inexpensive and can easily be stored if your work area is limited. Kitchen-table jewelsmithing is entirely practical.

The basic precious metals are platinum, gold, and silver. As with other metals there are many grades and alloys of each.

It is said that the best precious metal for the beginner to use is platinum. Platinum is easily worked, but it is not too soft. It doesn't oxidize and has a high melting point, and is therefore soldered easily. And it doesn't tarnish. Jewelry-grade platinum is normally quite pure, up to 97%. For a slight color enhancement, copper may be added, or, for increased hardness, it may be alloyed with iridium or rhodium.

Gold, for the craft worker, is usually understood to be slightly alloyed. Pure, 24-carat gold is much too soft and weak for practical use. The addition of two parts silver or copper produces a 22-carat gold much more suited for working. Each point below 24 means that one part (one twenty-fourth) of alloying metal has been added.

Silver, much lighter than gold and less costly, is recommended for the beginning worker in precious metals. Professionals prefer platinum for serious jewelry work, but the readily available silver alloys may be a better choice at first.

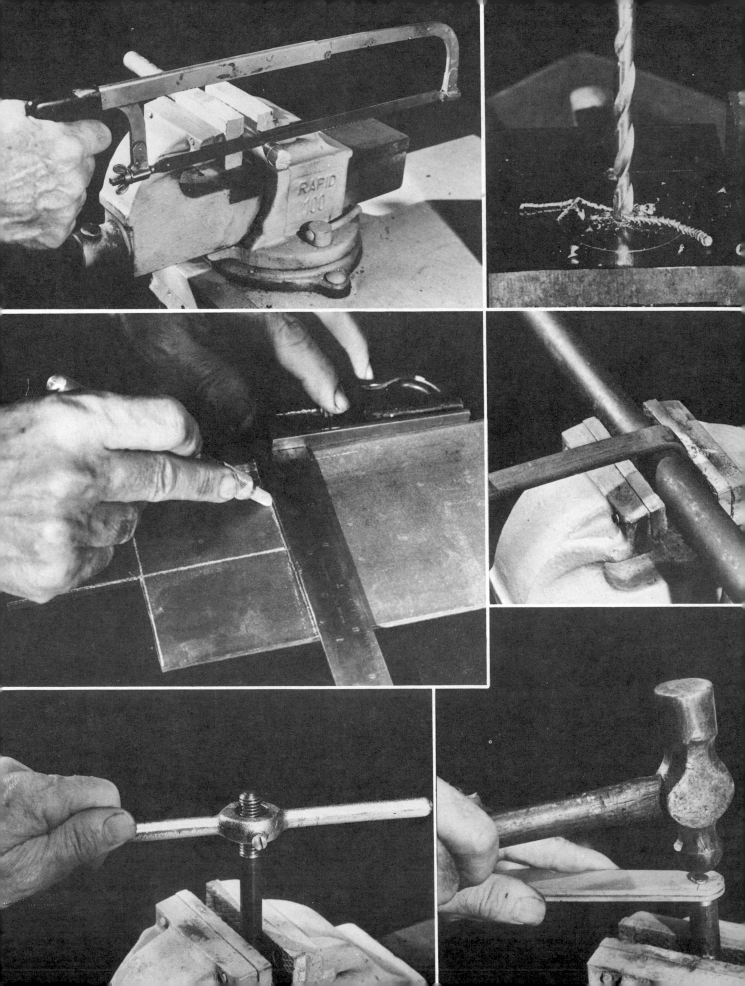

PART II
BASIC METALWORKING TOOLS AND TECHNIQUES

4. BASIC TOOLS

Were you to visit a metal-training shop in a vocational school, you would be amazed at the number and variety of tools. Even visiting the basement shop of a home metalworker like myself, who owns a multitude of tools bought randomly over the years on impulse or for certain jobs, or inherited from another generation, could be dismaying. Actually, beginners do just as well and have equal fun doing it with a few basic tools.

This is true of nearly any hobby or craft. For example, many years ago I developed my first pictures, taken with a little folding camera, in gravy dishes on the pantry counter, with a rug kicked against the door to shut out light. Surprisingly, the pictures turned out pretty well; good enough, at least, to satisfy an editor. Today, my darkroom equipment is more extensive, but the processes are the same. It still boils down to the basics of immersing the film in the proper chemicals for a specific time. The film doesn't really care how you do it.

In metalworking, too, most operations end up being very basic actions unchanged in hundreds of years. No matter how many tools you have, strip away the fancy names and convenience features and you find that there are only a few limited needs. There are holding and gripping devices such as wrenches, vises, and drill chucks. And there are tools to remove metal such

Simple drilling operation illustrates the basic requirements of most metalworking. The chuck holds and drives the cutting tool, in this case a twist drill. The drill-press vise, clamped to the table, holds the work and resists the thrust and twisting forces of the drill.

as drills, files, and abrasives. Metalworking usually gets down to a cutting edge in contact with a workpiece.

If you think of tools in three groups—holders of work, holders of tools, and movers or removers of metal—you've made a big step. You'll also spend some pre-sleep hours visualizing just how you're going to go about a certain job. In your mind's eye you'll somehow clamp or support your work. And, you'll mentally sort through the choice of cutting methods, such as filing or grinding, to remove metal if that's what is needed.

As an example, try to imagine the simple act of sharpening an old-fashioned garden hoe. You could, of course, hold the shank of the hoe in one hand and stroke a file across the edge with the other hand. But maybe you shudder as you picture the hoe pivoting around in your hand

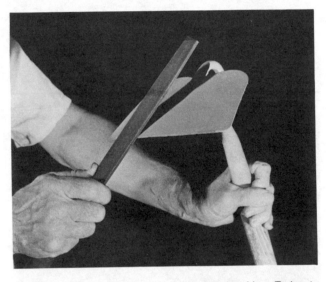

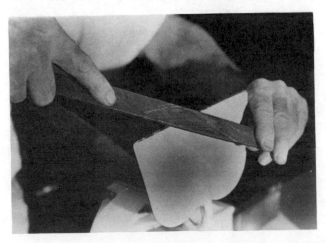

Holding your work properly is vital to metalworking. Trying to hand-hold a hoe for sharpening with a file, above, is both awkward and dangerous. The same filing operation, with the hoe firmly gripped in a vise, below, goes much better.

and cutting your knuckles. Searching for a better way, you picture your hoe clamped in vise jaws. Now you can stroke the file with an angled cut across the edge and apply your weight and shoulder muscles to the action.

But why choose a file? You could possibly use a portable disc grinder, a whetstone (slow), or maybe a small grinding stone in an electric drill. But considering the small amount of metal to be removed, a few strokes with a flat, 10″ mill file fitted with a wooden handle (the tool holder) will get the job done in less time than it would take to mount and plug in a grinder. Thus, choosing the procedures and equipment will soon become automatic as you gain experience in metalworking.

Unless you jump directly into some specialized hobby type of metalworking your first jobs will almost certainly be repairs on small appliances, home plumbing, fixing lawn and garden machines, or maybe patching up metal lawn or patio furniture. Most such tasks can be handled by the limited number of tools you could store in a kitchen cabinet drawer. For domestic reasons, however, I suggest a tool box since few spouses react favorably to keeping pipe wrenches with the silverware. The following list suggests both the basic tool and the advanced version or accessory you might like to have.

Each of the tools and their options shown in the table deserves discussion. Over the years you discover secrets not readily apparent to the beginner shopping from the hardware store shelf. Here are some important slants on selecting certain tools.

HOLDING TOOLS
Clamping devices for gripping the workpiece are as old as the arts of working stone, bone, wood, or leather. Early craftsmen may have been frus-

If you picture the frustration of a primitive worker trying to hold his workpiece and apply muscle power, it becomes apparent why even the crudest holding device such as this split log was a huge technical step forward.

BASIC METALWORKING TOOLS

You Really Need	Good Options	Common Uses	Hints & Suggestions
Bench vise	C-clamps	Holding all work	Try for at least 4″ wide jaws and solid mounting on bench
Slip-joint pliers	Vise grips	Gripping work, bending	Buy very best with wire cutting feature
Adjustable 10″ wrench	4″	Indispensable	Crescent type; 12″ is also recommended
Socket wrenches, 3/8″ drive	1/4″ drive	Also vital to most jobs	Ratchet handles are extremely useful
Hex-key (Allen) wrenches	None	Socket head screws	Get very small up through 3/8″ if you can
14″ pipe wrenches	24″ wrenches	Pipe joints	Steel pipe only
Ball-pein hammer	Soft-face hammer	Bending, riveting, chiseling	Medium weight
Screwdrivers	Very small screwdrivers	Appliance and mechanical jobs	Buy quality; at least four sizes
Cross-slot screwdrivers	As above	As above	Not all alike; see text about differences
Mill files	Round files	Shaping, sharpening, burr removal	Start collecting files of all shapes & sizes
Hacksaw	Jeweler's saw	Cutting off metal	Get variety of blades from 14 through 34 teeth per inch.
Metal snips	Aircraft snips	Sheet metal	Get the best forged type
Breast drill	1/4″ electric drill	Drilling driving small cutters	Good manual drill will cost more than electric
Twist drills	None	Drilling	Buy only high-speed steel, 1/6″–1/2″
Center punch	Drift punches	Locating holes to start drill	Kit of punches and cold chisels best way to buy
Taps and dies	None	Cutting and cleaning threads	Get 6–32 through 1/2–20

trated for ages and it must have been a glorious moment when the first primitive worker found that by gripping his work in some sort of jaws, perhaps a partially split log, he could apply both hands and the weight of his body to his work. Later, workers in many trades arranged a seat or bench on which they could sit and either exert body weight or foot treadle pressure to clamp their work. Eventually vises evolved from jaws which could be tightened by twisting thongs, and in due course screw jacks came into common use by carpenters and woodcarvers.

Bench Vises

Several things are wrong with a typical woodworker's vise when you try to use it for metalworking. As always, the forces you must apply tend to be greater. Wood deforms slightly to permit a tight grip in a woodworking vise, but most metalwork cannot accept significant deforming without marring or damage. Vise-jaw covers of soft metal are routinely used to protect metal surfaces, but the fact remains that a good metalworking vise must exert a very positive, nonspringing pressure. Moreover, metal is often

thinner than an equivalent wooden workpiece, and there are many times when you want to apply heat from a torch. All of this means that your metalworking vise must be very rigid, rather precise in its jaw action, and strong enough to resist forces in almost any direction without releasing the work or failing.

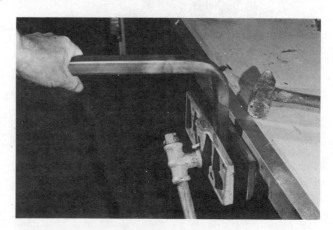

Woodworking vises lack the rigidity needed for metalwork. In this example, a poor choice of vise, tool, and method resulted in nothing but scrap metal.

It also helps enormously if the vise is securely bolted to a heavy workbench or other structure so you can apply full force to it. Unfortunately, many beginning metalworkers lack such a bench and must choose the type of vise which clamps on the edge of a light bench or table. For light work, this is better than nothing, of course, but at the first opportunity to get a better vise and anchor point it's wise to do so.

Unless you're into really heavy work, a vise with 4"-wide jaws is about right. Monster types, seen in some machine shops, tend to be clumsy and are seldom needed. However, if after reading the section on blacksmithing you decide you'd like to try it, you might want to pick up a big vise just to hold smithy tools.

Before buying a vise turn it upside down and examine the large, central sliding member. This is the backbone of your vise. If it fits loosely in the vise body or is springy, you'll frequently come to address it harshly with sharp words. You'll find some low-cost vises with this backbone formed of heavy, folded sheet metal. Avoid them. This all-important part should be a heavy casting or forging, machined smooth on all surfaces to mate quite snugly in an equally well-finished bore in the vise body. To test this, open the jaws a few inches and try shaking the outer jaw up and down and sideways. Some clearance is necessary, naturally, but if it feels sloppy and moves freely you don't want it.

Also, look for a flat working surface behind the rear jaw to provide a handy, light anvil for riveting and similar hammer work. Never hammer on the sliding portion which projects to the rear. Remember, a good bench vise will last a lifetime; buy accordingly.

Smaller vises. There are times when even the most gentle bite in a 4" bench vise is far too much. You would not, for examle, find it either handy or wise to grip a fine piece of jewelry, a

Two high-quality metalworking vises. Vise at top, with more open area under jaws, is a general-purpose type. The open area is often handy. But, if you frequently want to grip pipe or non-flat objects, a second pair of gripping surfaces in the vise throat, above, may be the best choice.

Delicate jobs require delicate holding. Small vise shown here has self-aligning jaws and grips ring adequately without damage. This vise may be bolted down, but it also has a suction-cup base for tabletop work.

Called pin vises, these tools are actually small chucks. The top one has jaws of several sizes stored in handle. Use them to hold small drills, as shown, or for picks, cutters, or small watch or clock staffs.

small model engine part, or the like, in a big machinist's vise. Over the years some clever specialty vises have been devised. Some have very delicate grips, others permit work to be rotated and positioned for filing, soldering, and drilling,

Positioning is important when working with small rotary or jeweler's tools. This Dremel vise lets you swing and cant work for most comfortable hand and tool position.

and others, called pin vises, permit very small, round parts or tools to be griped in a small chuck like the lead in an automatic pencil. If your metal shop is confined to the kitchen table, one of these small vises with a suction cup base may be ideal.

Drill-press vise.   If you have a drill press, a special vise, called a drill-press vise, is a necessity. Such a vise holds the work squarely, or with some types at a selected angle, and is routinely used with small parts you can't grip with C-clamps. The vise itself has lugs for bolting or clamping to the table. A drill-press vise is also a convenient method for holding work while feeding it through a band saw, grinder, or disc sander. Not only does it hold the metal squarely and firmly, but it also keeps your fingers from getting nicked or burned. Many metalworking operations heat the work metal enough to cause painful burns.

Clamps
Although not truly vises, there are a large number of clamps which are almost indispensable. The most common is the C-clamp, so-called because of its shape. C-clamps are commonly used, for example, when you want to drill through two pieces and finish up with the holes aligned. You simply clamp and drill through both at the same

Some drill-press vises permit angling work position as needed. Such vises can also be used as work holders for grinding and band-sawing. Note that protractor is used against work face, not against vise, since metal may misalign slightly in the jaws.

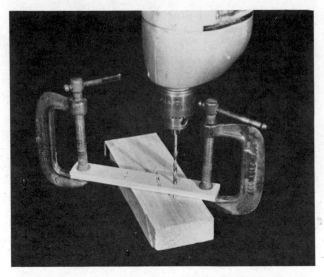

C-clamps, shown here holding two pieces for drilling so the holes will align, are among the most useful shop tools. You can never have too many on hand.

Ubiquitous slip-joint pliers are handy for a thousand shop jobs but are too often misused. Avoid the cheap, sloppy kind. Look for forged jaws, well-formed gripping surfaces, and slick-working slip joints.

time. A second routine use is to hold metal while drilling, flycutting, or grinding, especially on a drill press. This is another place where metal's resistance to cutting action enters the picture. Although you might easily hold a piece of wood with your hand on a drill-press table, hand holding a piece of metal becomes very dangerous. If the drill snags, or if the flycutter or hole saw grabs, the metal can instantly become a whirling, slashing knife. Or, it may be thrown off the tool and fly into your face or around the room. The least damaging but most common accident that occurs when you fail to clamp is to have the drill or other tool drift off center and wind up drilling a hole where you don't want it. C-clamps, among their multitude of other uses, are cheap insurance against such accidents.

Pliers

Common slip-joint pliers in sizes of about 6" to 10" have their place in any shop. Some, however, are a bit too common—cheap, wobbly, and crudely made. Look for forged pliers, smooth-working slip-joints and pivots, and neatly ground, well-fitted jaws. Such pliers can be used for a multitude of jobs where fingers just won't do: stretching a spring into place; twisting wire; even opening stubborn caps on cans and bottles. Even so, most skilled mechanics are profoundly scornful of persons who use pliers when they should use an end wrench or a socket wrench. Pliers normally have hard serrated jaws which tend to bite and mar surfaces and round off the corners on nuts. Do not use them to loosen

chromed and polished nuts and caps on plumbing fixtures.

Special Pliers

If slip-joint pliers are the tool of the amateur, specialized pliers are necessary in many trades and many forms of metalworking. So-called gas pliers were apparently devised as a rough and ready tool to heat parts in a gas flame. Such pliers are a refinement of a blacksmith's tongs, but anyone who heats parts with a propane torch, solders, or needs to grip a piece of metal for coarse grinding will want such pliers.

Electrician's pliers, with a portion of the jaws shaped to cut wire, are designed to trim wire and twist the ends together for splices. The jaws are often used to tug a snake or wire end through a conduit and sometimes to tighten conduit fittings and similar hardware where a tool mark hurts nothing.

Once you go beyond the common pliers we've discussed, there are many special types ranging from very delicate jeweler's pliers, pliers for forming small wire parts, longnose duckbills for probing deeply into narrow passages, and massive pliers for tugging fence wire tight. Many home metalworkers have found surgical gripping tools such as hemostats to be remarkably convenient for gripping tiny parts. They have selective locking notches to provide just the right gripping force and excel in working and retrieving small parts.

Vise Grips

This term is commonly used to refer to any toggle-action locking pliers, but it is actually the brand name of a specific line of high-quality locking pliers made by the Petersen Mfg. Co. I make this point first of all because this type of pliers is extremely useful, and secondly, because some of the bargain-basket imitations are of very poor quality. Vise Grips have an adjustment screw at the rear of the handle which allows you to adjust both the fit and the pressure level to suit whatever you want to grip. When they're

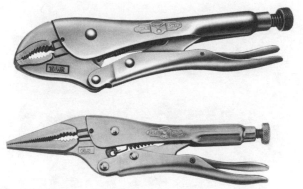

Vise Grips can be adjusted to snap over center and lock onto work with a powerful toggle action. Standard jaw shape or long nose is available with or without wire-cutter feature.

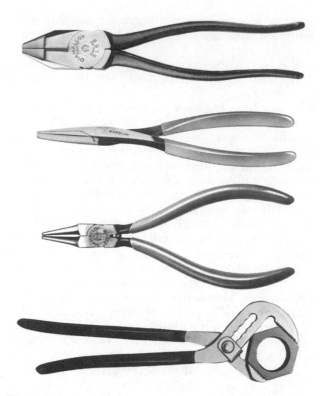

Pliers come in hundreds of special types. Examples are, from top, electrician's pliers with cutting edges and broad gripping surfaces on jaws for pulling wire through conduit; duckbills for reaching into narrow areas and twisting lockwire; round-nose for forming loops in wire; and adjustable, often called "water pump" pliers because they were used for tightening the packing nuts on pumps.

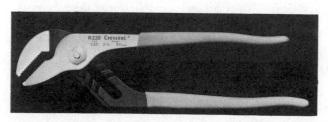

Large adjustable-jaw pliers can often speed work on conduit clamps, pipe, and couplings. Final tightening, however, should be done with a wrench.

properly set, you'll feel the toggle action snap over center when you close the jaws. The toggle action is extremely powerful. Vise Grips can sometimes be used as wrenches on damaged nuts and bolts which cannot be gripped by anything else. They do less damage than slip-joint pliers, and can substitute for C-clamps or welding clamps. Although a properly fitting wrench is preferable, if it can be used, Vise Grips are often real problem solvers.

TURNING AND TWISTING TOOLS

Since so many metalworking operations involve turning a screw, a bolt, a piece of pipe, or a fitting, a special class of turning tools has evolved that goes far beyond the simple plow wrenches of fifty years ago. Some are extremely specialized for factory production use. Knowing what tools are available to turn a difficult fastener can make the difference between a fast, neat job and utter frustration.

Screwdrivers

"Sharpen a screwdriver?" More than one person has asked me that when I interrupted a job momentarily to touch up a worn screwdriver on the bench grinder. But such persons probably never thought of a screwdriver as a precision turning tool. They may have grown up in a family where a single twenty-five-cent screwdriver was kept in the kitchen cabinet or garage and used for everything from opening paint cans to prying tacks. Thus, it comes as a surprise when I point out that a screwdriver must fit the screw slot just as closely as a socket wrench fits a nut. This applies to all screwdrivers, both for ordinary slotted screws and for so-called Phillips screws. We'll talk about the latter in a moment, but for now let's stick to slotted screws.

When buying screwdrivers, it is worthwhile to buy a matching set. There is no such thing as a universal, "average" size. To see why this is so, examine a screw large enough for you to see the slot clearly. Note that the vertical sides of the slot are flat and parallel. The slot is also quite shallow. This means that the entire force used for tightening or loosening the screw must be applied to these two flat sides.

Now, examine a screwdriver you might use to drive this screw. Is the tip thick enough to fill

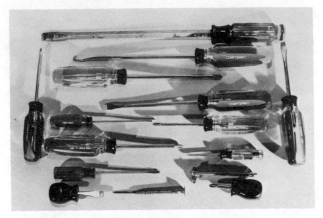

Screwdrivers come in large, medium, small, and very small, such as jeweler's tool, bottom center. They also vary in tip form to fit standard or cross-recessed screws. Often you need the "shorty" type in tight places and sometimes you need an angle type with a ratchet. The most important thing is to select a screwdriver which fits the slot snugly.

the entire screw slot? Are the sides of the tip also flat and parallel or are they worn round? Actually, exacting metalworkers will usually grind the tip to a slight hollow grind so the bottom edges flare just enough to bite into the screw slot right down at the base of the slot. This concentrates the driving force at the strongest part of the slot. It also helps to keep the tip from developing a wedging action which lifts the tip out of the slot as you twist.

To assure an accurate fit in many different sizes of screws, I recommend buying a set of screwdrivers. Even so, you will still find it im-

portant to grind them to size for critical jobs. Summed up, here are the guidelines for buying screwdrivers:

● Buy screwdrivers made of high-quality steel that will resist wear and accept repeated resharpening.

● A long handle offers the best grip and the most powerful turning action, but space often demands a "shorty" style. Buy a few of these stub screwdrivers for smaller screws.

● In metalworking, screws are often located down in a hole. A tip that flares out won't fit and will damage the threads in the hole. Screwdrivers with almost straight flanks are best.

● Tips for very small screws, such as in clockworks, are commonly custom sized on the job. Jeweler's screwdriver blades which fit in a handle or pin vise are the best choice for such work, but they must be ground before using.

Cross-recess screwdrivers.   Some years ago the increasing use of power screwdrivers on assembly lines brought about the development of cross-recessed screws with two slots 90° to each other. Neither slot extends to the outer edge, and this helps to prevent the screwdriver blade from sliding out and damaging the work. However, there are several reasons why cross-recessed screws can pose a problem in the home shop.

For one thing, although such screws are commonly called Phillips screws, there are at least two recess forms. These forms are not quite the same, but it's often difficult to identify them. Unless you are buying screwdrivers for an assembly line, it may be hard to buy exactly the right tip. Consequently, most of us make do with cross-recessed drivers which approximate the slot. Eventually, this causes the tip to wear in a nibbled-away pattern and the tool becomes use-

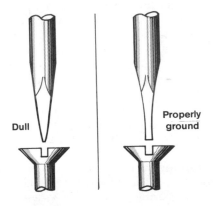

Dull, rounded-off edges on a screwdriver make it difficult or impossible to turn a screw since the tip tends to work out of the slot. This damages the slot and makes the problem worse. A well-sharpened screwdriver which just fits the slot will concentrate the twisting action at the bottom of the slot and "bite in" enough to prevent slipping. Don't be afraid to grind a screwdriver to fit a critical job. Eventually you'll have to replace the tool, but the improved performance is worth it.

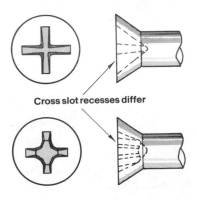

Cross slot recesses differ

Although cross-slotted screws may look alike, there are two different recess shapes. Most hardware-store screwdrivers are compromises and will handle both types—for a while. Expect to replace these screwdrivers occasionally.

less. It is very difficult to reshape such tips. I recommend buying new ones of the proper configuration and using them only in screws of matching configuration. Again, a high-quality screwdriver with a properly heat-treated alloy-steel blade will outlast any cheap, soft-metal tool many times over.

Adjustable Wrenches

Right in the beginning, let it be said that if you have a choice, a fixed-jaw, open-end wrench is greatly preferable to any adjustable wrench. A fully closed box-end or socket is still better. In fact, the mechanic who habitually uses adjustable wrenches is a subject of derision by his more professional fellows. Nevertheless, the adjustable wrench is such a handy tool around the shop that every metalworker has a few of them. There are any number of jobs from tightening the packing on a faucet to snugging down clamp bolts on a drill-press table where you just don't need to pull full torque. Here, the adjustable wrench is quick and adequate.

The old-time "monkey" wrench with jaws at 90° to the handle was never a very practical tool and has long been replaced by the much more useful Crescent wrench. This was the brand name of the original maker, the Crescent Tool Co. of Jamestown, N.Y. Other makers of long-standing: Diamond Tool & Horseshoe Co., of Duluth, Minn., and the Utica Tool & Drop Forge Co. of Utica, N.Y. These wrenches, and others made by reputable tool makers are drop-forged, alloy steel. The buyer should beware of cheap,

Although its makers call it an "auto" wrench, this is an old-fashioned monkey wrench. It has numerous uses for twisting, bending, and shaping, especially in wrought-iron work.

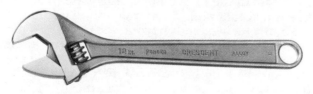

Better and handier than the monkey wrench, this adjustable type wrench is commonly called "A Cresent" wrench. Every shop needs a few, ranging from very small to 12" like this one.

cast wrenches. Not only are they apt to break suddenly, but the results of such a break can be badly injured fingers or a strained back.

Adjustable wrenches are available in little 4" models up to huge sizes used industrially. For the home shop, a 4", an 8", and a 12" will suffice. These wrenches are particularly useful on brass nuts and plumbing fixtures where the exact size end wrenches never quite seem to fit. If the adjustment nut is kept squared up so the jaws are firmly squared on the work, they do very well. If you are too casual and let the jaws work loose, they will often round off the hex and damage the work. Although not necessarily made for the purpose, adjustable wrenches are also handy for griping the edge of sheet metal, square bars, and the like for bending and twisting.

Socket and Box Wrenches

Since so many metalworking jobs around the home require disassembling and reassembling various mechanisms, an investment in a set of quality sockets and box-end wrenches will pay off many times over. Both sockets and box ends are fully closed wrenches which have female cavities of the exact size of the nut or bolt head. Exact, that is, plus a little clearance so they fit over the hex easily.

Such wrenches are available in both 6-point and 12-point models. The 6-points, logically, have six indentations to fit the standard six-sided, hexagonal nut or bolt. The 12-points have twelve indentations but fit the same size hex. Why the difference? The 6-point is a bit stronger in the sense that more wrench metal actually bears on the sides of the hex. But often working space limits aligning the wrench to fit over the hex. The 12-point is much more convenient in this respect and can be worked where the swing angle is quite limited. Most home-shop workers will prefer the 12-point. On the production line, with power-driven wrenches, the 6-point lasts longer. If you must loosen an extremely tight nut, bolt, or pipe plug, use a 6-point since it is less likely to round off the corners of the hex.

The table shown earlier suggested the drive sizes for sockets as starting at ¼" and going up through ⅜" and ½". There are also ¾" and 1" drives, but they are extremely expensive and needed only if you are repairing old steam engines or construction equipment. If you're not at all familiar with socket wrenches, the drive size refers to the square hole into which the wrench handle or ratchet fits. My choice, for starters, would be a little kit of ¼" drive sockets which extend up to ½" nut capacity. These small sockets are extremely practical for working on many

Small, ¼"-drive sockets are useful for repairing appliances and making electrical adjustments, such as on this pump control.

modern appliances and yard tools, plus the little hex-head sheet-metal screws and electrical screws so common today. However, they are not strong enough to torque tightly or break loose a very tight ½" nut.

Most nuts up to ⅝" can be handled by ⅜" drive sockets and, unless you're into engine work and similar projects requiring heavy torques on cylinder-head and connecting-rod bolts, the ⅜" drive is a good all-around choice. Heavier jobs do require ½" drives.

The wrench size refers to the measured distance across the flats of the hex. A ¼"-diameter bolt, for example, has a ⁷⁄₁₆" head. The common U.S. standard sizes are listed as follows.

Bolt Diameter	Diam. Across Flats	Socket Size
¼"	⁷⁄₁₆"	⁷⁄₁₆"
⁵⁄₁₆"	½"	½"
⅜"	⁹⁄₁₆"	⁹⁄₁₆"
½"	¾"	¾"

Thus, if you have to limit your purchases initially, these sizes, plus the midget sockets in a ¼"-drive set, will handle about 90% of the nuts and bolts you'll encounter. The exceptions are the "funny" sizes sometimes used, for reasons unknown, by some manufacturers. Occasionally,

you meet up with sizes you can't fit, perhaps ¹¹⁄₁₆" or ²⁵⁄₃₂". You have to decide if the job is worth buying a special wrench for, or if you can get by with an adjustable.

Today, you'll encounter metric sizes as more and more foreign-made products appear and as U.S. manufacturers convert to metric. About the only size you can interchange is a ½" U.S. socket or box for a 13mm metric, and vice-versa. Otherwise, if you work on such products you will have to buy metric wrenches. Fortunately, at least as sold in this country, the drive portions are again ¼", ⅜", and ½", so you can use them with your standard drives, extensions, and ratchets.

Special Sockets

There are two other important variations in socket wrenches. The first involves depth. Standard-depth sockets are fine for most jobs, and the depth of the forged hex is adequate to fit the nut and accommodate any remaining portion of the bolt which extends beyond the nut. But some assemblies, for example U-bolts that are used for muffler clamps or for mounting antenna masts, have long bolt extensions which prevent the socket from getting down over the nut. Spark plugs are another example. Such jobs require deep sockets. Why not just buy and use deep sockets all the time? As a matter of fact, this is

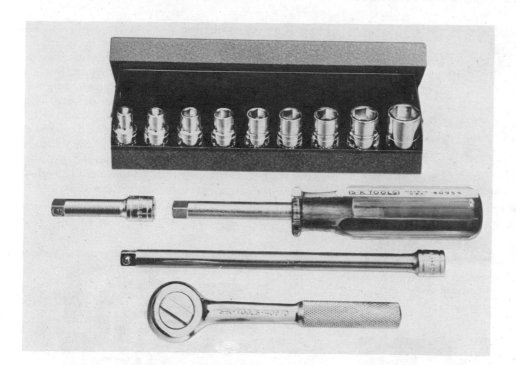

In kit form, small sockets range down to those which fit sheet-metal screws and up to ½". Don't count on them, however, for tightening or breaking loose nuts from ⅜" up.

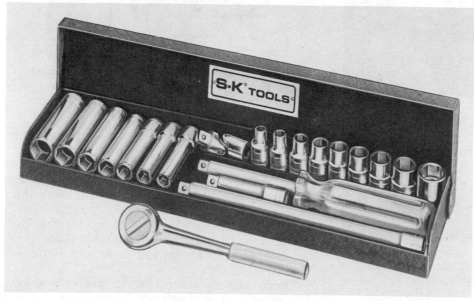

Typical utility socket set in ⅜"-drive size is probably the most practical for general use. These are six-point sockets.

a good idea except for one thing. Some nuts and bolts that you want to get on are in close quarters and offer barely enough room for a standard socket and some sort of drive handle. Here, deep sockets are impossible to use.

The second variation mentioned applies to universal sockets which incorporate a universal joint in the shank. These tricky sockets allow you to angle the drive off to one side and still turn the wrench. There are tight locations where universals are absolutely necessary, but you'll probably regard them as options in the begin-

ning. Universal wrenches do solve problems but are annoying and awkward for general use.

Socket Drivers

Socket wrenches can be turned, or driven, by a number of different adapter handles. The most common is the simple flex handle, sometimes called a breaker bar. Flex handles are always best for breaking loose a tight nut or for heavy tightening. They are much stronger than ratchet wrenches. But flex handles are slow-working

Flex handle provides the needed leverage for loosening and tightening bolts. Using a ratchet can overload ratchet teeth.

Once bolt is loosened, the ratchet drive speeds the action. It's even more useful when you can swing in only a limited angle.

tools in places that limit your wrench swing. You can turn through only a limited arc before the handle strikes, and you then have to remove and reseat the socket for another bite. The same, of course, applies to a box or open-end wrench.

For this reason, the ratchet driver is a popular tool. Aside from the initial breaking loose or final tightening, the ratchet is faster and more convenient since you can flip the handle back and forth rapidly, without reseating the socket for each swing. Combined with extension shafts which allow you to select a working position away from interfering parts, the ratchet is a valuable tool.

Hex-Key Wrenches

Probably some of your shop tools came equipped with hex-key wrenches for the internal hex sockets in the heads of certain screws. Setscrews to hold pullies on shafts, blade-retainer screws, and other special screws have hex sockets. The typical hex-key wrench, often called an Allen wrench is L-shaped with a short leg and a longer shank. They're made, or should be, of very tough steel with a hexagonal form to fit snugly into the screw socket. More sophisticated wrenches may have tee-handles, ratchets, and other features.

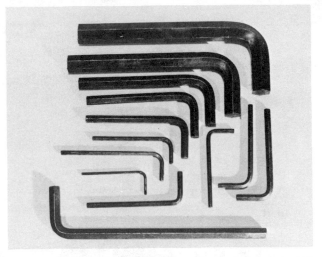

Individual hex-key wrenches are the most common, but you can also get them in fold-out cluster sets. Buy the best quality only.

The advantages of socket-head screws, in addition to requiring less space for the head than hex bolts, is their high torque capability. You'll nearly always find that socket-head screws are made of very high-grade steel and finished quite nicely. This is why they're expensive but often worth the money.

There is no substitute for the proper size hex-key wrench. Thus, you need a wide assortment ranging from very small, almost wirelike wrenches, for electronic gear knobs and adjustments to husky brutes ½" across the flats. Today, as with socket wrenches, you will find many metric socket-head screws. This is unfortunate because it results in dubious almost-fits. If a slightly small hex key is used, you may tear the hex out of the socket so nothing short of drilling it out will work. Rule number one in loosening a hex-socket screw is to feel the action very carefully. If it feels as if it's slipping, stop turning and investigate. You may have the wrong size wrench. Or, you may have a low-quality wrench. There are low-cost hex-key wrenches which simply lack the quality of steel required. Discard such wrenches because they'll also damage the screw sockets and cause you a great deal of trouble removing the screw.

Pipe Wrenches

The beginning metalworker will easily understand the principle of a wrench which grips the flat sides of a hex, but gripping a round pipe or bar may be more challenging. Sometimes, of course, some form of pliers will do, but often much greater force is required than can be resisted by the gripping action of pliers. And, more leverage may be needed than short pliers handles offer.

Many years ago this problem was solved by the invention of the pipe wrench, often called a stillson wrench. There are many versions and sizes of pipe wrenches but they all function on the principle of a pivoted lower jaw and gripping teeth which bite in one direction and release in the other. The pivoted jaw is usually lightly spring-loaded so you can pull and swing back, ratchetlike, for another turn without removing the wrench from the pipe.

Unless you expect to work with large pipe over

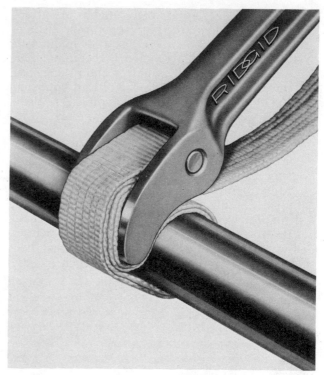

When you don't want to mar the pipe surface, use a strap wrench. It will grip tightly without teeth and protect chromed pipe from damage.

Best choice for hex-coupling nuts is this hex-jaw wrench. It will not, however, grip round pipe.

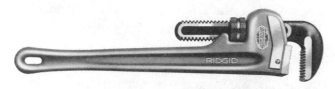

Modern, heavy-duty pipe wrench is huskily built. Again, buy the best, but remember that you usually need two of them, one to oppose the force of the other.

Large pipes often exceed the grip of a pipe wrench. Chain tong wraps around pipe and jaws bite in when force is applied.

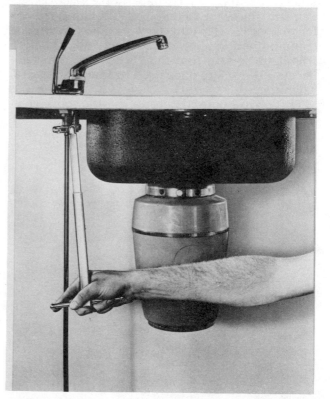

If you've ever tried to get at the nuts on a lavatory or sink you'll appreciate this basin wrench just made for that job.

1" or 1¼" in size, a pair of wrenches about 16" long will be adequate. For larger pipe fittings and couplings such as those used for home well systems, a pair of 24" wrenches is recommended. Note that one wrench is better than none, but on many occasions you must hold an opposing section of pipe against the force you exert. Without the second wrench it's easy to disturb joints that you don't want to loosen.

At the small end of the scale, one or two 6" or 8" wrenches will solve holding problems that nothing else will handle. One example might be an adjustment nut on a threaded rod. You can get an end wrench on the nut but the rod turns. A little pipe wrench will hold the rod. It will also get up into tight places under sinks and behind dishwashers. To put the hoary jokes to rest, neither monkey wrenches nor pipe wrenches come in right- and left-hand models.

CUTTING TOOLS

Files

The file may appear to be the least complicated tool in the shop, but its use can entail some of the most fincly developed skills of the human hand. Files range from coarse-toothed rasps intended for wood, or perhaps horse's hooves, to delicate, finely toothed and oddly shaped rifflers for precise jewelry and die work. In between are common mill files, the metalworker's best friends. It is said that they are called mill files because they were once used to sharpen saws in sawmills.

There are hundreds of file shapes, tooth configurations, and degrees of coarse and smooth cuts. For general metalwork, such as removing

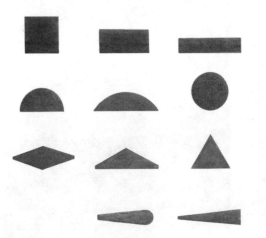

Common file shapes, shown in section by Nicholson, let you fit the file to the metal project you're working on.

burrs from sawed edges, rounding off sharp corners, sharpening garden tools, and dressing parts rotating in the lathe, the flat mill file, slightly tapered towards one end, and about 10" in working length, is a handy benchtop tool. A single-cut, long-angle tooth pattern will produce the smoothest surface, especially in lathework. A double-cut pattern removes metal somewhat faster. The latter are commonly called machinist's files.

The terminology used to describe the relative tooth coarseness is more picturesque than accurately descriptive. A rough-cut file is too rough for most work; so is a coarse-cut and a bastard cut. The bastard cut is often about right for heavy work on soft aluminum, soldered fills, and some plastics. Finer teeth are termed second-cut, smooth, and dead smooth. The reason this tends to be confusing is that the coarseness, or at least the size of the teeth, also depends on the size of the file. In general, the larger the file for any given type of tooth, the larger the teeth.

Another feature you should know about is called the "safe-edge." A safe-edge file may have any tooth formation, but one edge will have no teeth at all. This permits you to cut a surface which runs at an angle or corner to another surface without having the edge of the file bite in where you don't want it to.

You'll gradually acquire files of shapes and sizes that suit your jobs. For example, round files, often called rattail files, are extremely useful for cleaning up and enlarging holes, especially in thin metals. Triangular files, commonly used for sharpening carpenter's saws, are also useful for working into corners and squaring up openings. Half-rounds are clearly better for concave-curved surfaces, and so on. The rule is to approximate the shape of the work surface or the intended final shape with the file.

Files for special metals. If you choose to work in brass, buy files especially toothed for this metal. The file makers describe such files as having teeth with a short "upcut and a long-angle overcut." It may take a magnifying glass to see the difference, but your first trials will prove it's there.

Aluminum is another soft metal with peculiar working properties. You'll immediately notice that it clogs a file. Again, if aluminum is your specialty, invest in files made for it.

Vixen files, with deep, sharp, curved teeth, are familiar to all experienced auto-body metalworkers. At one time it was routine practice to fill dents and weld lines in auto bodies with soft solder. This is still done in car manufacturing. To smooth and shape this combination of very

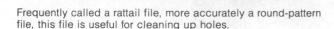

Frequently called a rattail file, more accurately a round-pattern file, this file is useful for cleaning up holes.

This flat mill-bastard file is a shop workhorse for fast metal removal. Although the teeth appear coarse, you can do fine work with it.

For all-round use on everything from your lawn mower blade to your garden hoe, this Handy File can't be beat.

Triangular file with a slight taper works neatly into corners. It's also used for sharpening wood saws.

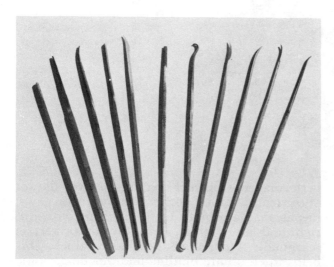

Specialty files, these bent rifflers are used for working down into cavities and odd shapes. Good for jewelry and art metal.

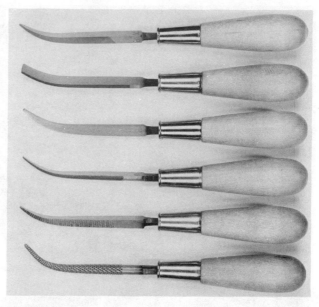

Swiss pattern or die-sinker's files are used to carve intricate forms and cavities in metal.

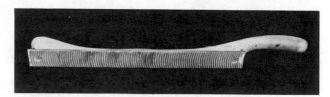

Vixen file, often used with a curved holder, works best for shaving auto-body filler solder or expoxy to form.

soft solder and body steel, a file had to shear off a different form of chip and leave a smooth surface behind. In spite of the use of epoxy body fillers today, the same tool is still needed. Vixen files are intended for mounting in a special handle and holder which allows them to be flexed to a convenient contour to match the curve of a body or fender. Vixen files, however, are really specialty files and are not generally required in the home shop.

Rotary files.   Many once-tedious filing jobs are now done quickly with rotary files or burrs rotated in a high-speed tool. Such cutters are available in a remarkable variety of shapes and sizes to fit nearly any need. They also vary in coarseness, flute configurations, and materials. Manufacturers offer extensive tables advising the correct burr type and rotating speed for different metals. Here, the problem of home-shop vs. factory equipment arises because, unlike air-driven factory tools which can run at speeds up to 30,000 or more rpm, about the best you can hope for is the top speed of your ¼″ electric drill—at best, probably below 200 rpm. For very small rotary files you can use a high-speed tool such as the Dremel.

Hacksaws
The standard tool, although not always the best, for cutting metal is the hand hacksaw. Configurations and handle patterns vary, but the com-

Rotary file in a drill press offers a high-speed metal forming tool that can save much hand filing time.

Even if your weld or braze joints aren't works of art, a rotary file in an electric drill can quickly smooth them out so they look good. Choose a shape that fits the work best.

mon hacksaw has a shallow, C-shaped frame which may be extended or shortened by a series of adjustment notches. The blade has a hole at each end to fit over mounting pins. Either a thumb screw or a threaded and rotatable handle is used to tighten the blade so it is taut and secure in the frame. Note that hacksaw blades of this type are almost always installed with the teeth pointing away from the handle so the cutting action takes place on the forward stroke.

Actually, almost any reasonably solid saw frame will do—the secret of successful cutting is in the blade selection. I strongly recommend buying the best-quality blades you can find. Industrial-tool and electrical supply houses generally have better blades than hardware stores.

Different saw manufacturers stress different features, probably more for sales reasons than because these features have much real effect on performance. One such feature involves the set of the teeth. Set, on both wood and metal saws, means that alternate teeth are bent outward, right and left, slightly. Thus, the cut, or kerf, is marginally wider than the blade is thick. This helps to eliminate binding and pinching. Some saws are set in a wave pattern, others in a conventional pattern, but it's hard to detect any difference. A good feature found on some saws is a short section of very fine teeth at the front of the saw to make it easier to get the cut started exactly where you want it.

The fineness or coarseness of the teeth is all-important. As a rule of thumb, there should always be at least two, preferably, three, teeth in contact with the cutting surface of the stock. This means that if you are cutting fairly thin stock such as sheet metal 1/16″ to 1/8″ thick, you should choose a blade with 24 to 32 teeth per inch. Trying to cut such material with a coarse blade is unpleasant because the saw tends to grab and buckle. Worse, individual teeth will catch and be broken out. On the other hand, using fine-tooth blades on thicker surfaces is frustrating because the cutting action is slow. Not only do the teeth lack bite; they also clog and the saw rides over the metal on the chips packed between the teeth. For average cutting of heavier stock and soft metals, 14 teeth per

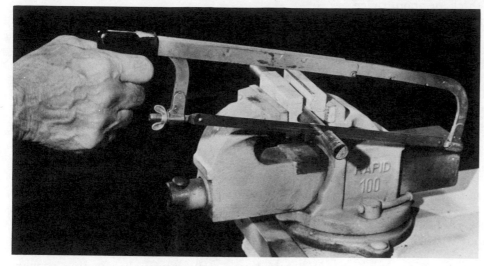

A hacksaw with a good blade is often the quickest and easiest way to cut metal such as conduit. Note that tubing is gripped in wooden blocks shaped to pad vise jaws.

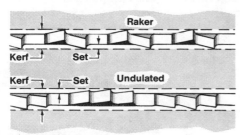

Like wood saws, hacksaws need some form of tooth offset to let the blade run freely. There are variations, but it's hard to detect the difference. Most important, buy high-quality blades.

inch is about right; for harder metals use 18 teeth per inch.

Saber Saws

In many projects you want to cut large pieces from a large sheet of metal. Here, the hacksaw is useless. One of the best tools for this job is a small, electric saber saw equipped with a metal-cutting blade. Choose a fine or coarse blade as needed, but if in doubt, choose the finer blade. A coarse blade may catch and kick the saw out of the cut or break the blade.

Jeweler's Saws

If you get into model making or jewelry work, you'll soon discover that even the finest hacksaw blades are too coarse and that the common shop saw is too clumsy. A special form of hacksaw called a jeweler's saw is the answer. Much

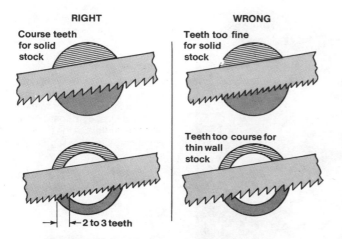

When buying hacksaw blades, avoid getting all one tooth count. You need at least two or three in contact with the metal for thin stock and tubing and you need coarser teeth for thick stock. Changing blades to suit the metal thickness is worth the time.

Delicate, fine sawing requires a saw, a blade, and a touch quite different from heavy sawing. This jeweler's saw takes blades down to almost hairlike dimensions.

lighter and smaller than the conventional hacksaw, the jeweler's saw operates in the same way with one important difference—the blades are installed so they cut on the pull rather than the push stroke. This is because the blades are so fine. The finest is only .006″ thick, or about twice the thickness of the human hair. They must be loaded in tension.

Jeweler's blades are graduated in about nineteen thicknesses and widths with the coarsest approximating a fine woodworker's coping saw. Most jobs, other than the very finest, can be handled by sizes (grade numbers) from 4/0 to #2, that is, with blade thicknesses from .008″ to .014″. On the smallest of these, the teeth are so fine that they are difficult to see clearly. These minute teeth are very sharp, however, and in spite of their apparent lack of bite they cut very rapidly. Obviously, a delicate touch is needed to avoid breaking them. The saw frame is adjustable for just that reason. By shortening it you can use broken pieces without wasting them.

Metal Snips

Most metals in thinner sheets, and soft aluminum in thicknesses up to about 1/16″, are most easily cut with shears called "snips." Conventional tinner's snips are basically heavily built scissors. You can buy them in sizes from about 6″ long to monsters 14″ to 16″ long. For ordinary shop use a 7″ pair is handy for cutting small pieces, gaskets, shims, cardboard, etc. Never use them for cutting wire since that will nick the edges. Although such small snips may be forced through fairly heavy metal, the length of the handles offers little leverage, and if you plan to

work larger sheet-metal projects, invest in a 12″ pair. Larger snips will cut roofing and gutter materials, screen wire, and automotive and aircraft metals.

Aviation Snips

Ordinary snips are simply not made for cutting around curves unless the radius is quite large. Try it and you'll find that they twist stubbornly in the metal and tend to kink and ripple the work. Such jobs call for aircraft snips, contrived in the early days of aviation for shaping the forms of aluminum fairings, wheelpants, and the like.

Aircraft snips have two advantages. First, they have a toggle-action handle linkage which greatly increases cutting power and reduces your effort. Secondly, unlike monkey wrenches, they do come in right- and left-hand models for cutting along curved lines. Thus, you need at least two pairs; most metalworkers acquire a third pair made for straight cutting. Incidentally, the latter make extremely effective kitchen

Aviation snips come in right-hand, left-hand, and straight-cutting patterns. Toggle action boosts cutting power.

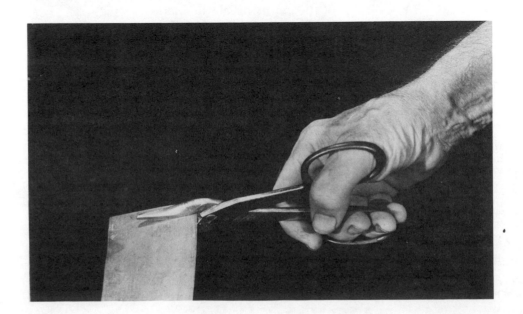

Every metalworker's shop needs a pair of small tinsnips for routine trimming of metal, cutting shims, cardboard, and other materials. Don't force small snips to do a big job.

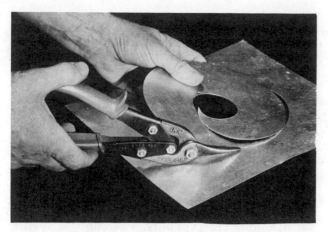

Left-hand aviation snips are designed to cut curves, so waste metal curls freely on left side.

shears for trimming such tough things as lobsters, stems, fowl, and other foods too hard to cut with ordinary shears. In any case, the secret to successful cutting of metal with snips is the way the waste metal curls up and out of the way. Aviation snips are shaped to aid this process.

Duct Snips
Nevertheless, when cutting straight lines in larger sheets or around a metal duct, for example, there are times when the curling action interferes with your hand. For this type of cut a

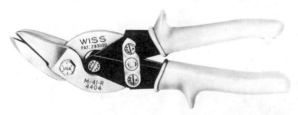

Duct snips are made for difficult cuts into closed metal structures which are not free to curl waste on one side. Cutting blade works between two fixed jaws to curl out narrow strip.

special snip called a "duct snip" is called for. Such snips have two stationary blades with an open throat and the movable blade works between them to cut out and curl up a narrow ribbon of waste metal. There are variations on this type of tool such as the Bernz cutter which work well under some conditions and poorly under others. Experienced metalworkers try to avoid this type of cut if at all possible.

High-Speed Rotary Tools
Someplace among files, grinders, drills, and a miscellany of other tools, you must class the small, hand-held rotary tool as a cutting tool. Such tools often have a very high-speed capability up to 30,000 rpm. They can be fitted with literally hundreds of small bits, grinders, and cutters, as well as polishers and surface cleaners.

In the home shop the name Dremel has become almost synonymous with electrically-powered units able to perform many tasks which would be unpleasantly tedious by hand methods. Since the maximum-diameter tool shank

High-speed rotary tools such as this Dremel have made many older methods of metal removal with chisels, files, or hand stones obsolete. Kit contains a starter group of abrasive stones, cutters, buffers, and drills, but there are many more you'll want.

Delicate silverware or jewelry can be safely cleaned and buffed with light pressure using rotary tool. Speed is the secret.

accepted by the chuck is only ⅛″, you cannot mount heavy, conventional tools. In part, this is a safety factor since the extreme high speed could easily cause oversize grinding wheels and the like to disintegrate.

This speed is the secret of the Dremel tool. It is one of the few metalworking tools where heavy pressure against the workpiece is unnecessary. Just a touch of the high-speed cutter is all it takes. Some jobs such as polishing do require lower speeds, and plastics tend to gum and melt at high speed, so if you acquire such a tool, and I recommend it for the beginning metalworker, try to choose a model on which you can dial in the right speed for the work.

Electric Drills

The hand-held electric drill has become the tool of all uses, and abuses, in the home shop. Originally massive, heavy, and very expensive, this ubiquitous tool has evolved into the amazingly light and inexpensive models found in every hardware store today. That doesn't mean that all are equally good in either quality or performance but most will do a reasonable job simply because they put a rotating shaft with lots of speed and power in your hands.

Nearly all metalworkers start with a size known as a ¼″ drill, which simply means that the chuck will open far enough to accept a drill ¼″ in diameter. Typically, you can use such a

Author's hand-crank breast drill, with right and left-hand ratchets, is about seventy years old but still operates smoothly. It's good for quick jobs where running a power cord would be a bother.

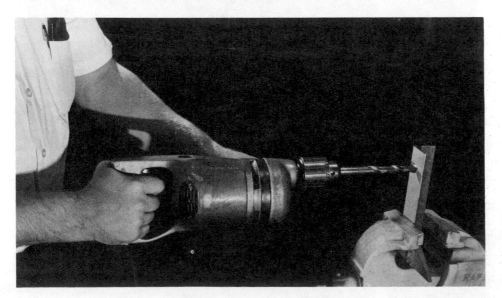

If you have a choice, a modern electric drill will save time and energy. This powerful ½″ drill is useful for large twist drills and hole saws.

drill for holes from $\frac{1}{16}''$ to $\frac{1}{4}''$ in diameter. For these relatively small hole sizes the single-speed drill, although often too fast, allows you to drill holes in most metals including mild steel. The excess speed often burns drills, especially if you don't use a lubricant. Now, with the advent of

A $\frac{3}{8}''$ drill is a good choice for the beginning metalworker since it handles larger twist drills without overloading and can still accept small ones.

variable-speed drills, it is possible to hold down the speed and get better results. Variable speeds also brought about the era of turned-down drill shanks. Drill owners started grinding or turning down drills larger than $\frac{1}{4}''$ so they would fit in the small drill chucks. Drill makers soon caught on and started selling drills with undersized shanks. I recently bought a $\frac{5}{8}''$ carbide-tipped drill (for drilling concrete) with a $\frac{1}{4}''$ shank. This is a ridiculous combination. The drill chuck and the gearing inside which drives it are simply not made for such service; neither is the motor. In brief, the $\frac{1}{4}''$ drill is a fine starter tool, and it will also handle burrs, rotary files, and small grinding stones fairly well, but respect its limitations.

Choosing a drill. If you have a choice, a $\frac{3}{8}''$ chuck size and drill is better for general metalwork unless you're really staying small. For drills above $\frac{3}{8}''$, a husky $\frac{1}{2}''$, lower-speed drill is still better. But at this point you again start to exceed the power resources of the human body. The force needed to keep a $\frac{1}{2}''$ twist drill biting is more than most of us can apply for very long.[69] The answer, of course, is a drill press, and I'll discuss that later. If you can't afford, or have no place for, a drill press, investigate the drill-press

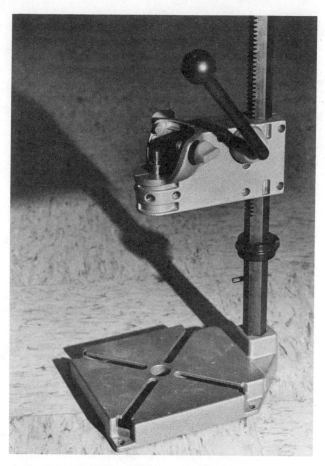

A stand such as this can convert your portable electric drill for drill-press action. Note that with this stand the drill actually threads onto a shank with a separate bearing. This is better than a cradle mount which requires careful alignment of drill in cradle.

stands onto which you can clamp a hand-held drill and apply pressure with a lever. Such stands are not really accurate as a machinist thinks of accuracy, but they are much better at keeping holes going into metal squarely than a fatigued human frame.

Breast Drills

The hand-cranked breast drill is to the metalworker what the auger brace is to the woodworker—slow, sure, but lots of work. The name comes from the broad plate on the handle against which you lean your chest to apply pressure for heavy cutting. The best breast drills were probably made fifty or more years ago when workmen spent all day drilling holes by hand. I have an old one with finely cut gears, ratchets, two speeds forward and reverse, and other features probably once of great importance. Today, smaller breast drills, or at least hand-crank drills, have their uses, usually for small or delicate jobs, or where it's bothersome or impossible to run an extension cord. If you have no choice, use a hand-crank d...l; otherwise, even the least expensive ¼" electric drill is better and faster.

This gets back to the points I made earlier about more force being needed to drill metal than wood. A carpenter's auger will bite cleanly and rapidly into wood with little effort, but a metal-cutting twist drill requires pressure to bite in and curl out metal chips.

Twist Drills

Probably no single metal cutting tool in your shop, whether you're old timer or beginner, will be used as often as the twist drill in its many sizes. For the beginner, it's also probably the tool he'll least understand. The common twist drill, so called because some of them are manufactured by twisting, appears to be a simple tool. Actually, it is not; nor is the size numbering and lettering system for some drills very logical.

Fractional drill sizes.   If you're just starting your metalworking shop, you'll do well to buy a complete set of drills in fractional size, of *high-speed steel*, in an indexed holder or plastic box. The holder should have a close-fitting hole marked for each drill size. Drills stored loosely either get lost or have to be checked for size each time you use them.

It may be that the cost of a full drill set, normally sold in sizes from ⅟₁₆" to ½", in steps of ⅟₆₄", is more than you want to spend at first. Unless you work on heavy structures, you'll probably be able to get by for a while with drills from ⅟₁₆" through ¼", plus a ⁵⁄₁₆" and a ⅜". Later you can fill out the larger sizes as you need them. You'll also find that drills are sold in rather short standard lengths and longer commercial lengths. The latter are sometimes handy but seldom necessary. If you intend to do small model work or jewelry work, you may want the very small fractional drills starting with ⅟₆₄". These fine drills are not really suited for use in an ordinary hand-held electric drill because of their delicacy. A small jeweler's breast drill is better, and a precision drill press is still better.

Number drills.   As soon as you get started in metalworking and need to drill holes into which you'll later tap threads, you'll need a tap-drill chart. It will tell you exactly the proper drill size for a given thread. But you'll also find that your fractional drills do not match the sizes called for on the chart. Instead, you'll find drill sizes iden- tified by numbers and letters. They're in-between sizes and are the ideal drills for approximately 75% thread engagement. This is the engagement commonly used for most work.

But, there are compromises which are practical and which will usually let you get by with your fractional drills as I'll explain later.

Letter drills.   Another sizing system, this one by letters, has been around a long time. You'll find letter drills called for on your tap-drill chart. I'll tell you how you can, and when you can't, compromise around these odd sizes later when I discuss tapping and cutting threads. In any case, you will find that you need only a few letter or number drills on hand for most jobs.

Measuring drills.   Nearly all drills, until you get down to the really small sizes, have stamped or etched size markings on their shanks, but such markings tend to become unreadable from chucking and wear. Although a good drill-storage box with exact-size holes is a fine way to keep drills separated by sizes, it's easy to make a mistake. A tiny burr from chuck slippage may cause you to insert a drill in the wrong hole.

Careful metalworkers use a drill plate to check size before drilling. You can get such plates, made of hardened steel, for fractional, number, and letter drills. Each hole is marked; it takes only a second to insert the drill in the hole to see if it fits. Always try the next smaller hole, too. If the drill won't go, you've got the right size.

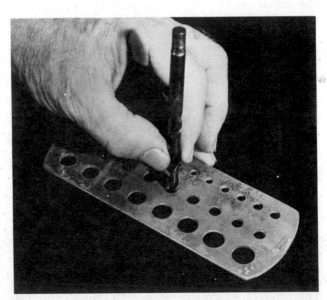

Steel drill plate gives you a quick check of drill size. It's good practice to use it whenever you select a drill.

Even so, if a drill has quite a bit of wear, the ribbed edges which establish the working diameter, called the "margins" of a drill, may be undersized enough to be misleading. The only sure check of such a drill is to take a micrometer measurement of the shank just above the flutes. If the drill is badly worn it should be discarded. If the severe wear is limited to a short portion, you can grind off the worn part and use it as a shorter drill.

Taps and Dies

You can't get into metalworking very far without getting acquainted with bolts, nuts, and screws. They're the most common devices for holding things together. For those of technical bent, it's worth noting that a thread is actually an inclined plane or wedge coiled around a central support. It's important to keep this wedge image in mind since the act of tightening a bolt or nut really amounts to driving a wedge tighter and tighter until the fastener metal is slightly stretched and the elasticity of the bolt metal acts as a permanent retaining force.

As with any wedge introduced between two surfaces, anything which might interfere with the sliding action, such as dirt, rust, burrs, or a poorly shaped taper, will also impair the tightening action. In short, it makes it harder, perhaps impossible, to drive the wedge. Taps, which create the internal threads in a hole, and dies, which cut the external threads on a bolt, actually form the working wedge surfaces, and understanding them is basic to the metalworker.

Although it's hard to imagine today, in the early days of the Industrial Revolution there were almost as many different thread forms and twists as there were manufacturers. There were no real standards establishing the same thread shape, diameter, or number of threads per inch. Some manufacturers thought it advantageous to use threads no one else could match.

Out of this confusion there evolved a number of standardized and foreign thread configurations still used today—British Whitworth, British Association, French Standard, International Metric, and Acme, the last for square threads. One notable difference is the vee-shape of the Whitworth British thread, which is 55°, while nearly all others are 60°. None of these is interchangeable with U.S. Standard threads.

U.S. Standard Threads. Fortunately, shortly before World War I, the United States established the American National Thread, later called U.S. Standard. For most home-shop use you will need only taps and dies meeting Na-

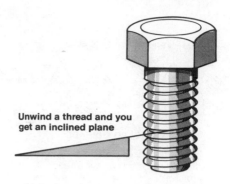

Unless you think about it, you may not picture a screw thread as a wedge or an inclined plane. Before machines made it easy to cut screw threads, however, wedges were commonly used to secure parts together. The screw form simply spirals the inclined plane around a central axis.

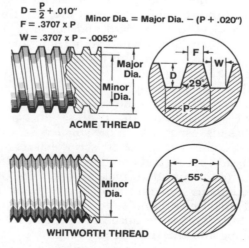

For a wedge to work properly it must slide freely between the working surfaces. This is also true of threads. Dirt or rust will interfere with the tightening action. Also, the threads must be clean and free from deformation to perform well.

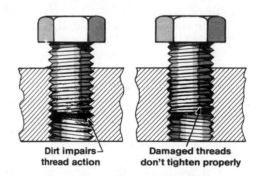

$$D = \frac{P}{2} + .010''$$
$$F = .3707 \times P$$
$$W = .3707 \times P - .0052''$$

Minor Dia. = Major Dia. − (P + .020'')

ACME THREAD

WHITWORTH THREAD

If you work on British products such as cars you'll probably encounter the Whitworth thread. You'll find Acme threads used on vises and presses where great strength is needed.

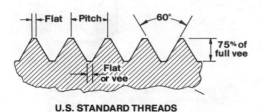

U.S. STANDARD THREADS

The American National (U.S. Standard) thread form uses a 60° vee and has a flat crest on top of the thread. On some mass-produced bolts this crest may be slightly rounded. Also, when you use a vee-shaped tool to lathe-cut a thread, the bottom will be a vee form, but you can leave the top of the thread flat.

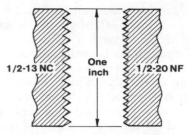

Learn to think of nuts and bolts according to their major diameter and pitch or number of threads per inch. After a while you'll be able to identify most common threads by eye.

tional Fine (once called SAE) or National Coarse standards. These are often abbreviated N.F. and N.C. on drawings. Also, you'll encounter metric threads more and more and eventually you will probably invest in a small set of metric taps and dies. One other thread form, interchangeable with U.S. Standard, is the so-called Unified Thread, UNF or UNC, intended for ease of interchange in military equipment and used jointly by several nations. If your metalworking hobby is gunsmithing, you may run into it.

U.S. Standard threads are described according to the diameter of the screw or bolt body and the number of threads per inch. The first number is the diameter of the fastener. For example, a ½"-20 thread is for a ½"-diameter bolt and has 20 threads per inch. This holds true down to ¼" diameter. Below that, number sizes are used and you'll commonly encounter 6-32, 8-32, and 10-32 or other sizes. To be certain of the diameter, you'll have to check a chart listing these sizes. To get an idea, a small screw such as you might find in a clock or an electrical appliance could be a 6-32, which means the body diameter of the screw is .138", just over ⅛". But it might also be 6-36 or 6-40 and not have 32 threads per inch. Thus, when your repair work calls for tapping new threads for old screws the system can be a challenge.

The above system applies to both fine and coarse threads. It is easy, however, for the inexperienced metalworker to confuse fine and coarse threads, especially in the smaller sizes. A common coarse-thread ¼"-20 screw has eight fewer threads per inch than a fine-thread ¼"-28. Thus, it's not unusual to pick up a ¼" nut by visual judgment and find that it will go on a thread a turn or two and suddenly become too tight to turn. This is because the wedge has the wrong slope and the spacing is wrong.

Choosing taps and dies. The most frequent use of hand-operated taps and dies in the home shop

is cleaning up existing threads. If you're repairing a lawnmower or restoring an antique car, your first job, after segregating the fasteners as to use, locations, and length, is to clean them up in solvent so you can inspect them carefully for damage. If rust and corrosion are a factor, you should probably clean them individually with a wire brush wheel in a bench grinder. Then, to be certain that each will screw smoothly into its tapped hole, you should run a die of the correct size and thread over them to clean up and reshape any threads which are nicked, battered, or deformed. It's even more important that you run a tap into the threaded holes to remove dirt and debris which would interfere with future seating of the bolt and perhaps give an illusion of tightness.

If you work in a tool room making precision parts you'll soon become acquainted with the four fits of threads. They range from Class 1 (loose) to Class 4 (close). For ordinary work in the home shop the taps and dies you buy at the hardware store, as well as the nuts and bolts, are usually a Class 2 (free) fit.

Moreover, you will probably find that a set or kit of small taps and dies going up to ½" is adequate. The two largest would be ½"-20NF and

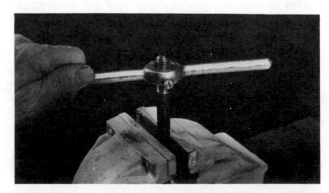

It takes only a minute to clean up the threads on a critical fastener with a small die, and it makes assembly easier.

DECIMAL EQUIVALENTS
of Wire, Letter and Fractional Size Drills

Drill Size	Decimal	Drill Size	Decimal	Drill Size	Decimal
80	.0135	1/8	.1250	O	.3160
79	.0145	30	.1285	P	.3230
1/64	.0156	29	.1360	21/64	.3281
78	.0160	28	.1405	Q	.3320
77	.0180	9/64	.1406	R	.3390
76	.0200	27	.1440	11/32	.3438
75	.0210	26	.1470	S	.3480
74	.0225	25	.1495	T	.3580
73	.0240	24	.1520	23/64	.3594
72	.0250	23	.1540	U	.3680
71	.0260	5/32	.1562	3/8	.3750
70	.0280	22	.1570	V	.3770
69	.0292	21	.1590	W	.3860
68	.0310	20	.1610	25/64	.3906
1/32	.0313	19	.1660	X	.3970
67	.0320	18	.1695	Y	.4040
66	.0330	11/64	.1719	13/32	.4062
65	.0350	17	.1730	Z	.4130
64	.0360	16	.1770	27/64	.4219
63	.0370	15	.1800	7/16	.4375
62	.0380	14	.1820	29/64	.4531
61	.0390	13	.1850	15/32	.4688
60	.0400	3/16	.1875	31/64	.4844
59	.0410	12	.1890	1/2	.5000
58	.0420	11	.1910	33/64	.5156
57	.0430	10	.1935	17/32	.5313
56	.0465	9	.1960	35/64	.5469
3/64	.0469	8	.1990	9/16	.5625
55	.0520	7	.2010	37/64	.5781
54	.0550	13/64	.2031	19/32	.5938
53	.0595	6	.2040	39/64	.6094
1/16	.0625	5	.2055	5/8	.6250
52	.0635	4	.2090	41/64	.6406
51	.0670	3	.2130	21/32	.6562
50	.0700	7/32	.2188	43/64	.6719
49	.0730	2	.2210	11/16	.6875
48	.0760	1	.2280	45/64	.7031
5/64	.0781	A	.2340	23/32	.7188
47	.0785	15/64	.2344	47/64	.7344
46	.0810	B	.2380	3/4	.7500
45	.0820	C	.2420	49/64	.7656
44	.0860	D	.2460	25/32	.7812
43	.0890	E 1/4	.2500	51/64	.7969
42	.0935	F	.2570	13/16	.8125
3/32	.0938	G	.2610	53/64	.8281
41	.0960	17/64	.2656	27/32	.8438
40	.0980	H	.2660	55/64	.8594
39	.0995	I	.2720	7/8	.8750
38	.1015	J	.2770	57/64	.8906
37	.1040	K	.2810	29/32	.9062
36	.1065	9/32	.2812	59/64	.9219
7/64	.1094	L	.2900	15/16	.9375
35	.1100	M	.2950	61/64	.9531
34	.1110	19/64	.2969	31/32	.9688
33	.1130	N	.3020	63/64	.9844
32	.1160	5/16	.3125	1	1.000
31	.1200				

TAP DRILL SIZES
Based on Approximately
75% Full Thread

Thread	Drill	Thread	Drill
#0–80	3/64	1-3/4–5	1-35/64
#1–64	No. 53	1-3/4–12	1-43/64
#1–72	No. 53	2-4-1/2	1-25/32
#2–56	No. 51	2–12	1-59/64
#2–64	No. 50	2-1/4-4-1/2	2-1/32
#3–48	5/64	2-1/2–4	2-1/4
#3–56	No. 46	2-3/4–4	2-1/2
#4–40	No. 43	3–4	2-3/4
#4–48	No. 42		
#5–40	No. 39		
#5–44	No. 37	**Taper Pipe**	
#6–32	No. 36		
#6–40	No. 33	1/8–27	R
#8–32	No. 29	1/4–18	7/16
#8–36	No. 29	3/8–18	37/64
#10–24	No. 25	1/2–14	23/32
#10–32	No. 21	3/4–14	59/64
#12–24	No. 17	1–11-1/2	1-5/32
#12–28	No. 15	1-1/4–11-1/2	1-1/2
1/4–20	No. 8	1-1/2–11-1/2	1-47/64
1/4–28	No. 3	2–11-1/2	2-7/32
5/16–18	F	2-1/2–8	2-5/8
5/16–24	I	3–8	3-1/4
3/8–16	5/16	3-1/2–8	3-3/4
3/8–24	Q	4–8	4-1/4
7/16–14	U	5–8	5-9/32
7/16–20	W	6–8	6-11/32
1/2–12	27/64		
1/2–13	27/64		
1/2–20	29/64	**Straight Pipe**	
9/16–12	31/64		
9/16–18	33/64	1/8–27	S
5/8–11	17/32	1/4–18	29/64
5/8–18	37/64	3/8–18	19/32
3/4–10	21/32	1/2–14	47/64
3/4–16	11/16	3/4–14	15/16
7/8–9	49/64	1–11-1/2	1-3/16
7/8–14	13/16	1-1/4–11-1/2	1-33/64
1–8	7/8	1-1/2–11-1/2	1-3/4
1–12	59/64	2–11-1/2	2-7/32
1–14	15/16	2-1/2–8	2-21/32
1-1/8–7	63/64	3–8	3-9/32
1-1/8–12	1-3/64	3-1/2–8	3-25/32
1-1/4–7	1-7/64	4–8	4-9/32
1-1/2–6	1-11/32	5–8	5-11/32
1-1/2–12	1-27/64	6–8	6-13/32

Tap-drill sizes and their relationships to fractional, number, and letter drills are something you'll refer to constantly in metalworking. This chart will guide you in selecting twist drills for your shop.

1/2"-13NC; the smallest 6-32. Although you may have occasion to buy larger sizes for special jobs, certain facts will have a bearing on your choice. The first point is that even though it's fairly easy to hand-run taps and dies up to 1/2" for cleaning up existing threads, it's quite a chore to hand-cut threads even 5/8" in diameter from scratch.

Types of taps.   You will probably find that your hardware-store taps will be tapered back quite a few threads from the tip. This makes hand-tapping easier since the tap enters the hole gradually and the amount of metal removed near the tip of the tap is not full thread depth. As you progress into the metal, each successive cutting edge cuts the threads deeper. Such taps are fine for cutting a thread all the way through a workpiece and emerging on the opposite side. But if you are tapping into a blind hole you must, if possible, drill the hole quite a bit deeper than needed. This allows the tap to be run deep enough so the partial threads at the bottom do not interfere with the bolt later. In many cases,

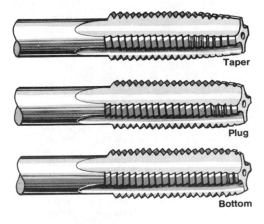

If you're tapping straight through a workpiece, a taper tap is fine, but if you're tapping into a blind hole the taper tap leaves partial threads at the bottom. A follow-up with a plug tap or a bottoming tap will clean them up.

however, such an extra-deep hole is not practical. Here, the usual practice is to follow the original tap with one having somewhat less taper, called a "plug" tap. You can buy plug taps, of course, and you can buy "bottoming" taps which will cut threads almost to the bottom of a blind hole, but it's just as easy to grind off the first few tapered threads from a tapered tap. Very often, most of the wear on a tap takes place right at the bottom so such grinding is a practical salvage operation.

Types of dies.   If you buy the usual tap and die set, the dies will probably be "solid" dies. These are often called "thread-chasers" since they serve best for cleaning up existing threads. They also work reasonably well for cutting new threads in fairly soft metal, including mild steel, as long as they are new and sharp. But after solid dies are slightly worn they will produce oversize threads which may be very tight or impossible to thread into a tapped hole or nut. Thus, if you do quite a bit of thread cutting you'll probably want to buy a set of adjustable dies. Often such dies are split or slotted at one point, and the die holder has a screw to allow adjustment by squeezing the slot together slightly. There are variations on this, because some metalworkers prefer to cut the threads slightly oversize at first and then follow with a final finishing and sizing cut after adjusting the die.

Pipe Thread Cutters

Pipe threads are used on pipes and fittings which will contain liquids or gas under pressure. You'll find them on the brass and aluminum fittings used on fuel and hydraulic lines, oil lines, and the like on automobiles, boats, airplanes, and outdoor power equipment. Don't be surprised if one end of such an elbow or fitting has tapered pipe threads and another end has a straight SAE thread. Straight threads are used to couple onto flared fittings and other connections. You will always find pipe threads on common galvanized and black-iron water and gas pipes.

One of the first surprises the beginning metalworker gets is when he encounters tapered pipe threads. As the name implies, the thread starts out small in diameter at the entering end of the pipe and tapers out to the full diameter of the pipe. You might compare it to a tapered cork with threads. The principle is the same since both cork and pipe thread are intended as much for sealing as for holding things together.

A few years ago cutting and threading galvanized pipe was a routine metalworking job in the home shop. Installation of a sink, water

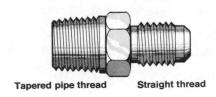

Tapered pipe thread   Straight thread

Almost all conventional plumbing fittings and many automotive fittings use tapered pipe threads for sealing against leakage. Pipe threads and straight threads, however, are incompatible.

Large holes are difficult to cut without hole saws. Note the firm clamping to resist powerful cutting action.

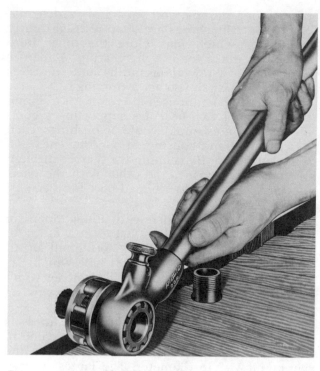

This compact pipe-threading die holder is made for working in tight spots. Ratchet permits limited handle swing.

heater, or simple connection for a garden hose always involved such pipe. To a large extent, the use of copper and plastic pipe has reduced the need for threading such pipe. Moreover, most hardware and plumbing shops will cut pipe to length and thread it for a minimal charge and use fast-cutting power machinery to do it.

Nevertheless, there are enough occasions to clean up thread-tapped holes for pipes and pipe plugs that you will sooner or later need pipe taps in ⅛″, ¼″, ⅜″, and ½″ sizes. I cannot, however, recommend buying pipe dies for hand threading. These dies are costly and their use involves a lot of muscle, especially in the common ¾″ and 1″ sizes.

Hole Saws

Up to ½″ it's a simple process to drill a hole in metal with a twist drill and electric drill or drill press. Go much larger and you run into trouble with the chuck sizes and pressures needed, not to mention the cost of the twist drill. There are often better and less costly options. For holes of standard fractional sizes, tubular-shaped saws called hole saws work well unless you want to cut to very accurate dimensions. Hole saws will cut a pluglike piece of waste out of most metals except hardened steel, and they can be used in

hand-held drills although a drill press is better. You can buy them in fractional sizes from about ½″ up to 3″ or more in diameter. Do not, however, expect to get good results in metal with the type sold with a series of ring shaped saws nested in a die-cast holder with concentric grooves. Such saws may serve for cutting holes in wooden bird houses, but they are not of high enough quality for metal work.

Quality hole saws come as individual tools and are screwed onto an adapter or shank which fits the drill chuck. It pays to buy a good industrial brand such as Milwaukee.

Fly Cutters

Sometimes you have to drill an off-size hole. That's when you need a fly cutter. Fly cutters are like expansion auger bits for woodworking;

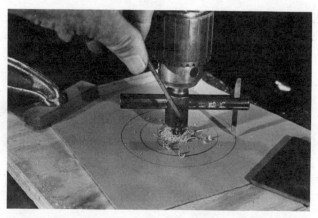

Fly cutter is another way to open up large holes. Diameter of cut can be adjusted by sliding the beam, shown here being adjusted with hex-key wrench. Best advice—try it first on scrap.

they can be adjusted to produce a hole of non-standard diameter. Basically, they consist of a hardened, sharp-cornered tool bit mounted in a beam extending from a central driving member. The bit is adjustable. A small twist drill, usually about ¼", extends from the central member and acts as a stabilizing center in a pilot hole.

Fly cutters have definite limitations and work best in softer metals such as aluminum. They are almost useless in hard steel. They also work best in relatively thin stock but are difficult and dangerous to use in a hand-held electic drill. For safety, if possible use a fly cutter in a drill press. Clamp the work firmly, with a piece of wood underneath it to protect the table.

Reamers

The reamer is the metalworker's tool for producing an accurate and finely finished hole, usually after drilling the hole slightly (.005" to .010") undersize. Reamers have a scraping action and are not intended to remove large amounts of metal. The flutes are commonly straight but are sometimes spiral if the hole to be reamed has an interruption such as a keyway.

Unless you have to produce many precise fits, you will almost certainly acquire reamers as you need them for specific jobs. One routine use is the final sizing of bushing-type bearings in elec-

tric motors, pumps, and yard and garden machines. Such bushings are often pressed tightly into place which may close the inner bore enough to make for a tight bearing. A reamer will remove a few thousandths and whatever high spots exist so you get a running fit.

Another important use for a reamer is aligning the centers of two bearings supporting a common shaft. An example would be bushings, each in a separate end housing, at opposite ends of a motor or pump. By running the reamer through one and directly into the other with the parts assembled, a straight, aligned bore for the shaft is created.

Taper reamers. Reamers with a long taper can sometimes be used when you're in a hurry to haggle out a hole which is too small or ill formed. A simple rivet or bolt hole which has somehow become battered so the fastener won't pass through can be opened up with a few twists of a taper reamer.

A more important use for taper reamers is sizing holes for taper pins. Taper pins come in numbered sizes. The smallest is 7/0, with the large end ¹⁄₁₆" in diameter. The largest is #10 with a large-end diameter of .706". They all have a standard taper of ¼" per foot, but for each size there are many selective lengths available. This means that if you disassemble a gear or shaft by driving out the taper pin, you should save the

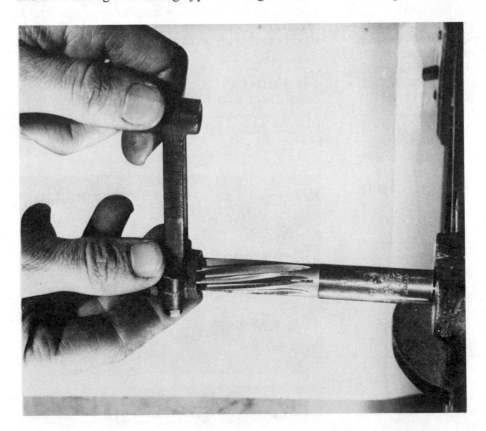

There are better ways to re-size this small connecting rod, but a spiral reamer works well. The object: to obtain a fit on the crankpin with about a .0015" clearance.

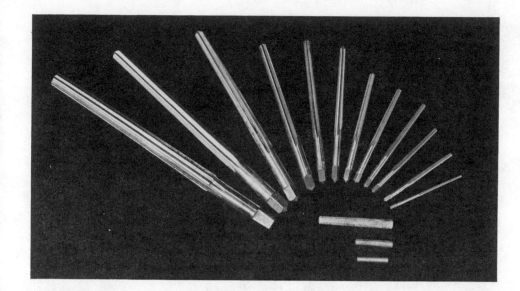

Taper-pin reamers are available in full sets, but few home shops need the larger ones. Typical pins are at bottom.

This handy set contains two cold chisels, center punches, pin punches, and drift pin. The straight sides of the pin punches let you follow the pin through the hole as you tap it out. Tapered drift pin aligns two holes in mating parts.

old pin for matching an exact replacement or an oversize one on reassembly.

A taper pin does its job only if the taper of the hole is an exact fit for the pin. You must select the reamer and size the hole carefully so that the pin enters the hole most of the way and may be driven tight the rest of the way. For most home-shop work, taper reamers in the 3/0 to #4 size range will suffice unless you are working with very small or very large pins. The sizes given range roughly from 1/8" to 1/4" at the large end.

Cold Chisels

All metalwork is not delicate or precise. Times arise when some fairly heavy-handed action is the best approach. Examples: removing old rivets from angle iron, whacking out a rough opening in a drum, or chopping off lengths of metal rod for garden supports. Cold chisels are ideal for such jobs. They are called cold chisels because they are intended for shearing cold metal rather than metal heated and softened in a forge.

Old-time metalworking books aimed at apprentices made much of many sizes and shapes

Taper or straight pins can be driven out with a pin punch. With taper pins you must determine large and small ends.

of cold chisels and the techniques of using them for opening cavities and actually carving into metal. This type of strong-arm operation has little place in the home shop. Today there are usually better ways, such as using a rotary file in a hand grinder to do the same job. If you doubt this, try hand chiseling a 1"-deep slot about ⅜" wide in a block of steel.

It is best to buy general-purpose chisels in a set of selected sizes, together with a variety of punches, from a reputable source. The cutting edge must be hard; but not so hard it chips. The striking end must be soft to avoid chipping, but not so soft it batters and mushes out into potential fragments.

Eye protection in the form of strong goggles is essential. So are gloves. A flying fragment from a chisel can penetrate your eye or your hand.

The most common accident with a cold chisel, however, is striking your hand or knuckle with the hammer. Since you're usually using a heavy hammer or small, single-hand sledge, this can be extremely painful. I learned long ago to hold the chisel with some sort of holding device. One such is a length of ³⁄₁₆" or ¼" rod wound once or twice around the chisel shank with the two ends extending for a handle. A simpler, and better, holder is about 8" of large size car heater hose. Drill a hole through the hose about 1½" from the end and force the chisel through it. You can now hold and aim the chisel firmly without getting your hand too close to the action.

The punches mentioned above as commonly sold with the chisel sets are called pin punches and are used for driving out retaining pins. You may also find your set includes one or two center punches for layout work, which I'll discuss later.

Bolt Cutters

There are other rough-cutting operations where a cold chisel won't work because there's no way to back up the cut with the equivalent of an anvil. If there's no handy way to hold the work for hacksawing, your best choice is a powerful set of toggle-levered cutting jaws called bolt cutters.

Bolt cutters are available as small bench tools for cutting heavy wire to enormous models for cutting heavy reinforcing bars. A pair about 22" long will take care of most of your home cutting needs. You'll be amazed at the power of their toggle action. If you let it get out that you own a pair you'll also be surprised how often the neighbors want to borrow them.

STRIKING TOOLS

The first working tools of mankind were probably stones gripped and used as hammers. Simple though the concept of a hammer seems, there

Bolt cutters come much larger than this, but the size shown is about right for the home shop. It easily cuts 5/16" mild steel.

When a rusted nut won't budge, a nut splitter with a powerful screw action will split it free without damaging bolt thread.

are a number of physical principles involved which go beyond the obvious. Over the years, thousands of different forms and shapes have evolved for striking tools.

Hammers

The common carpenter's nail hammer has a single purpose, to bring the concentrated force of the blow onto a nail head. But a silversmith or worker in copper or sheet metal may need a hammer with a striking face shaped quite dif-

ferently. He uses his hammer for forming metal. And the silversmith's hammer would be ill-suited to peening over a rivet or striking heavy blows on a cold chisel.

All of this involves something more than the shape of the striking face. The Stone Age man instinctively recognized that the stone he used had mass or weight. The principle is one of ballistics. Move a given weight through a given distance at a given velocity and you develop so many pound/feet of energy. Thus, the hammer may, like a small bullet, be relatively light but swung or moved very rapidly to generate and concentrate the desired force. Or, it may be a heavy sledge swung quite slowly. In theory, both could develop the same energy, but in practice

When push and pressure wouldn't do the job, early man learned that impact, mass plus velocity, often would. Some of man's earliest tools were crude hammers.

the metalworker chooses according to the job.

Other details also respect the laws of physics. The craftsman may talk of the "feel" or balance of a hammer. What he's really saying is that the shape of the head or the placement of the handle locates the center of gravity in a comfortable spot. The handle is equally important. For some jobs a light, springy handle may be just right. For others, delivering a heavy blow, for example, a thick, rigid handle is better.

In general, claw hammers intended for driving and pulling nails are not well suited to metalwork. A better choice is the machinist's hammer or ball-pein hammer with a rounded head opposite the striking face. The rounded pein has many uses, from forming rivet heads to shaping metal. A second choice might be the cross-pein hammer with a rounded wedge shape opposite the striking face.

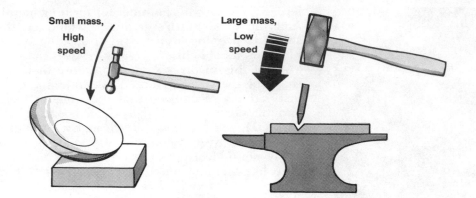

Small mass, High speed

Large mass, Low speed

Impact force must match the job. Sometimes heavy blows from a slow-moving tool work best as with a cold chisel, but other projects are better handled by a light, rapidly moving tool. Art-metal workers, for example, use a wide variety of hammers carefully selected to permit just the right impact to shape the metal.

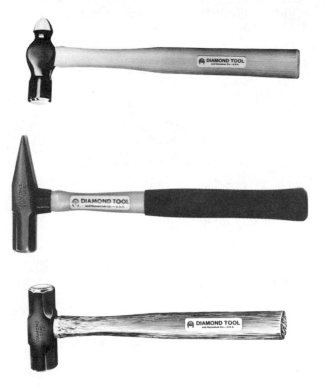

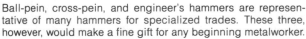
Ball-pein, cross-pein, and engineer's hammers are representative of many hammers for specialized trades. These three, however, would make a fine gift for any beginning metalworker.

Able to bump without battering, the soft-faced hammer has many uses in the shop.

If you get into forging and shaping metals with a hammer, you will probably acquire many hammers with special features. One could be a planishing hammer with a broad, almost flat, striking surface. Another might be an auto-body hammer with a pick-like extension of the head. But for getting started in metalwork, a medium-weight ball-pein is the most practical.

Special hammer faces. Still more physics, reflecting the elastic characteristics of materials, are mixed into a class of hammers often called

soft-face hammers. In many instances you'll find that you want to deliver a heavy blow, but you don't want to dent or batter the work. One of the best hammers for this is a simple cylinder of lead cast in a tin can (later removed) with a short piece of pipe cast in the lead for a handle. A lead hammer delivers a heavy "thud"-type blow rather than the ringing blow of a steel hammer. Such a blow is preferable for shifting a heavy object or locating a polished, finished piece. An example might be seating a bearing race in a press fit hole. For a somewhat snappier

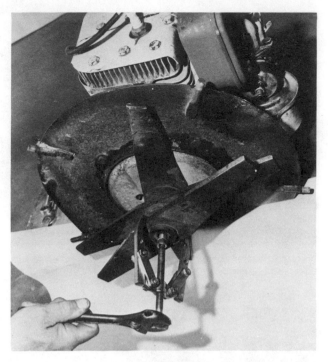

blow, a hammer of brass or copper is recommended. The brass is more elastic than lead and the impact is sharper, but most hard metals are not damaged.

For the beginner, a soft-face hammer with plastic striking surfaces is adequate. Plastic-face hammers seldom mar surfaces and they do deliver a dull blow.

PULLERS

I've mentioned several times that the beginning metalworker will almost certainly start with small repair jobs on appliances, yard and garden tools, perhaps small engines, and other devices which must be disassembled and reassembled.

The comparison with woodworking is interesting. With wood it's common practice to mortise-and-tenon or dowel a joint and secure it with glue. The process is a forgiving one with room for a little snugness or looseness. Metal parts which must transmit a load, such as pullies and gears, are fitted much more closely and many times are assembled with pressure, called a "press-fit," to actually stretch the metal slightly. Such press-fits, and others which are almost press-fits, cannot be disassembled without damage unless you have a special type of tool called a puller. This tool applies a powerful

Although this small, two-jaw puller exerts only moderate force, it is effective on many stubborn parts which would be damaged by hammering or prying. Most important—the force is directly in line with the shaft. Sometimes a tap with a hammer on the head of the puller screw will help, or a little heat from a torch may pop it loose.

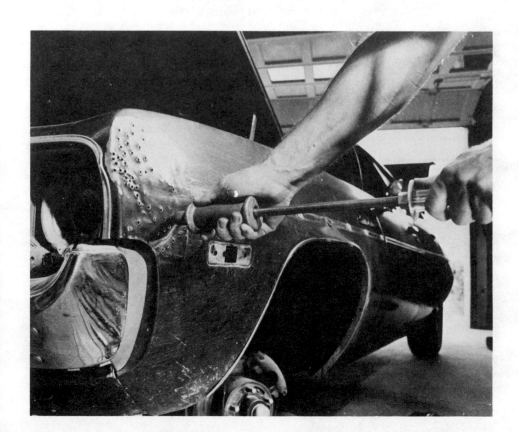

Impact, or slide-hammer, puller with a screw-in tip gets its power from the inertia of the sliding weight. In spite of appearance here, finished fender looked fine.

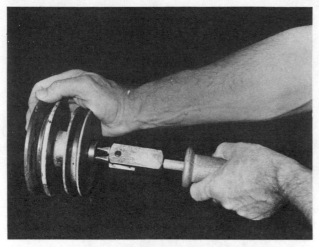

An impact puller combined with an internal jaw puller makes quick work of removing bearing from this pulley.

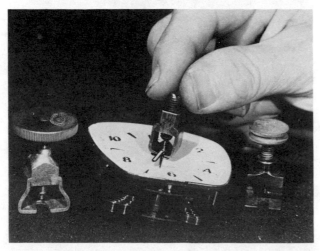

Miniature pullers are especially made for removing delicate hands from clocks and instruments.

Often you'll chip out pulley flanges or be unable to pull a small gear or pulley by direct jaw action. A backing plate slipped behind or into pulley groove distributes the force evenly.

force directly in line with the desired direction of movement.

Some pullers fit or grip the outer edges of the object to be removed. An example would be a two- or three-jaw puller on a gear. Other pullers work down internally to remove parts such as bearing outer races. We'll look at several types of pullers. Most of them use screw pressure, some use inertia or impact pressure, and some even use extremely powerful hydraulic cylinders. For the type of tool you'll keep in a kitchen drawer, the smaller, external-jaw pullers are good starter choices.

Jaw Pullers

The most common job of pulling you'll meet is removing a small pulley from an appliance, motor, engine, or workshop machine. Such pulleys are normally assembled with a slip fit or no more than a modest tap to locate them on the shaft. Unfortunately, they seldom come off as easily as it's presumed they went on at the factory. Setscrew scars, rust, and corrosion, and perhaps damage from previous poor workmanship, make them too tight to pull by hand.

Often nothing more than a small two-jaw puller gripping the hub or flange will remove such parts easily. The puller jaws simply hook behind the part, and tightening the screw forces the movement. But, if you have a choice, gripping near the hub is better than gripping the outer edge, and three jaws are better than two. The three jaws pull more evenly. Later, as you grow into more difficult jobs, you'll want to assemble a group of larger and heavier jaw pullers. I suggest that whenever you feel you owe yourself a little present you buy the next size up. The economics favor pullers. One job, impossible without a puller, will pay its cost.

Internal Pullers

Unless you expect to do a lot of motor or engine repair, or work on other equipment with bearings inside housings, internal pullers are less useful in the average shop. They, too, are jaw pullers, but the jaws open outward under the pressure of a screw to grip the internal bore of a bearing race or like part. The pulling force may be a pair of screws on each side, but quite often a device called a slide hammer is used to deliver a sharp blow and, in a sense, drive the part out in reverse.

Face Pullers

Perhaps the best example of a face puller is the tiny U-shaped puller used to pull pressed-on hands from clocks or instruments. Such pullers slip in behind the workpiece and bear against it with a flat face rather than gripping it with jaws.

The same principle, on a larger scale, is often necessary to pull certain kinds of pulleys from shafts. The concentrated force of the jaw-type pullers will often break or distort the pulley. By slipping a pair of plates behind the part the pressure can be brought to bear near the hub where damage is less likely to occur.

MEASURING TOOLS

Metalworking usually requires closer dimensions than does woodworking. This does not apply to hammering and forming art metal or wrought iron, or blacksmithing. It does apply to most repair work, model work, and machine-tool operations. Note how often when discussing tools and materials and drill sizes I have had to resort to decimal dimensions. Although the woodworker might talk of ¼" or ⅜" plywood, the metalworker is more likely to speak of "0-62" aluminum, for example. What he means is aluminum about 1/16" thick—thus, .062 or 62 thousandths.

To the beginner, the whole idea of dividing an inch into one thousand, or even ten thousand, parts for close work, seems almost ridiculous. If you're used to rough carpentry, 1/32" of an inch may seem more than close enough. Actually a good cabinetmaker will usually work to less than 1/32", but one-thousandth of an inch (.001)

is hard to picture. For a mental image, the page you are reading is probably three to four thousandths (.003-.004") thick. So is a human hair. Thus, it seems unlikely that you'll ever be able to work to such fine dimensions. There are, however, tools which make it easy.

Industry has literally thousands of special and general-purpose measuring tools for precision work. Most of them are far beyond the scope of the home metalworker. For practical purposes the following tools are adequate, at least for starters.

Combination square.   The rigid steel rule with a sliding square head, and sometimes a bevel protractor and center finder, is the tool of all uses in the metal shop. Although in no sense a real precision tool, it is used routinely for layout work, squaring drills and taps with a work surface, measuring, and even leveling. Most squares have a small bubble level built in. Typically, such rules are graduated in 1/16" and 1/8" on one side and 1/32" and 1/64" on the other. By sliding the square head to a given mark, using a magnifier if necessary, it is possible to work quite closely. Some workers prefer a decimal scale of tenths and hundredths.

Centers and angles.   The vee-shaped center finder is a standard part of a combination square. Its most common use is locating the approximate center on round stock for lathe and machine work. The bevel protractor head, which both slides on the rule and pivots within its own

A steel square and sharp steel scribe are the common layout tools of metalworker. Layout fluid makes lines visible.

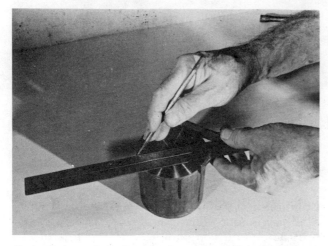

Center finder and steel square are used to scribe several lines across round stock. Intersection of lines is the center.

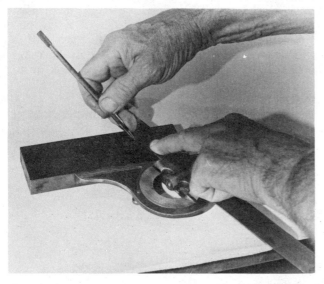

The steel square, this time fitted with a protractor head, is basic tool for laying out angles.

frame, is handy for laying out and checking angles. Since most protractors have a bubble level, you can use the tool to set up angle work from a level base.

Steel rules.   The thickness of the combination square's rule makes it difficult to view the markings versus a layout line without placing it on edge. Such measuring is much easier with a thin steel rule. There are a great many configurations and sizes of steel rules. Some have hooked ends for measuring in from edges. Others have sliding members, and some are narrow for measuring holes. Graduations may be fractional, decimal, or mixed. The finest graduations are one-hun-

dredths of an inch. Some form of magnifying aid is essential for reading such graduations accurately.

Outside micrometers.   Even though the square and rule are essential to the metalworker, measuring with them remains a judgment call and depends on your eyesight. Micrometers greatly reduce this judgment factor and let you read the dimensions directly in thousandths of an inch. There are many forms of micrometers, but in the home shop your greatest need will be for the standard one-inch, outside "mike." It will measure from .000″ to 1.000″. Later, if you get into larger work, you may want to get a one-to-two-inch or even larger micrometer.

Micrometers have a rotatable outer barrel, or thimble, with a central, precisely threaded, spindle screw. Each full turn of the thimble moves the spindle twenty-five thousandths (.025″) of an inch. Therefore, each of the markings around the outside of the thimble represents one-thousandth of an inch. The main frame, or hub, of the micrometer also has markings of .025″, these along the longitudinal axis. These are numbered and four, of course, make up one-hundred thousandths. Some micrometers also have another scale, called a vernier, on the hub, which makes it possible to divide the single one-thousandths markings by ten and read to one ten-thousandth of an inch (.0001″).

The standard micrometer has two hardened and polished flat surfaces to contact the work. The lower, fixed one is called the anvil. The work to be measured is placed between the end of the spindle and the anvil and the thimble turned down until a slight drag is felt. This requires both the feel of the contact with the work and the amount of turning pressure on the thimble. Again, judgment, skill, and practice enter the picture. Heavy-handed tightening will spring the micrometer frame and give a false reading. So will too loose a contact with the work. To reduce this error, many micrometers have a small knob at the upper end with a spring-loaded slip-ratchet. You tighten this knob until you feel and hear the ratchet slip. This feature makes it possible to control the tightening action mechanically and consistently rather than by feel.

Inside micrometers.   Inside micrometers and depth gages are marked and read just like outside types. Instead of being C-shaped, they have projecting tips and rods to bear against inner surfaces. The depth gage has a flat surface to bridge the top of the workpiece and a rod to contact the bottom of the hole.

Inside micrometers are used for measuring

Author's father at work adjusting a large micrometer. Gage blocks in tray on bench are masters, accurate within millionths of an inch. Even so, feel and judgment are part of precision measuring.

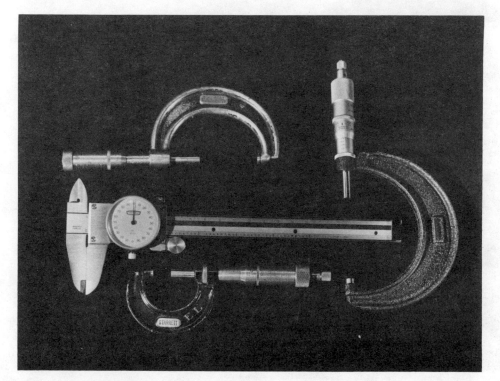

Measuring tools you'll probably want for your home shop are micrometers and dial calipers. In the beginning, one-inch range "mikes" at bottom will handle most jobs.

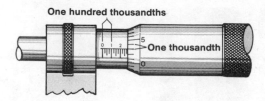

One hundred thousandths

One thousandth

Reading a micrometer is not difficult. One rotation of the thimble moves the spindle anvil twenty-five thousandths of an inch and each thousandth is marked on the thimble. Think of them as minute hand markings on a clock face. Here, we read .278".

bore diameters or the distance between two parts. They are more difficult to use than outside micrometers. Unless you work with a metal-cutting lathe, your need for inside mikes in the home shop will be limited.

Dial indicators. Every metalworker (and woodworker, too) should eventually obtain a dial indicator. I'll explain why in a moment. There are many varieties of dial measuring instruments, but the basic feature is a small, clocklike dial divided into one-thousandth-inch, sometimes

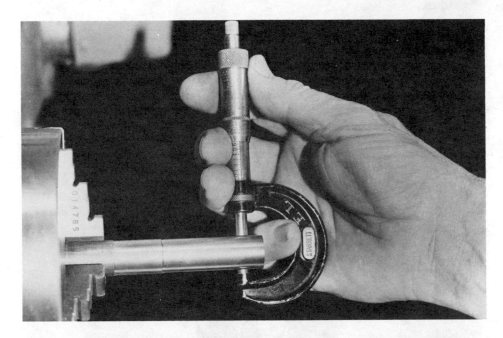

The usual way to grip a micrometer is shown here. Thumb and forefinger turn the barrel and feel for contact. Third finger can turn knurled spindle lock.

If you prefer to use the ratchet to be sure of uniform measurements, a two-handed grip is necessary.

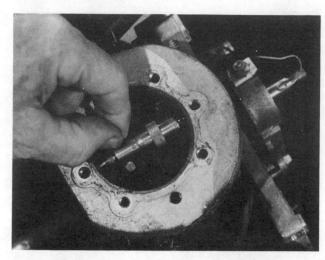

Inside micrometer is not as easy to use as outside type. In this picture, micrometer is set up for its shortest range. By using selected extension rods in end at left, range can be extended up to 12".

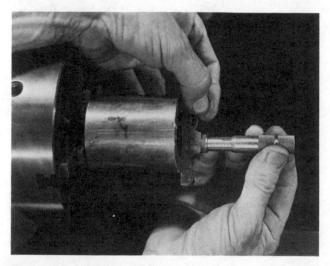

Depth micrometer extends inward to measure a location such as a shoulder or the bottom of a bored hole. A delicate touch is needed.

.0001", markings, and a movable hand which swings around the dial. The hand is connected to the indicator contact through a precise, clockwork-type linkage.

The dial indicator measures movement. With it, you can check a table saw for blade wobble, a drill press with a movable spindle for looseness, runout, and lack of squareness.

The delicacy of the dial and its sensitivity to the slightest movement means that it must be rigidly supported relative to the work. Beginning metalworkers are often amazed when they see a movement of several thousandths of an inch on the dial when they exert moderate mus-

Two styles of dial indicators. Larger one at left has a sensing rod extending directly from the back. Dial at right has an extended finger and is more easily positioned for many jobs. Faces rotate for zero setting.

cle power on an apparently husky part. You can, for example, flex a heavy cast-iron flywheel housing as much as three or four thousandths with your hands.

Dial calipers. Common calipers with a scaled beam and a sliding member are quite useful for comparative readings such as rough-sizing a piece of metal being turned or comparing two pieces of stock for size. They do, however, suffer the same problems as other rule-type tools in requiring a visual reading against fine graduations. Dial calipers combine a dial indicator with a caliper. Gross readings of inches and fractions are read on the rule and the dial, precisely

Dial caliper is extremely useful when bringing work to size. Scale readings on frame give gross dimensions and dial reads in thousandths of an inch over that.

geared to the rule, provides the easily read numbers of additional thousandths of an inch to be added to the gross reading. One advantage of this tool is that even in modest size it can measure from .001″ up to 6″, outside, and to shallow depths inside, thus supplanting several other more limited gages.

Thread gages.   Under the topic of taps and dies I mentioned that it is relatively easy to be confused by threads. An inexpensive thread gage is the best way to determine the number of threads per inch on a bolt or screw. The gage has a number of small leaves, each cut on one edge with a specific number of threads per inch and so marked. By holding the threaded fastener

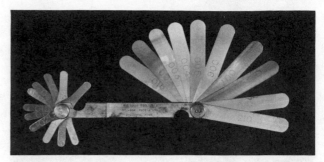

Feeler gages come in many styles, but this fold-out type is common. Thinnest leaf here is .001″. By adding them together you can come up with almost any desired thickness.

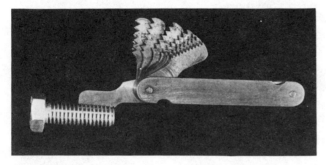

Using a thread gage is simply a matter of matching a tooth profile on the gage to the thread. Similar assortment on opposite end cover fine thread range.

against the gage, and holding both against the light if need be, you can readily see if they match. When you get a perfect fit you know the thread pitch.

It's not unusual today to find a thread which simply doesn't seem to fit. Such threads usually turn out to be metric. A metric gage is recommended.

Feeler gages.   Some dimensions in metalworking are difficult to measure simply because there is no room to insert a conventional measuring tool. Feeler gages, made of thin, springy steel finished to a precise thickness and so marked, are a handy solution. Persons familiar with autombile or small-engine tuning will recognize the technique as the same one used to set spark-plug gaps and adjust valve clearances. Since feeler gages, made up as individual strips in a holder, are as thin as .001″, they may be inserted into very small spaces. By adding or subtracting from a pack of such strips it is possible to build up a thickness which just enters and pulls out with a moderate drag. Adding up the thicknesses

Often feeler gages are the only practical way to measure something like the ring gap in this engine.

tells you the dimension of the opening. Feeler-gage stock is also available in bulk and can be used for gaging or snipped off and used as shims. In special cases—spark plugs and ignition points, for example—the contours of the surfaces to be measured are not suited to flat feeler gages. Round wire feeler gages or stock must be used here.

HEAT SOURCES
If you associate metalworking with a fiery forge, you are not far wrong. Heat is commonly needed for bending metal, loosening stuck parts, softening (annealing) and hardening, as well as for soldering, brazing, and melting metals for casting. For the beginning metalworker, many of these needs are easily satisfied with an inexpen-

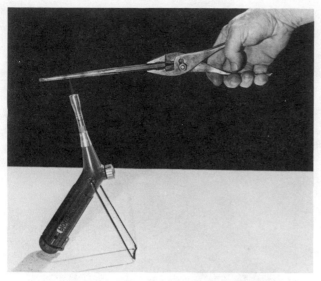

This small propane torch, recharged from a standard propane bottle, is handy for bench-top jobs such as hardening and tempering this punch to convert it to a special-use chisel.

sive and clean-burning propane torch. MAPP gas (stabilized methylacetylene and propadiene) provides a hotter flame. Both of these convenient bottle gases are sold widely. All you have to do is screw on the torch head and light.

Oxyacetylene and electric arc.   For actually welding steel, a still hotter source is needed such as the oxyacetylene torch or the electric arc. This type of equipment and its use is sufficiently specialized to be beyond the scope of this book. If you wish to extend your metalworking skills to welding, it is suggested that you refer to my *Electric and Gas Welding,* a Popular Science Book.

Soldering irons.   Soft soldering is another routine method of joining both ferrous and nonferrous metals. The jobs may range from securing hairlike wires in electronic gear to joining galvanized roofing and rain gutters. The latter type

Brazing outdoors, even in the wind, is possible as on this antenna ground connection. Torch is MAPP fueled.

Miniature butane torch is hot and precise for silver-soldering these tubing parts for a model engine.

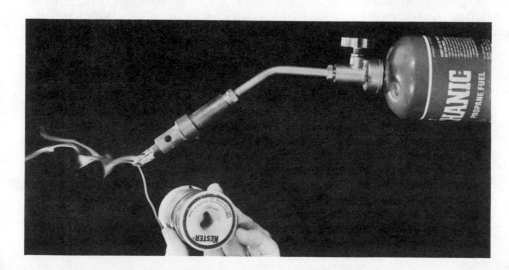

For heavier soldering, especially outside, this combination of propane torch and a soldering tip is inexpensive and very capable since the heat remains constant.

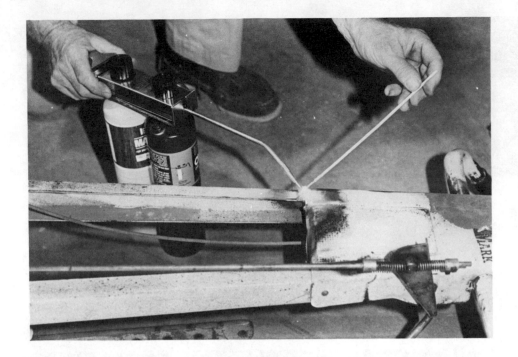

MAPP and oxygen provide a hot enough flame to braze light metal parts on this garden tiller. Beware, however, of trying to do heavy brazing on castings and the like with such torches.

An antique today, the old-fashioned soldering "iron," actually made of copper, was a practical way to carry heat from a flame source to the surface of the metal. Although crude, one might credit it with being a trouble-free tool that didn't burn out.

of soldering, as well as that done by the old-time tinker who soldered up leaks in pots and kettles, was done with a relatively heavy soldering "iron." The handle of this tool was wood to prevent burning your hand, the shank was steel, and the heavy, taper-ended iron was actually copper. In truth, soldering copper was a more accurate term, but even today they are called irons.

Such irons were heated externally in a blowtorch, plumber's pot, or gas flame. The copper absorbed and delivered a huge amount of heat but cooled in a relatively short time. Obviously, the heat was not constant. You started out too hot and ended up too cold. Such irons are inconvenient, but for really heavy jobs they sometimes work better than modern electric irons. For steady soldering, perhaps along the copper flashing of a building, it was common to have two or three irons so at least one was reheating while the other was in use. The apprentice ran up and down the ladder with the irons.

Electric soldering irons. As more and more soldering of a more delicate nature was required for electrical work, the big irons were found to be too clumsy and the smaller ones cooled too fast. Electric irons were developed with an internal resistance element to heat a copper tip.

As you get started in metalworking, you'll probably need this handy, general-purpose iron. When buying an iron, select a size suitable for your work, but pay special attention to the wattage rating. As with light bulbs, the higher the wattage the greater the output. Two electric irons may appear to be quite similar and of equal size, but a 200-watt iron will usually perform much better than a 125- or 150-watt tool. Low-wattage irons tend to soften but not really flow the solder and the result is a "cold" joint which is both weak and a poor seal.

At the other end of the scale, the type of iron with a small, rodlike tip for poking into tightly wired electrical circuits may be rated at 25 watts and still smaller ones may have only 18 or 20

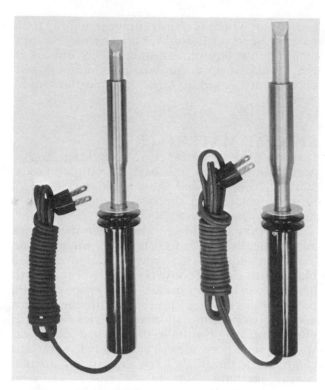

Two husky bench-top soldering irons for serious work. Iron on left is 120 watts; on right, 175 watts. Few home metalworking jobs require more than this.

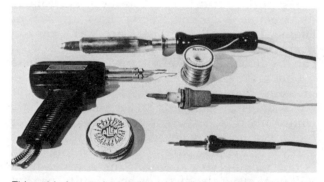

This soldering equipment is typical of most metalworking home shops. A large iron, two smaller irons, and a trigger-operated gun, plus resin-core solder and flux will handle most routine soft soldering.

If soldering small electrical connections is part of your work, don't try to do them with an oversize iron. Get a fine-tip iron like this one.

watts. These irons are not intended for heavy work but are essential for delicate soldering.

Soldering guns. In between the large and small soldering jobs you will find many middle-range, on-and-off jobs where you'll solder a joint or two, proceed with the next step, and solder again. Here, a trigger-operated soldering gun is handy since it produces almost instant heat at the touch of the trigger and shuts off when you release it. This avoids having a hot iron somewhere in your work area for long periods of time.

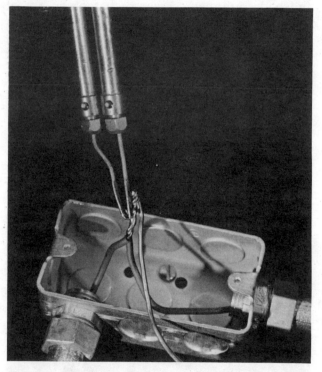

Gun-type soldering iron is ideal for quick-on, quick-off use on soldered wire connections. Apply solder to wire opposite iron so it melts and "soaks" into joint.

Most such guns have a two-position trigger for two levels of heating with a maximum wattage rating of about 125.

PROTECTING YOUR TOOLS
Since high-quality metalworking tools will easily last for a generation or more, it pays to protect them. Drawer or box storage is not a good practice because it too often means mixing sharp files with reamers, drills, and other tools easily damaged by nicks and scrapes.

Tool boards. If you have a permanent shop, you'll want to arrange tool boards with either homemade or pegboard supports to keep bench-top tools handy and separated. Some home-shop owners make a practice of spraying or wiping a light coat of oil on tools to keep them from rusting. I dislike picking up a tool which leaves oil on my hand and I've found that a coat of old-fashioned pastewax wiped on and later wiped dry and polished works better. You may want to install a dehumidifier to reduce the humidity in your shop.

Vapor-phase protection. Wax or oil is even less desirable on precision tools such as micrometers, lathe chucks, fine reamers, and other highly finished equipment. Keep such tools in a tool box whose drawer bottoms are lined with felt. When tools are kept in a closed tool chest, the finest protection is a unique chemical process called vapor-phase inhibition. If you've ever bought a new tool and found it wrapped in an odd paper which appeared to have a thin coating on it you were probably looking at vapor-phase-inhibiting paper. Industrially, this paper is widely used for wrapping finished parts. It functions by giving off an invisible and odorless vapor of molecules which coat the metal and in-

Lining storage areas for bright, precision tools with VPI (Vapor Phase Inhibiting) paper will keep them gleaming but free of messy oil. Change paper about once a year.

hibit corrosion. You will never see any trace of this protection on the tool, but lining the bottom of the tool drawers with this paper and changing it once a year or so will keep your fine equipment safe for years.

A similar product is V.P.I. oil, actually a light oil with the same chemical in it. A cloth or paper towel soaked with this oil and strategically placed in a closed storage cabinet is effective protection. There is no advantage in wiping tools with it. Such oil is sold for storing engines and construction equipment since a few ounces in the crankcase and combustion chambers will protect an engine stored outside for many months.

SPECIAL MATERIALS

It doesn't take long for a woodworking shop to accumulate bottles and cans of paint remover, stains, glues, and polishes. Metalworking, too, is made easier and the results improved by a number of products.

There may have been a time when metalwork automatically included grubby fingers and blackened nails. That was a hangover from blacksmith days. Today, no metalworker worth his salt works with grease- and grime-covered parts. Besides being unpleasant, the dirt makes accurate work impossible and carries over with often damaging results to the finished job. If you want to get a good idea of what a clean shop and clean parts should be, try to visit an airline-engine overhaul shop. In any case, there's no harm, and much to be gained, in cleaning all work to bright and sparkling clean metal and laying it out on clean towels or paper.

Degreasers. The best time to get rid of heavy grease, oil, and dirt is before even starting to disassemble a garden tractor, lawn mower, or engine. For small jobs there are spray cans of degreaser which soften and emulsify grease so it can be flushed off with a garden hose. These products are good but expensive. Less costly degreasing agents are available at automotive parts shops in gallon or larger cans. These are commonly mixed at about ten parts kerosene or fuel oil to one part degreaser. A small pressure sprayer or a coarse paintbrush or cleaning brush is fine for applying them. Again, a water flush will float away the dirt. For best results, use hot water but do not connect the common variety of plastic garden hose to a hot-water tap. It will almost certainly swell like a balloon and burst. Rubber hose works fine. If you have an air compressor, follow up with an air blast to get rid of small dirt residues and water.

The foregoing procedures work well for heavy cleaning; the same agents can be used in a small tray or bucket to clean parts as you disassemble. The parts can then be washed off in a laundry tub.

Never, however, resort to water-flush degreasers intended for castings and heavy parts when cleaning electrical devices such as motors. There are special, and much better, cleaners for electrical parts which will not harm the insulation or leave moisture to corrode contacts. For tiny, delicate jobs, kitchen-table-type repairs of appliances, for example, a small pressure can of TV tuner contact cleaner is very handy. These cans have fine discharge tubes to get the solvent into important areas. Larger cans are more economical, of course. The important thing is that these solvents are noncombustible and, in normal use, not toxic or offensive. Above all, never resort to gasoline as a cleaner. The hazards are just too great.

Rust removers.   Sometimes metalworkers become involved in cleaning and restoring badly rusted antiques, old hardware, or works of art. Or a spell of damp weather or a leaking water pipe causes some of your tools to rust. Rust can be removed several ways depending on the equipment you have and the end result you want. Mechanical removal with abrasive discs, power-driven wire brushes, and files and scrapers is sometimes practical for rusted outdoor equipment such as lawn furniture and wrought-iron gates. In fact, if the work is to be painted later with a rust-inhibiting paint this is usually all that's necessary.

If painting is not desirable, I recommend a small sandblast rig if you have an air compressor with at least a 1-hp motor. The alternative, often extremely worthwhile, is to take the project to a commercial shop with heavy-duty sandblast equipment. The finished surface, of course, will be slightly rough and have a frosty appearance.

On the other hand, you don't want to sandblast a precision tool or a handful of rusty twist drills. Such jobs call for a chemical rust remover. You have undoubtedly seen the advertisements for many popular rust removers; paint and hardware stores have large numbers of them on their shelves. None, at least none of the many I've tried over the years, really performs as advertised. Some are intended to leave a paintable surface behind by chemically combining with the surface of the metal. Most require some help with stainless-steel wool, very fine abrasive paper, or a wire brush to really get rid of rust. Most leave a dark coating of some kind. The best leave a coating which is easily buffed away on a cloth buffing wheel to reveal bright, gleaming metal again.

The best rust remover I've found, if the tool or parts can be immersed, is odorless, nontoxic, and so harmless to the skin you can even taste it. You mix a small amount with water and soak the rusted article overnight. The results are worth it.

PROTECTING YOURSELF

Metalworking is no more dangerous than woodworking, with a few exceptions. Wood splinters are no fun, but a minute metal splinter or fragment can be worse, especially in your eye. Since many metalworking operations generate grindings, chips, sharp strands, filing debris, and abrasive particles it is imperative to use eye protection at all times.

Eye protection.   Most metalworkers who require prescription glasses will order lenses of so-called safety glass. While not a total protection,

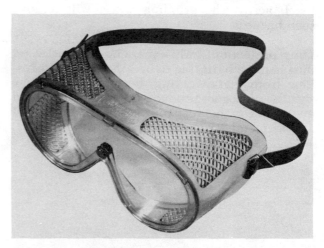

Safety goggles, large enough to wear over glasses if necessary, are by no means options. If they keep only one chip out of your eye in a lifetime, they're worth it.

such glasses are required in most industries and offer much better protection than ordinary glasses. Coupled with clear goggles with side covers, or a face shield, they are almost certain protection. I also make a point to keep a small, powerful magnet clean of dust and chips in a plastic bag but always at hand. In the event small grindings or other particles get in your eye, the magnet will often pick them out quicker than any other method. Nonferrous and stainless-steel chips, of course, are nonmagnetic, but since most of the grinding operations which throw off such chips are on iron or steel, there's nothing lost by keeping the magnet handy.

Hand protection.   For most small metalworking operations there is no real need to protect your hands, and in many cases a delicate touch is essential. But for those operations using heat, such as bending and annealing, a pair of weldor's gloves can prevent painful burns. The usual cause of such burns is distraction or simply forgetting which end is hot. Aluminum and copper are especially hazardous since neither changes color when hot and both conduct heat very rapidly to unheated sections.

Cutting sheets of metal often produces wire edges of knifelike keenness; these can cause severe slashing wounds. A good pair of leather-faced work gloves should be kept handy for such metal handling. And, just as a wise carpenter never leaves a nail protruding from a scrap of discarded lumber, a wise metalworker never cuts a piece of metal without checking afterwards for sharp burrs, little projecting spurs, and wire edges. A quick strike with a file or a touch across the grinding wheel will remove such hazards.

Lung protection.   My experience is that wood dust is more irritating to breathe than most residue from metalworking, but there are a few special airborne products which you should avoid. One is the dust you may grind or sand off an old metal structure such as lawn furniture, power equipment, or simply structural metal you want to salvage. Such dust is probably mostly iron rust and scale, but it may also contain old paint residues heavily laced with lead. Lead was long a favorite paint base for protecting metal, and it was used long after it was banned from house paints. Be aware of it especially when restoring old metalwork.

Many metal surfaces have also been galvanized; again, if you're using an abrasive disc or wire brush you should avoid breathing in what is probably zinc dust. Other metals, often called terneplate, were actually steel coated with lead. Again, avoid the dust. A lightweight protector with a replaceable filter is always worthwhile.

Many metalworking jobs require cleaning and degreasing the work before you even start. There are many powerful cleaners for this purpose, and some use toxic solvents or strong alkaline bases or lye. Use such cleaners out of doors, wear rubber gloves, and avoid getting the least drop in your eyes. Remember, too, that although respirators will keep out dust, they do not protect against toxic fumes.

5.
LAYING OUT THE JOB

A metalworking project may originate in any of several ways. Sometimes a repair is needed to make a piece of household equipment function again. All metalworkers enjoy such projects occasionally. But as you advance in skills you'll find plans in magazines, hobby books, and material suppliers' literature for projects that catch your fancy. Eventually you will originate your own ideas for metal projects.

WORKING FROM PLANS

One of the first skills you'll acquire, almost automatically, when working with metal is the ability to read a drawing. Over the years, designers of woodworking projects for the home shop learned to simplify their plans so even an inexperienced builder would have little trouble. This is less true of plans for metal projects. Usually the designer assumes that the builder will understand the meaning of dotted, hidden-object lines and the terminology of threads, fasteners, and metalworking operations.

Basic to all of this is the three-view drawing, the standard language of metalworking. The three views, each revealing something the others can't, are the front, side, and top view. Visualizing the final shape of a workpiece from complex engineering drawings, as is required of patternmakers and tool- and diemakers, takes experience and training, but most amateur metalworkers will find that a little practice is sufficient for ordinary projects.

To understand how three-view drawings are made and how they are interpreted, picture yourself with a need to show a handyman how you want him to build two concrete steps. Viewed from the front, straight on, your sketch would show a simple rectangle; the width and height of the steps would be designated in feet and inches. Halfway up, if the steps are of equal height, a single horizontal line would show the edge of the top of the lower step. Again, its height would be shown. This single drawing wouldn't make things clear for your workman. A second view, from the top, would convey more information such as the width of the treads. But, it, too, would appear as a simple rectangle with a line across the middle. Presuming your handyman had never seen a set of steps he'd still be puzzled. So, let's add a third view, this one as the steps would appear from the end. The final shape now becomes apparent. Moreover, if you want the treads to slope slightly for drainage, and if you want to round the edge of the step a bit to prevent chipping, you can add that to the end view. Your three-view drawing is now essentially complete.

Note that at this point two complications have been added. If you indicated the drainage slope

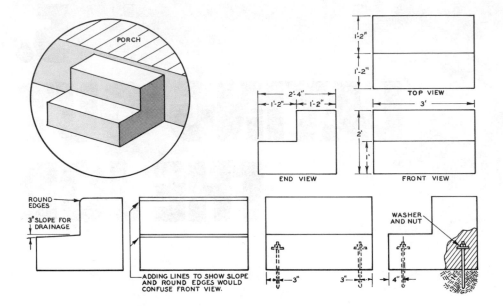

Making a three-view drawing of something as simple as a pair of concrete steps involves a little thought, particularly about details which might be confusing in one view and better shown in another, or perhaps called out by a note.

on the front view you'd have a second horizontal line very close to the first, one for the front edge and one where the lower step joins the riser at the rear. Also, the rounded edge would require another line. For practical purposes, you could well eliminate this confusion of closely spaced lines and rely on the information in the end view to clarify these details. For reasons just like these, most three-view drawings require a detailed study to understand the shape of the object presented.

You also might want your handyman to install a pair of steel rods extending into the ground and up into the concrete to anchor the steps. This means you must resort to dashed, invisible-object lines to show the location of the rods. Dashed lines are the common way to show the viewer that there's a part that is invisible in the external view but important to the project. Just to be certain that your man understands, you could draw a cross-sectional view of the anchor rods to show further detail. Conventionally, such sections are crosshatched to show that something is cut away.

Although usually, but not always, all of the information you need is in the drawing, you should spend some time studying each part closely and clarifying just what sequence of operations you'll follow to make it. This can save many scrapped pieces as well as time. I mentioned that the forces and pressures of metalworking tools require tool setups and holding methods more extensive than woodworking. It makes sense that once you've made a setup you should try to make use of it for similar operations, perhaps on other parts, before tearing

it down and putting away the equipment. All of this comes under planning your work and performing it mentally, step by step, before starting.

DRAWING YOUR OWN PLANS

When you start working from original ideas it may be enough to follow a rough, mind's-eye image of what you want to make. If the metal doesn't quite respond to your hand the way you expected, you can simply alter your project to fit. Few projects, however, can be accomplished successfully with this type of artistic abandon. That's why putting your ideas on paper is important—it often brings you up cold against a factor you'd overlooked in your creative enthusiasm. If you have an idea for a metal project, the first step is to make a sketch, even if it's a rough one. At the same time, consider the materials which might work best, if you can obtain them, and what might have to be substituted. Once you have a rough sketch showing the general shape and form of your project, it's time to translate it into a scale drawing. The easiest scale is, of course, 1:1, or full size. This is often impractical because the project is simply larger than any reasonable-size paper or drawing board. An example might be a backyard swing set 10 feet high. Conversely, a very small part for a model may be impossible to draw in minute life size and you'd want to scale up your drawing to show the details clearly.

Both of these problems are easily solved by using a draftman's triangular rule. Such rules have a conventional inch scale along one edge,

A triangular scale with proportional scales along its edges is basic tool for drawing plans. Shop drawing board need not be elaborate.

but each of the other edges shows reduced or expanded scales. Thus, if you chose a scale of 1″=1′, your 10′ high swing set would be drawn 10″ high on your planning paper. Other common scales are ¼, ½, ¾, and so on. Pick out a scale of a size which lets you make the largest practical drawing on your paper and which will show you the problems you may encounter. Unless you intend to submit the finished drawing for professional use or reproduction, there's seldom reason to show full details of each part. Most experienced metalworkers will establish center lines for the parts and pieces. Such centers will ordinarily be measured upwards from a bottom base line and right or left from a vertical base line. The usual technique is to outline your project and its centers first within a box of correct size and then fill in the details. To avoid confusion, pencil in the dimension you used as you locate each detail. This will save coming back later and attempting to measure it from the drawing. Also, don't be surprised to find that as you go you have to backtrack occasionally as an unanticipated problem arises. That's one of the reasons for making the drawing.

A Real-Life Example

To make the material above less academic, let's follow one metalworking project, a steel rail and bannister I made for a front porch from inception to completion.

1. With a mental image of the finished rail, I made an accurate drawing of an inaccurate object. Houses are seldom perfectly square, at least as a metalworker thinks of square, and here the porch, steps, and walk all sloped slightly for drainage. I used a level to establish a horizontal base line for each and ignored the angle initially since they were not significant and would have been confusing to measure.

2. On site, a sketch at ⅜ scale was made of the step profile and the dimensions were recorded to the nearest ¹⁄₁₆″. Also, the angle and locations of the clapboards were noted. Looking ahead, I didn't want the top and bottom rails to end smack on a clapboard overlap step.

3. Back in my shop I made a full-size layout of the steps and the proposed bannister. A piece of chipboard served as a drawing board. Shelf paper, if you don't have anything else, will do for such layouts. Tape it together as needed. The outline and the center lines of the pieces were drawn in after establishing the base lines at the porch and walk levels.

4. Suddenly, the value of a drawing became apparent. My planning was faulty because I'd intended to run the lower, sloping member straight up to the corner post. The drawing made it obvious that doing so would put the lower horizontal rail of the straight section ridiculously high.

5. Several trial configurations were drawn and each looked "funny." Finally, I settled on a dogleg in the lower sloping rail and it worked out fine.

6. Since my drawing board was scrap chipboard, I wasn't concerned about a little heat damage so I blocked and wedged the parts right on the drawing while tack welding. Brazing would have done as well.

7. The finished and painted rail was brought to the job site and dropped into place exactly.

Obviously, no two projects are alike, but note

To transfer real-world dimensions to paper often requires deciding what's important and what's not. Here, even though porch, steps, and walk sloped slightly, a level was used to measure the heights as though they were square. I made a sketch and dimensioned it as I went along.

The scaled, on-site drawing was worked up to full size and the problems became apparent. Even projects as simple as this may have aspects you hadn't considered.

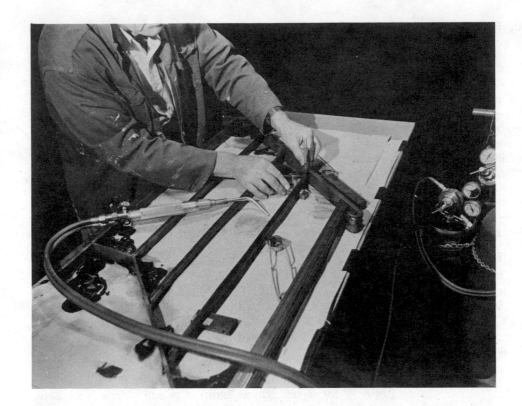

My full-scale layout permitted easy marking and cutting of the metal to the desired size and angles. Then with props and shims the parts were tacked together right over the drawing. Either brazing or welding will serve on such projects.

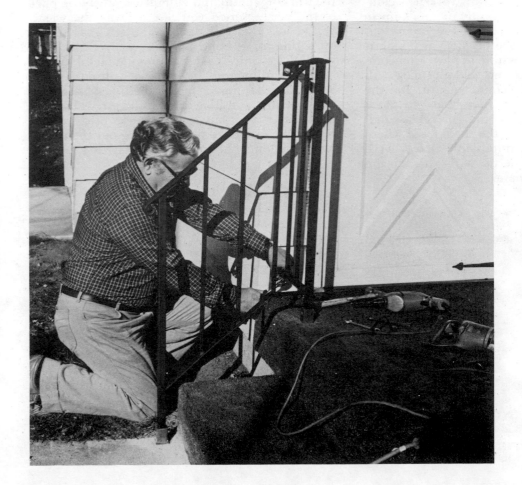

The finished railing was taken to the job and dropped into place perfectly. It's better to discover errors and problems on paper than to find them in the finished metal.

that a problem I hadn't foreseen cropped up when making the drawing.

Lofting

Some metal projects are simply too large for full-size drawings, but do require a layout to cut and fit. An example is the sheet-metal parts used to modify and fit out a camper van, as shown in the accompanying photographs. Such parts compare with the huge pieces often used in aircraft and ship construction. In the old-time shipyards, the ribs and curved stem and stern pieces were actually drawn full size on the floors of huge, barnlike lofts. The same method works well for large metalworking projects such as the swing set mentioned. Chalk marks on a garage floor or driveway, or perhaps on a sheet of plywood, can be used to check the dimensions and placement of components. Often a small error in a scaled-down drawing becomes magnified as you go full scale. A working layup of parts on a "lofted" drawing is the best way to check before cutting metal.

Mock-ups

In both automotive and aircraft work it is common practice to make a dummy or mock-up in some easily worked material before laying out metal. In part, this is done because although it may be geometrically possible to plot out a complex shape, it is difficult and seldom takes real-life inaccuracies into account. Again, for the camper van, I used stiff poster board to mock up the forms I wanted. I could correct a small interference with a snip of the shears, see where unwanted buckles and impossible bends were likely to occur, and come up with an accurate pattern to lay out the metal.

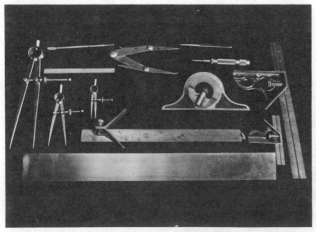

Typical layout tools for metalworking: squares, rules, and straightedges, plus dividers, scribe, and punches.

In some instances, I constructed whole models by using light metal strips as stiffeners with the poster board stapled or taped in place. If this seems time consuming it's far better than the jolt that comes from cutting a large piece of metal and finding you've cut it ¼" too short.

This same technique of cut-and-try patterns in cardboard, wood, composition board, or plastic works just as well, for example, for establishing the shape and fit of the handle on a gracefully contoured silversmithed or pewter vessel. When measuring won't work, especially in items with irregular shapes, try a mock-up pattern. Sometimes just a piece of wire solder can be bent around a curve and then transferred to a drawing or layout.

MARKING ON METAL

Before you can cut, drill, or bend your work metal, you must first locate the edges, drill centers, and bend points. These steps may seem to belabor the obvious, but many metal projects go wrong because the metalworker failed to observe them. Sometimes a radius, for example, must be drawn from a point which is outside the working metal and will ultimately be on part of the waste. Once you've cut away the waste you've lost this reference point. It's easy to lay off a line for a bend and forget that the bend itself will require that you provide metal for the "bending allowance," which we'll discuss later. When this happens, the finished part seems to have shrunk, or a hole or other feature is located improperly. In many projects, be prepared to accept the fact that simply laying out the metal may take longer than the work itself.

Layout Tools

Many of the tools used for layout, such as the ball-pein hammer, measuring rule, combination square, and protractor, have already been discussed. For most layout work you'll also need a large and small pair of spring dividers, a scriber for marking, a straightedge or long steel rule, a prick punch and a center punch, and perhaps some ships curves.

The prick punch is usually a center punch sharpened to a very acute point. The center punch has a point angled at about 60° to withstand being tapped with a hammer. There are two reasons for the sharply pointed prick punch. One is that once you have scribed two or more thin lines to form an intersection or center, it is important to locate the point of the punch exactly on the intersection. This requires a good light and a magnifying aid for accuracy. The center punch is too blunt for easy viewing. The second reason is that quite often all you want is a minute dimple to locate one leg of the dividers and have no need for a deeper depression in the metal.

On the other hand, after a center for drilling has been located with the prick punch it is good practice, unless the drill is very small, to use a center punch to enlarge the mark and provide good centering action for the drill. Either the prick punch or the center punch may be of one-piece construction for tapping with a hammer. An automatic prick punch, however, is handier. This tool has a replaceable point in a handle containing a spring and release mechanism. To use it, you place the point on the desired location and press straight down until the internal trigger releases. At that moment you feel an impact and the point is driven lightly into the metal.

There are several common methods of drawing curves ranging from flexing a thin stick or rule between two points to the use of a long flexible spline held in place by weights. The weights are often called ducks because they slightly resemble a duck at rest on the water. Where the duck's beak would be there is a hooked metal tip that bears on the spline to hold it down. Splines are made of plastic or rubber-like material flexible enough to curve but rigid enough to curve smoothly without kinks or wiggles. The duck and spline system was probably borrowed from ancient shipbuilding practice and refined for laying out larger panels for aircraft. You will seldom work with large enough pieces to require these items.

For smaller curves, however, such as might be used in wrought-iron forming, making artistic planter hangers, boxes, and the like, the draftsman's French curve is quite suitable. A set of plastic ship's curves with longer, sweeping patterns is best for larger shapes. Ship's curves are available at low cost from art-supply stores.

Seeing the Marks

Metal, in general, is not as easy to mark as clearly as wood where an ordinary pencil or a sharp knife blade usually suffices. Some sort of coating or marking medium is sometimes needed to make fine scribe marks visible. The marking medium you choose depends on the work-metal surface and your requirements for accuracy. If you are laying out a part to be machined from clean, bright steel, and you expect to work to close limits, a simple line with a felt-tip pen or pencil would be too crude. Such layouts are usually scratched into the metal surface with a needle-sharp, hardened point called a scriber. The brightness of the metal, however, makes these scribe marks hard to see. For this reason most metalworkers first coat the surface with some type of layout fluid.

Layout fluid can be brushed or sprayed on a metal surface which has been cleansed of all oil and grease. It dries quickly to a dark-blue color against which the scribe marks stand out crisply. Sometimes, for a quick mark in a small area, such as locating a lathe center, all that's needed is a dab from a black, felt-tipped marker which dries almost instantly but will show up scribe marks. If you feel inclined to try a layout method favored by old-time toolmakers, a solution of copper sulfate in water can be brushed or swabbed on and will leave a very light coating of copper on bright steel.

Many jobs, especially those laid out on black iron, do not require such accuracy. Here, the commonly used marker is soapstone, which

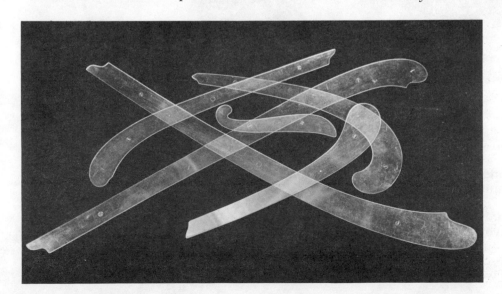

A typical assortment of ship's curves, the longest about 24", will handle most home metal-working layouts. The trick is to blend curves, or curves into straights, smoothly.

Blue layout fluid is the standard material to make scribe marks stand out brightly. Brush or spray applications are both fine but spray is handier. Clean surface of oil or grease first.

Blue surface makes layout marks clear on bright steel surface.

leaves a white mark. Soapstone markers are available at welding supply houses. If critical centers are involved, it is routine to make the rough layout with soapstone and follow up with scribe marks or center-punch marks where needed.

In other types of metalwork, any type of scratch or mark must be avoided. Plainly, no one wants to produce a handsome copper or pewter article with layout marks scratched deeply into the surface. And if you're working with a finely polished aluminum you don't want to mar it. Moreover, if the finished work is a structural part, such as an aircraft fitting, scratches which localize stress can cause cracks and ultimate failure. Aircraft sheet-metal workers often tape nonwork surfaces and cover the workbench with clean, grit-free paper to avoid scratching the metal.

Since a scriber is unsuitable for marking these surfaces, a sharp, soft pencil can be used. Pencil marks, however, tend to smear on bright metal.

A soapstone marker is adequate and easily seen on black iron surfaces if the layout does not need a high level of accuracy.

Spray-can automotive gray primer surfacer dries quickly and forms an ideal flat, non-reflecting surface for layout. Here, on sheet aluminum, pencil marks can be seen but do not scratch metal. Note that layout is made from the single straight edge.

Again, cleaning the metal and applying a white layout fluid will help. I keep a spray can of light, gray automotive primer surfacer handy and spray the metal lightly after degreasing. The primer dries in a minute or two and has just enough tooth to take a pencil line. Since it's flat it reduces glare, so it's easier to follow the line later. Lacquer-base zinc-chromate primer also works well and leaves a light greenish-yellow surface. Zinc-chromate is commonly used as a protective finish for aluminum parts in aircraft, thus serving a double purpose. The dull, lacquer-primed surfaces readily accept colored pencil lines and fine felt-tipped pen marks. You can mark or shade waste areas, identify rights and lefts and opposite sides with different colors. When the cutting and forming is complete, the primer wipes off cleanly with lacquer thinner.

Finding a Starting Point

If every piece of metal was perfectly square and precisely dimensioned, it might be possible to measure and square from any edge and have your layout come out right. In the home shop this is hardly ever the case. We all pick up materials wherever we can, keep waste cut-offs and use them when they're large enough, and when roughing out working-size pieces from larger stock we leave rough edges.

To lay out on such stock means you've somehow got to establish a working edge from which other points and edges can be located. In most cases a second edge or base at right angles, in effect a bottom and side, will be needed. The easiest way, of course, on sheet metal, is to find an edge which was sheared true and straight at the mill. Check with a steel straightedge. And be sure it runs at the right angle to the grain of the metal.

Although speaking of metal grain may sound odd, if you examine most mill rolled sheets, especially aluminum, you'll see a fine pattern running in one direction much like wood grain. Most metalworkers prefer to make bends across such grains for better strength in the finished part.

Ideally, you could establish a true edge on sheet metal with a squaring shear. Such huge shears, which chop down with a long, heavy blade, are common in commercial shops but rare in home shops. If you're working with a block of metal thicker than sheet, you might use a planer, milling machine, or surface grinder to true up an edge or working face. Again, you'll probably lack the luxury of this equipment, although a metalworking lathe, as we'll discuss later, will sometimes serve quite well.

Truing an Edge

On sheet aluminum, brass, copper, and soft steel you can resort to a crude but effective truing method. An initial roughout cut, made with snips, saber saw, or band saw, just outside a marked base line, will always be less than straight and true. One way to straighten it is to clamp the metal securely between two lengths of angle iron 1¼" or larger, with just the high points along the edge projecting. The angle iron

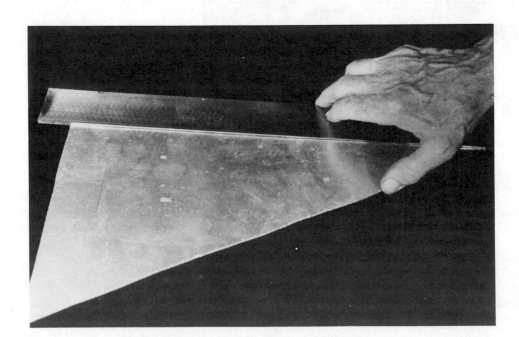

Most of us save and use scraps and trimmings, but before starting a new layout be sure that you have at least one true working edge. There's a slight bow in edge shown here against straightedge, and it must be dressed out.

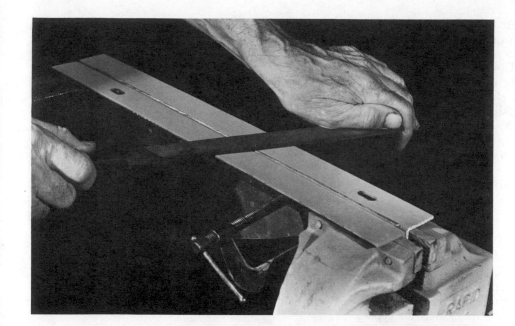

Two pieces of angle iron clamped, one on each side, of work metal serve as a file guide to dress edge ready for layout.

Carbide-toothed table saw will easily cut aluminum, but don't try it hand-held. Home-made rig seen here guides in the table slot and clamps sheet metal firmly. In this photo the blade was intentionally set slightly high to show cut. It's better practice to cut just shy of coming through.

will serve as a guide while you file—in metal-worker's terms, "dress down"—the high spots until the edge is smooth and flush with the top of the guides. This can be speeded with an abrasive disc in a rotary grinder or even an electric drill.

If you have a belt sander or a disc sander, it is also possible to clean up the worst of an uneven edge by working against the belt table or using the guide with the disc sander. This often results in a smooth but slightly curved edge and still requires a final dressing with the file and the angle-iron guides.

To produce a true edge on soft aluminum, you can use a carbide-tipped blade in a bench saw. If your stock is ⅛″ or ³⁄₃₂″ thick, you can bring the blade up until it is just a few thousandths lower than the thickness of the stock so it will cut almost, but not quite, through. For very short cuts of an inch or two the crosscut guide can be used, if your saw has clamps, to hold the metal securely. *Never attempt to hand-hold metal when sawing this way!* The slightest misalignment will snatch the metal from your hands and turn it into a slashing knife which can hurt you badly. This goes back to my earlier remarks about the forces involved in cutting metal and the importance of holding it securely. In this case, the carbide saw cuts aluminum like butter, but rigid holding is vital.

If you have many long cuts to make in aluminum I suggest making the guide shown in the accompanying photo. It slides in the longitudinal slot in the table, and a series of clamp screws lock the sheet metal firmly. After sawing, the metal can be separated easily, leaving a strip of tinsel-like scrap. Use a file or abrasive paper at once to soften the razor-sharp edges left by the saw.

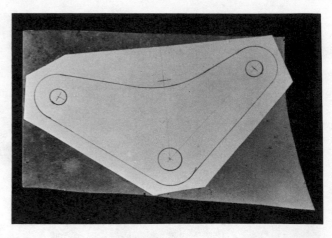

A fast way to make layouts on irregular scrap is to draw a paper pattern on a drawing board and rubber cement it to metal. Once firmly adhered, use pattern to locate and prick punch center holes so they won't be lost if paper loosens.

Paper Patterns
Depending on the nature of the job, the methods described for establishing an edge and laying out the work may exceed the need for accuracy entailed in the job. An alternate method is simply to tape a sheet of sturdy paper such as typewriter bond to a drawing board and make your layout on the paper using a square and triangle in the usual way. From here, it's a simple matter to clean the metal, coat it and the reverse side of the paper with a quick-drying cement such as Plio-Bond, and adhere the paper to the metal. When the paper is smooth and dry, use a prick punch to establish the hole centers and cut the metal. Peel off the paper later.

Working from Center
Most metalworkers, after establishing an edge, will work from it to set up a center line or working centers, usually both a vertical and horizon-

tal line as a reference point for other lines and dimensions. These center lines may not be in the geometrical center of the work but are chosen for any of several reasons. First, the lines may be through hole centers or other locations totally critical to the performance of the finished part. In short, everything must work, pivot, or be supported from such an axis. Or the location may be the most convenient one to use later when measuring and cutting the metal. In any case, think of center lines as the lines from which all is to be measured.

The advantage in working from centers is that

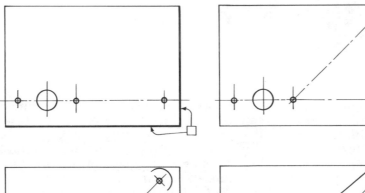

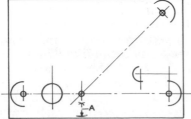

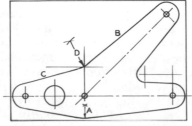

Making a layout of a flat part such as this requires several logical steps after squaring at least two edges of the stock. Start by locating the horizontal center line and hole centers. Next, establish the 45° center line and hole. You can now swing the arcs for the ends and bottom, and connect the tangent lines for the sides. Lines drawn parallel to B and C intersect outside the piece. Use the intersection as a center for arc D.

it avoids the creeping accumulation of little errors which are normal if you work out from an edge and build your layout progressively in a stepping-stone fashion. Moreover, if you must establish angles with a protractor, the center line will usually be the best base line for the angle even though you may have to draw the final angle parallel to the first one. None of the above may seem quite clear until you actually make a few such layouts, but then the logic of it all will become immediately apparent.

BENDING METAL

If you bend a piece aluminum foil, you would be able to make a perfectly sharp, 90° corner. But since most metal you'll use will be much thicker, probably 1/32" (.032") to 1/8" (.125"), you will find it very difficult to make such a bend. Even if you accomplished it on the inside of the bend, the outside corner would be curved; in short, it would have a radius. Even worse, if you were to examine such a bend under a microscope, or by etching, or even to test it by flexing, you'd almost certainly find that your sharp corner bend had weakened the metal badly. The outside would have been stretched and cracked.

Yet, beginning metalworkers who would never attempt to bend a piece of wood around a square corner, knowing full well that it would break, will often try such corners in metal. The truth is, however, that all metals with significant thickness greater than that of foil must be limited in the sharpness of the bend to a suitable bending radius.

Just what radius you should choose will depend on the metal you're working and the method of bending. A piece of 3/16" soft steel strip for a wrought-iron project could be heated until it is red and bent sharply in the jaws of a vise. You might even hammer the corner square if needed. But that's forging, not cold bending.

And cold bending the sides of a box or channel from 3/32" soft aluminum or copper would be different from making the same bends in sheet steel or hard aluminum alloy.

My own experience is that a bend radius of one, two, or three times the metal thickness is generally satisfactory and is in line with long-standing aircraft practices. Even thin stock, such as 1/32", needs at least a 1/32" radius and 1/16" is recommended. The harder aluminum alloys, and this also applies to brass, copper, and thin steel, require a larger radius than soft aluminum. Most important, the radius needed increases with the thickness of the metal. As a rule of thumb, soft metals can be bent to a radius of their own thickness. Harder metals should usually have at least two or three times their thickness for safe bending and it's good practice to lean towards the larger radius even for soft metals if the part will be loaded in use. Remember, the radius is measured on the inside of the bend. Summed up, deciding upon a suitable bending radius is essential before you continue laying out sheet metal which will be bent.

Bending Allowance

All of the previous discussion on bending radii has been leading up to an aspect of bending metal which often remains a mystery even to experienced metalworkers. Technically, it's called "bending allowance."

The reason for the "mystery" is that it takes different amounts of metal to go around curves of different radii. If you draw layout lines on paper and bend and crease the paper sharply along the lines, you do not need a bending allowance. But if you bend a piece of metal, say 1/8" thick, around a 1/4" radius it will take a different amount of metal to go around the curve than it would to make a dead sharp corner. If your radius was 1/8" or 3/8", it would in each case take a different amount.

Bending metal over a square corner is almost impossible and if forced will weaken the metal so it will probably fail later.

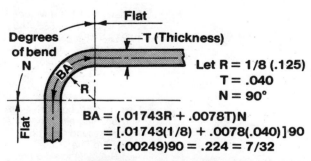

$$BA = (.01743R + .0078T)N$$
$$= [.01743(1/8) + .0078(.040)]90$$
$$= (.00249)90 = .224 = 7/32$$

Let R = 1/8 (.125)
T = .040
N = 90°

One way to determine how much metal will be required for a given bend and metal thickness is shown here.

This means two things when you're laying out metal for bending. First, you must decide what radius you'll use. Secondly, you must provide the amount of metal in the bend area needed to go around that particular radius. Thus, when you lay out your project it will be divided into "flats," the areas not bent, and bend areas of the width calculated for the bend allowance. The bend line, actually the center of the bend, will be the center line of the bend allowance. The following explanations of bending allowance and two ways to arrive at it, one mathematically accurate and the other simple, have been worked out over the years.

Bending Allowance =

$(.01743 \times radius + .0078 \times thickness) \times degrees$

Thus, if we were planning to bend a sheet of ⅛″ (.125″) thick aluminum over a ¼″ (.250″) radius to 90°, our formula would be:

$$BA = (.01743 \times .250 + .0078 \times .125) \times 90.$$

It is usually stated:

$$BA = (.01743R + .0078T)N$$

Knowing the metal thickness and having chosen a bending radius, and knowing the angular degrees of the bend, you could, with a handy calculator, come up with a dimension for the metal which will be used in the bend. Most workers, however, will simply consult a table made up by calculating the bending allowance for all common thicknesses and values of R (radius) and N (degrees).

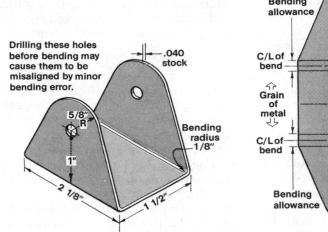

Drilling these holes before bending may cause them to be misaligned by minor bending error.

.040 stock

5/8″ R

Bending radius 1/8″

1″

2 1/8″

1 1/2″

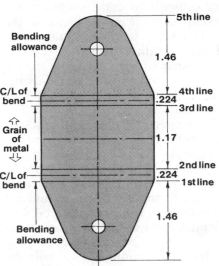

5th line

Bending allowance

1.46

C/L of bend

4th line
.224
3rd line

Grain of metal

1.17

C/L of bend

2nd line
.224
1st line

1.46

Bending allowance

To make a layout using bending allowance perform the following steps:
Metal thickness *(T)* = .040″
Bending radius *(R)* = ⅛″ = .125″
Angle of bend *(N)* = 90°
Bending allowance, the material needed to make the bend:
B.A. = (.01743 *R* + .0078 *T*) *N*
Thus: *B.A.* = (.01743 × .125 + .0078 × .040) × 90
B.A. = .224″

To determine full developed width of layout in the flat:
1″ + ⅝″ = 1 + .625. Thus: 1.625 − *(R+T)* + *B.A.* =
1.625 − .162 + .224 = 1.684″ (first leg)
1.5 − (.250 + .080) + .224 = 1.394″ (center area)
1.625 − (.125 + .040) = 1.46″ (second leg)
1.684″ + 1.394″ + 1.46″ = 4.538—Total width of flat layout

To locate bend lines:
First line from bottom—1 − ⅝″ − *(R+T)* = 1.625 − .165 = 1.46
Add bending allowance B.A., .224 to locate second line
Add to second line 1.5 − (2R + 2T) = 1.5 − .330 = 1.17 to locate 3rd line
Add *B.A.* .224 to third line to locate fourth line
Add to fourth line 1.625 − *(R+T)* = 1.625 − .165 = 1.46 to locate fifth line.

The Easy Way

In practice, since many bends are 90° or thereabouts, metalworkers often bypass the precise calculations or tables and use the method shown below. It's based on the common practice of using a bending radius of 1, 2, or 3 times the metal thickness.

A = Length of stock required
$A = B + C + t/2$
$A = B + C$
$A = B + C - t/2$

When R is equal to t (Steel)
When R is equal to $2t$ (Alum. alloy)
When R is equal to $3t$ (Hard alum. alloy)

From: *Aircraft Mechanic's Pocket Manual*

This simple procedure will give you the dimension of the stock you will need. It works very well when bends are made over accurately shaped radius blocks in a professional metal brake. In making up a single piece or two for a home-shop project, it may not work out quite so nicely if your forming equipment is less than professional. Your radius block may be a block of hard maple with a corner rounded off to approximately the desired radius. And you may make the bend in a vise by hand pressure followed by tapping a wooden block held against the metal.

For these reasons, if it's important that holes or other features in the piece be accurately located after bending, it may be best to make the bend first and accept variations from perfection. Then, with the bends finished, check and change, if necessary, the hole centers and other critical locations. There's no question that drill-

ing or cutting on a bent piece is not as easy as working in the flat. But it's worse to locate and drill holes accurately and then find that they don't line up properly after bending. So, bend first, then drill. By judicious use of wooden blocks to stiffen the work under the drill or saw, you can produce the final piece and have the critical locations accurate.

Precision Layouts

The methods described for laying out sheet metal and ironwork will suffice for most jobs which do not involve working to extremely accurate dimensions. If, however, you are going to machine a block of metal, as we'll discuss later, a higher level of accuracy is necessary. The easiest way to establish such layout marks is to work from a surface plate.

A commercial machine shop or tool room is equipped with a massive steel or granite plate with the top surface finished perfectly smooth and flat. Such a surface plate forms an ideal base for layout work, especially if you have precision measuring equipment.

Unfortunately, costly surface plates are usually outside the realm of home shops but often you can find a workable substitute. For example,

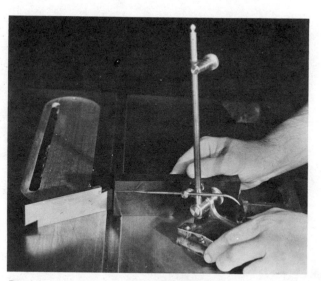

Precision layouts for machining are different from sheet metal. A smooth, flat surface such as a benchsaw top and a surface gage with a scribe provide a constant base reference.

the cast-iron tops of my table saw, drill press, and jointer are flat within one or two thousandths of an inch. Periodically, I wash them clean with solvent, coat them with kerosene, and polish off any nicks or blemishes with a flat hone.

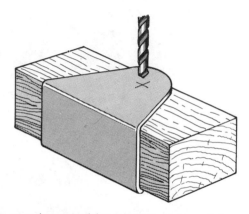

Unless you have precision bending equipment, two opposing holes which should align will be misaligned if drilled in the flat. One solution, less than perfect, is to drill both holes in one operation after the bend is complete.

This method of layout requires clamping the work metal very firmly and squarely to the table surface. You will be working against the vertical face of the metal rather than working flat down, as with sheet metal. The table surface is now a base line. The needle-point scriber is mounted in a holder with a heavy base generally called a surface gage. The base is precisely finished on the bottom to slide over your "surface plate," whatever it is. The base supports a vertical member with a clamp to secure the scriber. The scriber support is moveable and the scriber point may be set to a precise dimension, often taken from a steel rule or square, by using a magnifying glass. In some cases you may set the scriber against another surface known to be accurate. Or, if you are duplicating an existing piece, you may set the scriber from selected points on it. By sliding the surface gage from the reference to the work and moving the sharp point across the work you can scribe a line very accurately.

6.
CUTTING METAL

All metalworking except casting and forging involves cutting and drilling. Metal may be cut with many different tools ranging from saws to drills, taps, and files. The choice of tool, as I'll explain, depends on your own judgment and the tools you have to work with in your home shop. Thus, it is far more common in the home shop, as compared to a factory, to improvise and make do, sometimes using a tool in a manner for which it was not really intended. An example is the use of a carbide saw, intended for wood, for cutting aluminum.

With due precautions and common sense it is possible to adapt other woodworking and home-shop tools to metal cutting. Almost always, however, you must recognize the points made earlier about the higher forces required and the need for holding the work firmly. Many jobs where you might routinely hold a piece of wood in your hand for power sawing, drilling, or routing become exceedingly dangerous with metal.

In other respects, cutting metal and cutting wood are quite similar. Normally, you work to the final finish and dimensions in progressive stages. Just as you might rough-cut a piece of plywood or lumber stock to approximate dimensions and finish with a plane and sandpaper, you'll rough-out metal and gradually take finer cuts to final size.

In the home shop you're seldom blessed with exact size stock. You'll use scrap, salvaged metal, even pieces off a discarded part or an old tool. Knife makers, for example, often cut pieces from old saw blades, mower blades, and car or truck springs because such metal is usually high-carbon steel and can be hardened when finished. Many carving chisels and other cutters are made from junk auto spring stock. But herein is another difference between working metal and wood. Wood cannot be changed in its hardness and other characteristics, but a piece of carbon steel can be made glass hard or relatively soft by heating and cooling processes.

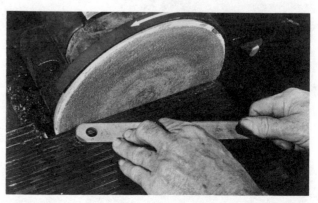

You'll find that your woodworking belt sander and disc sander serve almost as well on metal as on wood for general shaping and cleanup.

Although less than an ideal procedure, soft aluminum can be cut with a woodsaw. Use a saw with fine teeth and secure metal with a clamp since it tends to slide around more than wood.

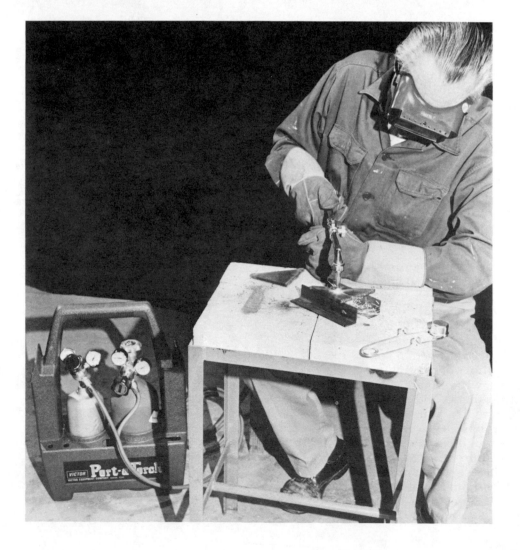

Sometimes a torch is the best way to cut heavy stock. Here, an oxyacetylene torch is used, but inexpensive propane or MAPP/oxygen torches will do as well.

It follows that if you wish to cut stock for a project and the material has previously been hardened, it will be almost impossible to saw, chisel, or shear. One possibility is to use an ox-yacetylene cutting torch or a propane/oxygen or MAPP/oxygen cutting torch. Lacking this equipment, you can have the cut made at the local welding shop. Bear in mind, however, that the torch heat will alter the hardness of the metal unpredictably and you will later have to heat-treat it. Also, be sure there is plenty of rough stock left around the edges to cut back from the burned kerf left by the torch.

HACKSAWING

Most of the metals you'll work with can be sawed. As pointed out under the discussion of hacksaws, the choice of sawblades is important and depending on the thickness of the thinnest section of stock you should always use a blade which will always have at least two teeth in contact with the metal. For sawing off a thick piece of bar stock such as 1"-diameter cold-rolled steel rod, a coarse saw blade with 14 teeth per inch would speed the cut. But such a blade would be totally unsuited to cutting pipe, tubing, conduit, or sheet metal. Here, a fine-toothed saw with 32 teeth per inch would be much better.

In those instances where even a fine-tooth blade bites and catches, as might happen with thin sheet metal or thin-wall tubing, some sort of support is recommended. A piece of wooden dowel tapped inside the tubing works well, and clamping thin sheet between scraps of hard-

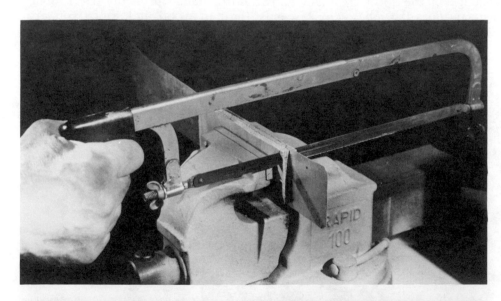

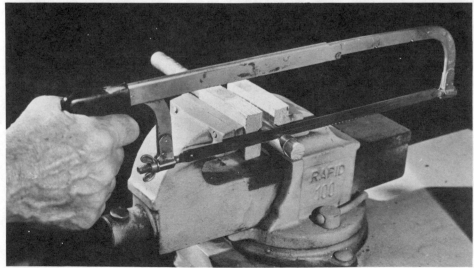

When sawing thin metal, either flat stock or tubing, you'll get a smoother, neater job by backing metal with scrap wood or a plug for tubing. Protect metal from vise jaws.

board will do the trick there. Nearly all hacksaw cuts require clamping the work, usually in a vise but sometimes with C-clamps or other means. Try to clamp the work so that the cut is as close to the vise jaws as possible to prevent the metal from wobbling and vibrating.

Since the hacksaw cuts in only one direction it is important to learn the proper stroke. Always use enough pressure on the forward stroke to bite in and remove metal. Overly light pressure simply dulls the saw. Ease off all pressure and lift the saw slightly on the return stroke. On long cuts where the frame would contact the metal, the blade may be turned 90° to permit access at least to the depth of the frame.

Hand hacksawing with a good blade can be surprisingly effective, but I have never deemed it a pleasure. It also has severe limitations because of the saw frame which limits the ability to get in very far from the edge of the sheet metal. A small electric saber saw does the job faster and allows you unlimited freedom to cut

any shape or in any area. If, for example, you had a large sheet of aluminum and wanted to cut out a smaller piece of work stock, or even wanted to cut an opening near the center of the large piece, you could do it with a saber saw. In the latter case you must first drill or hole-saw a starting hole.

Again, the blade must be well chosen. Be sure, of course, that it is intended for cutting metal and that the number of teeth per inch suits the metal thickness. Moreover, makers of high quality saw blades list them according to the type of metal they're suited for. The alloy of the blade and the tooth forms vary.

Once more, the forces required and the resistance of metal to cutting must be considered. You might, for instance, select a blade which would be about right for hand hacksawing but too coarse for power sawing. That's because the blade can catch or hang up in the metal much more easily than in wood and, since you are resisting the saw action with your hand, it's pos-

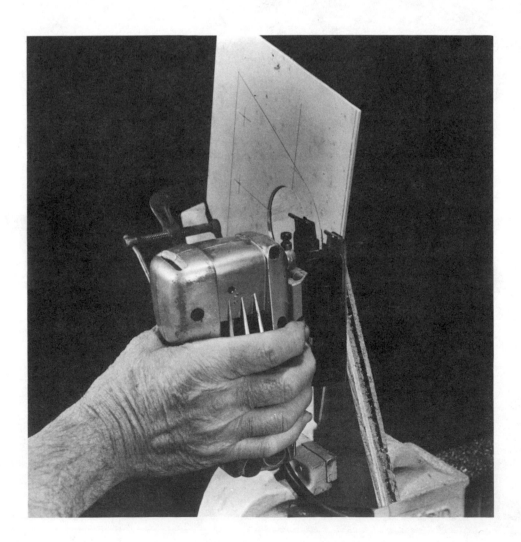

Saber saw with a suitable metal-cutting blade is an efficient way to cut metal, but first secure metal to wood backing. Vertical mounting lets cutting fall away for better visibility of layout lines.

sible for the blade to kick out of the kerf and break or hurt you. My suggestion is to use a finer blade than really seems necessary until you become thoroughly familiar with metal cutting.

Saber-sawing metal requires special precautions. Sheet-metal stock is flexible and tends to flutter and spring under the saw. It is extremely important to hold the bottom plate of the saw firmly against the metal to avoid the jumping out described above. Large sheets are best sawed flat. If you have sawhorses, make a support with a piece of heavy plywood or a pair of 2×6 boards. Place the metal so the cut line is just to one side of the supporting wood. If you're making a straight cut, it is best to place another piece of wood on top of the metal and clamp it so one edge may be used to guide the saw. If you are making a curved cut, try to keep it closely between the support pieces and move them or the metal as needed as you proceed. You're probably going to have to make adjustments several times during longer cuts.

Another problem you may encounter is the tendency for the cut metal to buckle slightly and pinch the blade. Good support helps, but pinching can be reduced by dribbling a bead of cutting oil or even engine oil along the cut line to lubricate the blade.

Jeweler's Saws

Two different styles of saws are classified as jeweler's saws. One uses a blade about ³⁄₁₆″ to ¼″ wide and has a triangular shape with the blade in place. As with standard hacksaws, the blade is mounted so the teeth cut on the forward stroke. The width of the blade prevents cutting anything but straight lines so it is mainly useful for squaring off the edge of thin sheet stock or cutting delicate bar stock.

A distinctly different form of jeweler's saw, as described earlier, resembles a standard hacksaw except it's much smaller and the blades are much narrower, almost hairlike in some sizes.

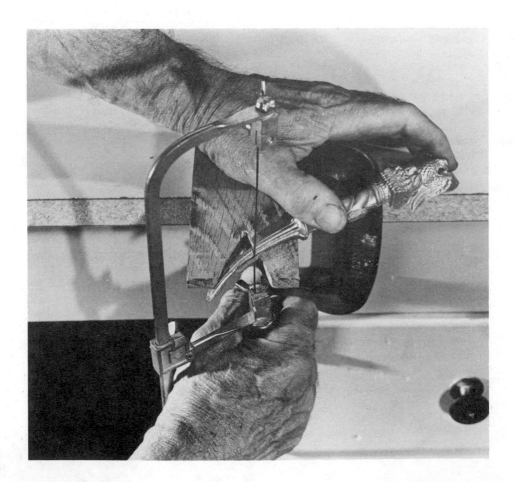

Jeweler's saw and jeweler's peg combine for fine sawing to trim this casting. Jeweler's saw cuts on down-pull stroke.

Since these blades are too small to mount with a hole in each end, they are simply clamped by a small lug and screw. Also, since even the most careful workman will break the thin blades frequently, long before it gets dull, the saw frame can be telescoped to a shorter length and the broken pieces used.

This type of jeweler's blade is mounted just the opposite of a hacksaw blade, so the teeth cut on the backpull rather than on the forward push. A jeweler's workbench is fitted with a little projecting workshelf which usually has a V-notch. Some jewelers call them bench pegs; others call them bench pins. In use, the metal is held on the peg with the cutting area over the throat of the V, and the saw is worked from below with gentle pulling motions. Cuts of this type are used to shape fine ring mounts and other jewelry filigree. With the work thus positioned, you can easily arrange a light above the work and watch the action through a magnifier. For occasional use you can make up such a bench peg and clamp it to the bench with a C-clamp.

SHEARING

Metal shears or snips will cut soft metal, especially aluminum, up to about $\frac{1}{16}''$ thick. For short cuts they are handy, but making long, straight cuts is often difficult because the snips must work in between two cut edges. When making such cuts, be sure to wear heavy work gloves since the cut edges may be slivered or razor sharp. The best technique is to work the metal well up into the throat of the snips, cut about two-thirds of the way towards the snip jaw tips, and then advance the shears again. If you make a full cut to the end of the jaws you will wind up with a series of little notches or jogs in the metal which are hard to clean up.

FILING

Biblical history has it that files were being used to sharpen agricultural tools about 1,000 years

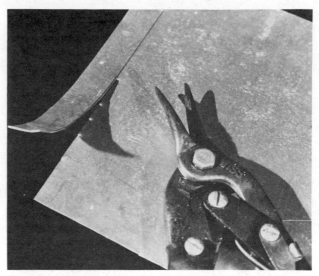

Closing snips all the way will leave a series of notches in cut edges of metal. Close snips only partially for a clean cut.

B.C. (I Samuel XIII:21). And about the time of Columbus, Leonardo da Vinci is reported to have devised a machine to produce the teeth on files. Thus, you are in time-honored company when you pick up a file to cut metal.

For most ordinary bench work, such as cleaning up a sawed edge or shaping a piece to your layout lines, a mill file or a faster cutting machinist's file will do. The trick is to handle it properly. Never use a file without a handle. Not only is it dangerous, but you simply cannot produce the proper, level cutting stroke. If you use a file correctly you can cut a flat, true surface. Done improperly, with a rocking motion, the result will be rounded edges and an uneven finish. Ideally, the work should be secured in a vise. Use soft, protective jaws if needed. The vise should be at about elbow height, lower for heavy work and higher for better vision if the work is light and delicate.

The method of holding a file, like holding a golf club or fishing rod, varies with position and

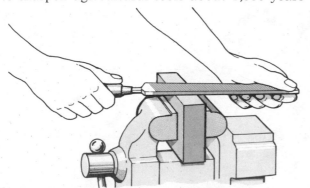

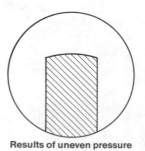

Results of uneven pressure

Holding a file so it cuts level is both a knack and the result of practice. The position of the work, your body, and your hands all have a bearing on your filing results.

your own sense of what feels right. Usually, the butt of the grip is held in the palm of your hand with your thumb extended along the top of the handle. The tip of the file is held by your other hand with your thumb on top and one or two fingers curled underneath. Such instructions may seem overly tedious for such an apparently simple tool, but they have been found important over the ages. This may be because of the peculiarities of the human joint structure. Holding a file in the manner I've described allows the forward thrust to be kept in a horizontal plane without a rocking motion. The secret is maintaining a balance between the pressure on the handle and the pressure on the tip of the file as the cutting teeth move across the metal. As with a good bowling swing, a metalworker's filing

Draw filing can produce and almost mirror finish with practice.

stroke is a combination of muscular adjustments which must become automatic.

Most filing is done by orienting the file straight across or at a slight angle to the work. Sometimes, however, a fine, almost polished finish is wanted, and this can be produced by skillful drawfiling. This is done with the file held and drawn at right angles to the work. For drawfil-

ing, a file with a long-angled tooth should be selected, and it should be a single-cut for the smoothest results. Experimenting is the best way to learn this technique.

File Care

As with any edge tool, files should be stored so they do not rub or batter against one another or other tools. Rust and corrosion will dull them quickly. To get a better view of how the fine cutting edges on a file work, examine them under a strong magnifying glass. One thing will

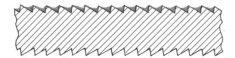

A sectional view of typical file teeth shows that they are actually multiple cutting edges. It also shows why metal packed in the gullets can prevent effective cutting.

immediately become apparent, and that is that cuttings packed down into the gullets of the teeth will prevent the file from biting in. A metalworker accustomed to filing will tap the tip of his file on the bench to free the cuttings after every few strokes. He will also use a file card, a wire-brush type of tool with short wire "bristles," to remove the cuttings. A handy trick for really getting down into the gullets of the file teeth is to use a short strip of brass, aluminum, or even soft iron, about $\frac{1}{16}''$ thick and $\frac{5}{8}''$ wide. Simply press the lower corner of the end of the strip down against the teeth and push it across in the same direction as the teeth are slanted. This will form a sawtoothed edge which will dig down into the teeth and clean them of packed metal. It can be used indefinitely.

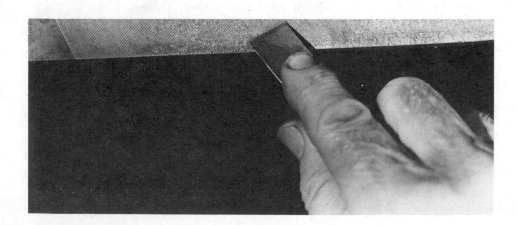

A quick way to clean the gullets of a file is to use a scrap of brass or copper pushed along the file teeth. Action will form grooves in the metal strip and force out the waste.

7.
DRILLING METAL

Many novices spend untold time trying to force a dull or improperly sharpened drill through metal. At times their efforts resemble a Boy Scout fire-by-friction test. They're amazed to see an experienced metalworker drill a hole quickly and effortlessly with the cuttings flowing smoothly out of the drill flutes.

There are many things to be learned about twist drills, including sizes, speed, lubricants, and the tricks of the trade, but before getting into these topics the most important thing is to learn how to grind a drill so it cuts easily.

It is worth the time to examine a new, factory-sharpened twist drill, preferably one ⅜" or larger in diameter, so you can see the details of the tip. Note that the center is not really a point like an auger bit, but is actually a sharpened flat. Technically, it is called a dead center because it does almost no cutting. This is why it is harder to start a twist drill dead on a center, and why a punch mark is almost always used. Notice also that the tip center is not at right angles to the cutting edges. If you look at the drill from the side you'll see that each cutting edge, or lip, has a slope of about 59° to the vertical axis of the drill. Most important, the shoulderlike portion of the drill tip or lips slopes, on each side, back and down from the actual cutting edge. This is called the "relief" or "clear-

Typical drill cuttings in mild steel indicate that this drill is properly sharpened and cutting evenly on center. Not all metals—for example, cast iron—will produce this type of chip.

ance angle" and is the most critical angle when sharpening a drill. Without this angle, usually 12° to 15°, the drill simply will not cut. I'll talk more about that under sharpening procedures.

SHARPENING DRILLS
Beginning metalworkers sometimes regard sharpening a twist drill as an arcane art. They

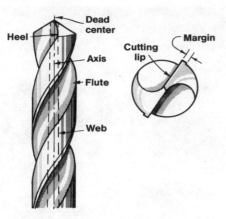

The tip of a twist drill is more complex than it first appears. Each part has a specific function to perform.

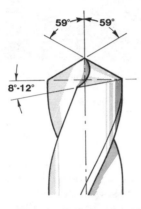

A simple taper will not work for a twist-drill point. The cutting action depends on presenting the cutting edge to the metal at a working angle without the metal behind the edge interfering. The 59° angle works best on most metals.

perceive that there's a secret to it, and they're right. Old-timers can flip on the bench grinder and grind a perfect drill point with the casual ease of a cowboy rolling a cigarette with one hand. The secret is thinking about the drill point as two separate angles and maintaining a mind's eye image of what's happening between the grinding wheel and the drill point as related to the two angles.

If there is any single power tool you cannot do without it's a grinder. Even in the most primitive of pioneer ventures you can be sure that a grindstone for sharpening tools and axes was loaded aboard the covered wagon. Although it was powered by muscle, the rotating abrasive stone was a necessity. Today, even though you do your metalworking on the kitchen table in an apartment, you can use electric power. A small aluminum-oxide wheel mounted in the chuck of an electric drill, the latter clamped in a support cradle, will sharpen drills, knives, chisels, etc.

It's not ideal, but it works, and it's better than trying to force a dull drill through metal. Later, we'll take another look at grinders.

Free-Hand Sharpening

All of the instructions you'll read on twist drills will talk about the 59° angle of the cutting lips. Actually, 59° is not all that sacred. In fact, for hand drilling with a breast drill it may ease your labor quite a bit to go to a steeper angle such as 65°. For electric drills or a drill press, however, 59° is a good starting point. If you err, try to err towards a sharper, not flatter, angle. In any case,

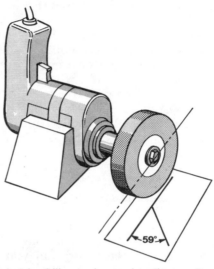

Even an electric drill may be used to sharpen its own twist drill bits. If you're unsure of your eye, make a 59° mark on the bench to sight against while you hold the drill.

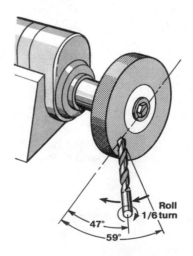

A swinging and rolling motion will produce the desired relief angle on the drill tip. Practice until you can sense that you're doing it right and can produce the same profile on both sides.

this angle at the cutting lips is the one you must grind first.

You'll soon find that you can judge this angle quite accurately by eye, but in the beginning it helps to draw or scribe a line on the grinder tool rest. If you're using an electric drill, a piece of stiff paper taped to the bench under the drill will serve as an eyeball guide. To grind this angle, hold the drill securely in the fingers of both hands so you can look directly down and observe the angle the drill makes with the side of the stone.

Hold the drill so it is horizontal, or with the shank end of the drill tipped down slightly. Look down at the cutting edge, not the back side of the flute. Grind each lip so they are equal in length and angle. If one lip is longer than the other, the drill will wobble and drill oversize.

When both lip angles are equal, the second angle must be ground to give a back relief. If that seems obscure, remember that you want the sharp edges of the lips to contact and bite into the metal. If the metal behind the lips is higher than, or even flush with, the cutting lips, the drill will simply burn, not cut. The metal must slope back slightly by about 12°–15° from each cutting edge.

Once again, bring the edge of the lip to the side of the stone at the same angle, but this time roll your hand slightly, about one-sixth turn, and swing the shank end of the drill towards you at the same time. This is the tricky part, and it's what I referred to when I said that you had to hold a mind's-eye picture of what's happening between the stone and the drill. Good light will help; so will a magnifier of the type you wear with a headband. In all cases, you should certainly be wearing eye protection. A good trick is to draw a second line at 47° if you are using a marked guide to help you judge angles. Theoretically, if you swing the drill to 47° while rolling it one-sixth turn, you'll produce the correct relief angle.

There's one other important point: Maintain a light touch and do not allow the drill to become so hot that it turns blue. Most drill manufacturers warn against dipping a hot, high-speed, steel drill into water for cooling since it is claimed that this sets up minute cracks in the metal. This is probably true, but I have cooled untold drills by dipping in water and had no problems. You can, therefore, allow the drill to cool in the air for a minute or dip it in water and take a chance.

Electric Drill Sharpener

Black and Decker offers a modestly priced electric drill sharpener somewhat resembling an

Black & Decker twist-drill sharpener works fairly well for medium-size drills, less well for small drills. The trick is to get both cutting edges alike since sharpener does one at a time.

electric pencil sharpener except that it has a series of holes to accept the drill sizes commonly used in the home shop. The sizes are limited, however, and the machine doesn't handle small-diameter drills very well. Otherwise, operation is simple and the tips produced are fairly satisfactory. The results are not automatic since you grind first one lip and then the other and must judge by eye if both lips are sharpened evenly.

Sharpening Guides

Another inexpensive sharpening guide is available to mount on, or next to, your bench grinder. The range of this tool is ⅛″ to ¾″ drills. Once again you must resort to hand and eye to sharpen very small drills. This guide is somewhat more difficult to use than Black and Decker's, but it offers a selection of tip angles and, as you learn its tricks, allows you to increase back relief a bit. Its great virtue is that it produces exactly the same lip lengths on both sides.

Special Grinds

The angles described, 59° and about 12° to 15° relief, serve well for steel, cast iron, and other hard metals. Brass and soft aluminum, however, tend to grab or "hog-in." To counter this the angle of the cutting lip should be flattened a trifle to give more of a scraping action. This must

This type of sharpening guide requires a very firm mount next to your bench grinder, but it handles large drills well and is so designed that it produces equal cutting edges.

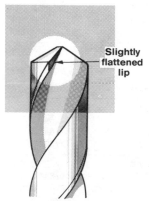

Slightly flattened lip

The difference between the grabbing action of a drill sharpened for steel but used in brass, and a drill with a slightly flattened cutting edge, will surprise you. Try it on aluminum, too.

be done by hand. On small drills it's easiest to hold the drill in a chuck or vise and flat the edge with a small hone. Note that it is not necessary to produce a wide, flat area. Doing so only means that you have that much more to grind away when you resharpen for other metals.

If you examine some professional metalworker's drills you may find that part of the backsides of the drill flute have been ground away. It is true that for some metals and some jobs, this reduction in bearing surface at the tip speeds penetration and allows the chips to flow more freely. It is also done to thin the center web on

drills which have been ground short. The center web thickens as it runs towards the shank of the drill.

A word of caution is in order about this grinding practice. A drill so sharpened will have a tendency in soft metals, even in wood, to grab and thread itself violently into the material. Damage to the work, drill breakage, and, with a powerful ⅜″ or ½″ drill, personal injury, can occur. Unless you have a lot of holes to drill in a hurry and are willing to experiment, I do not recommend cutting back the flutes.

TAP DRILLS

As mentioned earlier, when you start working with metal you'll need to drill holes which you'll later tap for threads. A tap is a thread-cutting tool, and I'll discuss it later. To select a drill for a hole to be tapped you consult your tap-drill chart. If, for example, you want to produce a hole to be threaded for a ¼″-20 bolt, you can't us a ¼″ drill. The ¼″ hole would have no metal for threads; the bolt would fall right in. Clearly, the hole must be smaller than ¼″, but the question is, how much smaller? If you make it too small the tap won't enter, or, if it does, it will break off. Make the hole too large and the threads will be loose and shallow and may strip out.

Fortunately, all of this was worked out for you ages ago. Your tap-drill chart will tell you exactly which drill will produce a thread to engage the bolt approximately 75%. That's the good news. A few special uses exist for tighter thread engagements, but unless you're into precision toolmaking, don't worry about them. Now, the bad news: For ¼″-20 thread your chart calls for a #7 drill. If you have only fractional drills you won't have a #7 because it belongs to the group called number drills, discussed in Chapter 4. As we explained, the diameters of number drills are not nice, simple fractions of an inch. Before giving up, however, always look for a compromise solution. If you follow out your chart you'll find that a #7 drill is .201″ in diameter. (Here's where you get used to thinking in thousandths of an inch.) Read .201″ as two-hundred and one thousandths.

If you think about it for a minute you'll realize that ¼″ converted to a decimal is .250″. Thus, .201″ is .049″ smaller than your bolt diameter and will leave .0245″ on each side for threads. Since you don't have a #7 drill, look at your chart and you will discover that a ¹³⁄₆₄″ fractional drill is .2031″ in diameter—close enough for practical purposes. The extra .0021″ is less than the diameter of a human hair and shouldn't be

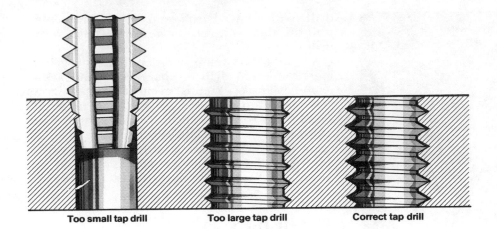

Too small tap drill   Too large tap drill   Correct tap drill

An oversize tap drill will produce a loose thread with low holding ability. Use too small a tap drill and you'll probably break the tap in the hole. Small compromises, however, are sometimes practical if you lack exactly the right drill.

THREAD DIMENSIONS AND TAP DRILL SIZES

Nominal Size	Threads per Inch	Major Diameter Inches	Minor Diameter Inches	Pitch Diameter Inches	Tap Drill for 75% Thread	Clearance Drill Size*
1	64	.0730	.0527	.0629	53	47
2	56	.0860	.0628	.0744	50	42
3	48	.0990	.0719	.0855	47	36
4	40	.1120	.0795	.0958	43	31
5-1/8"	40	.1250	.0925	.1088	38	29
6	32	.1380	.0974	.1177	36	25
8	32	.1640	.1234	.1437	29	16
10	24	.1900	.1359	.1629	25	13/64"
12	24	.2160	.1619	.1889	16	7/32"
1/4"	20	.2500	.1850	.2175	7	17/64"
5/16"	18	.3125	.2403	.2764	F	21/64"
3/8"	16	.3750	.2938	.3344	5/16"	25/64"
7/16"	14	.4375	.3447	.3911	U	29/64"
1/2"	13	.5000	.4001	.4500	27/64"	33/64"
9/16"	12	.5625	.4542	.5084	31/64"	37/64"
5/8"	11	.6250	.5069	.5660	17/32"	41/64"
3/4"	10	.7500	.6201	.6850	21/32"	49/64"
7/8"	9	.8750	.7301	.8028	49/64"	57/64"
1"	8	1.0000	.8376	.9188	7/8"	1- 1/64"
1-1/8"	7	1.1250	.9394	1.0322	63/64"	1- 9/64"
1-1/4"	7	1.2500	1.0644	1.1572	1- 7/64"	1-17/64"
1-3/8"	6	1.3750	1.1585	1.2667	1- 7/32"	1-25/64"
1-1/2"	6	1.5000	1.2835	1.3917	1-11/32"	1-33/64"
1-3/4"	5	1.7500	1.4902	1.6201	1- 9/16"	1-49/64"
2"	4-1/2	2.0000	1.7113	1.8557	1-25/32"	2- 1/32"
2-1/4"	4-1/2	2.2500	1.9613	2.1057	2- 1/32"	2- 9/32"
2-1/2"	4	2.5000	2.1752	2.3376	2- 1/4"	2-17/32"
2-3/4"	4	2.7500	2.4252	2.5876	2- 1/2"	2-25/32"
3"	4	3.0000	2.6752	2.8376	2- 3/4"	3- 1/32"
3-1/4"	4	3.2500	2.9252	3.0876	3"	3- 9/32"
3-1/2"	4	3.5000	3.1752	3.3376	3- 1/4"	3-17/32"
3-3/4"	4	3.7500	3.6752	3.5876	3- 1/2"	3-25/32"
4"	4	4.0000	3.6752	3.8376	3- 3/4"	4- 1/32"

*Clearance drill makes hole with standard clearance for diameter of nominal size.

Thread dimensions are important for both drilling and tapping, but they are even more important if you learn to cut threads on a lathe. The major and minor diameters are used to size the metal before threading. Clearance holes allow a threaded fastener to be inserted through a nonthreaded piece with a little to spare.

a problem unless you're a real fusspot. Go ahead and drill with the ¹³⁄₆₄″ drill and know that you're in good company. Industry uses such compromises routinely.

There are eighty sizes of number drills. You won't have occasion to use many of them. Beware of ads offering bargain prices for complete drill sets. They often turn out to be number or letter drills. Letter drills have also been around a long time, and you'll encounter these odd sizes when seeking out a tap drill. Suppose that you want to tap-drill for a ⁵⁄₁₆″-18 thread, a really common bolt size. This time your chart will call for a letter F drill with a diameter of .257″. Your best approximation is either ¼″ (.250″) or ¹⁷⁄₆₄″ (.2656″). For soft metal, plastic, or thin stock of ¼″ thickness or less, the ¼″ drill would probably be a fair compromise. True, it's slightly under size, and the tap would go in too tight for hard metal or deep holes. Small taps in such circumstances are easily broken off in the hole. The ¹⁷⁄₆₄″

CLASSES OF FIT—AMERICAN NATIONAL THREAD

Class 1	A loose fit.
	Thread must assembly easily.
Class 2	A free fit.
	Most interchangeable screw-thread work falls into this class.
Class 3	A medium fit.
	Highest grade of practical and economical screw-thread work.
Class 4	A close fit.
	Produces a fine, snug fit, but selective assembly may be necessary.
Class 5	An interference fit.
	Where wrench-tight fit is required. Here there is interference between maximum nut and minimum screw.

Courtesy of American Twist Drill Co.

Most of the threaded fasteners and the taps and dies you buy at the hardware store will be for a Class 2 fit. For closer fits you'll need more costly industrial taps and dies. Or you might want to produce them in your lathe for special uses. An example might be an adjustment screw for a gunsight where you don't want looseness or backlash.

LETTER SIZE DRILLS

A	0.234	J	0.277	S	0.348
B	0.238	K	0.281	T	0.358
C	0.242	L	0.290	U	0.368
D	0.246	M	0.295	V	0.377
E	0.250	N	0.302	W	0.386
F	0.257	O	0.316	X	0.397
G	0.261	P	0.323	Y	0.404
H	0.266	Q	0.332	Z	0.413
I	0.272	R	0.339		

Letter size drills are needed less often. For tap drilling, only sizes F and U are commonly required.

DECIMAL EQUIVALENTS NUMBER SIZE DRILLS

No.	Size of Drill in Inches	No.	Size of Drill in Inches	No.	Size of Drill in Inches	No.	Size of Drill in Inches
1	.2280	21	.1590	41	.0960	61	.0390
2	.2210	22	.1570	42	.0935	62	.0380
3	.2130	23	.1540	43	.0890	63	.0370
4	.2090	24	.1520	44	.0860	64	.0360
5	.2055	25	.1495	45	.0820	65	.0350
6	.2040	26	.1470	46	.0810	66	.0330
7	.2010	27	.1440	47	.0785	67	.0320
8	.1990	28	.1405	48	.0760	68	.0310
9	.1960	29	.1360	49	.0730	69	.0292
10	.1935	30	.1285	50	.0700	70	.0280
11	.1910	31	.1200	51	.0670	71	.0260
12	.1890	32	.1160	52	.0635	72	.0250
13	.1850	33	.1130	53	.0595	73	.0240
14	.1820	34	.1110	54	.0550	74	.0225
15	.1800	35	.1100	55	.0520	75	.0210
16	.1770	36	.1065	56	.0465	76	.0200
17	.1730	37	.1040	57	.0430	77	.0180
18	.1695	38	.1015	58	.0420	78	.0160
19	.1660	39	.0995	59	.0410	79	.0145
20	.1610	40	.0980	60	.0400	80	.0135

For tap drilling at the smaller end of the scale, you'll find that some number drills are useful. Or by careful matching of their diameters with fractional drills, in decimals, you can often find substitutes.

DECIMAL EQUIVALENTS OF PARTS OF AN INCH

1/64	0.015625	33/64	0.515625
1/32	0.03125	17/32	0.53125
3/64	0.046875	35/64	0.546875
1/16	0.0625	9/16	0.5625
5/64	0.078125	37/64	0.578125
3/32	0.09375	19/32	0.59375
7/64	0.109375	39/64	0.609375
1/8	0.125	5/8	0.625
7/64	0.140625	41/64	0.640625
5/32	0.15625	21/32	0.65625
11/64	0.171875	43/64	0.671875
3/16	0.1875	11/16	0.6875
13/64	0.203125	45/64	0.703125
7/32	0.21875	23/32	0.71875
15/64	0.234375	47/64	0.734375
1/4	0.25	3/4	0.75
17/64	0.265625	49/64	0.765625
9/32	0.28125	25/32	0.78125
19/64	0.296875	51/64	0.796875
5/16	0.3125	13/16	0.8125
21/64	0.328125	53/64	0.828125
11/32	0.34375	27/32	0.84375
23/64	0.359375	55/64	0.859375
3/8	0.375	7/8	0.875
25/64	0.390625	57/64	0.890625
13/32	0.40625	29.32	0.90625
27/64	0.421875	59/64	0.921875
7/16	0.4375	15/16	0.9375
29/64	0.453125	61/64	0.953125
15/32	0.46875	31/32	0.96875
31/64	0.484375	63/64	0.984375
1/2	0.500	1	1.000

Since so many metalworking dimensions, and so many tools are given and sized in decimals, a table of decimal equivalents should be posted at a handy place in your shop.

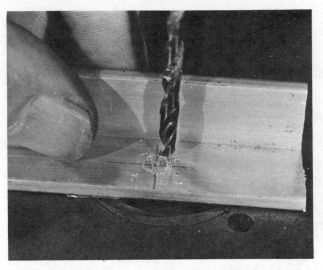

Poor center punching, an improperly sharpened drill, or attempting to hand-hold work can cause a twist drill to drift around dead center.

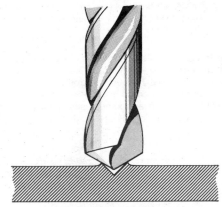

Punch mark lets drill cut

A center-punch dimple allows the cutting edges of the drill to engage the metal, stabilizing the drill so it doesn't drift.

drill is a bit loose but a reasonable, although not ideal, choice for hard steel or deep holes. In due course, since a 5/16″-18 thread is so common, you'll probably buy a letter F drill.

DRILLING TECHNIQUE

Starting the Drill

Sometimes getting a hole located precisely is extremely important and sometimes, of course, it can be a matter of more-or-less. Whatever the demands for accuracy, a twist drill, unlike a pointed wood bit, will wander or drift on the work surface rather than biting in exactly where you want it to. If the work is rigidly clamped on a drill-press table and the drill firmly chucked in a husky, solid drill press, the drill may not appear to wander perceptibly, especially if it is of small diameter. On the other hand, the same drill used in a hand-held electric drill may be almost impossible to start where you want it unless you center-punch the location first. As a

rule, all drilling center locations should be center-punched.

The center-punch dimple provides a little cavity for the small flat at the tip of the drill. This allows the sharp cutting lips to engage the metal and start the hole. Once cutting has started well, all that's needed is a steady pressure suited to the size of the drill and the hardness of the metal. At least that's true with drills up to about 5/16″. But even with drills as small as 3/16″, and almost always with drills larger than 5/16″, the operation will go much faster and be more accurate if you first drill a small pilot hole. A pilot hole is a hole slightly larger than the tip of the drill. The tip will run freely in the pilot hole and the cutting lips will get a better bite into the metal on each side. If you have reason to drill fairly large holes, up to or even over ½", with a handheld electric drill, you'll soon come to appreciate how much hard work a pilot hole can save.

Breaking Through

I have no idea what the statistics are, so I'm free to say that I suspect that more drilling accidents—broken drills, work torn from your hands or clamps, and personal injuries—occur at the moment the drill breaks through the other side of the metal than at any other time. These misfortunes result from the lips of the drill suddenly engaging the thin edges of the remaining metal and the spiral flutes acting like a coarse thread to pull the drill into and through the workpiece. There are many techniques for avoiding this grabbing action. If you are just starting in metal-

Violent breakthrough occurs when the drill flutes wind into the remaining thin web of metal in a hole and act like coarse threads to pull the drill.

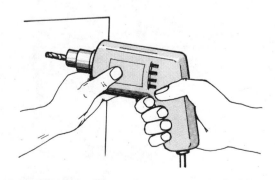

One way to reduce the effect of violent breakthrough with a hand-held drill is to wedge your hand ahead of the drill body and against the work surface.

working, be aware of this hazard when you drill through a piece of metal.

As you gain experience, even with a small ¼" electric drill, you will learn to sense when the drill is cutting well, when you need to apply more or less pressure, and when the drill is about to break through. If you feel unsure of yourself, make or buy a stop collar which can be secured on the drill and prevent it from breaking through. Another precaution is to stop drilling when you know you are about to penetrate and look into the hole to detect the beginnings of breakthrough. Of course, if you can see the reverse side of the work you can watch for the little dimple that is the first sign of the drill tip.

However you determine that you're about to pop the drill tip through the metal, the urgent thing is to reduce pressure and hold back on the drill. With a ¼" electric drill, you can grasp the front of the drill body with your left hand (if you're righthanded), and wedge the thumb and fingers between the drill and the work. The idea is to limit the forward motion of the drill so that the last few chips are cleaned out with a very light cut. If you are using a drill press you can do the same thing by getting a good grip on the handle and actually holding up rather than pulling down as the drill makes its final penetration. Another good method, if you have access to the back of the work, is to clamp a backup plate of scrap metal behind the hole so when you penetrate the drill is just starting a hole in the backup piece.

Drilling Don'ts

Good twist drills are expensive, especially in the larger sizes. It pays to take care of them and it pays to avoid destructive practices.

One very destructive use of a drill is to use it to enlarge a hole just a trifle smaller than the drill. You might, for example, have a ½" hole that you want to open up to %₁₆". Trying to run a larger drill into such a hole concentrates all of the cutting action on the extreme outer corners

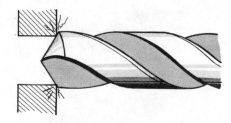

The reduced bearing surface you get when you try to use a drill just slightly larger than the hole will almost certainly damage the outer margins of the drill.

of the lips and flute margins. This usually causes a wedging and wearing action which reduces the diameter of the drill and causes it to bind unless the damaged area is cut off and the drill resharpened. A typical job is drilling out a piece of steel pipe to produce a smooth bore which will slide over another piece. This job can sometimes be done with a reamer, or perhaps a succession of progressively larger reamers. Lacking reamers, it's better to find a friend with a metal-cutting lathe in which the pipe can be mounted and bored out with a boring bar.

Drills are also ruined by bending. This occurs with a hand-held drill when you attempt to cut sideways. For example, when drilling through two or more pieces with holes which should align but don't. There's a temptation to apply side pressure to the drill but the result is seldom good. Such misalignments are better solved with a taper reamer gradually worked through the holes until a line up is gained. Follow this with a straight reamer to produce a straight passage and use an oversize pin or bolt as needed.

Another way to damage a drill is to strike a glancing blow against an unseen part, flange, or casting bulge in a blind area. This kind of interference forces the drill to bend while rotating and will either wear away the margins or break the drill. Experienced metalworkers try to anticipate the possibility of hitting an obstacle like this and will probe gently as the drill proceeds to feel out the drill path before pressing ahead. Obstructions you can't see, or can't even imagine, are very common inside castings.

Drilling Speeds
It is tempting to say that more drills are ruined by running them too fast than by rotating them too slowly. But that's only partially true. The cutting engagement of the drill lips and the metal, the actual force that tends to burn or break the drill, is a combination of both speed and feed. You'll find many charts and guides recommending the speed and feed rates for various drill sizes, metals, and lubricants. My own experience is that these tables are fine for production operations in commercial shops with automatic and adjustable tool feeds. They are not very useful in the home shop with either a hand-held drill or a drill press since both are hand fed. There is really no control for the rate

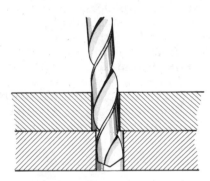

Attempting to use the sides of a twist drill to bring two out-of-line holes back into line is a good way to break the drill in the hole. Removing the broken stub can be trying.

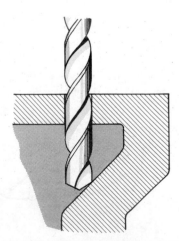

If you must drill into a blind area in a structure or casting, try to probe cautiously to avoid encountering an obstruction which would bend the drill and break it off inside the work.

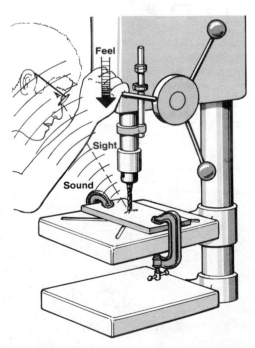

Lacking the precision feed control and repetitive operations of mass production, the home-shop metalworker must attune his sense of feel, his observation of the chips, and the sound of the drill to establish the right feed pressure and speed.

of feed with such tools other than your own judgment and the pressure you apply manually.

And, although variable-speed electric drills offer an infinite speed selection, there is no instantaneous way to know exactly what speed the drill is turning. On the typical shop drill press, speed changes are made by adjusting the belt between stepped V-pulleys, so the best you can do is approximate the recommended speed. Some recently introduced small drill presses have computers which read out digitally for speed. They do not, however, control feed.

Thus, operating an electric tool is a matter of skill. The metalworker should learn when a drill is cutting properly by the appearance of the chips, the rate at which the drill seems to penetrate easily without forcing, and by that all-important sense of feel.

Quite honestly, my drill press has the belt set on the lowest-speed pulley combination, 625 rpm, most of the time. The exceptions might be when I want to drill a large number of small holes for a riveted assembly, or use a small drill, 1/16" or 3/32". Although my drilling may not always attain production speeds, I don't burn or break many drills. Very small drills, however, work best at higher speeds and light feeds. Sometimes the lowest speed on the drill press is too fast for larger drills such as 1/2". If possible, I drill larger holes in the lathe and cut down the speed until I get smooth chip production rather than the chattering you can experience at higher speed in the drill press.

Drilling Problems

Twist drills are easily dulled in spite of their high-speed steel. Sometimes when drilling low-grade angle iron and strip stock, you'll hit inclusions or spots which are glassy hard. Past welding can also produce hard spots. When sharp, and rotating at a proper speed for the drill size and metal, a twist drill will produce curling chips or flowing broken chips neatly emerging from each drill flute. Some metals, such as cast iron, do not produce the same kinds of chips but you can easily tell if the drill is moving into the metal as it should. At the first hint that it's requiring too much time and pressure to drill a hole, stop and examine the drill point. Pressing on with a dull drill is not only tedious but will make the drill duller and burn the point. Do not, however, mistake a drill that's clogged with chips for a dull drill. If progress seems hard or you hear a squeaking sound, back out immediately and allow the chips packed in the flutes to clear. Forcing a clogged drill will either break

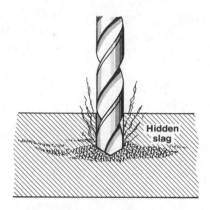

Striking a slag inclusion or hard spot in metal with a drill is like sawing into an unseen nail with a wood saw.

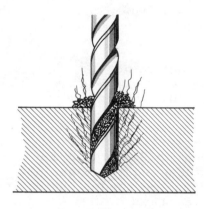

Squeaking and slow progress are often signs of chip-packed drill flutes. The heat expands the metal, tightening the flutes even more until the drill twists off.

Drill "chatter" usually results from rotating a large drill so fast that vibrations are set up at the cutting edges.

off the drill in the hole or cause it to slip in the chuck.

There are many reasons for clogging. These are some of the more common:

- The nature of the metal or drilled material
- Wrong drill speed
- Inadequate lubrication
- Deep hole

Often brass, art metals, aluminum, and plastics behave like sticky materials and the chips pack rather than slide up and out of the flutes. As soon as they start to pack tightly the drill and work metal get hot. The drill expands. This causes squeaking and drill breakage. To avoid this, enter the drill for short distances at a time, withdraw it and clear the chips, and repeat. If you have compressed air, blow the chips clear and cool the drill. Often, slowing down the drill speed will help.

Drilling Lubricants

Many times drilling can be helped by a lubricant which cools the drill and lets the chips slide more freely. Over the years a great number of lubricants have been tried and a vast variety of charts published listing a bewildering array of exotic lubricants. It is true, of course, that industrial drilling and cutting operations pushing for maximum speeds and tool life on automatic machines can benefit greatly from a professional

Although not always needed, cutting oil cools a drill, aids free flow of cuttings, and reduces wear. If in doubt, try drilling with and without it.

analysis of lubricant requirements. Since your work in the home shop is seldom, if ever, a repetitive process hour after hour, you can forget about such lubricants.

Old-timers often recommended lard oil, lard oil and kerosene, or lard oil and turpentine for lubricating drills. Try all of these if you wish, and any of the other ancient mixes, but the likelihood is that you'll eventually reach the conclusion that for most ordinary drilling you'll do just as well with a good grade of SAE 10 or 20 automobile engine oil. Such oils are highly compounded, resist heat well, contain lubricity additives, and do not gum. Automatic transmission fluid also works well.

An equally good, possibly better, lubricant for all-round bench-top use, including machining and thread cutting, is the sulfur-based type lubricant sold as threading and cutting oil.

COMMON DRILL LUBRICANTS

Hard, tough steels	Turpentine or kerosene
Softer steels	Lard oil or equivalent
Aluminum and other soft alloys	Kerosene
Brass	Drill dry or use paraffin oil
Die castings	Drill dry or use kerosene
Cast iron	Drill dry

This list is typical of the common drill lubricants used by the old-time machinists. There are many others. You can test them against modern lubricants to decide if they are better or worse.

8.
BENDING METAL

The methods of bending metal in the home shop are almost always different from those practiced in the factory or professional shop equipped with powerful presses, precision stamping dies, bending brakes, and forming tools. Nevertheless, you can approximate the action of an industrial press with a vise, and bend metal with a hardwood block and a hammer. This is one of the challenges and satisfactions of metalwork. Remember, most of the products that we live with were, at one time, made by hand with fairly crude tools.

ANNEALING

As pointed out, metal, unlike wood, can be altered in character by either softening, commonly called annealing, or by hardening and tempering. Moreover, most metal almost always hardens as it is worked cold by bending or hammering. For this reason, some jobs require repeated annealing as you proceed just to maintain the metal in workable state. This applies particularly to aluminum, copper, brass, and silver since continued working after the metal becomes work-hardened will cause splitting and damage.

All of the above metals except aluminum are easily annealed by heating to a dull red and quenching in water. Since aluminum does not change color when heated, a different method is used, which I'll describe next. Brass seems to anneal better if the quench is held off until the red color starts to dull.

For annealing smaller pieces of metal, it is relatively easy to place the work on a fire brick or even hold it in tongs or pliers and play a torch along it until the metal is evenly heated to a dull red. This is more difficult with larger pieces, such as circular work being made into bowl shapes or the like. The metal tends to cool in one spot while you're heating in another. Metalworkers who often encounter this problem use a rotating table supported on a bearing to spin the work under the torch flame for even heating.

Unlike hardening and tempering steel, discussed in another section, quenching of soft metals when annealing is not a critical process. In fact, there are some who say quenching is not really necessary but merely a convenience to cool off the metal so you can get on with your work. You might want to try quenching and nonquenching and determine for yourself if it makes a significant difference. Any suitable bucket or plastic container filled with water is suitable for quenching if it is large enough to hold the work. Lacking that, simply holding the work in tongs or pliers under running cold water until it is comfortable to touch is adequate. The main thing is to hold the work so your hand is not in the path of the rising steam.

If you are interested in doing hammered metalwork, you'll probably want to make a pickling bath for oxide removal. A sturdy plastic, wide-mouthed container or pan is required. Never use glass; the pickling solution is basically sulphuric acid in water (4 parts water to 1 part sulphuric acid) and an accident might break the glass and splash the acid. This acid solution is extremely dangerous. Even a small splatter will burn your skin or your eyes, and the fumes are equally hazardous. If you insist on using such a pickling solution in your shop, obtain a premixed solution from a chemical supply house, or one of the less hazardous products from a jeweler's supply house.

Annealing Aluminum

Aluminum is also annealed by heating to a critical temperature, but quenching is unnecessary. The tricky part is that aluminum doesn't turn

Annealing aluminum is a two-step process. First use a yellow flame to coat metal with carbon. Follow with a clean flame to burn away carbon. Aluminum will be dead soft.

red to tell you when it's reached the annealing temperature. Various methods have been offered to determine when hot is hot-enough without melting the metal, but the old-time aircraft mechanic's technique is simple and reliable.

If you have an oxyacetylene torch, the first step is to light a small acetylene flame without oxygen. Quickly play the flame over the aluminum to leave a thoroughly blacked surface of carbon. Now, open the oxygen valve to a neutral flame. Carefully burn off the carbon by holding the torch well away and "painting" the flame over the metal. You'll see the carbon magically disappear and the aluminum will return to its original bright state. The metal is now soft. The process can be repeated as often as needed. Be aware, however, that aluminum also time-hardens to some degree. The piece you annealed last week won't be as soft today. For this reason, aluminum rivets for aircraft work were often annealed and then kept refrigerated to retard time-hardening.

The same method can be used with a propane or MAPP torch. To blacken the metal, block off the air holes in the torch burner with tape or a small hose clamp. Use the yellow flame to provide the carbon. Then open up the air holes and burn off the carbon as described. Whichever method you use, do not try to concentrate the heat in one place since aluminum melts very quickly and uneven heating can distort it.

BENDING TUBING

Both copper and aluminum tubing are common materials in the home shop that must often be bent. After annealing, gentle, long-radius bends are easily made by careful hand pressure and the use of a form of the right diameter, such as a basement Lally column. There is always a limit to how much of this kind of bending you can get away with without buckling, crimping, or ovalizing the tubing. Not only does this reduce the diameter and restrict flow, it also con-

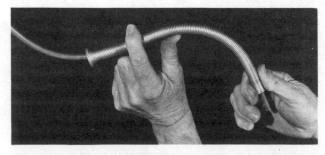

Spring-type tubing bender works quite well within limits. For best results anneal tubing first.

centrates stress. Many fires and disasters in aircraft and boats have been caused when a slightly buckled fuel or oil line ultimately failed from vibration concentrated right at the damaged point.

Over the years many methods have been devised for bending tubing and each has good and bad points. One old technique is to fill the tubing with soft sand, hot resin, or even hot lead. If you use sand, the ends must be plugged tightly. The tube then becomes a fairly solid rod and bends without collapsing. This method is a little better for larger tubing, over ½'' diameter, since it is easier to pack the sand (or other material) solidly inside. It is difficult to pour sand or even

molten resin or lead into a small tube without getting voids.

One major flaw in filling tubing to bend it is the difficulty of completely cleaning the inside later. Sand often hangs in the bends, and material which requires melting can leave residues which cause trouble. Such debris is naturally undesirable in a carburetor, hydraulic cylinder, water valve, or similar device.

Tube-Bending Tools
For the common sizes of tubing up to ½", the best tools for bending are probably the spring

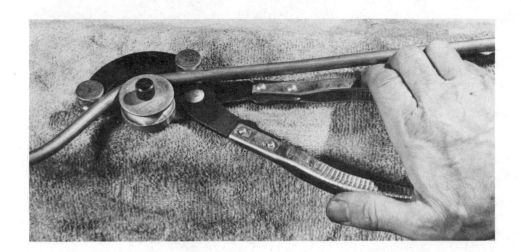

Delicate bends in fuel lines and the like can be made with this type of bender. Practice on scrap tubing to get the feel.

Conduit bender, commonly known as a "hicky," will bend both heavy and thinwall tubing. This one has a jaw insert to match both types.

coils which slip over the tubing and support the walls. These tools are inexpensive. You need one of the proper diameter for each size of tubing.

Other tools which produce more intricate bends, but require a little more care in use, resemble a pair of pliers or tongs with a trio of grooved spools where the jaws would be. The grooves in the spools fit the tubing wall. One of the spools must be changed to suit different tubing sizes. These tools are available at auto parts houses and are used to shape fuel lines, brake lines, etc. Refrigeration supply houses also offer tubing tools of this type. Larger tubing and pipe, such as electrical conduit, is easily bent with a conduit bender commonly called a "hicky."

BENDING RODS AND BARS

Many decorative items and project components are made up of aluminum or soft steel rods or bars. Some projects use brass but it is costly. Many times the desired form is a curled or spiral pattern. Ideally, bends of this type are made around forms of the proper size and curvature minus a small amount for the inevitable "spring back" of all metal. This is fine for production, and if you elect to produce a dozen candle sconces for Christmas gifts you'll do well to make such a pattern from hardwood blocks or chipboard. Generally, however, the final curvature is elective, and pleasing the eye the main concern. For this level of work rather minimal forming tools do just as well.

Many simple bending forms are made of hard metal pins placed in a mount to hold them in rigid spacings. Even two bolts clamped in your vise jaws will often do the trick. But, if you're using a soft metal rod the pins will leave a slight dent at each point of contact pressure. You can eliminate the denting and the occasional sharp overbends caused by pins by using a grooved form which accepts the rod stock into a groove or between flanges for an even contact. Roller-type forming tools are available, but for home-shop use a very practical bending form can usu-

Repeat operation in step 1 three or more times until you've come all the way around. This may be as far as you want to go for a decorative eye. Remember, at each step check to be sure you are coming around square.

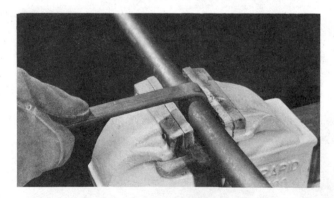

Bending an eye in mild steel strap is a typical operation where a bending form is needed. Here, a steel bar is used for a form. By just nipping the end of the strap between the bar and the vise you can start the bend. If you do this cold with just hand strength and a hammer, the spring-back will cause the eye to be larger than the forming bar. By heating area to be bent red hot, and then pulling down quickly, you can get a snugger wrap. Tap with hammer if necessary while metal is still red. The secret to a good bend is to be certain top of bar is exactly parallel to top of vise jaw, and metal strap is exactly at right angles to jaw so you start off square.

To make a closed eye with a shank, clamp straight portion of strap in vise and hammer eye, with bar inside, over and down.

Flat bends are easily made with vise and hammer in mild steel strap. You can do it without heat, but it goes so much better and easier when red hot that it's worth the trouble. Always try to provide a radius in the bend rather than a sharp corner.

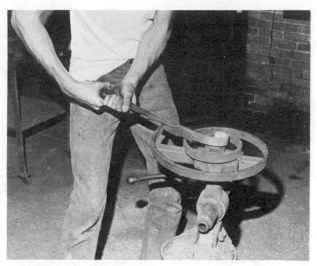

Blacksmith's scroll bender also locks the end of the stock at the center, but the forming action is simply muscle power. Hot iron, however, bends easily.

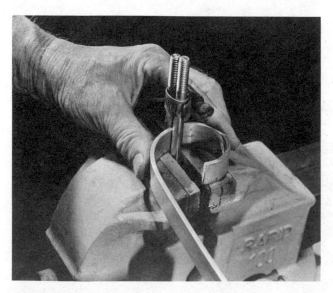

Aluminum strip is easily formed cold after annealing. There are many ways to form spirals, but one of simplest is to use two bolts clamped in the vise jaws so work metal pushes between them snugly. Be assured the bolts will spread if you don't secure them somehow above the work. Small hose clamp shown here holds firmly but allows slight loosening so you can slide stock along for a fresh bite. Work in small bites, bending and shifting metal. You can judge scroll by eye or lift it out and check against a pattern or template.

ally be made of a V-belt pulley of the approximate diameter needed. Such a pulley, firmly anchored, can be used to pull the rod around the desired curvature by hand. You can even make up a roller with a ball bearing to force the metal tightly around the groove. Because of spring-

back you will probably find it best to choose a pulley slightly smaller than your finished diameter. Only trial and experience will show you this.

MACHINE BENDING

Although it is relatively easy to cobble up some sort of bending rig for an occasional job, this can be a tedious and time-consuming approach. There is considerable fun and sometimes profit in making wrought ware, tubing products, wire hardware, etc. For many years the Di-Acro Div. of Houdaille Industries, Inc. has offered a series of manually operated bending machines. The smallest of these is an ideal home-shop tool. Examining its design and construction is an education in the art of bending metal.

The machine is basically a heavy baseplate with a central hole, a series of holes spiraling outward from the center, and a swinging arm which pivots about the center. A radius pin of the radius size desired mounts in the center hole. This might be compared to the V-pulley shown in the crude setup for making croquet wickets. When a piece of metal is placed against the radius pin, a locking pin is inserted in one of the spiral holes chosen to suit the metal thickness. A forming nose is then brought to bear on the work metal and the handle swung to bend the metal neatly around the radius pin.

In some applications a roller rather than the noselike former is used, and for tubing and round stock suitably grooved center pins and

Even a crude bending rig, such as this one made from a vee pulley and an old ball bearing, can turn out neat bends. This rig has made dozens of croquet wickets from ⅜" aluminum rod.

This small, manual Di-Acro bending machine can be set up to bend wire or flat stock. The basic principle involves a rotating arm with a nose bearing against the work metal to force it into shape.

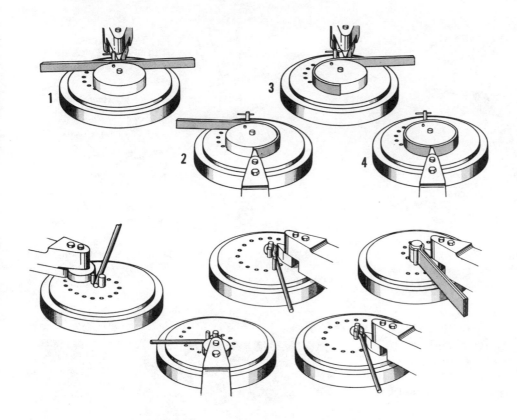

Di-Acro bender is capable of many forming operations on both flat and round stock. Step 1, for flat stock, clamps the metal against the central member and brings the forming nose in firm contact. Step 2 swings the forming nose around halfway. In Step 3 the process is repeated on the unbent end so the finished piece froms a complete ring as in Step 4. The illustrations with round stock show the various steps used to make eyes on center. Flat stock can be shaped much the same.

rollers are available. Stops and setting gages may also be used for repetitive operations. Even if such a machine is beyond the scope of your needs, it is an excellent illustration of the principles of bending metal cold.

HOT BENDING
Soft metals, properly annealed, are readily formed cold if the curve is not too tight and if the stock is not too heavy. But even mild steel can prove difficult to wrap into a snug curve, especially if it's more than ⅛'' or so thick. On the other hand, such steel is wonderfully malleable at red heat. It can be bent, hammered, twisted, and pulled like taffy. To produce a controlled bend, however, you really need some sort of bending jig. Again, as with the Di-Acro tool, the jig must provide a space into which the end of the metal can be inserted and more or less locked, plus a curved face around which to pull the hot metal.

Actually, there are two methods for forming such scrolls and curves. Note that many scroll shapes are made by progressively increasing the radius of the bend so no single form short of a reproduction of the finished scroll would be right. For a single, fixed radius, of course, all that's necessary is to heat the metal, slip it into the jig, and pull it around the form with a smooth, deliberate sweep. But for scrolls with expanding curves, although you may start with a tight curlicue, you'll want to heat and bend alternately in a progressive fashion which inches the metal along and allows a series of small pressure applications to develop a generally expanding curve. This requires a degree of judgment, since an extra-strong pull at one point will produce a visible sharp point in the bend which destroys its grace. The trick is to keep the heat of the metal fairly even so you develop a feel for it.

TWISTING
As with other bends, soft metals in lighter gages can be twisted cold. One end must be anchored in a vise. Usually an adjustable-jaw wrench is used as a twisting lever and moved along as each twist develops. This is not as easy as it sounds. You'll find yourself bending as well as twisting and the result will be crooked and unevenly twisted.

Before starting serious twisting, you should practice on scraps, watching not only the twist but the straightness of the metal. With heavier

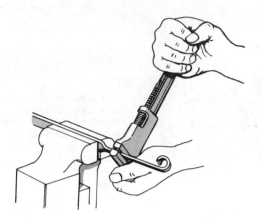

Twisting iron into a spiral requires a solid grip at one end and some sort of wrench for turning. Often soft steel can be bent cold, but even heating is better.

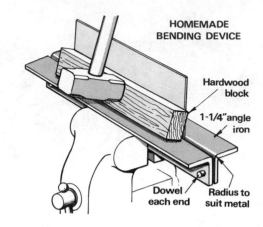

HOMEMADE BENDING DEVICE

Hardwood block

1-1/4" angle iron

Dowel each end

Radius to suit metal

Angle iron and wooden block are effective for bending light metal. If angle corners are sharp, file them to a suitable bending radius first.

steel, you'll have to learn to work with the torch in one hand and the twisting tool in the other to maintain an even heat and a smooth, constant twist. Uneven heating causes some turns of the spiral to be tighter than others.

A little-known trick of the trade used by old-time smith workers specializing in iron rails and the like was to arrange a vise or clamp above their heads and provide a clamp-on weight for the opposite, or lower, end. After heating the metal evenly in the forge, they quickly suspended and weighted the hot metal. It only took a few spins of the weight to spiral the work as desired. If you want to try this, you'll probably suspend and weight the metal first and then play a torch along the stock until it is an even red.

BENDING SHEET METAL

You can bend sheet metal simply by placing it between two pieces of wood in a vise and folding it over with hand pressure on another block of wood. Some jobs, however, are very demanding and require careful layout. Some form of metal or hardwood radius form must be provided, and the exact placement and clamping of the work metal must be worked out before bending. There are also practical limitations in the home shop. A long, narrow strip, such as a drip-edge molding for a roof, is almost impossible to form without a professional metal brake long enough to accept the full piece in one bite. This kind of work is best taken to the local tin shop.

Smaller projects, up to about 24'' long, however, can be bent, and the limitations are only those of your own ingenuity. Since you won't

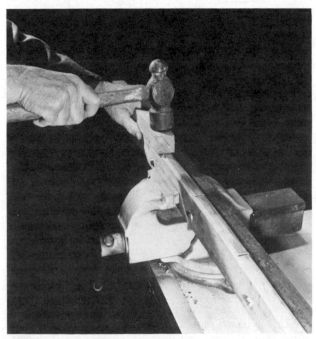

Bending and shaping long pieces such as this deck beam for an aluminum boat modification require more than casual methods. This piece was roughed out and one edge trued for layout. Too long for home bending, the lower edge was bent at a sheet-metal shop. Then a hardwood form with the proper bending radius was made and a length of angle iron was drilled to match holes in the metal and the form. After the metal was annealed, it was clamped between the angle iron and the forms with bolts which passed through all three pieces. The assembly was clamped in a vise at progressive points for bending. The angle iron held the metal flat against the form and prevented distortion and bulging. A maple block the length of the bent segments was held against the metal and struck a few sharp blows with the hammer for each bend. Pressure was applied evenly along the bend, and repeated hammering, which would have distorted the metal, was kept to a minimum.

have the force and power of commercial bending machines, it always helps to anneal those metals I've discussed.

For small pieces, the vise method works as well as anything. The secret, here, as with nearly all bending, is to bend the entire face of the metal evenly and at one time. If you start bending at one end and work along the bend towards the opposite end, you'll almost certainly wind up with a mess. This means that some sort of pressure block is needed to distribute the bending force evenly over the face of the metal.

For longer pieces, the vise jaws can be extended with hardwood blocks. But, unless such bending is a rare thing, it's better to get two sections of 1¼″ angle iron about 24″ long and make a set of extensions by doweling them as shown. Use C-clamps at several points on each side to make certain of a firm grip on the metal. One of the sections should be filed to a radius suited to the metal thickness you work most often. By providing several interchangeable sections of angle iron, you can have a selection of bending radii for different thicknesses.

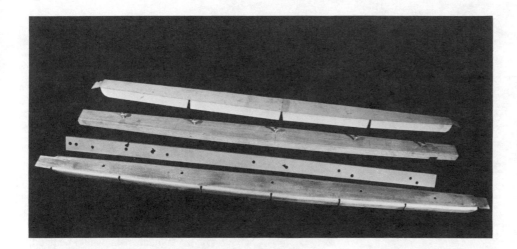

Steps in making the deck beam: First a cardboard mock-up (top) was made to fit the boat. The wooden form and back-up angle iron are seen between the cardboard and the finished beam (bottom). Also, the face of the iron which contacted the aluminum was polished free of burrs and nicks. Two tabs were left unfinished at each end. Later, these would be bent to fit the boat contours and then riveted in place.

After installing the deck beam made in the previous steps, a second, shorter beam was mocked up in cardboard and clamped in place.

With the cardboard as a template, the second deck beam was cut and bent to shape. Since cardboard can be bent sharply, you must compensate for bending radius and allowance in metal part.

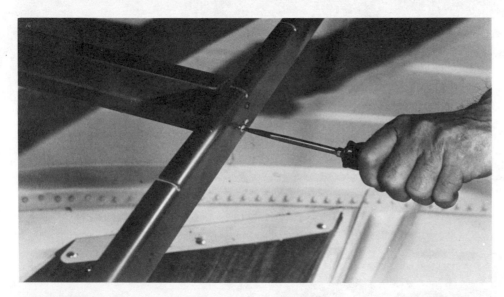

After priming with zinc chromate primer, beams are given a check assembly with self-tapping screws. Here, the important factor was aligning the faces to which the large sheet of deck metal would be fitted.

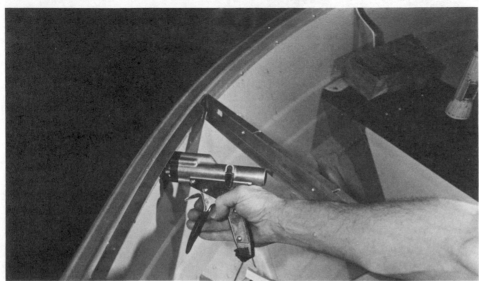

To support edges and front of deck, aluminum angle was annealed, bent gently, and carefully located, again with self-tapping screws. Screws were removed and blind rivets installed one at a time.

A pattern for the deck piece, to be made from ³⁄₃₂″ aluminum, was first roughed out in cardboard and secured by two screws and wooden strip for marking. Screw holes were center reference points and were used several times in later steps. Here, inner contour of boat is marked in pencil on pattern.

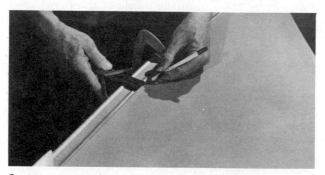

Contour was transferred from cardboard to aluminum slightly oversized and metal was band-sawed to shape. Again using the screw holes, the metal was fastened down and a rule with a vee-shaped center-finder head was carefully moved along boat's gunwale to give a final trim mark. Metal was trimmed on a disk sander, smoothed with a file and orbital sander.

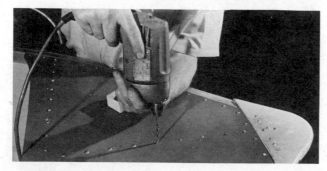

After final fitting, deck metal was drilled, deburred, and again located with reference screws for drilling deck supports. As drilling progressed, screws were installed to pull metal into shape. After all holes were drilled and all the screws installed, the screws were removed and rivets driven one by one. The procedure sounds tedious, but it prevented the metal from creeping out of position. Since deck was crowned in the center, initial riveting started down center beam. Screw holes were smaller than rivet holes so the latter had to be redrilled to size.

With deck riveted in place, it was ready for finishing by spraying with automotive primer surfacer over the zinc chromate. This was followed by finish coat of acrylic lacquer. Masking with tape and paper was necessary for color coats. Since rivets made it difficult to rub out finish, a final spray, seen here, was applied with mixed thinner and retarder after masking was removed. This improved gloss and blended any ragged edges left from masking tape.

Curves and Cylinders

There are many projects that call for large-radius bends or closed tubular forms. If you were making a panlike bottom for a flower planter or a bird feeder, specific dimension is unimportant. Almost any gentle curve which pleased your eye would be satisfactory. You could make a forming block of hard wood, clamp the metal against it with a backup block, and bend it the same way as you would a right-angle bend. Here, you would not be concerned about spring back. Even though the natural spring of the metal results in the final curve having a slightly larger radius than planned, nothing is lost.

However, if it is important that the finished radius be accurate, you must make the curve of the forming block sharper than the finished radius so the spring back will bring the finished bend to the proper contour.

In practice, it's almost always easier to open up a large-radius bend than to tighten it up if you don't allow enough for spring back. Err, therefore, on the tight side. Some metals, such as aluminum annealed dead soft, may spring back very little. Others, such as springy brass or copper, may be quite stubborn about taking a

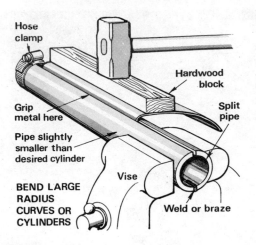

One way to form a tubular or curved sheet without a commercial roller is by bending it over a pipe or bar. Doing this without some way to grip it in a fixed relationship to the form, however, usually results in buckles and a poor job. This split-pipe mandrel grips one edge and lets you form the metal squarely aligned with the form. Always use a block to avoid dimpling or stretching pockets into the stock.

curve. It's always best to make a few trial bends before going ahead with a finished piece.

The same concerns apply to bending up a cylinder. Typically, in the home shop such a job will not turn out as well as it would if it were bent in a commercial roller. If you have need for an accurately formed cylinder, the local tin shop is still your best option. For decorative pieces and the like, especially if evident marks of hand fabrication enhance rather than detract, you can form cylinders around mandrels of suitably sized pipe or bar stock.

Heavy bar stock has the advantage of anvil-like rigidity if you form with a block and hammer. Pipe, however, works adequately and if split can serve to grip one edge of the cylinder. One way to make such a split mandrel is to saw the pipe lengthwise and then tack one side of the split back together by welding or brazing. Grind or file the seam down flush with the pipe. To use the mandrel, wedge the pipe open slightly, insert one edge of the metal sheet, and clamp one end of the pipe firmly in a vise. Clamp the outer end with a C-clamp or other means so the grip on the metal is even, to prevent skewing.

Duplicating curves.   In some projects, such as restoring an antique car or airplane, you may want to make a new piece that matches the original contours. There are many ways to make a forming block, but if you can find an area where the old metal retains most of the original contour, you can use it as a starting point. Use wax

paper or the like to avoid adhesion and build up a block of plaster of Paris or body-repair plastic against the metal. When this has hardened firmly, you can then use it as a mold into which to pour aluminum, type metal, or even lead. You will now have a forming block against which to work.

Forming Edges

The edges of sheet metal can be made stronger, safer, and more attractive by bending them over. This means that you almost always form the edge first and do final shaping later. It also means that you must provide extra metal for the bend-over when making the layout.

Allow at least a one-thickness bending radius on the initial right-angle bend to start a fold-over edge. This will soften the appearance of the finished edge. Follow the right-angle bend by clamping a piece of metal, the thickness a matter of your choice, in the angle of the bend, and use a block and mallet to fold the metal over. This will leave a folded edge, but you'll have a gap at the bottom of the edge the thickness of the metal used to form the bend. The edge may now be tapped flush with the main workpiece using the edge of a block and a mallet.

The edge formed in this manner is often adequate, but what you've formed is essentially a narrow box or tube. If you now attempt to shape the metal around a curve or bend, there's a good chance the result will be unsightly buckles and crimps in the edge.

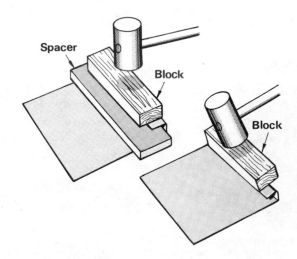

There are three steps to making a folded edge. First, make a right-angle bend by one of the methods shown elsewhere. Next, close the edge over against a spacer of scrap metal of a thickness suitable to soften the edge. Finally, close down the raw edge against the face of the workpiece.

Wire edges. A stronger edge, and one less prone to buckling, can be formed by rolling the edge metal over a piece of fairly heavy wire. The wire should be compatible with the workpiece metal to avoid electrolytic corrosion—aluminum with aluminum, copper with copper, and so on. Dissimilar metals will eventually corrode.

A rolled edge will require more extra metal than you think. Picture the edge metal you're going to wrap around the wire as going completely around to form a tube. You would now require an amount of metal equivalent to the circumference of the wire. If you wished to calculate this you'd use *Pi (3.1416)* × *D* (wire diameter). But in practice the metal will not wrap totally around the wire so you can use a rule of thumb and multiply the wire diameter by 2.5.

Start the wire edge with a right-angle bend over a forming block which will produce an inner radius to match the wire. Complete the fold-over against a spacer piece the same thickness or slightly less than the diameter of the wire. A piece a few thousandths less will help compensate for spring-back if the metal is springy.

The final folding must, of course, be done with the wire in place. It's important that the wire be retained well back against the fold during the folding process. If it starts to skew or angle out, the result will be an unsightly and uneven edge. A good way to avoid this, if possible, is to clamp both wire and work metal firmly to the bench top using blocks or pads to avoid marring the metal. The important thing is that the wire and the metal must not slide around.

Strike down the edge over the wire using a narrow, blunt-wedge-shaped piece of wood or metal and a mallet. Try to distribute the force evenly so the entire edge folds evenly and at the same time. By working carefully, you should be able to close the metal snugly against the wire.

Some metalworkers use a special hammer with a cross-pen head to drive the metal home, but this is poor practice and almost inevitably leaves hammer marks and scars on the finished work. If you can avoid striking the metal directly with a hammer, it's always better. For a final tightening of the roll, place the work so the metal overhangs a forming bloc or angle-iron edge, and use a block and mallet to tap the edge down tightly on the wire.

Bent-metal joints. In the past, it was common for tinsmiths to use joints or seams made by folding metal so it interlocked. Although such seams have their place in furnace ducts, aircon-ditioning ducts, and "tin" cans, they are seldom used in the home shop. If you can find an old-time sheet-metal shop and look at the equipment you'll see why. Almost without exception, forming such joints required heavy and highly specialized equipment ranging from long bending brakes to rollers, crimpers, and other forming tools, the latter often hand-cranked.

It is, of course, quite possible to make such a joint—for example, for the side of a fireplace bucket or floral bucket—if the edge of the joint is quite short. You simply make a right-angle bend between two pieces of angle iron, fold the edge over as described under forming edges, interlock the two opposite folds, and close the joint by tapping with a block. With any project over the limited length, perhaps 18'', it's practical to

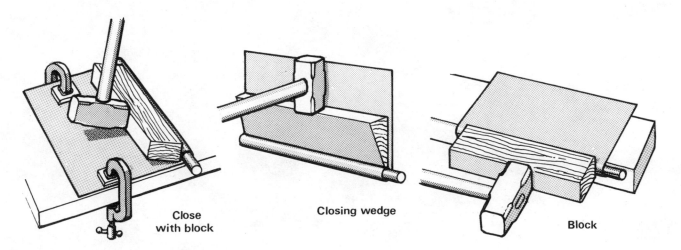

Close with block

Closing wedge

Block

Forming an edge with an enclosed wire starts with the first two steps for making a folded edge. Use a spacer the thickness of the wire. Secure the metal from slipping and close the edge around the wire by driving with a block. To finish curling the edge, use a wedge-shaped closer tool. Finally, to snug and finish the work, place closed edge against a block or bench edge and tap evenly.

Folded seam

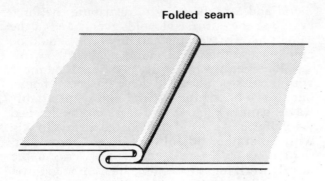

Although folded seams are common in commercial sheet-metal work, they are seldom used in the home shop. One reason is few of us get into projects of the size and shape where they're suited. The other reason is that they require large and accurate forming brakes to make the folds.

clamp and fold by hand methods. Such joints, if of significant length, require that the folds be very straight and accurate. This requires a bending brake. It may be that some craftsmen can hand fold a long edge in the home shop, but unless you have a lot of experience, or just an urge to experiment, try to avoid such bent-metal joints or swallow your pride and go to a shop with the necessary equipment. I did this even to get a right angle bend in a 36″ piece of ⅛″ aluminum.

An equally good joint can be made with pop rivets, sheet-metal screws, or tinner's rivets, followed, if necessary for water or air tightness, by soldering or brazing. Note that bent-metal joints are not used in a 747 jetliner.

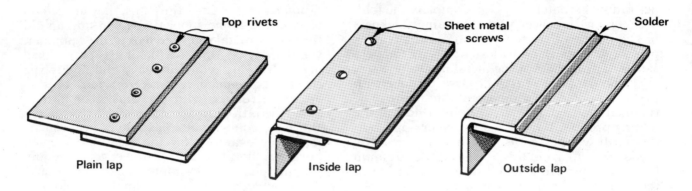

Pop rivets   **Sheet metal screws**   **Solder**

Plain lap   **Inside lap**   **Outside lap**

In the home shop you can make simple lap joints with rivets, screws, solder, or brazing. Refer to the Chapter 9 and you'll see that the solder should be between the two faces as well as along the edge.

9.
SOLDERING AND BRAZING

Soft solder is to metal what glue is to wood. Clean the metal, touch it with the solder and soldering iron, let it cool, and the two become as one, almost instantly. Solder, a name for many metals with low melting points but for the moment referring to a mix of tin and lead, melts and "wets," or flows, freely over the joint. When it cools it adheres firmly.

Nearly all of the jewelry craft metals such as gold, silver, and platinum are easily soldered, but for reasons of color, melting points for successive joints, and strength, soft solder is seldom used. The more common metals—copper, brass, tinned steel, and galvanized steel—are also easily soldered and soft solder is routinely used. Chromed metal, stainless steels, and plain, mild steel are less readily soldered although it is not impossible. Aluminum is very difficult to solder, but there are materials and techniques which make it possible even in the home shop.

Soft solder. Appropriately named because of the soft metals in its makeup, soft solder is a mixture of tin and lead in proportions ranging from 30/70, 30% tin and 70% lead, to 63/37, 63% tin and 37% lead. The latter has an extremely low melting point, 361°F, for special electronic use. The former, which melts at 491°F, is used where cost is a factor. The most common, general-purpose solder is 50/50. It melts at 421°F. Obviously, soft solder is not an ideal fastening material if the project is going to be subjected to heat. A cooking vessel for oven application would be a poor choice. On an eave gutter, however, this would not be a concern.

Also, since soft solder is a mix of soft metals, it is not particularly strong in certain types of joints. An example might be the snaps on a coin purse where the actual contact and bond area is quite small. On the other hand, for electrical connections where there is no real load, or for the lapped edges of sheet-metal roof flashing, soft solder is perfectly adequate.

Flux. This is a chemically active material which removes the oxide, occludes air, and produces a good wetting or flow action of the solder on the metal. The choice of flux depends very much on the nature of the work.

For many years tinsmiths soldering galvanized-iron eave gutters and the like, and workers in copperware and tinware, prepared a liquid flux by dropping bits of zinc into muriatic (hydrochloric) acid until the foaming reaction stopped. The flux was brushed along the joint area and the tip of the soldering iron dipped into it to brighten it. This flux works well and is still quite suitable for jobs requiring a large bar of solder. Another form of such flux is soldering paste, very useful for most home-shop jobs where the work can be washed clean later.

Acid flux and paste, however, are totally unsuited for electrical work or fine work where corrosion of either the work or surrounding parts would be very serious. For this reason, a less aggressive flux, commonly a resin-base material, is always used for electrical work.

Wire solder. Handling liquid, paste, or resin fluxes in crude form is not easy. Most home metalworkers choose a wire solder with a hollow core filled with the desired flux. For working ordinary sheet metal, which can be cleaned later, an acid-core solder which automatically fluxes as it melts is very satisfactory. Electrical and electronic jobs should always be done with a resin-core solder. Note that even here, especially in electronics work, there are special solders which are better.

Silver-bearing solder. Soft solder is often used for copper tubing joints, but where somewhat more strength is desired, a silver-bearing solder is preferable. Many builders of model engines also prefer "silver solder." Note that this solder, offered at hardware stores, is basically a tin solder with about 4% silver. The melting point is 430°F. Do not confuse this with jeweler's silver solders which have a much higher silver content and a considerably higher melting point. Low-melting, silver-bearing solder would not, for example, be a good choice for soldering the boiler tubes in a model steam engine because of the heat factor.

SOLDERING TECHNIQUES

Although soldering is easy, actually fun if the metal is clean and the right flux is used, it can also be frustrating unless you learn the proper techniques. The best way to learn is to practice on scrap metal before trying a serious project. Don't worry about faulty results, just analyze what went wrong and how you can improve your next trial. Although there are two common methods of soldering, torch soldering and soldering with an iron or gun, it is best to practice first with a conventional electric soldering iron. You'll need:

● A soldering iron with a 150 to 200-watt rating.
● A spool of acid-core solder, another spool of resin-core solder, and, for experiment, a spool with no flux core. A 50/50 or 40/60 wire solder .093″ diameter will do fine.
● A small can of soldering paste.

● Fine abrasive paper: 240-grit wet-or-dry.
● Scraps of copper or brass, about 2″ by 2″ and, for experiment, similar scraps of galvanized iron.
● A work surface such as a fire brick.
● Safety glasses to protect against flux and metal spatter.

The tip of the iron should be wedge shaped for most flat work, although later you may wish to acquire other tips with four-sided or even round shapes. The tip needs flat areas so you can establish good heat contact over enough area to heat the work to soldering temperature.

One way to reshape a badly worn iron tip is to remove the tip from the iron, heat the working end red with a torch, and forge it out into a wedge shape with a hammer and some sort of anvil surface. Do not try to do this with the tip still in the iron since you will probably damage the internal heating element. For a less worn tip, or after hammering one into shape, use a coarse-cut rasp to finish off the surfaces smooth, flat, and perfectly bright. The iron is now ready for tinning, the term used to describe coating

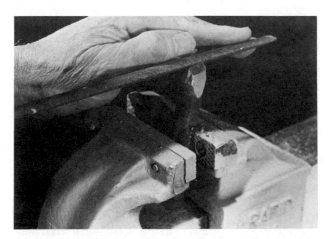

To shape the tip of your soldering iron, remove it, if possible, from the handle and heating element section, and grip it securely in a vise. The exact contour you choose may depend on the type of work, but the shape shown here, being finished off with a coarse file, is practical for most jobs. Note that the flats at the tip form an angle of about 90°.

the working tip with solder. An untinned iron, or one that's tinned spottily or has pits and black spots, will not work well. Replace the tip in the iron. To tin the iron:

1. Allow the iron to heat until solder touched to it flows freely. Polish away any discoloration from heating with abrasive.

2. Coat the tip with acid-core solder and work the tip around on abrasive paper or the fire brick until the surface is brightly coated with solder all around. Lacking acid-core solder, you can dip the tip in soldering paste and get the same result. The flux aids adhesion and even flow.

3. Snap the tip sharply towards the floor or wipe it with a dry cloth to remove excess solder and allow inspection for faulty tinning. The iron is now ready for use. Retinning is needed only at infrequent intervals.

As an experiment, try depositing solder on a piece of dull, oxidized copper without brightening it first. You'll find it impossible, even with flux, to get flow and adhesion. Note how solder sought out and adhered to one part of freshly cut edge—the only bright part of the metal.

Proper tinning to a bright, clean surface is vital to good soldering. Usually the flux in the solder will suffice to make the solder flow and adhere neatly to the tip. A block of salammoniac, available at hardware stores, is shown here; it has been the standby tinning flux for many years.

You are now ready to practice soldering on your scrap metal. As an experiment, and so you'll recognize the problem in the future, try first to solder a piece of copper or brass that is oxidized and darkened. Make your experiment this way:

● Using solid-core, no-flux solder, bring the iron into contact with the metal until solder touched to the metal melts. You will see that although the solder melts and forms globules, it will not adhere to the metal and flow evenly because of the oxide coat.

● Try the same experiment with acid-core solder. This time you'll probably see the solder adhere in some spots because the acid breaks down some of the oxide coating. It is unlikely, however, that the solder will flow evenly and adhere over the entire surface.

● Repeat the experiment after coating the metal with soldering paste and on another piece with resin-core solder. Your results are not likely to be good.

After cleaning and brightening, solder flows and coats the metal like molten paint.

What you have just proven is that solder will not adhere and flow on dirty or oxide-coated metal. Now, use abrasive paper to clean a section of the metal to full brightness and repeat the steps above. You'll probably discover:

● Solid-core solder without flux still does not adhere or flow well, even on bright metal, without some sort of flux.

● Brushing or swabbing a little soldering paste

on the metal will make a great difference and you should be able to flow a smooth, mirror-bright coating of solder on the brightened area.
● Both the acid-core and the resin-core solder will do equally well.

In summary, both a bright surface and some form of flux are necessary for successful soft soldering.

Later, you'll find that even after you have cleaned and brightened the metal, you'll sometimes have a problem from materials which contaminate the metal. Examples are: wire insulation which melts or burns and works onto the surface while you're soldering; grease, oil, or other coatings which heat and flow into the joint. The only solution is to scrape or solvent-clean well back from the area to be soldered.

Before going on, try this experiment to show how the iron conducts heat to the solder area. Take one of the pieces on which you got a good solder flow and coating and arrange it so you can apply the iron against the solder-free side. Now try touching just a corner of the iron to the backside of the metal. The heat will eventually penetrate and a small area will melt and grow bright, but the melting will be marginal. Repeat the procedure but bring one flat face of the tip fully flush against the back of the metal. This time you'll see much faster heating and a much larger area of melting. Good heat conduction depends on good contact between the iron and the metal.

So far, you've only experimented with flowing solder but have not made a solder joint. For practice, take one of your scrap pieces and bend it to a sharp vee shape down the center. Brighten both of the edges and brighten matching areas where the scrap rests when inverted on another scrap. Now, using flux paste, resin core, or acid-core solder, apply the tip of the iron to the juncture where the vee-shaped piece and the flat piece meet. Although you'll probably be able to bring the area to the point where it melts solder touched to it, you'll also find it hard to keep the upper piece in place when you press the iron against it.

You've learned one of the important rules of soldering—you must support the workpieces so they don't move and will resist the pressure of the iron and your own accidental bumpings and unsteadiness. To carry on your learning, try resting something fairly heavy, such as a bar of iron or a heavy wrench handle, on the top of the vee. Now you have stabilized the joint. The next step:

Again apply the iron, and when the solder melts when touched to the metal, flow it into the joint and move the iron along so the solder follows the heat. You should produce a perfect fillet with the solder surface concave and smoothly blended into the work metal at top and bottom. If you don't, there's no law that says you can't run the iron back over the joint and smooth out your work.

Do not move the joint until the solder cools. This is evidenced by the bright, wet surface suddenly dulling and turning gray. Let it cool a few seconds longer before disturbing. You've now made a solder joint.

The type of joint described above, with two pieces more or less at right angles, is fairly common, but because the solder is soft, it depends considerably on the area of the joint for strength. Most experienced metalworkers will plan a solder joint so there is a flap or lap-over to increase the area the solder has to hold.

There are a number of ways to make such a lap joint and you should experiment with them. To start, again make a vee, tent-shaped scrap, and this time bend two flaps on the bottom legs. This time, brighten the areas of the contact with the flat piece and also both side of the flaps at the bottom. Support the piece firmly, as before.

1. Apply the iron along the edge of the joint and hold the iron so the flat, heating surface runs along the flap.

2. As the solder melts you'll see it form a small fillet along the thin edge of the flap, and you should see some of it flow under the flap between the two surfaces. Allow the joint to cool.

The joint you've made should have solder between the workpiece and the flat over the entire surface. To see if it does, clamp the work in a vise and pull it apart with a pair of pliers. You will probably find that the solder has penetrated between the pieces, but the penetration and adhesion are spotty. Try the procedure again. This time, before placing the vee piece on the flat piece, invert it and run the iron and solder along the flap to coat and tin the metal. Repeat this with the area on the flat piece where the flap will touch.

After flowing the solder onto the flap and the workpiece, while the metal is still molten, quickly wipe off the excess with a rag. Both surfaces should now be coated with a thin film of solder.

Again, place and secure the vee piece on the flat piece and provide yourself with something such as a piece of wood or a screwdriver to press down the joint later.

Heat the joint with the iron and, as before, add a small amount of solder. Work the iron to keep the entire joint hot and press down firmly until the joint cools thoroughly.

Again, pull the joint apart, if you can. This time there should be full and complete adhesion

This practice joint solders an edge to a flat surface. It is not particularly strong since the joint area is narrow, but it will teach you to distribute the heat from the iron to two pieces of metal equally. Steel block weights joint so pieces don't move.

For a stronger joint, increase the solder contact area with a flap which rests on bottom piece. The trick here is to be certain solder gets between flat surfaces. Some will flow in by capillary action but actual contact may be spotty.

For better joint, and to ensure full solder contact, try coating both contact faces with a light tinning coat of solder before assembling joint. Now apply heat from top and apply pressure so solder is forced from joint as heat penetrates from top and melts it. Run a little additional solder along the edge if gaps show.

between the two surfaces. If not, repeat until you can consistently produce a secure and total solder interface of minimum thickness between the two faces.

The above procedures are fine for fairly large soldering jobs and you should try them on various metals, especially galvanized iron. You'll probably find an acid-core solder works best. (Remember, work fluxed with acid-core or paste should be washed clean.) But not all soldering jobs fit this type of procedure. It's fine for eaves, chimney flashings, and repairing containers, but as often as not you'll find yourself trying to repair or construct delicate assemblies which require a little different touch.

To practice fine-joint soldering you'll need:

● A small electric iron of about 25 to 27 watts rating and with a tip about ⅛" in diameter at its thickest point.
● Smaller diameter, resin-core solder, about ¹⁄₁₆'' diameter, often called radio or electronic solder.
● About 10' of bare #12 or #14 copper wire. Strip the insulation from some old wire if necessary.
● A flat work surface such as a sheet of asbestos or even a scrap of plywood.
● Fine sandpaper such as #240.
● An assortment of weights such as square barstock about the size of your finger. Miscellaneous clamps—spring clothespins, bobby pins, hemostats, or small jeweler's pliers.

The best way to learn to solder small parts is to set out on a project into which you can introduce problems at will. An example, which I suggest to follow, is the little house of wire shown here. The dimensions aren't critical. The one I made is about 2" wide, 3" high, and 3¾" long. The important thing is that you start out with easy joints and proceed to more challenging joints as you go along.

1. Draw the wire through a folded sheet of fine abrasive paper several times to make it clean and bright. Snip off equal lengths for the bottom and top, verticals, and lengthwise members of the box-shaped structure you'll make first. Use a hardwood block to roll the wire lengths on a sheet of sandpaper so they're all fairly straight.

2. Place a long member and three vertical members flat on the work surface and weight them so all pieces are flat and square.

3. Touch the iron tip and the solder to each joint, depositing just enough solder to make a tiny filleted joint. Try to make the solder flow around the corners and all around the wires.

4. After the solder cools, turn the structure over, and if you don't have a full solder joint all around, weight the pieces again and solder lightly from the reverse side.

5. Duplicate the side you have just made.

6. You're ready to solder in the top and bottom cross members. Place the two sides parallel and square with each other, the cross members weighted flat on the work surface. You'll find that it's necessary to rig some support blocks or other devices to hold the sides vertical and square. This is where the challenge increases.

7. Solder in the bottom cross members. Try to do this without loosening or breaking the joints you made originally. This is where the proper touch with the torch becomes important. You must judge how much heat is enough and not too much.

8. Invert the structure and solder in the top cross members.

By now you'll have started to develop a feel for small, detailed soldering. I suggest you continue, adding a peak roof frame and ridge, some windows, a door or two, and whatever other embellishments strike you. As you do this, you'll find it necessary to work out your own ways of clamping and holding the bits and pieces of wire in the proper positions and angles.

Common Errors

One of the most common soldering errors is to melt the solder with the iron and flow or drip it into the joint. Some solder may adhere when you do this, but no real bond is formed. The proper method is to apply the iron or gun tip to the metal so it becomes hot enough to melt the solder when it touches. At least this is the recommendation you'll find in most books on soldering, and on a flat surface it works fine. But many real-world situations do not lend themselves well to such pre-heating with the iron because the metal is not flat and the iron doesn't make good heat contact. A simple example would be two wire ends twisted pigtail fashion in a junction box or radio chassis. The wiggles in the wire not only don't pick up the heat very quickly but the hot iron starts to melt insulation and other surrounding materials if held in position too long. My own experience has been that it works best to apply the iron to the work and the solder at almost the same time. Let a small amount of solder run into the joint; it adapts to the wiggles in the wire and becomes a heat conductor. The iron is held in position until the solder glob melts and flows freely into the joint. This action is apparent, as the solder blends into the work in a nicely contoured fillet.

The second cause of poor joints is movement,

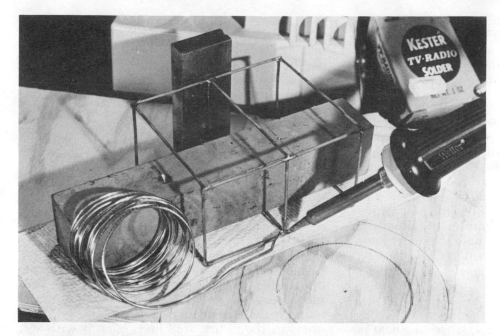

Soldering small joints is quite different from large surfaces. The problem often is one of introducing a new piece without having previous pieces break away. Iron shown has a 25-watt capacity, is made especially for small joints and electrical connections. Two steel blocks serve to hold down and square up our little house of wire. When possible, solder against a flat surface.

After a little practice, try soldering "the hard way" rather than against a flat surface. Your own imagination is the only limit on clamping methods. Clothespin and wood scraps serve here to align and hold this piece of wire.

even a minute, fractional movement of the joint before the solder is totally cold. When solder is first applied and still molten, it has a very bright appearance. If you watch it cool you'll notice that it quite suddenly dulls. The dull surface means that the solder has cooled and is now fairly solid. If you move the joint at this moment you may see a mushy appearing metal. This seriously damages the joint. The trick is to hold

the joint motionless until it dulls and then a little longer for full cooling.

Clamping solder joints. The movement problem often results from trying to hold the soldering iron in one hand and the solder in the other, with perhaps a finger or two around the work. Since you are not holding anything very steady when you start, it is unlikely that you'll keep the joint rigid until it cools.

There are a number of ways to solve this. Some metalworkers make up or buy clamping devices with swivel arms and grips, essentially mechanical hands, with which to hold the work. Another method is simply to pull a short length of solder out from the coil, place the coil on the bench, and bend the tip of the solder down against the joint. This frees up one hand. Other simple arrangements are spring-clip clothespins to hold the work and small weights to stabilize them and free both hands. Electronic workers are familiar with various clamps which not only hold the work but also act as heat-sinks to prevent soldering heat from reaching sensitive solid-state components. Whatever the situation, work out an arrangement to hold the solder joint securely until it cools.

SWEATED JOINTS

Joints in copper tubing or other metal with considerable thickness and mass, where the heat is conducted away faster than the contact with the iron can supply it, are usually made with the direct flame from a propane, MAPP, or oxyacetylene torch. Seldom is the extreme heat of the last heat source needed.

A sweated joint is usually defined as one made between two surfaces not exposed to the air. If you polish the external end of a length of copper tubing and the inside of a fitting, coat them lightly with flux and push them together, you are ready to make a sweated joint. To finish off the sweated joint, torch heat is applied to the fitting and tubing evenly until wire solder touched to the joint area melts freely and runs, by capillary action, into the hairline space between the tube and the fitting. Once you've made a few such sweat joints you'll find it fast and easy. The solder should be clearly visible as a complete ring around the juncture. Remove excess hot solder with a cloth.

Another type of sweated joint is made by first coating each surface to be joined with a thin layer of solder. The pieces are then positioned with the solder coatings together and heat from the torch applied until the solder flows. Sometimes a weight or clamp is used to press and hold the parts firmly together until the solder cools.

In all of the above examples of torch soldering there is one important point to keep in mind. Although you do need sufficient heat to melt the solder and heat the work, excessive heat will cause damage to both the solder and the work metal and may make the joint impossible.

There are a number of propane and MAPP torches offered today that are billed as being much hotter than torches previously available. In fact, their makers seem to view maximum heat as the only significant feature of a torch. Do not be misled. These torches make a roaring sound, but they have to be operated wide open. If you turn down the gas flow to produce a smaller flame, the torch end gets red hot and more or less self-destructs. A more useful, although less expensive torch, will let you adjust the flame intensity from the merest flicker to wide open. This type of torch is much better for soldering.

Safety Precautions

When torch-soldering copper tubing, plumbing, or roof and gutter flashing, consider flammable materials in the surrounding areas. A pipe running under floor joists or back in a wall can start a fire. If there appears to be the least chance of fire, wet the entire area first, pack it with wet asbestos paper, slide a metal shield behind it, or, safest of all, use a flared coupling rather than a solder joint.

Another serious hazard exists if you attempt to solder a pipe filled with water or containing residual water. Such water can quickly flash into steam under enormous pressure, burst the pipe, and scald you. Always be certain that one end of the pipe is open. If necessary, open a tap or valve to release the steam. Don't overlook an adjoining pipe with water in it. If you hear gurgling sounds, stop and investigate where the steam can be relieved safely.

HARD SOLDERING

Most of what I've said about soldering relates to soft tin/lead or silver-bearing solders which melt at low temperatures. But some piping and even model work often need extra-strong joints and heat resistance. Such joints must either be brazed with a brass-type alloy or soldered with one of the higher temperature industrial products available from refrigeration supply stores.

These specialty solders are expensive and most require a torch rather than an iron or gun. Some are coated with special fluxing agents. Others come with bottles of flux. Although the techniques for using them generally follow those for a sweated joint, there may be special instructions which must be observed. Also, in many cases post-soldering cleaning is required. In all cases there is likely to be some degree of toxicity associated with the fumes from the flux and the cleaning agent. Take no chances. Ventilate well and follow instructions to the letter.

SILVER SPECIALTY SOLDERS

ASTM Spec #B-73-29	Silver	Cu	Percent Zinc	Cadmium	Melts °F	Flows °F	Color
	9	53	38		1450	1565	
1	10	52		.05	1510	1600	Yellow
	*15	80		(5% Phos)	1185	1300	Gray
2	20	45	35	.05	1430	1500	Yellow
3	20	45	30	.05	1430	1500	Yellow
	30	38	32		1370	1410	
	**35	26	21	18	1125	1295	Almost white
	40				1135	1205	Almost white
4	45	30	25		1250	1370	Almost white
	**45	15	16	24	1125	1145	Almost white
5	50	34	16		1280	1425	Almost white
	**50	15.5	16.5	18	1160	1175	Almost white
	**50	15.5	15.5	16 (3% Ni)	1195	1270	White
6	65	20	15		1280	1325	White
7	70	20	10		1335	1390	White
8	80	16	4		1360	1490	White

*A special alloy containing phosphorous and used only on nonferrous metals.

**Some special alloys of silver using a fairly high cadmium content.

Although not commonly available in hardware stores, these alloys and many others are available from jewelry and trade specialty supply houses for high-temperature soldering. For many jobs, the critical factors are the temperature required to flow the metal and the color of the finished joint. When using these materials, especially those containing cadmium, take added precautions to ensure that your work area is well ventilated.

BRAZING

Brazing is generally considered to mean joining metals with an alloy, usually copper/zinc, at a temperature above 800°F. In terms of strength, brazing, or braze welding as it is sometimes called, is not as strong as welding, but for many uses it is more than adequate. Moreover, it is less likely to damage high-alloy steels than welding. Bicycle frames are often assembled by brazing. The wrought-iron porch railing discussed earlier was brazed. By the same token, many small, delicate jobs which would be difficult or impossible to weld are handled without problem by brazing. Examples would be the snap locks on a purse, thin art-metal structures, and repairs to tanks and water containers. Brazing is both strong and heat resistant.

Brazing Practice

As with soldering, the best way to learn how to braze is to do it. Also, in the case of brazing you will learn the limitations of your equipment. Just as a too small iron will make an inferior solder joint, an inadequate heat source will prevent satisfactory brazing. By making practice joints on scrap metal and breaking them apart, you can determine if you really have made a brazed joint or have just melted the brazing rod into a pretty puddle. With suitable oxyacetylene equipment or a carbon-arc torch feeding from a small transformer welder, you will almost always have enough heat for good brazing of even fairly heavy castings and wrought iron. This is not true with small MAPP or MAPP/oxygen torches which can braze only limited metal thicknesses and mass. For this reason the following suggested practice steps are limited to metal 1/16″ thick or less. Do not attempt to use such torches to braze critical assemblies such as playground equipment, trailer hitches, or mobile or marine components. For brazing practice you will need:

● A good quality MAPP or MAPP/oxygen torch.

● Some scraps of thin, sheet steel about 1/16″ thick.

● Some steel tubing with thin walls. Electrical conduit is fine, but before brazing sand off the cadmium coating and braze it outdoors or in a well-ventilated shop. The fumes are toxic.

● A work table with a top of fire brick or asbestos board.

● A wire brush and abrasive cloth or paper, the latter about 100 grit.

● Some lengths of uncoated brazing rod, either 1/16″ or 3/32″ will do.

● A small can of brazing flux powder.

● A weldor's chipping hammer or other chisel edge hammer.

● Weldor's gloves and goggles, nonflammable clothes, closed shoes.

To get started with a practice braze, cut two

With flux lines on your practice metal, heat and dip rod into flux to collect a small cluster on end. Apply torch heat until flux on metal starts to melt and flow. Hold rod clear but in heat path until flux melts.

Dip rod tip into heated area, and as soon as a puddle of bright metal appears, start moving rod and torch along at an even pace.

Repeat the above process on second line of flux. Run practice beads like this until you can produce an even bead without skips or burn areas.

pieces of sheet steel roughly 2″ × 3″. Brighten the entire surface of one with abrasive paper. Brighten about ½″ along the edge of the other on both sides but put it aside for the moment. If you have a belt sander it will do a good job of brightening.

1. Clamp or weight the first piece to the work table and light the torch with a standard torch lighter. Never use a match or cigarette lighter. If you're using MAPP/oxygen, adjust the torch, according to instructions, for a conelike flame. If you're using one of the super-hot MAPP torches adjust it wide open.

2. Play the flame over the metal for a few seconds to heat it. Sprinkle several lines of flux powder along the length of the workpiece. If the metal is warm enough, the flux will melt slightly and adhere.

3. Now select one line of flux and start at one end, usually from the right if you're right-handed, and with the torch canted slightly to direct the flame in the direction of movement, towards the left in the above case, start to heat the metal near the edge.

4. At the same time, hold the brazing rod in the flame briefly and immediately dip it in the flux can. If it's hot enough, a cluster of flux about an inch long will adhere.

5. Observe the flux on the metal. When the metal approaches brazing heat the flux will melt and appear glassy. The metal will start to show a dull red.

6. Bring the tip of the rod against the metal and into the torch flame. It should melt and flow almost instantly, leaving a bright spot or puddle on the metal.

7. Continue to heat and move the rod along to deposit a bead or line of metal as you go. Remember, if the metal doesn't flow freely it's slightly cold; if it sputters and forms globules it's too hot or the metal is dirty.

8. Repeat this practice bead in the other places where you placed a row of flux powder. The powder will have melted, but the flux will remain and save you the trouble of recleaning the metal.

9. Chip and brush away the slag residue from the flux. Repeat until you can consistently run a smooth bead of braze metal, of controlled width. With a MAPP torch, the bead area will probably be wider than necessary since the flame discharge is so broad. This is a limitation of the equipment.

The next step is to make a joint:

1. Heat one brightened edge of the other piece of metal previously cut and coat it with flux.

2. Place it over one of the beads you've just

run and weight it down or clamp it with weldor's clamps or C-clamps.

3. Start heating at one edge, flux the rod, and proceed as before. The braze metal in the bead under the edge of the new piece should melt and the two pieces should settle together. You can add a little rod along the edge as you go, but you shouldn't need as much as before.

4. Let the work cool a few minutes, and cool it in water for safe handling. Grip one piece in a vise, and with Vise-Grips or pliers peel the joint apart or wedge it apart with a cold chisel.

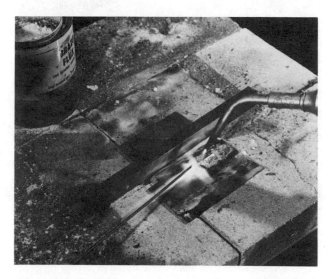

Now, try making an actual joint by overlapping pieces and runing a bead along the edge. Metal should flow into joint. It will work better if you first adhere some flux to the contact side of the upper piece.

You may find the adhesion between the pieces spotty. If you placed the second piece flux-side up this is likely. Repeat with the flux-side down and note the difference.

Practice with the above system of running beads and making an overlap joint until you acquire a feel for the heat needed and the flow of the metal. You'll find that you can "lead" the metal around with the heat. Lap joints, much like tubing fitting joints, are quite easily made by this technique.

For practicing right-angle joints, again cut scrap pieces to a convenient size and brighten them. This time you are going to deposit braze metal on one face of a vertical piece as well as on the flat face of a horizontal piece and, as you learn the art, form a fillet of metal in the corner formed by the two pieces. To start:

1. Clamp or weight one piece on the work surface and clamp or weight the second piece on

edge so the two pieces are at approximate right angles. A weldor's clamp is handy for this but not really necessary as long as the two pieces are stabilized and held together firmly.

2. Again, play the torch along the joint and sprinkle flux so it adheres to both pieces.

3. Heat the rod tip and flux it, and start heating the joint at one end as before. This time you'll have to cant the torch so some of the heat strikes the vertical face and some strikes the flat face.

A right-angle joint requires distributing torch heat so both pieces are heated evenly. Since torch flame is confined somewhat by vertical member, heat ahead of the torch may build up to high. The technique to avoid this is to raise torch flame momentarily, as shown, so metal ahead of bead cools slightly.

4. Try to apply just enough heat to develop a small puddle of braze metal bridging the two pieces at one edge. This is called tacking and helps keep the melt from distorting from heat expansion.

5. While the other end is still hot, deposit another spot of tack metal at the opposite end. Let both tacks cool for a minute. If you're using a conventional MAPP torch you may find it hard to confine the heat to a small tack area.

6. Now, start at the first end and try to run a bead which is evenly distributed on both vertical and flat face with a curved fillet of metal in the corner. When cooled, chip away the slag and examine your job for unevenness, heavy and light deposits, slag deposits, and other imperfections. Be assured that your first attempts will have such flaws but practice will teach you how to avoid them.

The fillet, or corner reinforcement, in a braze joint greatly increases its strength over two pieces which are merely bonded along a thin edge area. There may be times when such joints with a minimum of braze metal are desirable in art metalwork and the like, but if you expect the joint to resist a load a fillet is desired.

Since many braze joints involve tubing, you should now practice with round thin-wall stock.

1. Saw a short length—an inch or so—from tubing about 1″ in diameter. Brighten the end you will be brazing. Use a flat piece, brightened at the center, as a base, and stand the tubing vertically on the brightened area. Clamp or weight it in place.

2. Heat and flux the joint where the tubing rests on the flat and proceed as before. Now, you will find that you must maintain the torch angle and move around the work at the same time. This requires concentrated thinking about just where your torch flame is striking, but in a short time you'll find that you've developed reflexes that make flame control almost automatic.

Manipulating torch flame around tubing requires new skills in observing flame, metal flow, and in positioning. Practice until moving your body, torch, and rod become reflex actions.

Depending on the extent of brazing you plan to do, you can expand any of the above exercises to develop greater skill. If at all possible, before attempting a serious job, try mocking up an equivalent joint of flat metal or tubing and running a few practice beads to get the feel.

10. THREADED FASTENERS

Many of the metalworking jobs you'll do with small tools involve threaded fasteners—that is, nuts and bolts. Cutting new threads or cleaning up old ones that are damaged by corrosion or battering is routine in metalworking. Watch an experienced metalworker restore an antique car, engine, airplane, or artifact, and you'll see that he devotes considerable care and respect to threaded fasteners.

When removing threaded fasteners, you should be careful not to mix them so they can be returned to the same places. For example, if you remove the cylinder head from a lawnmower engine you'll probably find that all the bolts are not the same length. Mixing them can cause serious trouble later. For this reason, the experienced metalworker will make a rough sketch showing where the longs and the shorts go, or he'll push them into a piece of cardboard to retain them in order.

There is another reason for segregating fasteners. In many pieces of equipment, the bolt quality, alloy, and hardness are specifically chosen to carry special loads, resist corrosion, or endure wear. Use of ordinary grade fasteners can be highly destructive or hazardous.

These precautions also apply to lock washers, locking devices, and special nuts and bolts with locking features formed or built in. If you notice that a nut seems to remain snug after breaking it loose, always inspect it for a locking feature. This may be no more than a tool mark or dimple on the outside of the nut to deform it slightly and make it snug. Sometimes you'll find a plastic or fiber block or ring inside the thread area. Whatever locking means were used, you should replace such fasteners in exactly the same way. Few manufacturers spend money without reason, so if they deemed it worth the expense to use a locking fastener they may know something that you don't.

You'll occasionally see shreds of plastic-like material as you remove the fastener. This is usually a locking agent such as Loctite applied during assembly. This type of locking agent does not set when exposed to air and is put on the threads as a thin liquid. When air is excluded after the fastener is installed, it sets up and grips the fastener very tightly. If the maker of a product thought it important, you should use it in that location. It's available at automobile-supply stores.

In addition to segregating nuts and bolts according to use and location, it is good practice to wash them clean of grease, dirt, or paint in a solvent such as lacquer thinner. If they come out clean and dry but rusty, wire-brush them bright and inspect the threads.

Earlier, I pointed out that a thread is actually

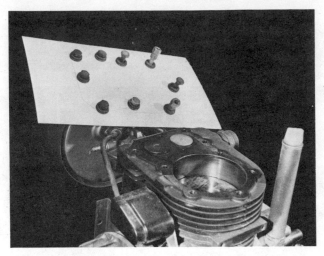

Mixing bolts can cause serious problems. A scrap of cardboard with holes punched in it can keep them in order.

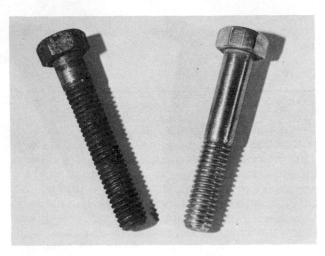

Bolt at left is unlikely to torque down properly on reassembly. A wire brush in a bench grinder should be used to clean up critical bolts so they look like the one at right.

an inclined plane or wedge. But there is more to threads, especially in metalworking, than may be immediately apparent. Screws and bolts securing an assembly together must often be tightened enough actually to stretch the metal in the fastener. This produces a tension which is maintained in the assembly to hold the parts together just as though the bolt was an extremely stiff spring. The same effect is seldom present in wooden parts since the softness and elasticity of the wood serves the same purpose.

Torque value. Only a very few bolts can readily be measured for stretch. It is possible, though, to measure the force applied to a bolt or nut when you tighten it. In metalworker's terms,

this is called "torque value." If you're following instructions for a critical assembly, this force will be specified in either inch-pounds or foot-pounds, depending on the size of the bolt and the wrench. A special type of wrench, called a torque wrench, is used to measure this twisting effort.

In theory, if we establish by many experiments just how much twisting force, or torque, is needed to stretch a bolt or snug up a nut to produce a given tension or stretch, we can make up a table which all will follow and there should be no problem. But problems arise very quickly. If we go back to the concept of a thread as an inclined plane or wedge, it becomes apparent that driving a greased wedge will probably be easier than driving a dry one, since the grease

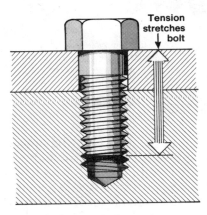

Only holding action of a bolt that is not stretched to induce tension is light friction between the parts. To really hold parts together against a force which would separate them, the bolt must be physically stretched a small amount to provide a countering tension.

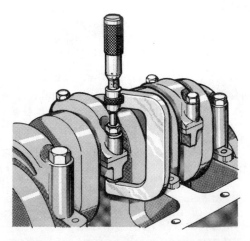

One indirect but accurate way to measure the tension on a bolt is to take a micrometer measurement of the stretch, as on this Mercedes connecting-rod bolt.

Another indirect measurement of bolt tension is the force required to turn it. A torque wrench has a scale to show how hard you are pulling, and the handle provides a lever of a fixed, known length.

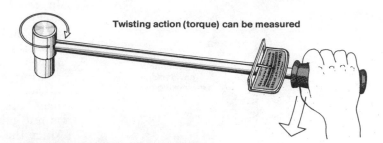

Twisting action (torque) can be measured

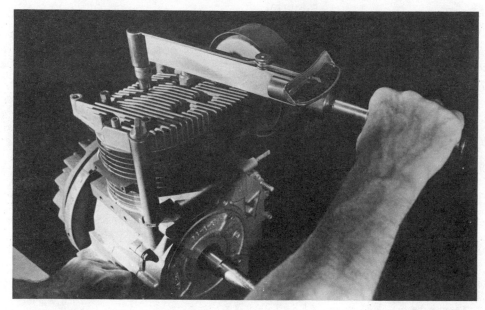

Although torque wrenches vary in size, range, and type, this beam type is reliable. You can use the visual scale or, for repeated torquing to the same value, set a click stop which signals when you've reached correct tension. Always work back and forth; reach final tightness in a few stages.

reduces the friction between the wedge and the surface it's working against. This also means that it's easier to turn an oiled bolt in a thread than a dry one. Thus, the force, or torque, needed to produce a given tension can be different according to whether it's specified as "dry" or "oiled."

Even worse problems arise if you fail to clean dirt, rust, or other interfering material out of a bolt hole; or if the threads themselves are burred, deformed, or filled with rust at the bottom. It may be that you won't have many occasions to use a torque wrench, but if you rely on the "feel" of a wrench to determine tightness, remember that the force needed to overcome the above conditions may be deceptive. A fastener may feel tight when it actually has very little tension at all.

Chasing threads.   One way to secure threaded fasteners is to inspect critical threads before assembling them. Even the simple act of running each bolt into a new, clean nut is worthwhile. If the fasteners have been used before, you may be surprised to find out how many have minor thread damage. Solid dies, as described earlier,

should be used to "chase" or clean up such threads. Taps, of course, should be used to clean up nuts and threaded holes.

One caution about cleaning up threads is in order. Do not run a tap through a nut which has been dimpled or has a fiber or plastic locking feature. Doing so will cut out the locking action.

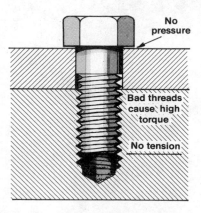

If bad threads or dirt impair the freedom of a thread to turn, you might get the specified torque reading on the wrench but actually produce little or no tension in the fastener.

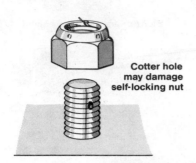

Cotter hole
may damage
self-locking nut

Stick with the original locking method used in the equipment you're reassembling. Replacing a slotted nut intended for lockwire, or a cotter pin with a plastic insert lock nut, can destroy the locking ability by gouging out the locking material.

In general, it is accepted practice to use such locking nuts a second time if they are not damaged and show significant locking drag when turned on a bolt. If there is the slightest doubt, however, and the fastener is in a critical place—a wing spar, engine mount, or similar part—always use a new nut. If the bolt or stud was originally drilled for a cotter pin or lockwire, it is not good practice to substitute a locking nut since the drilled hole may cut away the locking material.

Shortening bolts. If you don't have a bolt of the proper size, it is not unusual to shorten a

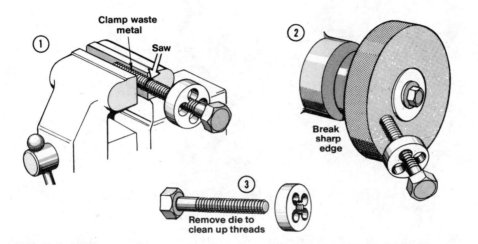

① Clamp waste metal   Saw

② Break sharp edge

③ Remove die to clean up threads

Reestablishing the damaged threads on a sawed-off bolt can be frustrating. To avoid the problem, spin a die on the bolt before sawing and then back it off after dressing sawed end.

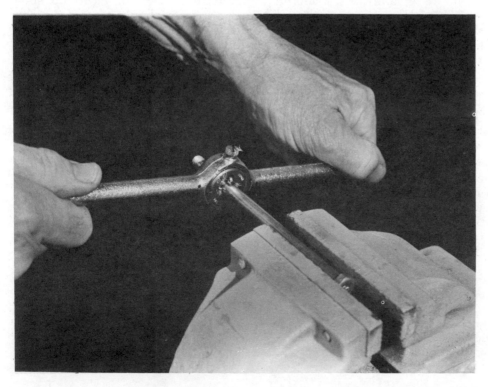

To add extra threads, use plenty of cutting oil and reverse the rotation of the die intermittently to break chips.

long one. This is easily done with a hacksaw. Here's how:

Before clamping the bolt in the vise, run a die onto the bolt far enough to be out of the way. Clamp the bolt by the extended portion which will be cut off as waste. Cut the bolt. Then dress the saw burr with a grinder or file to approximate the slight taper on the end of a new bolt. Now, backing off the die will clean up any residual damage from the saw and the bolt will enter and thread normally.

THREADING NEW STOCK

It takes considerable force to cut threads, so you must lock the stock firmly in a vise. To avoid marring the stock, use a piece of soft aluminum or brass to pad the vise jaws.

Use a grinder or a file to establish an even, short taper on the end of the stock so the die slips over easily and can start cutting without struggling to get a bite. Starting a thread on a square end is very difficult.

Make the first few turns with the heel of your palm pressing firmly on the center of the die. After you feel the die bite in and start to cut, check carefully to be certain that the die is started squarely and not canted. If you detect a cant, continue the pressure with your hand while you turn but gradually adjust the die back to true. By the time half the depth of the die is

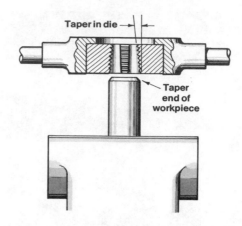

Starting a die would be very difficult without an internal taper in the die threads. Partial threads allow an initial bite. This works best if the stock is beveled slightly on the end so the die seats down over it.

entered, the cutting action should be squared up. If things are still running at an angle it may be necessary to cut off the bad threads and start over.

This problem becomes more acute as you try to thread larger-diameter stock. You can solve it readily with either a woodworking or metal-working lathe. Chuck the stock in the headstock and bring the tailstock up against the face of the die. Keep pressure on the tailstock while you turn the headstock by hand and the die will be

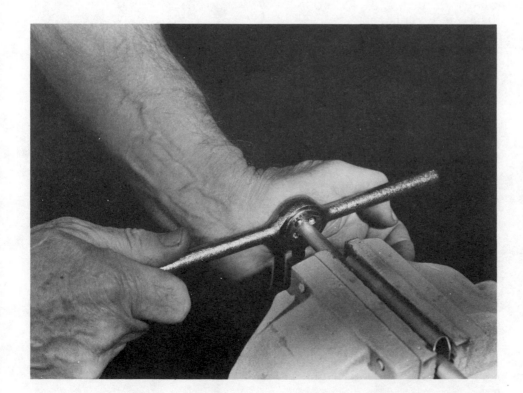

Getting a die started squarely by hand pressure can be difficult. Before starting, form an even taper on the end of the stock so die fits over metal. Cut a thread or two and check to be sure you're square in all directions. Recheck and correct as you proceed.

If you have a lathe, use the tailstock to square and feed the die for starting. Rotate work by hand. Once started, you may be able to run the lathe at low speed and brace the die holder against the carriage for power threading.

held squarely in position. Thread-cutting lube is very necessary for this operation, and one or two turns forward and a turn back are often needed to break the chips.

Tapping in Threads

Tapping internal threads requires most of the same procedures of lubrication, breaking chips, and getting started squarely as threading with a die. Ideally, if you drilled the tap-drill hole on the drill press, you simply remove the drill and replace it with your tap. The piece remains aligned under the same center and with gentle pressure on the feed lever you can hand-start the tap squarely until it is well into the threads. Do this by gripping the chuck by hand or by using

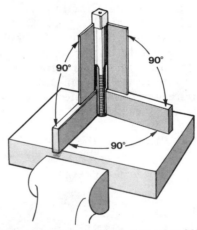

Use a small square or squared tab of metal at 90° locations to check the tap for squareness after starting initial threads.

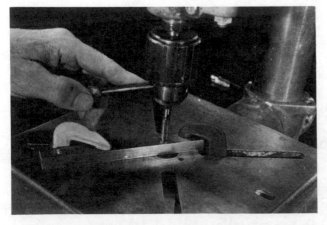

With a drill press the best way to start a tap is to remove the tap drill and install the tap without moving the work. Use gentle hand pressure to turn tap. Never try power tapping.

the chuck key for a little leverage. *Never* try to tap with power. Once the tap is well started you can loosen the chuck and proceed with a hand tap wrench.

The above procedure is easy because the tap is perfectly centered and squared. If you don't have or can't use a drill press and must start the tap into a hole drilled with a hand-held drill, you have to use some other means to get a square start. A taper tap helps a lot and so does a short tab of squared-off metal between the surface of the work and the tap. Remember to square at 90° and to check for tilt in two directions. Some pieces, such as curved or irregular castings, don't even offer this much flat surface for squaring. This becomes strictly a matter of eyeball and feel to get the tap started right.

Broken Taps

The biggest difference between die-cutting threads and tapping is the ever-present danger of breaking the tap off in the hole. Taps are extremely hard and brittle. You can twist on them just so much and they will snap without warning. A broken tap will almost always be a perfect example of Murphy's law. It will break at the most inconvenient time; it will break just at the surface and leave no stub to grip, and it will be so tight you'll swear it's welded itself in. The smaller the tap, the harder it will be to remove the broken part. This is partly because the grooves between the flutes are too small to work a tap-removing tool into them, and partly because the small diameter offers little twisting leverage to rotate the stub against the chips that are binding it. You may stop reading here if you wish, because the rest is not pleasant, but you'll come back and look it up someday.

A fairly large tap, ⅜" and up, can often be worked out by fairly easy methods. Bear in mind that the tap is much too hard to drill out. If a broken stub protrudes you may be able to get a grip with Vise Grips and wiggle it out. Or, you may be able to get the tip of a pin punch against the flutes and tap it one way and then another to compact and loosen the chips. A dribble of penetrating oil may help, but I've never found it did much good. On taps of this size I will normally try to loosen them with a punch as described. You can even try to drive them out backwards with the punch. The next step, failing the above, is to get something into a pair of opposite grooves. Hard steel wire is fine if you have some that just fits. Two matching hex-key wrenches (Allen wrenches) are also good. If you can get these well down into the grooves, you may then be able to get a grip across them with

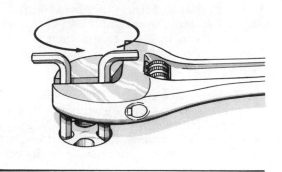

Another way to grip and turn a tap stub is to slip hex-key wrenches into the side grooves and turn them with a wrench.

an adjustable wrench and start worrying the tap in each direction until it can be backed out.

Small taps can be more difficult. If they are too small or deep in the hole to be joggled with a pin punch, you might try the hex-key wrenches as described. Unfortunately, in these sizes you lose real twisting effect. Another strategy is to pick a small drill and gently run it down the space between the flutes to remove the chips. Use a hand-powered drill. Follow with a slightly larger drill which will barely cut into the work metal and then follow with a still larger drill

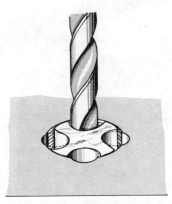

Careful drilling between the tap flutes to clear chips may loosen a small tap. Use slightly larger drills in steps if needed until the tap can be loosened.

until you have removed all, or most of, the threads you originally cut. Now, all that's holding the tap is the area in contact with the cutting teeth, and by going into the open slots with a pair of hex keys you can probably work it around so the teeth are in the open spaces.

By this time I hope you've removed the tap stub. If you used the drill-out procedure, the hole will now lack threads at four points. You have the choice of going oversize and using a larger

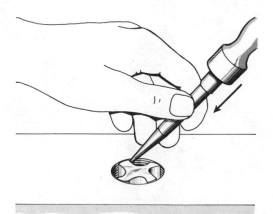

If you can get the tip of a punch on the flutes of a broken tap, you may be able to work it loose by tapping one way and then the other to free the chips which bind it.

bolt or, perhaps, filling the hole with braze metal and starting over. You might even oversize the hole, thread in a plug, and then go back to the original size and try not to break the tap this time.

Clean holes.   A common source of broken taps is simply failure to clean out chips or dirt ahead of the tap. Dirt and chips are also a prime cause of a bolt that becomes tight but doesn't hold because it's jammed against trash in the bottom of the hole. The handiest way to get rid of this trash is with a jet of compressed air. If your shop lacks an air compressor, you can do a surprisingly good job with the pressurized air or gas

equipped to do so. You can then drill and tap to the original size. This technique, while often used, is not recommended for beginners. Moreover, die-cast metal, aluminum, and many cast-iron articles cannot withstand the heat or will not accept braze metal.

Still another approach is to oversize the hole two or more sizes and tap for a threaded bushing, which may then be drilled and tapped to the original size. If, for example, a 5/16″ thread was stripped out, you might drill and tap for a 1/2″-20 thread. Then a section from a 1/2″-20 bolt could be threaded in, sawed off flush, and staked to prevent turning. Staking is the term used to describe making light indentations or notches

![photo of drill press with pressurized cannister]

A small tank-type compressor is enormously useful in any metalworking shop, but if you don't have one a pressurized cannister such as this can help. Protect your eyes against chips.

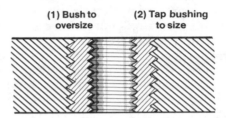

(1) Bush to oversize   (2) Tap bushing to size

A bushing threaded into an oversize hole is one way to handle a stripped-out thread.

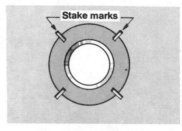

Stake marks

Staking with a small punch so the workpiece metal and the bushing engage will help keep the bushing from turning.

bottles sold at camera stores for cleaning negatives and photo gear. Some bottles have a small plastic nozzle which can be worked right into the bottom of the hole. Since thread-cutting oil sticks the chips in the hole, try working in solvent first with a small brush. Above all, never get your eyes down close to the blowing operation and be sure of your eye protection. Metal chips can be ejected with dangerous force.

Stripped threads.   When a tapped thread is damaged so the threads are stripped out and will no longer hold a bolt, you have several choices. The obvious one is to tap-drill the hole and cut new threads to the next oversize. Go from 1/4″-20 to 5/16″-18, for example. Another possibility is to close up the hole with braze metal if you're

Helical coil insert

Commercial thread-repair tools and coil-like insert provide the most workmanlike repair and in some cases mean the difference between saving and junking an expensive part.

around two mating surfaces with a light punch or chisel. The stake marks act as little teeth which engage to secure the parts. Now, the new section can be drilled and tapped.

Clearly, not all situations lend themselves to such patchwork. An example would be the sparkplug thread in a cast-iron or aluminum cylinder head. Your best chance of doing a workmanlike job of salvaging this type of part is to purchase a repair kit at your local auto-supply house. These kits contain special taps to cut a nonstandard thread in the stripped hole. A coil-like insert is then installed with a special tool, and the threads are instantly back to standard.

SELF-THREADING SCREWS

After soldering, the most common assembly device for home-shop projects is probably the self-threading screw. If your shop is typical, you have a jar or container somewhere filled with a miscellaneous collection of what are generally called "sheet-metal" screws. Over the years you may have salvaged these screws from aluminum furniture, screen doors, eaves and gutters, toys, appliances, and even drapery installations and weather stripping. If you sort them out a bit you'll see that there is a wide variety of head styles ranging from button to oval and countersunk, to small hex-heads, cross-slotted, and recess-slotted. Examine the tips and you'll find that some are simply screw points; others are tapered, blunt, or have grooves, slots, or flats. The one thing they all have in common is that they are hardened and made of very tough steel.

The outstanding feature of these screws is their ability to enter a small, unthreaded hole and force the metal into a thread form. This very act of forcing means that the screw will be tight and will probably withstand vibration without any locking device.

There are a few not-so-obvious factors you should be aware of when choosing and using such screws. The most common type is called a "thread-rolling screw." Drive it into a punched or drilled hole in two pieces of soft sheet metal and it will roll the edges of the hole to form threads. Normally, the size of the unthreaded hole is the same, or slightly under, the root diameter of the screw thread. If the screw seems to go in only with extreme effort, go up one step in drill size. You should, of course, expect to meet some fairly high resistance until a full thread is formed. These screws can be snugged down very firmly, but care must be taken not to tighten them to a point where they tear out the threads. Remember, in thin metal there isn't much to work with.

If you attempt to use thread-rolling screws in

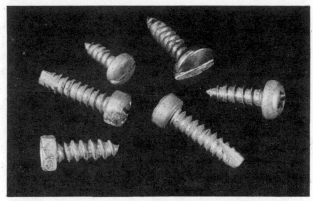

Self-threading screws, often called sheet-metal screws, come in a multitude of shapes, sizes, and features. These, however, are typical of those you can buy locally; industry uses many types not offered at the hardware store. These are hexhead for miniature socket drive, slotted-head for a screwdriver, cross-recessed for Phillips driver. They also vary from button head to fillister and round head. Note that two have a chip relief for thread cutting; others are thread-rolling types.

deeper holes and solid material, you'll probably find that they get tighter and tighter, and if you persist you'll twist them off. Such applications call for a thread-*cutting* screw with a cutout slot at the tip which resembles a partial tap. These screws cut, rather than roll, a thread for themselves. The cutout at the tip provides a cutting edge and clearance for the chips. In some industrial applications, the tapping section is preceded by a drill-like point with cutting lips resembling a twist drill. Such screws are strictly for high-production, machine driving. They have little use in the home shop. For the others, if you have a choice, select those with a hex head as well as a screwdriver slot. They are much easier to drive with a miniature socket and ratchet than with a screwdriver.

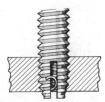

Most common sheet-metal screws form their own threads by a forcing action of the hardened screw. This one, however, has a taplike action to cut threads. The important thing is to size the hole so enough metal is available to form the threads. Too small a hole makes driving hard.

Another type of thread-cutting screw is actually a miniature tap with cutting edges and a space for chips. You'll find such screws used in mass-produced products because they can be driven into soft metal or plastic without the cost of cutting threads first.

11. RIVETS

Riveted joints have long been popular for fastening metal assemblies together, but now, with the exception of "pop" rivets, they've dropped somewhat from favor. Basically, a rivet is a round pin with a head on one end. When inserted in a hole which just allows it to enter freely, the end opposite the head must be formed into a more or less matching head. This driving, or "setting" process should draw the pieces snugly together and expand the rivet firmly in the hole. It follows that since the important part of installing a rivet is the setting operation to form a new head, the quality of a riveted joint depends very much on the skill of the metalworker.

There were several reasons for the popularity of rivets in the past. First, they were easily made and inexpensive since they did not have to be threaded in a day when automatic threading machines were rare. Secondly, they did not require tapped threads, or even precise holes, in workpieces. This suited the early blacksmith, since he didn't have the drills or taps to make such threads. Another factor may have been purely a consumer reaction. Anything studded with rivets looked strong and sturdy. It was also true that before the days of self-locking nuts, fancy lock washers, welding, and other modern fastening methods, rivets did not tend to vibrate loose or fail totally in wagons jolting over rough roads. Vibration resistance, to some extent, is

one reason for the thousands of rivets used in present-day aircraft. In any case, there are many occasions when the metalworker will still find rivets the preferred method of assembly. The problem is chosing the right rivets.

You can sort out rivets according to the materials of which they're made, the shape of the head, and the type of shank—solid, tubular, or split. And, of course, you can sort them according to length and diameter. The common fractional dimensions used in the home shop extend from 3/32" to 1/4" or 5/16". There are also a number of special-purpose rivets and sizes.

If there's any basic rule in making a riveted joint, it's being sure the rivet material is the same metal as the workpiece. Using aluminum or brass rivets in steel, or vice versa, is an invitation to galvanic corrosion action since the dissimilar metals behave like electrodes in a battery. Use steel with ferrous materials, aluminum with aluminum, brass with brass. For some assemblies, a decorative sconce, for example, this may not be important, but for a flower-planter box, on the other hand, corrosion must be considered.

Black-iron rivets. The most commonly used rivets for metalwork in the past were soft steel (iron), usually with a black-oxide coating, and with any of a half-dozen or more different heads.

Hardware stores often called these "wagon-box" rivets since they were routinely used to hold the metal and wooden parts of wagons and carriages together. They were also used to assemble almost any type of blacksmithed ironwork, farm equipment, kitchen pots and kettles, and stoves. Black-iron rivets are still available but are hard to find in modern hardware stores.

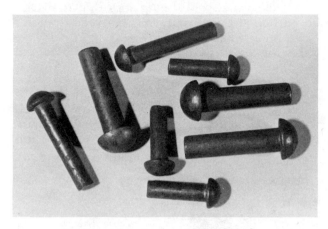

You may find it hard to buy black iron rivets at your hardware store. They're still made, however, and they're useful for some jobs, especially if there is a pivoting action.

Tinner's rivets. Another common rivet has a rather broad, flat head and is known as a tinner's rivet since it was used to assemble gutters, stove and heating ducts, and the like. These are semi-

tubular rivets with a hollow part way down the shank. They are seated by flaring over the tubular section. Although any of these rivets can easily be headed by peening the extended shank to form a head, a more finished job can be done with a setting tool.

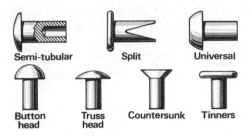

Rivets are sufficiently handy around the shop to justify an assortment ranging from tinner's rivets, tubular rivets, and black iron rivets to some of the more exotic.

Blind rivets. In the home shop a great many of the functions once served by the type of rivets discussed above have now been taken over by blind rivets. The common name for these is pop rivets; however, this is the trade name for blind rivets made by USM Corp.

Actually, there are a large number of makes and types of blind rivets, each with some special feature. Blind rivets are tubular rivets, usually of aluminum or steel, but also available in other materials, with a central mandrel which often resembles a finishing nail and which extends from the rivet an inch or more. These rivets are

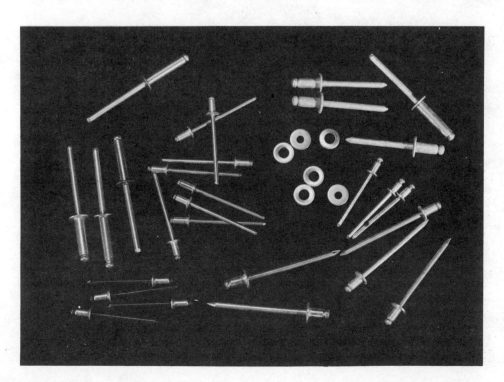

Blind rivets come in many different sizes, lengths, and materials. Match rivet material to metal in your workpiece. Washers are used to reinforce joint in soft material where the rivet might pull through.

especially handy because they can be set without access to the inner, or blind, side of the joint; hence, the name "blind." To set such a rivet you simply poke it through a drilled hole, grip the mandrel with a special puller tool, and squeeze the tool to pull the mandrel up into the hollow rivet. The enlarged head of the mandrel on the blind side pulls into the rivet and expands it to form a head. Just as the right tension is reached, the mandrel snaps (pops) off and leaves a neatly set rivet. The operation is fast and practically foolproof.

How to Rivet

Regardless of the type of material or rivets you use, there are a few basic practices to follow:
● The rivet diameter should be at least 2.5 times the thickness of the metal in the joint.

● The rivet should be located at least two rivet diameters from the edge of the joint.
● Space the rivets at least three, better four, diameters apart.
● Rivets to be set by hammering should project through the joint about 1.5 times their diameter.

The secret to a sound, neat joint is having the rivet holes in both pieces aligned exactly, drilling holes which fit the rivets closely without excess clearance, and being sure that there are no burrs or foreign materials between the joint faces. As an example, follow through the procedures for a riveted joint between two pieces of aluminum or steel sheet.

Drilling rivet holes.   Lay out, mark off, and center-punch the rivet locations on the piece which will be exposed to view and will have the finished rivet head visible. Drill each rivet hole and

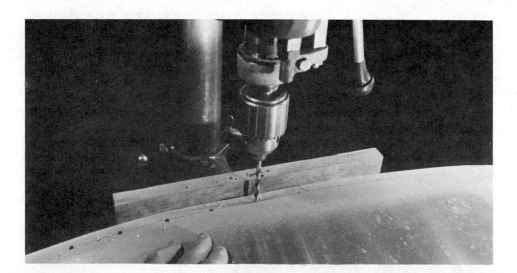

Rivets look best when they align neatly. One way to true up rivet holes is with a drilling fence clamped to the drill-press table. The support block underneath is part of fence and is slightly arched to drape metal over it.

Burrs must be removed if the riveted joint is to be smooth and tight. They are easily trimmed from aluminum with sharp chisel.

One way to form a head on an iron rivet is simply to peen it into shape with a ball-pein hammer. If backed up by a flat surface the head will also be flattened. Here, a piece of scrap stock has been turned out to fit the head and seat it for peening.

remove the burrs from the backside. With soft aluminum you can easily shear away the drilling burrs with a sharp wood chisel. On steel or other metals a file or sanding belt will clean them up.

Now, locate and clamp the two pieces together. Use the predrilled outer piece as a drill guide and drill the back piece at one end. Install one or two rivets to secure the two pieces together and prevent them from shifting. Next clamp the pieces so the faces are firmly together over the undrilled portion. Drill the remaining rivet holes. It is important that there are no buckles or open spaces between the pieces. After drilling, clean all chips away which may have intruded between the faces and remove all burrs from the second piece. The two pieces should now be ready for riveting.

The above system has some weaknesses for really fine work such as aircraft or boat building. It is always better to drill both pieces in the assembled position in shaped and contoured curved pieces. Do this by drilling several locating holes in the corners of the outer piece. Assemble the outer piece in exact position with temporary retainers. These may be aircraft-type CleCo fasteners, spring-loaded buttons which are inserted through both pieces to draw and lock them together. Or you can use sheet-metal screws or blind rivets which will be drilled out later.

Now, the rivet holes may be drilled through both pieces using a slightly undersized drill. As you go along install a CleCo or blind rivet every few holes to prevent creeping. When these holes are drilled, remove the piece and clean away all burrs and chips. Again replace the piece and secure it with temporary fasteners. You may now drill or ream the holes to final size. Finally, after once more deburring and removing chips, you are ready to clamp and rivet. The method is time consuming but produces high-quality joints suitable for aircraft or marine demands. Note that far more time is spent getting ready to rivet than actually riveting.

Heading rivets. Soft-iron rivets, copper rivets, and aluminum rivets can be headed simply by placing the existing head on a flat, anvil-like surface, or holding a bucking bar behind them, and whacking them down with a hammer. This rough and ready method can be improved on if the backup anvil or bar has a concave dimple in it to match the rivet head. And instead of hammering the new head flat, it's easy to use a ball-pein or cross-pein hammer to form a rounded head.

The use of a rivet set is still better. You can buy or make such a set. A rivet set is simply a metal bar with a hole in it slightly larger than the rivet shank and with another dimple to

For a neater result in forming rivets use a rivet set. The pocket which forms the head is on the left. The hole at the right is for placing over the rivet shank so you can drive the pieces together for a tight fit.

match the head. To use it, you back up the original head as described, slip the hole over the shank, and hit the tool to drive the two faces together. This is a precautionary measure and reflects the fact that the old blacksmith punched his holes and usually had a raised edge on the back face which prevented good interface contact. If you compare this with the lengthy procedure previously detailed for making rivet holes (essentially handcrafted aircraft) it becomes apparent why an airplane costs more than a one-horse shay.

In any case, after driving the faces together,

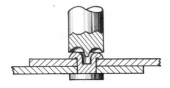

A tubular rivet works best when the solid portion of its shank is matched to the joint thickness. The setting tool should flare out and curl over the tubular portion neatly and evenly all around.

you can now tap down the end of the rivet to establish an initial set and finish off with the dimple in the set to form the rounded head.

The above procedures do not apply to aircraft work. Aluminum-alloy aircraft rivets are often heat-treated or annealed and are driven with two operators, one with a small air-powered gun and the other with a bucking bar. Aircraft riveting is a critical technique and requires training and practice to ensure an airworthy joint.

Using tubular rivets. A different type of rivet set is used with tubular rivets. Here, the dimple in the set must have a raised center point to align with the hole in the shank. When struck, the central point of the set forces the metal out so it curls over into a flange or flare and draws down evenly all around. In many instances a squeezing tool is used rather than a hammer.

Tubular rivets are a little tricky since the solid portion of the shank should be about the same thickness as the pieces of metal to be joined. If too much of the tubular portion extends, the rivet will split; if too little extends, the rivet will lack draw down and holding power.

Using blind rivets. If you like a play on words, you'll love blind rivets—they're on your side. Which is simply a whimsical way of saying that you don't have to get to the opposite side of your work, inside a pipe, behind a panel, or underneath anything to buck them and form a head. All of the installing and heading is done from your side of the work.

Moreover, the heading action doesn't require hammering or backing them up. Thus, they can be used on thin sheet metal and other light structures where hammering would do more harm than good.

As described earlier, blind rivets, at least the ordinary hardware store variety, have a hollow center and are headed by pulling a central mandrel into them to expand the backside and form a head. The mandrel snaps off and is discarded when the correct tension is reached. As long as the preparation of the rivet holes is well done, no special skill is required.

Blind rivets come in four common diameters—3/32", 1/8", 5/32", and 3/16". They are also available, but seldom at hardware stores, in 1/4" diameter. Hardware stores normally stock only aluminum or steel rivets. The lengths you choose depend on work thickness. Typically, you'll find the package labeled, "For work up to 1/8", 1/4", 3/8", and 1/2" thickness." In most cases, since you won't see the reverse side, the important thing is to have them long enough. If the reverse side is visible, be warned that there's nothing more unsightly and unworkmanlike than the contorted shanks of excessively long rivets.

HOLE SIZES FOR BLIND RIVETS

Rivet Diameter	Preferred Drill	Optional Drill
3/32"	#41	3/32"
1/8"	#30	1/8"
5/32"	#20	5/32"
3/16"	#11	3/16"
1/4"	F	1/4"

Blind rivets with flush heads make a neat job, but it's best to confine them to thicker metal because the hole must be countersunk with a special tool which would simply enlarge the hole in thin stock. After countersinking, flush-head blind rivets are installed like standard type. This is how they look. ▼

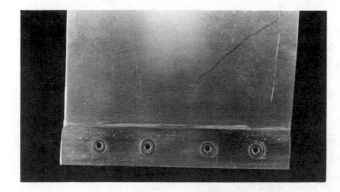

For most jobs in soft metal such as aluminum it works out fairly well if you use a drill of the same fractional size as the rivet diameter. In harder metals, or even thick aluminum joints, however, you can have trouble with the rivets catching and binding when you insert them. Sometimes you just can't get them through the holes, and sometimes metal will be shaved off and intrude between the joint faces. For this reason it's good practice to use the drill sizes shown in the chart. If you refer to drill size listings vs. a table of decimal equivalents you'll see that the next larger fractional size tends to be somewhat on the sloppy side. If you're mounting a license plate on a bicycle, it may not matter at all. If you're building a home-built airplane, it matters a lot.

Unless you have special industrial requirements, your choice of blind-rivet heads is limited to a rather shallow dome head or a flush head which seats in a 120° countersunk hole. The hole requires a special countersinking bit which is trifling in cost but hard to find. The flush heads do, however, produce a smooth, neat appearance.

If there is any single fault with the garden variety of blind rivets it's that they are nonsealing. Usually the head of the mandrel will pull into the rivet body and stay there, but they often fall or vibrate out. Special sealing rivets are available which do lock the mandrel in place, but even these cannot be counted on to hold liquid or air pressure. In short, don't use them to repair the bottom of your aluminum canoe. Closed-end special rivets without a hole all the way through are available, however, and these could be used. In this case, sealing will depend on how well the rivets fit the holes and the integrity of the joint.

Blind-rivet tools. Drawing the mandrel into the rivet hard enough to force the rivet to expand and later snap the mandrel requires substantial power. The tool used must have a gripping chuck which grasps and locks onto the mandrel firmly and, for the home shop, must have sufficient leverage or hydraulic power to pull without tiring your hand. Power riveters are normally used industrially.

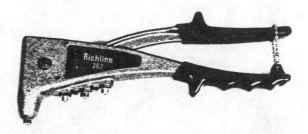

Two blind riveting tools of the many types available. One is fine for flat work. Different diameter mandrels are stored on bottom side of handle. Extended-nose riveter is more convenient for many jobs and will get into channels and boxes where shorter nose won't go.

You will find many very inexpensive blind-rivet tools in hardware stores, but buy them in full recognition that they are inadequate for more than the most casual jobs. These tools resemble pliers and require a full, strong grip to operate. Even worse, the working nose of the tool which grips the mandrel is almost flush with the handle. This puts your knuckles down against the workpiece, and when the mandrel snaps it can hurt. Moreover, it makes it impossible to rivet down in a channel or a recess. Better-quality tools have extended noses which will go down into channels and will also protect your knuckles.

Note, also, that each rivet size has a different mandrel diameter. The tip of the tool should have a bore size which just slips over the mandrel. This means that you need at least three interchangeable tip pieces. Some low-grade tools offer only one or two, but they are troublesome and should be avoided.

Removing rivets.   Blind rivets are easily drilled out by using a drill the same size as the rivet. This is one reason why they are often used as temporary fasteners while drilling other holes.

If ordinary iron, aluminum, or other rivets are accessible from the reverse side in rough work, a cold chisel can be used to remove the headed portion and a punch to drive them out. Or you can use a portable grinder to grind away the headed shank.

In other situations, however, you may want to remove rivets from the head side without marring the work metal. This requires carefully centered drilling to remove the head so the shank can be tapped out with a punch. You'll find it almost impossible to center-punch by hand the top of a round or button-head rivet. For critical

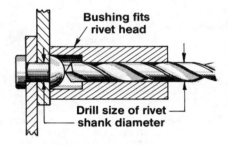

Bushing fits rivet head

Drill size of rivet shank diameter

Instead of skittering off the head of a rivet which must be drilled out, you can make up a drill guide to center the drill. Proceed with caution and check frequently; the head may be off-center with the shank.

Blind riveter with a hydraulic boost is a hand saver if you have a lot of rivets to pop.

jobs of this kind, make up a centering guide by drilling a short length of bar stock or rod to the rivet-head diameter, but only slightly deeper than the rivet head. Drill a second hole on the same center to accept and guide a drill the diameter of the rivet body. By placing this tool over the head, you can now guide the drill. Be aware, however, that rivet heads often shift off center when the rivet is headed. Thus, the procedure requires careful observation. Do not attempt to drill out the entire rivet shank. You will almost certainly enlarge or ovalize the hole. Drill only deep enough to cut into the area where the rivet head shoulders with the shank.

12. OTHER FASTENERS

M ost home metalworkers think in terms of assembling their projects with such basic fasteners as nuts and bolts, rivets, or machine screws. Actually, according to the publications of fastener makers, there are over 500,000 special fasteners used industrially. Most are intended to speed production or solve a special assembly problem. Some make it exceedingly difficult to disassemble and repair common household appliances. Others make it easy.

An example of the latter might be the kind of spring nut which clips to the edge of a panel and provides a threading means for a screw in a place where holding such a nut would be impossible. There is nothing more disheartening than removing a screw or bolt and hearing the nut on the opposite side go jingling down deep inside a door panel or into a gearbox. One way to avoid this mishap is to loosen the bolt partially, and then try to move it lengthwise. If the nut on the inside is loose and not attached to the structure in some way, you will probably be able to move the bolt by the amount you have loosened it. If it still feels as though it was threaded into something solid it's probably safe to go ahead. The chances are that the nut is a captive type.

There is not room enough in this book to discuss all metal fasteners, but it will save you an enormous amount of time and frustration if you become familiar with some of the basic types.

RETAINING RINGS

Retaining rings are known by a variety of names—snap rings, circlips, crescent rings, D-rings, E-rings, and !X!!X! rings when they snap free of your tool and fly into the nether regions of your shop. Most such rings are made of spring steel. They are narrow, thin, flat or round wire rings with one side open, and they seat in grooves in shafts or expand into grooves in cavities such as those used for ball bearings.

One type, called "axially installed," must be sprung either inward or outward to fit in a groove down in a cavity or bore, or over a shaft and into an annular groove around the shaft. Such retaining rings usually have two small holes into which the tips on a pair of special pliers fit. Depending on the pivot linkage of the pliers (called lock-ring pliers), squeezing the handles either expands or contracts the rings.

Another type of retaining ring, called "radially installed," has a larger opening on the side and is pushed onto a shaft from the side. After springing for assembly, the ring contracts and grips the groove in the shaft. These can often be pried free and pushed on without special tools.

By mounting a snap ring on a shaft, a manu-

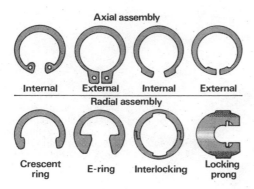

Axial assembly
Internal   External   Internal   External
Radial assembly
Crescent ring   E-ring   Interlocking   Locking prong

Snap rings come in many sizes and variations. To install, most of them must be squeezed or expanded, or pushed in from the side against spring tension. These are axial and radial rings.

facturer of a motor, pump, garden tractor, or whatever can locate a bearing against it or prevent the shaft from moving endways. This makes it possible to use a shaft of the same diameter for the full length, either from stock shafting or after centerless grinding. Without the handy snap ring some sort of shoulder would have to be turned to serve the purpose, and this increases the cost of the shaft enormously. Thus, such rings are basically locating devices.

In many cases, a second ring will be located on the opposite side to keep the bearing, wheel, gear, or other part from sliding off. That's why it's important to think like a manufacturer's engineer when disassembling such equipment. Think this way and you'll be able to anticipate where snap rings may be hidden. But never underestimate the ability of a snap ring to conceal itself. This is especially true of rings made of small wire. Very often attempts to pull a bearing

or gear are mysteriously blocked until you locate the little ring in the groove that is resisting your efforts. The rule—look, don't force.

Radially installed rings are usually removed by gentle prying with the tip of a small screwdriver or similar tool. It is wise to wrap a cloth around the area while removing such rings since they tend to fly off into outer space when they release. This is especially true of the very small ones. This should not, theoretically, be important since it is always good practice to use a new

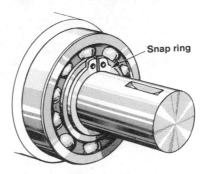

Snap ring

You'll find snap rings, sometimes no more than a thin ring or spring wire, used to locate bearings. If you're disassembling a bearing and it doesn't move, look for a hidden snap ring.

ring on reassembly. This rule applies to any part which locks by distorting, but in the real world you may not have a new ring handy. And the old one is a useful guide to size even if you do buy a new one.

Snap-Ring Pliers
Axially installed rings usually can be dug out with a pointed tool, but it is not easy, and it

Snap rings are popular retaining devices on axles. Pliers are outward-opening type to expand ring so it lifts free.

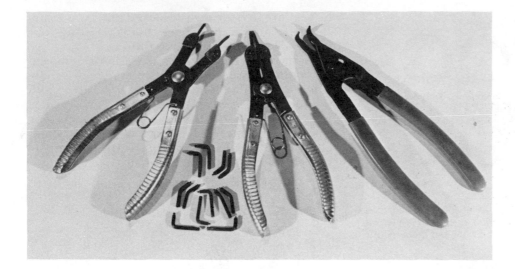

Snap rings come in so many sizes that it's hard to have enough single-size pliers such as those at right. Kit at left, however, with inward and outward opening handles, offers a wide range of fits simply by changing tips.

usually distorts the ring badly, not to mention nicking the groove. You really need a pair of snap-ring pliers, either inward or outward opening, to spread or contract the ring. Since the holes in the ring are quite small and the rings are thin, there's not much metal to engage. The tips of the pliers must be exactly the right size and must also be square, not worn, in the engaging area. Worn, or undersized, tips will slip out of the holes and frustrate your best efforts.

It would take a fairly large set of pliers to cover all of the sizes, plus inward and outward opening, to fit all the snap rings you'll find over the years. The less expensive approach is to buy a pair of pliers which can be adjusted for either opening direction and which has a kit of exchangeable tips for different hole sizes and working angles. Look for these tools on the special-tool display boards at automotive supply shops.

At the same time, you might want to buy an assortment of rings. Since axially installed rings are distorted significantly when removed, it is always better to replace them with new. This is especially true if you dig them out by spiraling one side up and around a shaft.

PINS

These range from clevis and cotter pins to hardened and ground dowels, taper pins, grooved pins, and spring pins. All are used to resist shear loads. A shear load acts against the pin in one direction—sideways. A cotter pin thus prevents a nut from turning by passing through a hole or slots in the nut and bolt; a taper pin, or any of the other varieties, may be used to keep a gear or pulley from turning on a shaft. Each type of pin has certain installation requirements if it is

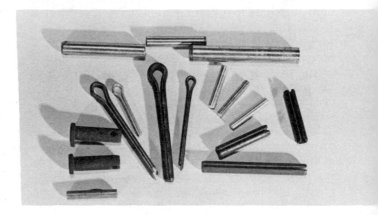

Straight pins, top, taper and groove pins, split tubular pins, clevis pins, and cotter pins are all common hardware in metalworking. In some places—for example, on some outboard motor propellers—a soft brass or aluminum shear pin may be used as a safety factor so it breaks before serious damage occurs.

to be effective. In an earlier section of this book I described the reaming of a drilled hole to accept a taper pin. As a rule, snug, precision fits are very important.

Cotter Pins

Although widely used for many years, cotter pins are also widely abused and improperly installed. Typically, a cotter pin passes through the slots of a nut as well as through the drilled bolt on which the nut is threaded. On a child's wagon the fit and alignment of the pin passages may not be critical. On an automobile wheel-bearing nut, a marine propeller shaft, or an aircraft assembly, life itself may be at stake.

Cotter pins, in a variety of materials, are available in 18 standardized sizes with fractional di-

(1) Pin should fit snugly
(2) Hole must align
(3) Pin split horizontal

Simple, and often abused, cotter pins have definite installation details you must observe if they are at critical locations. The pin should fit the hole and the slot in the fastener snugly; hole and slot must be aligned; split line should be as shown so it's parallel to the plane of the nut.

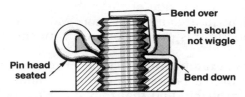

Bend over
Pin should not wiggle
Pin head seated
Bend down

A properly installed cotter pin should be so snug you can't wiggle it. The head should seat well into the nut slot and the legs should be drawn tight and bent as shown.

ameter dimensions from ⅓" to ¾". Lengths, of course, are selective. The diameter of the pin should match the diameter of the whole in the shaft or bolt so it fits snugly. Since, in many cases, the nut must be tightened to a specified torque, the nut slot may be too high, or, less likely, too low, for proper installation. The answer is not an undersize pin. In such cases selective spacer washers or other adjustments are needed. It is also common for the correct tightening torque to result in misalignment of the nut slots and the hole. It is usually acceptable to move the nut slightly in the tightening direction to align the slots. This situation often arises, for example, on connecting-rod bolts. If you have misgivings about overtightening, try backing off and retorquing the nut, or dress the bottom face of the nut lightly on abrasive paper, supported by a smooth surface, to remove a very small amount of metal.

Dowel Pins

Dowels are used in metalworking as well as in woodworking. The difference is that metalworking dowels are hardened and ground to very accurate dimensions. They are used in two ways. One is as a locating device. You'll find dowels used to locate gear covers, flywheel housings, flywheels, and other parts where a piece is precisely aligned at assembly and doweled so it can be reassembled in exactly the same location.

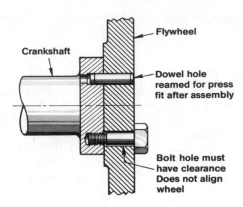

Crankshaft
Flywheel
Dowel hole reamed for press fit after assembly
Bolt hole must have clearance Does not align wheel

Metal dowels are precision fasteners and are commonly used to align critical parts such as flywheels and bearing plates so they can be reassembled in exactly the same place. Dowels are ordinarily snug fits in closely reamed holes.

Their second use is to resist shear loads, and although they are probably the best and strongest device for this purpose, they depend totally on a press fit for security.

This means that the holes which receive them must be drilled and reamed to exact size. Dowel-pin nominal diameters extend from ⅛" to ⅞" in lengths from ½" to 5½". The actual diameters of standard pins are .0002" (two-tenths of a thousandth) over nominal for a light drive or press fit. Oversize pins are .001" larger.

Such close fits are seldom needed in routine home-shop metalworking. My point in discussing them is that when you encounter dowel pins, be assured that the manufacturer felt they were vital. Failure to respect them can result in injury or death. If you must remove such a pin, be sure the work is well supported and a properly fitting punch is used to drive it out. If there is any suggestion of looseness, install an oversize pin.

Groove Pins

Less challenging to install than straight, hardened dowels, groove pins can often serve as effectively. Groove pins also lock in the work by being forced or driven into closely fitted holes, but since they have raised areas or grooves running lengthwise, thereby expanding their nominal diameter, they have more tolerance for slight inaccuracies in the hole diameter. To install them, normally all that is required is to drill to their nominal diameter and tap them home. They are not to be used as a substitute for hardened dowels because there is less assurance of their true bearing area in shear. If they happen to be held by only a light engagement of the raised surface there may be enough clearance at the main body of the pin for them to start moving and eventually become battered loose.

Spring Pins

Two varieties of spring pins, sometimes called split pins, are very widely used. One is simply a tubular pin with a slot or split down one side. The other has the metal wrapped in a spiral pattern. Both types are made a trifle larger than the nominal hole diameters, and when driven home they squeeze down and press firmly against the sides of the hole.

Standard spring-pin diameters range from $\frac{1}{16}$″ to $\frac{1}{2}$″, but you may find your hardware-store selection limited to a maximum of $\frac{1}{4}$″ diameter. Unless damaged by wear, corrosion, or removal,

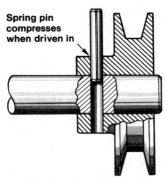

Spring pin compresses when driven in

A typical tubular spring pin compresses slightly as it's driven. You can use one inside another for extra shear strength.

spring pins can be reused. For additional shear strength it is acceptable to drive a smaller pin inside a larger one.

LOCKING DEVICES

A great many devices are made to lock parts together during use but still permit disassembly without driving out pins. One such common locking device is the setscrew.

Setscrews

Your first meeting with setscrews probably involved a vee-belt pulley on a shaft. Setscrews are universally used to hold pullies on everything from sewing machines to power tools. They are another of those deceptively simple items about which there are a number of fine points for the metalworker to learn. Setscrews are actually clamping devices. Installed from one side of a collar or hub, the screw itself contacts the metal of the shaft and inhibits rotation.

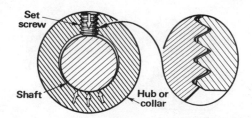

Set screw

Shaft

Hub or collar

Although you may think of a setscrew as being a holding device in itself, its main function is to force the opposite side of the part into a hard clamping action with much more gripping surface than the screw point.

Equally important, the screw pressure forces the opposite, inner side of the hub tightly against the shaft in a clamping action. Most setscrews function in this manner but not with equal efficiency.

If you examine the usual jar of setscrews collected over a period of time in the home shop you'll probably find that they differ not only in size and length but also in the type of point and the method used to drive them. The following types of setscrew points are fairly standard:
● Cup—the point is recessed in a cup shape and bites into the shaft.
● Cone—the point tapers to a sharp end intended to seat in a matching hole in the shaft.
● Oval—the screw ends in a smoothly rounded surface which can be loosened and shifted without significantly marring the shaft.
● Flat—also used where adjustment and retightening are expected, but a mating flat is usually provided for setscrew seating.
● Dog—the screw ends in a short (half-dog) or longer (full-dog) shanklike extension which should fit accurately in a matching hole in the shaft.

As may be seen, oval and flat screw ends permit the hub part to be relocated frequently and

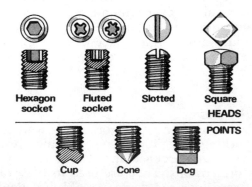

Hexagon socket   Fluted socket   Slotted   Square

HEADS

POINTS

Cup   Cone   Dog

Setscrews have many variations in heads and points. Those shown here, cup, cone, and dog, each have a purpose. Those points which do not engage or enter the metal are best where the screw must be loosened occasionally to adjust the location of a pulley or like part.

are, indeed, used for adjustment and alignment of the part on the shaft. They are not the best choice for securing a highly loaded member. The cone and the dog point have a maximum securing action against shifting in service but permit no adjustment.

The cup point is probably the most frequently used, scars the shaft, but secures quite well and allows shifting for adjustment. An example would be aligning the vee-pulley groove with a pulley on a motor shaft. Unfortunately, the biting action of the cup point often scars the shaft so badly that pulling the part after loosening the setscrew becomes extremely difficult. The scarred metal gouges into the hub and wedges the parts. A flat on the shaft to keep the scar damage below the surface is a good trick to ease pulley removal.

You'll also notice a difference in the heads of a random collection of setscrews. On some types of equipment, such as lawn or farm machinery, rotating parts were once routinely secured by square-head setscrews which could be tightened with an end wrench. Although square heads are easily tightened, they tend to throw any rotating assembly off balance because they project out from the hub. Even worse, such heads are very dangerous because clothing, wiping rags, or your hands can be drawn into them while the machine is running. Never use square-head setscrews in an exposed position. Replace them with the socket-head type.

Setscrews with screwdriver-slot heads are also common, and they can be set flush or slightly below flush for safety. They are not reliable,

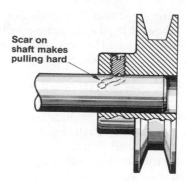

A common shop problem is removing a pulley over the burr raised by a setscrew. Before replacing the pulley, file a flat on the shaft to receive the setscrew next time.

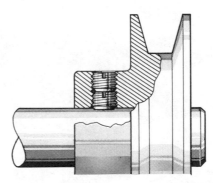

If a pesky setscrew keeps loosening up, maybe you can cure it by using two shorter ones, the second one snugged down on top to jam the bottom one.

however, for driving loads since the slot area limits the tightening torque you can apply. The holding capability of a setscrew is in almost direct relation to its tightness.

For most general metalworking applications, the socket-head setscrew with a hexagonal recess for a hex-key wrench is by far the best choice. Not only does the hex key allow maximum tightening, but it also is a better bet for removing a tight screw which has rusted in place. A trick of many metalworkers is to use tandem setscrews. If the threads into which you're installing the screw seem a little loose or worn, try installing a short screw as tightly as possible, then follow it with another one tightened jam-nut fashion against it. Conversely, if removal of a setscrew does not seem to free a hub on a shaft, look for a second screw at the bottom of the hole. Someone else may have used the same trick.

Lock Washers

The familiar split-circled lock washer with one side of the split canted up and the other down

Socket-head screws, ranging from fairly large to tiny setscrews, are often the fastener of choice because they are far less likely to cause trouble than slotted-head types which are difficult to tighten as securely as needed.

appears simple in its action. The ends of the split bite into the underside of the nut or bolt head and also into the face of the workpiece or a flat washer resting on the workpiece.

Actually, if you review the earlier material on threads and tapping, you'll recall that a bolt secures an assembly by stretching or tension. In service, many things can reduce this tension. Among them are gasket crush, heating and contraction, corrosion, and fretting wear between surfaces. The split lock washer is also a section of a spiral spring. When the fastener is tight-

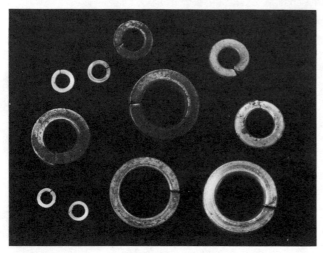

If you have a jar full of salvaged lock washers, look them over. You'll probably be surprised at how they vary in thickness, width, finish, spring offset, and other details.

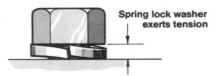

Spring lock washer exerts tension

A standard spring lock washer does no more than an ordinary flat washer as long as the assembly remains tightened to its original tension. If, for whatever reason, lower tension develops in the fastener, the spring action helps replace some of it and the ends of the split can now bite in.

ened, this spring is compressed and flattened. Later, if the bolt loses some tension, the spring action of the washer acts to retain a portion of this tension. It is only under these circumstances that the split ends are free to bite into the metal. At best, however, this can only constrain the fastener from turning and becoming completely loose. At worst, the biting and scarring of the workface and the underside of the nut or bolt head can groove out these surfaces so the lock washer will be ineffective in the future.

Toothed lock washers.   Commonly called star-washers, toothed lock washers are generally a better choice than split-ring washers. The small teeth engage, but seldom cut out, the mating surfaces. The teeth may be internal, to produce

Star or tooth-type lock washers also come in a wide variety. When disassembling equipment, take note of which type of lock washer is used in each location. There's generally a reason for choosing that particular style of washer.

a more finished appearance; external to gain the greatest radius for gripping, or even internal and external. The latter serve well between two clamped surfaces to inhibit sliding. They are also handy for securing electrical connection lugs or other tablike parts under a bolt head.

Locking Nuts

Hundreds of variations of nuts and bolts which lock and resist turning are used industrially. There are a few common ones you can buy readily, and I recommend their use on almost anything from a child's wheel toy to playground equipment, boats, and aircraft.

Lock nuts may be either "prevailing-torque" or "free-spinning" types. The former turns freely at first, then resistance sets in and a wrench is needed to seat the nut. To remove a lock nut, you have to use a wrench almost all the way. Free-spinning nuts can be run down easily by hand but lock when seated firmly. When loosened, they back off freely. Their greatest advantage is in speeding production.

Prevailing-torque nuts.   Probably the most familiar lock nuts are those with an inset ring of fiber or plastic material at the top. These nuts have standard threads in the metal portion, but the locking material is left unthreaded and the threads are forced into the material on installation. There is always a question about reusing such nuts. If age, heat, or thread burrs have effected the locking material, they may not lock effectively. If you feel they turn down much more easily than a new nut, they should be discarded. On the other hand, if the locking core still has a definite gripping action they can be reused. This also applies to another type of nut which has a plastic segment inserted like a small plug from

Self-locking nuts may have a plastic insert, left; a dimple mark, right; or an engaging surface, lower right. The first two types tend to hold even though not contacting the assembly tightly, but those with a surface-locking feature must be snugged down.

one side. As a general rule, such a nut should not be used in place of a slotted nut and cotter pin or lockwire if the plastic will be turned past the drilled hole in the bolt. The hole tends to shear away the locking material.

A second type of prevailing-torque lock nut depends on high friction between the nut metal and the bolt without any special plastic insert. One such nut has the appearance of a castle nut on which the slots are too narrow for a cotter pin. The castle portion is coned in slightly so the fingerlike segments grip the bolt as they are sprung open on installation.

Other locking nuts have a dimple or strike mark on one side to distort the thread or nut body just enough to build up an interference or binding action on the threads of the bolt. All such types are generally confined to less critical applications and unless evidently damaged may be reused.

Free-spinning lock nuts. Most nuts in this class are production rather than hardware items. Some have plastic inserts at the bottom which mash and grip on seating. Others are actually double nuts with the upper member acting as a check nut, and still others have a toothed bottom surface or permanently mounted, toothed lock washers. The important thing is for the metal-worker to accept the fact that the manufacturer deemed these nuts important in their given lo-

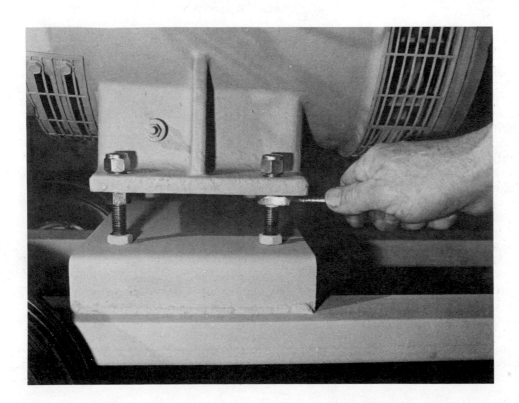

On this leveling and aligning system for a generator, lower nuts act as jacks and supports. Upper nuts are self-locking and are tightened down after adjustment to jam lower nuts and prevent turning.

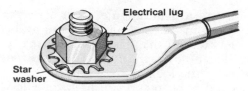

Electrical lug

Star washer

Electrical ground leads and similar connections must remain secure. When they loosen, mysterious electrical troubles develop. A star washer bites into a lug for good mechanical security and also helps improve electrical contact.

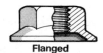

Plastic ring insert   Plug insert   Split crown

Distorted thread   Flanged

Dozens of self-locking nuts have been invented and are used industrially. These are types you can buy at the hardware store. Look for a plastic or fiber collar, a plastic side insert, or a dimple in the side of the nut. All apply extra friction to the threads and inhibit the nut from backing off.

cations. Segregate them and put them back in the same locations on reassembly.

Locking Materials

Many times you'll encounter an extremely tight bolt or nut, or even a series of them. Yet, on disassembly you find that they are not lock-type fasteners. Such fasteners have probably been installed with a locking chemical such as Loctite. There are a number of such products, each intended for specific applications. They are liquids which do not harden in the presence of air. Left in a partially filled bottle, they are always ready for use. When a small drop is applied to a nut or bolt during installation the liquid fills the voids between the thread faces. Since air is now excluded, they set into a tough, plasticlike adhesive. These materials are especially useful on any assembly subjected to vibration, such as a snowmobile, boat, or lawn mower.

The most important rule in using these agents is to be sure that the threads of both the nut and the bolt are clean, dry, and free of grease or oil. Wash the fasteners in a good solvent to be sure. A primer is also available in spray form to improve setting action.

Keys and Keyways

It is often necessary to lock a hub to a shaft against strong torque forces. Although setscrews, as discussed, can do this within limits, they are often not strong enough. Even the flywheel on a small lawn-mower engine develops very high inertia forces. This is a typical situation for a key. In other cases, an accurate, timed, relationship must be established and maintained between a shaft and other working parts. An example is the gears which time the valve-actuating camshaft to the crankshaft in an engine. These gears are almost always keyed.

Although metalworkers with milling equipment can and do cut keyway slots as needed, most are more often concerned with replacing worn or lost keys. This must be done with some thought and some analysis as to what has happened in the past because a keyed assembly is usually a critical assembly.

Typically, on disassembly, a key will show a jog or other deformation which makes it unsafe and unusable. This wear indicates that the hub has been moving on the shaft either under load or under vibrational impulses.

A worn key immediately suggests careful examination of the keyways in the shaft and hub. Use a magnifying glass. Look for rounded-over corners on the slots and signs of wear and fretting on the side of a keyway. A new key of the same size as the old one may be used for a gage. Keys are normally fitted to require a light tapping to seat. A key which drops in freely is too

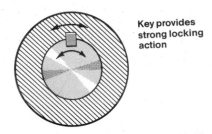

Key provides strong locking action

The greatest value of a key is in preventing two parts such as a gear or pulley on a shaft from rotating. This is technically a loading in shear where rotation would tend to shear the key in half if the parts moved.

loose. In some cases—a vee-belt drive, for example—you may elect to go ahead with the assembly using a new key. Later, you may have trouble, but if the part is noncritical it's worth the gamble. *Never* do this with an engine or other flywheel. The danger from a loose flywheel exceeds by far the cost of new parts or machining an oversize keyway in the old ones.

Why keyways wear. If you find a worn keyway you should then ask yourself the reason the hub moved and caused the wear. Many hubs such as flywheels and heavy-duty drive pulleys and gears are tapered as well as keyed. The retaining nut on the end of the shaft is usually torqued very tight. Sometimes you may remove a flywheel and fail to tighten the nut to its full tension. The usual cause is lack of some means to prevent the flywheel from turning when wrench force is applied.

In other cases, the hub is expanded by heating when it's installed, slipped over the shaft, and then shrunk as well as keyed. If some previous disassembly resulted in galling the shaft metal, cleanup operations may have destroyed the shrink fit. Never slight such considerations or

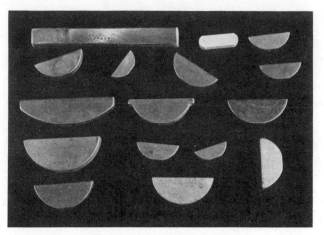

These half-moon-shaped keys are Woodruff keys of different types and sizes. Straight key, top, is the type used to secure pulleys and gears with heavy loads. Small, lozenge-shaped key is soft metal, intended to shear under excess load.

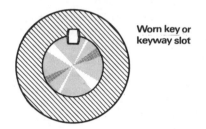

Worn key or keyway slot

Key action depends on square, flat sides and a snug fit in the shaft. When wear or looseness allows the key to roll in the slot the eventual result is deformation of both key and slot. The only real cure, if it's a critical assembly, is to remachine the keyway in both parts and install an oversize key.

try to get by if you are working with a high-speed, rotating part which might come loose in service and seek vengeance for your carelessness.

One other aspect of damaged keys should be known to you. In some applications where accidental high impact may occur, "soft" keys are often used to avoid serious damage to expensive parts. Rotary lawn-mower hubs are an example. Keys of softer metal are used so if the blade strikes something hard like a stump the key will shear rather than damage the engine shaft. Replace these keys with soft keys, never standard steel keys.

Woodruff keys. Shaped like a half-moon, woodruff keys range in fractional sizes from 1/16" thick by 1/4" high to a huge 3/4" thick by 3½" high size. Such keys may be full semicircle or flattened slightly on the bottom. This is not critical. Keys are made from tough steel and hardened to resist shearing. Their thickness tolerance is from −.001" to +.001". This allows you to make a

Basic purpose of a Woodruff key is to prevent one part from turning relative to another. A second purpose is often a timed relationship—for example, a timing gear on a camshaft.

selective fit by trial if you have a supply on hand. Lacking such a supply, it's a good idea to take the part with the keyway to the hardware store so you can select for the best fit.

Woodruff keys can sometimes be stubborn to remove. In most cases a light tap on one end will rock the key in its seat so you can get the tip of a chisel or a punch under it and tap or pry it free. At other times you'll find that the key is tight enough to require some more substantial, but careful, hammer and chisel action to lift it out of the slot. Don't reuse keys damaged by such removal action. Dressing them off or forcing them back in can only reduce their capability to resist loads.

Square and flat keys.   To increase the available loading area, square or flat keys are often used. The presence of such a key can be detected by the open ends of the key slot in both the hub and the shaft. In most cases the end of the key will also be visible. The same general rules of snug fit apply to square and flat keys as to woodruff keys. On installation and reassembly it is very important that the key slots align with the key. If you miss this alignment and try to drive or force the hub on, there is the probability that

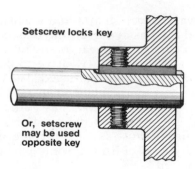

Another method of securing a part on a shaft is to combine the key with a setscrew. Placing the setscrew opposite the key is probably a better technique.

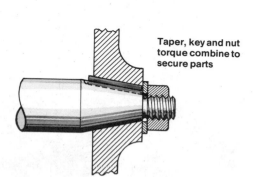

Many assemblies combine several retaining methods. Here, the shaft and part are tapered, keyed, and secured by a threaded fastener. In most cases the torque on the nut is critical.

you will force the key rearward so it rides up in the unfinished portion of the keyway. This wedges the hub so it can't seat. Use a new key and start over.

In some assemblies a setscrew is used above the key as a further insurance against loosening. In such cases it is still the key that carries the load. Do not count on the setscrew to secure a loose key which rocks in the keyway. Almost certainly the rocking will loosen the screw.

Shrink Fits

If a hub is extremely hard to pull, or if it required heat from a propane torch to free it, the

Sometimes keys can be bedded firmly in their slots. Basic removal technique is to get under them and tap so they rock up and out.

chances are it was either shrink fitted by heating or was pressed on with a heavy industrial press. In either case, reassembly will probably be much easier if the hub is heated to expand it before trying to reinstall it. Be very certain that all surfaces are clean and free of burrs. Many metalworkers will apply a light coat of lubricant such as Lubriplate to the shaft.

One way to heat the hub is to immerse it in a bath of lubricating oil over a hot plate. There is always a danger of the oil catching fire, so be prepared to smother the flame. The usual temperature for such shrink fits is about 400°F. In the case of hardened parts such as a gear or bearing race you certainly don't want to get it hot enough to impair the hardness.

If you use a torch for heating, be sure to play the torch over the surface evenly and build up

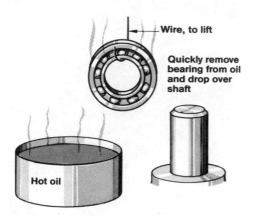

Shrink-fitting a bearing race or other part is always exciting because time is critical. The part must be transferred from the heat source, such as an oil bath, aligned in position, and dropped home before it cools. Wise metalworkers always have something on hand to fit over the shaft and against the hot part so it can be tapped down if it balks short of full seating. You have to judge when to drive it harder and when to just let it cool and try again. The latter is usually the wiser choice.

the heat gradually to avoid cracking or distortion. Touch a piece of wire soft-solder to the hub as you heat. When the solder melts it's hot enough.

A shrink fit occurs very rapidly so you must be prepared to pick up the hot part with asbestos gloves or other means. Align it instantly and squarely with the shaft and key and thrust it home with dispatch. Be prepared to drive it the last fraction with a soft-faced drift and heavy hammer. Any mistakes along the line will result in the part sticking. The only solution is to pull it and start over.

Cold shrink fits. Many times it is impractical to heat one of the workpieces because of its nature and size. An example would be installing valve-seat inserts in a cylinder block or head. Another might be an outer bearing race in a wheel. If you read the section on working-to-one-thousandth, you will recall that I shrunk a replacement liner for a motor end-plate and installed it while the end-plate was still centered in the lathe chuck.

Cold shrinking is a practical way to solve these problems. The trick, as with hot shrinking, is to have everything prepared for fast action. The part to be installed must be very cold. Dry ice is an ideal cooling agent. A pan full of dry ice and alcohol works best. Do not place your fingers in it. Also, do not get in the habit of using a carbon-dioxide fire extinguisher for shrinking parts. It works fine until you need it to put out a fire.

In the home shop adequate shrinking temperatures can often be obtained by placing the part in your home freezer.

It's interesting to reflect at this point—the shrinking technique was used to secure ancient chariot wheel rims. Among men who work metal, there's a bond over the ages. That's part of the mystique of metalworking.

PART III
THE FINE ARTS OF METALWORKING

13.
SHOP AND TOOLS

The term "fine metalwork" as I use it in this book refers to metalwork of a delicate nature that depends on a high degree of manual and/or artistic ability. This would include watchmaking, jewelry making, engraving, hand-forming vessels and decorative art objects, and some forms of casting.

Some of these crafts need a fairly large shop if they involve hammer work on large metal sheets, pickling, melting, and pouring metal. Fortunately, watchmaking and jewelry work can be done in small, even cramped quarters. How many times have you seen a watchmaker or jeweler working in a tiny space behind a counter or even in a subway stall? For this reason, fine metalworking is an ideal hobby for apartment dwellers or anyone with limited available space.

A few obvious precautions are in order. Whenever metal is cut, fine metal slivers and chips are produced which can work into places where they don't belong. Jewelers working with precious metals are cautious about such material, which some call "lemel," and try to salvage as much as possible. Even if the metal you work with is less costly, make some provision for catching these particles for they can be hazardous in food or flesh.

Nearly all the fine arts at some point require heat for annealing, tempering, or soldering. Frilly curtains, flammable plastics, papers, and modern synthetic fabrics must be kept well away from an errant sweep of the torch flame. Pickling solutions, used routinely for cleaning fine metalwork, must be stored in unbreakable containers far out of the reach of children's hands. *Never* store acid solutions in any container even resembling something commonly used for food or drink. A friend of mine died because he kept a chrome-plating solution in a beer bottle.

THE WORKBENCH

Typically, a bench for either watchmaking or jewelry making is arced inward or made with two extending sides so you can sit in very close, surrounded by your tools. Some watchmakers, however, prefer a straight bench. This reflects a need for steady hands. If you observe a watchmaker at work, you may notice that he rests his wrists, or even the fat of his hand, on the bench to prevent tremors. For comfort, the height of the bench should suit your own physical dimensions so you are not unnecessarily bent over. If you wear bifocals or trifocal eyeglasses, your bench, and your chair or stool, must be adjusted to permit you to work without fatigue.

Tool location is a matter of choice. Most jeweler's tools are quite small and are easily held

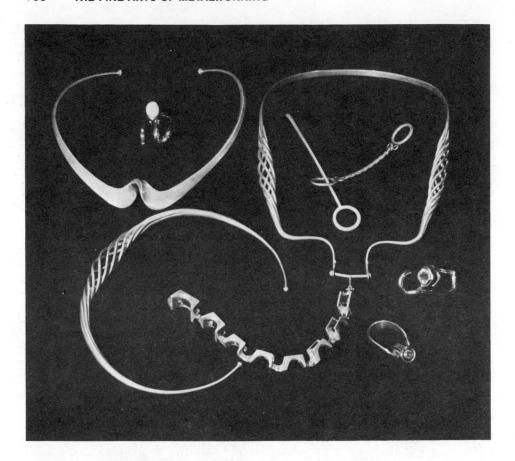

Handcrafted jewelry may involve forming metal, casting, joining many pieces, and setting gems. These personally conceived and designed pieces are examples of metalworking at its highest level of skill and creativity. *By Fred Fenster, University of Wisconsin, Dept. of Fine Arts.*

The glamor of the front-of-the-shop jewelry-display cases can change to the real-world workshop in cramped quarters at the rear. This bench belongs to a highly skilled working jeweler who moves from watch repair to ring sizing, engraving, gem setting, and frabrication of jewelry from raw precious metal stock. Note the tool and catch tray at lap height. Since the tools are small and light, jewelry crafts are ideal where heavy metalworking equipment is impossible. *Zag Jewelers, Waukesha, Wisc.*

in racks or trays within hand's reach. The work-pieces are difficult to pick up and hold with your fingers so tweezers or some equivalent are used constantly.

Naturally, there will be times when you'll accidentally drop a tiny part. The bench should be

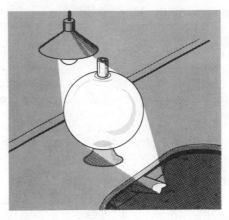

It's impossible to work on fine jewelry in dim light. Old-timers used a condenser lens of sorts, made by filling a glass globe with water. It provided a spotlight effect from a dim electric or gas light.

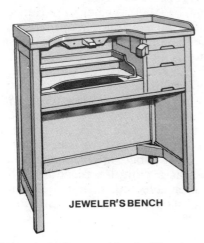

JEWELER'S BENCH

A jeweler's bench, for the pro at least, differs from an ordinary workbench. It is a support for hands and arms, a surface on which to spread out tools, and a catch device for dropped items; and it's at a height to prevent excessive stooping when working down close with the loupe.

equipped with a tray or canvas apron above your lap to catch both dropped pieces and metal scrap. It's quite possible to make a jeweler's bench which can be pulled down from the wall, or out of storage, but be sure it is heavy enough and firm enough to resist strong working pressure from your hands.

Old-time jewelers and watchmakers had a bad

Many secrets of the jeweler's craft can be observed in this picture of a jeweler at work. The height of the chair is just right for comfortable viewing through his loupe without awkward or tiring bending, which causes fatigue and unsteady hands. The tool tray and its catch surface prevent dropping and losing small parts, and it's also at the right height to support his elbows. Hands and wrists are easily rested on the bench top; another aid to steady hands. Although the bench appears cluttered, the jeweler actually has his needed tools within easy reach so he can pick them up without putting the work down. Draftsman's light can be moved around for close-in, glare-free lighting.

time obtaining the kind of light needed for good vision. They tried to use natural light to best advantage but resorted to novel strategies to use such artificial light as they had. One interesting gadget was a water-filled glass globe which acted as a sort of refractor to beam the light onto the work. Others used condenser lenses or mirrors. Fortunately, you have an excellent choice today, ranging from fluorescent draftsman's lights for general illumination to high-intensity spots for very small work. In addition, there are many industrial lights combined with magnifiers, ring lights, and other special lights made necessary by new technologies such as electronic chip assembly. Get the best you can afford.

Jeweler's peg.   A novel piece of equipment in the jeweler's trade is the "peg" or "bench pin," a tapered wooden block which projects from the front edge of the workbench. In some cases, the peg is forced into a mortise in the edge of the bench. Other jewelers prefer to use a sturdy holder which clamps onto the bench and accepts the peg. It provides a handy support during the delicate filing, fine sawing, and polishing and other handwork. The fact that it projects is important; many filing and cutting jobs require the tool hand to be underneath the work.

If you prowl around jeweler's shops you'll find that this peg, actually an expendable miniature workbench, is a highly individualized item. Some are clean and straight, some have the outer edges battered, and some have worn or cut notches reflecting the jeweler's specialty.

SOLDERING TORCHES

Soldering, in the jeweler's parlance, differs somewhat from routine sheet-metal or electrical-wire soldering. It refers almost exclusively to joining the small parts of a ring or other decorative article by melting a small bit of solder between them. The solder is hard solder made to closely controlled melting temperature and color specifications. Part of the jeweler's art is selecting just the right solder to make an invisible joint. Another part is selecting the right melting point. Since much of the soldering is sequential, as a complex piece is built up, solders are often selected so that the heat required for later joints will not cause a previously made joint to soften.

Moreover, the heat must be applied very delicately and confined to a small area. Such soldering is not a job for a garden variety propane torch, but propane and other gases are commonly used for torch fuels. The old-time jeweler

The jeweler's peg is actually a miniature workbench. This one clamps to the edge of the bench and is easily removed.

used a gas or alcohol torch with part of the combustion air supplied through a hose, and a mouthpiece into which he blew to control the flame. If you're good with a harmonica, able to blow out and breathe in at the same time, you might master this skill. Such torches or blowpipes can also be supplied with air from a small

Although later you may want to investigate some of the torches available from jeweler's supply houses, hose fed from bottle gases, for a beginning a small butane/oxygen torch such as this may be sufficient. Flame is needle fine and almost invisible. It's good for other soldering, too, as on this antenna connector.

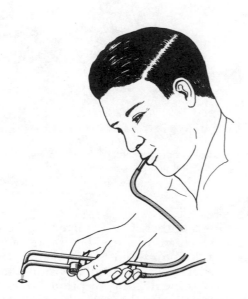

Another art you don't have to learn, unless you'd like to, is using your breath to control and direct a gas or alcohol flame for fine soldering work. Modern bottle gas makes it easier.

compressor or air bottle and regulated by a finger valve. Today, many jewelers prefer to use bottled oxygen and propane. You'll also find that many of them fabricate their own torch tips, sometimes from hypodermic needles. They take great pride in being able to demonstrate a minute, needle-sharp, intensely hot flame. For the beginner in jewelry work it may be best to investigate one of the miniature oxygen/butane torches available at most hardware stores.

Soldering supports.   Anyone who has tried to solder extremely small parts knows that holding these parts firmly and in the right relationship to each other can be very difficult. In addition, almost anything that you use to support the work tends to absorb more heat than the work itself. Attempts to remedy this with more heat can result in a melted disaster. Jewelry workers often use slate or carbon blocks to support work, but another old-time device called a "wig" often works very well in the home shop. A wig resembles a little scouring pad with a wire handle or stem. This device, about the size of the inner palm of your hand, can be made by wadding or packing soft steel wire snowball fashion and then tamping the wire mass into a dense, pancakelike shape. The wire should be compacted quite tightly. Used as a soldering support, the

One old-time rig that still works is the jeweler's wig for holding small jewelry items while soldering. Try it.

heat loss to the wig is less than to a solid, and the work can be arranged on the tangled surface advantageously.

HAND TOOLS

Both jewelers and watchmakers use tweezers and a wide variety of small gripping and forming pliers. Some are highly specialized; you'll find them in the supply catalogs of firms catering to these trades. If you take up one of these crafts, you'll soon learn just which pliers are important to you.

In addition to the common metalworking tools

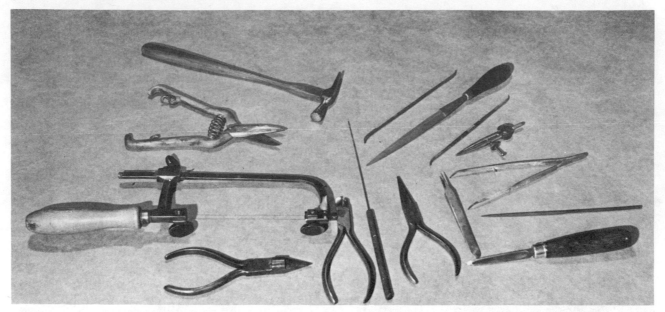

Jeweler's tools tend to be small and light, well suited for metalworking hobby where space is limited.

for rough-cutting stock, the art-metal worker also needs a good loupe, a jeweler's saw, small drills, hammer and mallets, and a Dremel-type tool for polishing, buffing, working into details, and drilling.

Tweezers. The universal fingers of the jeweler and watchmaker. For the watchmaker, in particular, it is absolutely necessary to be able to pick up very small parts and hold them firmly. One old watchmaker's criterion of good tweezers is that they must be able to pick up a human hair from a piece of glass.

I have suggested the use of some form of magnifying lens for several jobs, including reading scales graduated in hundredths, locating centers for punching, and sharpening drills. For watch and jewelry work magnification is essential. One look inside a small watch with normal vision and a second using a jeweler's loupe will quickly convince you of this.

Loupe. The conventional loupe, in short, medium, and fairly long focal lengths, has been a standby for years and it has the great advantage over a hand-held magnifying glass of freeing both hands. One manufacturer's loupes come in magnifications from 10X to 2.5X. Their working distances range from 1″ to 4″ respectively.

Unfortunately, many persons find it difficult to retain a loupe in the eye socket. And, if you customarily wear bifocal or trifocal glasses, removing the loupe and replacing the glasses every time you want to look up and locate a tool on

A jeweler learns to work with one eye using a loupe. If you wear glasses, get type that clamps to earpiece.

the bench is a bother. This is solved by the type of loupe which clips onto the frame of your glasses and flips up when not needed. Even so, the loupe offers only monocular vision and deprives you of some depth perception. Professionals who work constantly with a loupe undoubtedly compensate to some degree for this, but for the beginner a headband magnifier with dual lenses may be better.

For small metalworking jobs, a flip-up, headband magnifyer gives more comfortable viewing and retains the depth perception you may find you need. Lenses of different power may be used as required.

Such magnifiers, in the better grades, come with interchangeable lenses up to about 15 power. You'll probably find that, except for extremely fine work, even 3 or 4 power is an enormous help. You'll be able to see the tool and work clearly, watch a cut or chip if you're using a cutting tool, and spot lint and dirt you'd otherwise miss.

Fine drills.   It is one thing to shoot a hole in a piece of steel with a ¼″ drill or a drill press using a husky twist drill. It is quite another to drill a tiny hole .010″ or .015″ in diameter. Nevertheless, such holes, and much smaller ones, are routinely drilled by watchmakers and jewelers.

Watchmakers and jewelers used to make their own fine drills from needles by heating, flattening, and shaping the point to a flared diamond form. The cutting edges were honed flat and a small amount of relief was given exactly as on a twist drill or a lathe tool. In some instances, such as when enlarging a worn, existing hole slightly, or opening up a starting hole for a jeweler's saw blade, you can simply clamp such a drill in a pin vise and spin it through with your fingers. This somewhat rough and ready technique is not really necessary with today's power tools.

Conventional twist drills, in approximately 67 different sizes between ⅛″ (.125″) and #80 (.0135″) are available, mostly in number sizes. It is not likely that any home shop will need this many, but a well-spaced choice is extremely handy. These small drills can be mounted in a high-speed Dremel tool or flexible shaft for hand-held drilling. For more accuracy, the Dre-

mel tool can be mounted in an accessory drill-press stand. Or a miniature lathe can be used in either vertical or horizontal modes.

Drilling with such fine drills requires a degree of touch and patience. Proceed slowly and back out often to clear chips.

Rolling mill.   If you elect to work in gold, silver, platinum, and some of the other precious-metal alloys, you will probably find that it is best to buy presized metal in flat, wire, or other forms from a supply house. Later, you may want to work with sizes and forms less available.

Professional jewelry makers often size their metal by either rolling or drawing, both two rather ancient processes. Rolling reduces the thickness of metal and is done with two hardened steel rollers called a rolling mill. If you get into serious jewelry work you may want to acquire a rolling mill, or you may be able to use one at a local school shop or in a jeweler's back room. Rolling mills are heavy and expensive and are really seldom needed in home-shop jewelsmithing.

Draw plate.   Wire can be reduced in size and altered in shape by drawing it through a draw plate, a device with a series of progressively smaller holes. These plates can be purchased from supply houses and are perfectly suited to home-shop use.

Hammers and mallets.   An additional array of tools for hammering and forming is also needed. Since a great deal of shaping is done by hammer strokes, the shapes, weights, and faces of the hammers exceed those of the blacksmith. The difference is that the softer metal, worked cold, does not require the very heavy striking tools used for working heavier metal while hot. For the same reason, the art-metal worker uses many soft-face hammers of leather, plastic, rubber, synthetic compounds, or wood. These tools help to form metal without marking it.

Mallets are frequently used in conjunction with a sandbag to develop gentle curves. Such a bag, perhaps a foot square or slightly larger, is easily made from heavy canvas and filled with fine sand to the point where it can be plumped like a pillow. Some of the modern synthetic fabrics are probably better than canvas since they don't pick up water which may be slopped after annealing or pickling. The weave must be fine enough, and several layers may be used so sand grit does not work through.

Stakes.   Sandbag forming works well for shallow forming, but since many art-metal objects are hollowware they require more aggressive forming operations. For these, a large variety of stakes, actually anvil forms, are needed. Stakes can be mounted blacksmith-style in an anvil, but more commonly they are simply clamped in a vise. Part of the art of metal forming is selecting a stake form which gives the most convenient access and best produces the desired shape.

It is important to realize that forming art metal is almost always a progressive operation. Unlike commercial die forming where one, or sometimes two or three, swift strikes of the male and female dies stretch and squeeze the metal to shape, hand forming must be done gradually so the metal flows, stretches, and compacts without bulges, wrinkles, or distortion. Thus, a series of stake forms may be needed to bring the work gradually to form. Since the metal is impacted with a hammer on one side and backed on the other by a stake, the faces of the hammer and the stake must be smooth and free from nicks or raised spots. Accidentally striking something with a hammer or tossing in a stake with other tools can cause this. Such damaging marks will reproduce themselves hundreds of times as you hammer.

Forming blocks.   One of the things that you'll quickly discover in working art metal is that no matter how many stakes you have, it becomes necessary to make your own forming blocks. Hard maple, cherry, or other dense woods with a tight grain are ideal for these blocks. In some cases all you need is a sharp, straight edge to bend over the sides of a box or tray. In other cases you'll want a rounded corner; and in still others you'll want a depressed, concave pocket. Many simple projects can be made simply by sandwiching a piece of metal between two wooden discs and clamping the package tightly in a vise or C-clamp. Hammering the edge does the rest.

Any woodworker can easily make such forming blocks, sometimes by band-sawing and sanding the curves; or, more often, by turning in a lathe. Remember that metal hammered over a curved block will be larger than the block. This means that your forming block must be smaller than the desired finished size by the thickness of the metal. And, of course, forming inside a concave block requires that the form be larger than the inside of the finished work.

Chasing tools.   It is quite possible to take a bowl or other object spun to a smooth surface in a lathe and produce a highly artistic finished work by "chasing" decorative designs into the surface. Chasing work can even be combined with engraving. Some of the finest examples can be seen on old silverware.

Chasing tools are basically small punches often resembling the punches used for stamping letters or numerals into metal. But for chasing, sometimes called repoussé work, they have a huge variety of tips, each ground to shape to produce an equivalent raised pattern in the metal. Obviously, the choice of striking faces is very much a matter of the design or motif involved and the artist's fancy. Usually, chasing is done against a semisoft surface such as pitch or leather and the work is bedded so it is both held and supported during carefully delivered hammer taps.

14. HAND ENGRAVING

Although nearly all engraving done today is done by machine, hand engraving is a satisfying art form which allows considerable personal expression. Your work can be highly formal with Old English or German letters, crisply modern, or your own script. The important thing is that it be neatly cut into the metal after a very accurate layout.

Depending on the metal, the hand pressures needed to cut the design with an engraving tool can be quite high. This is true even for pewter and silver. Also, the pressures must be evenly graduated from a rather low initial bite into the metal to a sustained and guided pressure through the main cut, to a leveling off and easing of pressure as the tool leaves the cut. Without this smoothly graduated pressure the cut edges of the engraving will waver and the depth will be uneven. Even worse, you'll slip and make ruinous gouges.

Engraving Tools

For these reasons, the cutting tool must have a full and comfortable handle. The actual pressure to move the tool, called a "graver," through the metal and guide it around curves and sweeps, comes primarily from the wrist and forearm, not from the fingers. The engraving tool must seat well against the heel of your palm and must be large enough for the fingers to wrap around and control the motion. At the same time, the extension of the hard, steel cutter bit should not be so long as to prevent your knuckles and thumb from resting on or against the work table.

This is not only a steadying but a checking action. When you first attempt engraving, you will be proceeding nicely with a cut only to have the tool slip and cut wildly across the metal. In serious work all is lost by such slips. The checking action against the bench can help avoid them.

The gravers themselves are shaped to produce a large variety of cuts ranging from heavy, sharp, vee-bottom grooves, to shallow, rounded bottom curves and emphasis marks. Letters generally require outlining tools for the main letter structure and finer tools for hatching and shading. Some gravers for this shading effect actually have three or four minute, vee-shaped cutting edges and produce a series of fine parallel cuts.

Although you can make up your own gravers from stock tool-steel shapes, or reformed files, it is best, at the start, to purchase the basic tools from a supply house. Even so, although you get the metal graver—handles come separately—you'll probably have to sharpen it yourself. This consists of grinding off some metal from the top face, and grinding an angle of about 45° on the tip. For some gravers, a "belly" or shallow angle

175

on the bottom of the tip is ground in first and the tip then cut at 45° and shaped. The most important part is to finish the cutting surface and sides very sharp and clean on an oilstone. The sides should be polished bright and smooth. As you experiment, you will find that sharpness is vital and that slips start to occur if the graver dulls.

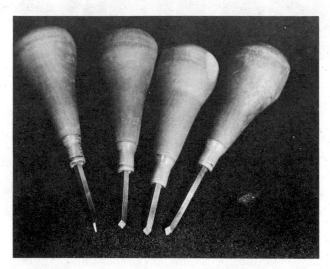

These basic engraving tools are typical of the points used for single lines, although the tool on the left is maneuvered with an oscillating or "walking" motion to produce a ripple cut.

The size of your hands will determine both the amount the graver projects from the handle and the tip angle that works best for you. Practice and trial are the keys—engraving is a highly personal art.

Holding Work
Hand engraving is very much a matter of guiding and controlling hand pressure. It follows that the work must be very solidly mounted to resist this pressure. At the same time, because of the limitations of human wrist motion, you must be able to align the direction of the cut comfortably with the pressure. For small engravings such as jewelry, trophy name plates, and the like, the professional engraver mounts the work in the jaws of a device called an "engraving block." This block, which commonly weighs about 18 or 19 pounds, is spherical on the bottom and has adjustable jaws with a selection of holding clamps for the top. This rather massive holding fixture is supported on the bench by a ring-shaped, leather pad. Thus, the spherical base is free to be canted in any direction. The upper half of the sphere is pivoted on the lower half on a smoothly working bearing. This allows the engraver to rotate the work with one hand and perform the cutting operation with the other. In a sense, the movement of the graver tool is almost in one direction while the metal is turned to make a curved cut.

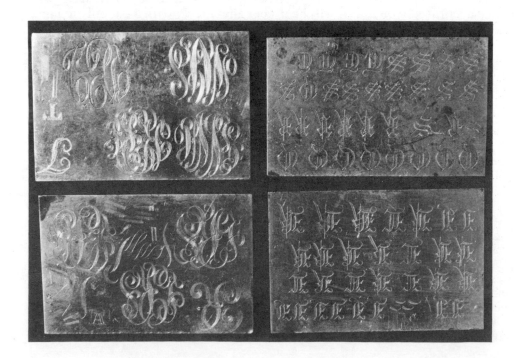

Typical practice plates of soft copper, about 2" × 4", show an advanced level of engraving skill and the wide variety of embellishments possible for a given letter.

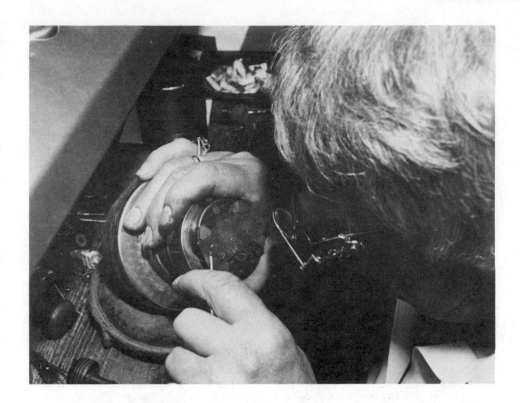

Professional engraver's block or pedestal has a very heavy, ball-shaped base seated in a soft leather, pillow-like pad, and may be tipped and turned freely. Since many engraving cuts are curved, engraver rotates work with opposite hand to produce curve.

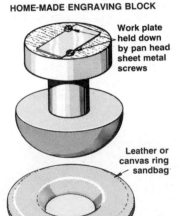

HOME-MADE ENGRAVING BLOCK

Work plate held down by pan head sheet metal screws

Leather or canvas ring sandbag

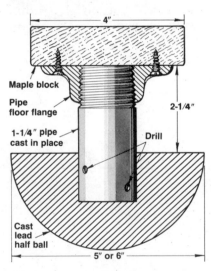

4"
Maple block
Pipe floor flange
1-1/4" pipe cast in place
Drill
2-1/4"
Cast lead half ball
5" or 6"

To get started, try making your own engraving block by casting a half-sphere of lead (see Chapter 22, Sand Casting) with a short length of metal pipe in it. A pipe flange and wooden top complete the outfit. When you mount it in a ring of leather or canvas filled with sand you'll be able to angle and position your work just as a professional engraver does. Polish ball surface and use talc or the like on the sandbag for smooth, easy swiveling.

Engraving blocks and their clamping attachments are rather costly if you just want to practice or try your hand at engraving. For this purpose you can make up a small, round work table of maple or oak and arrange a pivot bearing underneath on a base you can clamp to your bench. The pivot or bearing should have a provision to lock the table when a number of cuts are to be made in one direction. For practice, the metal can be held down by small pan-head screws, the heads just overlapping the edge. Small practice pieces of soft copper or alumi-

num about 1" × 2" will serve your purpose. The table should be of a size to permit you to work to the margins with the graver but keep your knuckles and thumb on the edge.

Laying Out Work

Even for practice, you should lay out the letters or design you wish to cut and try to follow it exactly. Such layouts are easily made if the workpiece is taped or secured to a small workboard with squared edges. Use a small square and draftsman's triangle. Steel rules and squares often scratch soft metal, so wood or plastic is better.

Lettering on bright metal is hard to follow. Spray automotive primer-surfacer or light-gray lacquer on the surface; pencil lines are easily seen on it. You can also use China white or even white shoe polish.

As with all lettering, you must resort to the sign painter's optical tricks to space the letters. If each letter is spaced exactly the same, the finished work will appear uneven. Books on lettering explain this. Above all, before cutting metal, get in the habit of checking spelling. There's nothing worse than completing a laborious job of engraving only to find a mispelled word. Remember, you can't erase engraving.

Engraving Round Objects

Although the pivoting table works fine for flat engravings, it is no good working on curved surfaces. Cups and goblets are also a challenge. Small, irregularly shaped articles are often set in jeweler's pitch in cast/iron pitch bowls. Any substantial bowl with a semispherical bottom will work. Again, a leather ring or pad into which the bowl can be nested will allow canting and turning.

For bands and round objects, you must arrange a drumlike mount on a rotating axis. As you work on each letter, the drum is rotated to bring the letter into cutting position, and locked to prevent it from rolling under the graver. Since this positioning deprives you of some hand support, I strongly recommend leaving such jobs to the pros until you have a lot of faith in your skill.

Engraving Practice

Learning to do a creditable job of engraving is no different from learning to oil paint, sculpture stone, or even make stone arrowheads. If you've ever tried the last, you may have concluded that it was impossible; yet the untold number of arrowheads found proves that it's a technique that can be learned. So it is with engraving. Try at first for full control of simple, straight cuts, even, square letters, and true vertical and horizontal lines of even depth. The fancy curliques and script can come only after you've mastered control of your hand and the graver. If you can find a teacher it will help, but only with the rudiments. After that, engraving is an individual art form.

15. LOST-WAX CASTING

For many years, the process by which the ancients made magnificent precious-metal artworks was, according to legend, a secret. Intricate figures, settings for royal jewels, and other exotic works appeared to have been formed by casting molten metal. But all the rules of conventional foundry practice were violated since these pieces were too intricate and were impossibly shaped to pack into sand and then withdrawn to leave a cavity into which metal could be poured. The truth was much less mysterious and the technique was surprisingly simple. While the art experts were wondering how it was done, roaming country dentists were trotting their horse-drawn workshops down dusty roads and making such castings every day—for tooth crowns.

The secret was a technique called "lost-wax casting," so named because the tooth crown had to be carved in wax. The wax pattern was then placed in a packing of plaster or soft clay which hardened around it. Then the mold was heated and the wax melted out. The remaining cavity exactly duplicated the original. Now, molten metal could be poured in. There were, of course, provisions for the hot wax to run out, and for hot metal to be poured or forced in. Vents were included for air and gas to escape. But that was really all there was to it.

Recently, this ancient process has been brought to an extremely high level of technology for the production of turbine blades from metals very difficult to form by other processes. It has the advantage of reproducing the original with great accuracy. If you try lost-wax casting, you may be amazed to see that minute scratches and details you hadn't noticed are reproduced cleanly.

Primitive peoples who used the wax process were artists of the first order since they had to carve the original in wax. There's nothing, of course, to keep you from doing the same. But today rings and other jewelry items are usually mass-produced from a metal form, often with multiple units of the same item "treed" together.

You, too, can produce a piece of jewelry, a small repair part for a machine, or even a copy of a rare coin with great exactitude. You will have to decide whether this is copying or creative art. In any case it's fun.

Making a Mold

When you have the object that you want to reproduce, the trick is to reproduce an exact duplicate in wax. Here, you have an advantage over the ancients. It's called molding rubber and comes in two parts like epoxy glue. After combining the two parts, you gently pour the mixture over the object, which you have confined in

You can buy RTV (Room Temperature Vulcanizing) mold rubber in quantities as small as this half-pint can. Curing agent is in bottle. Other items you'll need—wax, wax wire, and a release agent.

some sort of container—a small box or even a cardboard ring. The object must be covered on all sides and all air bubbles worked out. In 24 hours or less the mold will have cured into a tough block of rubbery material. You can make such a mold in two parts by using a parting material, but it's more common simply to slit it in half with a sharp craft knife.

Since the mold material is elastic, you can now remove the object, leaving a precisely matching cavity. If, for example, you wanted to mold something as convoluted as a walnut meat, you could, with a little care, remove it from the mold. This is impossible with sand casting.

The Wax Form

After removing the object, you can now make a duplicate, or duplicates, in wax. You must cut a passage for the wax to get in and a number of small vents for the air to get out. If you fail to vent adequately, you'll have problems with air bubbles. The two halves of the mold are now placed back together and clamped, wired, or taped firmly.

Molding wax is a special wax available in many degrees of hardness. This you buy from a jeweler's supply house together with the molding rubber and other items such as rods for

sprues and vents. The sprue is the hole into which the wax, and the metal, will be poured.

Serious lost-wax workers use a wax melting pot with a nozzle or tube to inject the hot wax under light air or hydraulic pressure. Only about 5 to 7 pounds per square inch are needed. For experimenting in the home shop, a good-sized oil can with a thumb-operated pump lever can be used to heat and inject the wax. This works fairly well if the wax is kept at flowing temperature, and if you work quickly. You simply pump the hollow mold full of wax until it exits at the vents. In a short time the wax cools and hardens. When you open the mold you should find a perfect wax duplicate of your original object.

The Plaster Mold

The next step is to make a plaster mold into which the molten metal can be poured. Although dental plaster was used for many years, and still can be, the same supply house that sold you the wax will have some improved products less given to bubbles and other problems.

Once again, you need a container, this time one that can endure heat. A clay flower pot which can be broken away later works well for experimenting. The sprues and vents can be left on the wax pattern, and you will probably want

Make up a small flask or container to receive mold rubber. Be sure rubber contacts the pattern all around without including air bubbles. Here, pattern was supported off mold board by three small brads and rubber poured in to level of top of gear

teeth. After curing and coating surface with mold release material, a second layer, seen here, was added. A sprue pin of round wax wire was then inserted and prevented from tipping by wire wax braces.

When two halves of mold have cured and been separated, the cavity should be an exact duplicate, in reverse, of pattern.

Before wax can enter mold the air must escape. Cut small channel on each edge for air passage to outside.

The methods shown here are definitely experimental. Pros would scoff at using an oil can to inject hot wax. This wax works at about 150°F. Use a glove and for best results warm the mold before injecting. Vented wax is seen at side of mold.

Crude or not, the wax pattern came out just fine. You can reuse rubber mold over and over. Make several wax patterns since you'll inevitably get good and bad castings.

Attach wax wire sprue and vents to pattern with a hot wire used like a soldering iron. Immerse pattern in plaster quickly.

Losing the Wax

The plaster must harden fully and, if possible, should be left in a warm place overnight to promote the escape of water. Water forms steam bubbles which leave voids in the casting. Now, all that's needed is to melt or burn the wax out of the plaster. Professionally, temperature controlled ovens are used for this purpose. The temperature of the mold is raised to approximately that of the metal which will be poured into it. This may require five to eight hours.

In the home shop you can at least make some experimental runs in a less sophisticated manner. Almost any convenient heat can be used, but a hot plate is recommended. Do your wax melting outdoors where the smoke and fumes can escape and where you don't have to worry about a fire hazard. Continue heating the mold

Melting and burning out the wax produces lots of smoke and smell. It's best to do it outdoors.

Add remaining plaster carefully to avoid trapping air. Use a spatula if necessary to work plaster in around wax pattern.

until all traces of wax, steam, and fumes are gone from the vents. In the meantime, start melting the metal.

Pouring the Metal

If you visit a jewelry-casting shop or a dentist's laboratory, or even the shop of a serious amateur, you'll find that the metal is forced into the mold cavity by centrifugal force. They don't, of course, use flower pots, and the mold box they use is made especially for mounting on one arm of a rig which will whirl it around while the metal is being poured. This device is counter-

to add some additional wax rods for further venting. After pouring in the plaster mix, check to be sure that all the vents reach the outside. The pattern must be completely surrounded by plaster. When mixing the plaster, it is important to avoid air bubbles and even more important to work out any that appear when you pour the plaster in.

Pour in the hot metal smoothly and without air-entraining breaks in the flow. If possible, pour while mold is still warm. Watch for metal to appear in and escape from vents, then top off with a small puddle of excess metal.

While puddle of metal is still molten, clap a container of wet asbestos over it firmly and abruptly to create steam pressure and drive metal into mold. Wear protective clothing, goggles, and gloves.

After mold is thoroughly cooled you can break away the plaster and see the result. This casting needs only the removal of the sprue and vents, plus minor cleaning, but it sometimes takes several tries to find just the right method for a given mold shape. Upper gear was from a previous mold.

balanced to run smoothly. The metal is poured into a funnel at the center and passes down the arm leading into the mold. Centrifugal force drives the metal in and forces air and gases out of the vents.

For serious lost-wax work such equipment is well worthwhile and greatly reduces the chances of spoiled castings. But for an occasional foray into lost-wax casting such equipment is costly and impractical.

Another crude but usually effective method is to use steam pressure to force the metal deep into the crannies and crevices inside the mold. To try this technique, find a shallow tin can and drive a nail through the bottom from the inside into the end of a short length of broomstick. The latter serves as a handle. Pack the can full of wet asbestos or even wet newspaper. Have it at hand as you pour the metal and allow a small puddle of molten metal to accumulate over the sprue hole. Now, instantly clamp the can over the molten metal and hold it firmly against the top of the mold. The result will be a rapid burst of steam which will drive the metal into the mold. Clearly, it pays to protect your eyes and wear gloves, but done quickly and neatly the steam process works very well.

FORMING ART METAL

Somewhere between bending sheet metal accurately for an aircraft-wing fitting and manipulating bits of gold or silver wire into decorative jewelry lies the craft of forming art metal. At its highest level, this would include silversmithing vessels and tableware; at its most modest, perhaps hammering an ash tray out of copper in a crafts class. This work is done by hand with simple tools. In short, you form a decorative or useful object by stretching or compacting metal in a cold state. Often the chosen shape is as much in your mind as on the plan, and variations by choice, accident, or creative impulse are quite acceptable.

For the home shop the use of precious metals such as gold, silver, and high-silver alloys is unlikely although they are fine working materials. Copper, brass, aluminum, nickle, silver, and pewter are less expensive and more practical, at least for the beginner. All but pewter must be worked in the soft, annealed state, and for projects requiring extended work must be annealed repeatedly. Annealing is described elsewhere in this book. With the exception of aluminum, pickling to clean and brighten the metal after annealing is routine.

Forming Operations

Before starting to form a sheet of metal into a concave-convex shape, it helps to visualize how the metal must be stretched or compacted to arrive at the final form. One way might be to think of the flat sheet as a limp, unbaked pie crust. You might drape the crust over the outside of an inverted pie tin and pull the edges down to form a pie-crust shape. Or, you might, more conventionally, place the crust inside the tin and let it sag into the depression with the edges sloping up. In both cases you'd wind up with about the same shape, and you'd have to use your hands to stretch the dough up around the rim and probably smooth out wrinkles in other areas. You might even picture another approach. Suppose that the dough is in a thick, round patty, not rolled out. Now, you could make a pie shape by molding a depression in the center and gradually working out to the edges with your fingers.

Metal, like dough, is elastic to some extent as long as it's in the annealed state. And there are usually several ways to produce the desired shape. There are also pitfalls—excessive stretching, wrinkling, buckling, and even break-

Most art-metal workers accumulate a wide variety of shaping hammers. Here are a few typical shapes. Working faces of the hammers should be kept polished and free of nicks, which would be impressed in the work metal.

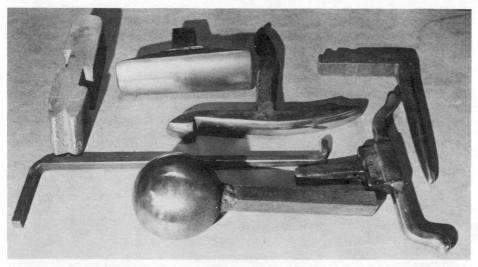

Forming stakes range from massive and solid to rather thin and springy. They may be purchased or homemade. Again, a smooth, bright surface avoids marks which would be hard to remove later.

You can make your own forming blocks with ordinary woodworking skills and equipment. These blocks are used to shape handles. Metal is silver.

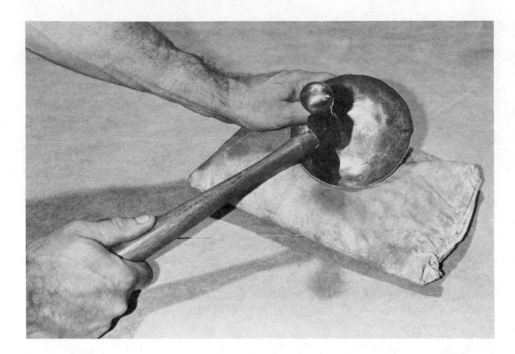

A sandbag is one type of forming backup for working soft metals with a hammer. This is primarily a roughing-out process.

throughs equivalent to sticking your thumb through dough.

Bearing the pie-crust analogy in mind, you might start forming a dish-shaped piece by using a concave depression turned, bowl-like, into a forming block. The usual technique is to hammer progressively, starting around the outer edge and moving inward in a series of concentric rings. The same results could be obtained by essentially the same procedure using a sandbag instead of a forming block. You can judge the two methods and their similarities and differences by actually trying them. Note that in both cases the inside metal is compacted and the outer surface stretched.

Exactly the opposite approach, but with es-

sentially the same results, would be using a domed, vertical stake, and hammering on the outside—stretching the metal over the the stake. All three of these methods are useful for producing relatively gentle, bowl-like curves.

Solidly mounted, firm support is helpful in forming bowl shapes by hammering. Short lengths of 4″ × 4″ lumber or larger are often available as scrap at woodworking shops. Or use a chunk of treetrunk or limb rescued from the fireplace. Develop the depressed area with a router and gouge and finish to a smooth surface with sandpaper. A few coats of linseed oil will help prevent checking and splitting:

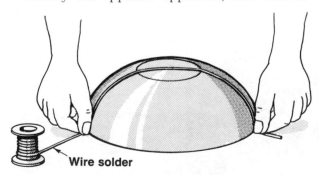

Wire solder

To determine size of flat metal stock you'll need to form an irregular or bowl-shaped piece, apply soft wire solder to the surface, pushing into curves; when straightened it will give you the size of the work metal. Provide an extra margin for trimming later rather than wind up slightly short.

Use your ingenuity to devise modifications of the basic process for concave forming. Here, again, a heavy piece of wood has been shaped as a form, but dowels act as a guide for the flat flange or rim. With this technique you'll tend to get buckling of the flat rim and inner face, and if allowed to continue while working you'll lose the accuracy of the rim dimension. To avoid this, flatten the rim and inner face periodically as you work by gentle tapping on a flat surface. Anneal frequently since this type of contour asks more flowing action of the metal than does a simple bowl with all surfaces curved.

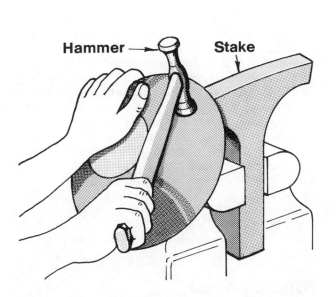

Hammer ← → **Stake**

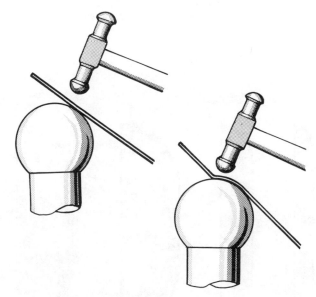

Forming a concave surface over a stake is just the opposite of forming into a depressed form. The process, sometimes called "raising," involves some of the same techniques—laying out the metal in concentric circles, working around each circle in turn, and avoiding overworking in spot areas. There are two tricks for successful raising: (1) start at the center and work out; (2) strike so the hammer impacts just "over the crest of the hill" and forces the metal down against the stake contour. If you hit right on the point of contact between metal and stake you'll only produce a thin spot. Beginners have trouble with the metal slipping so it slides on the stake as the hammer hits. Hold it firmly; in time your grip on the metal and the hammer blow will fall into an automatic rhythm of grip, strike, reposition, grip, and strike again.

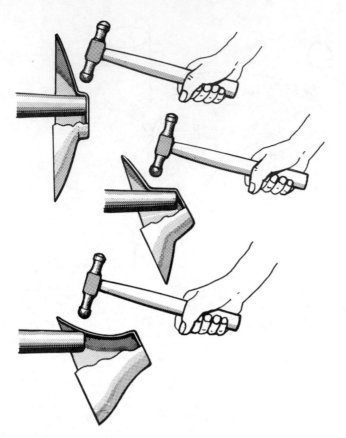

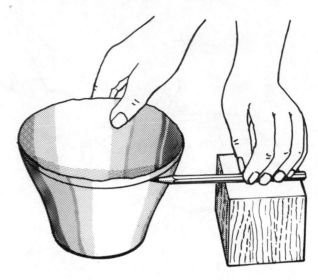

A pencil and a block make a sort of surface gage to establish a trim line for the finished edge. That part is easy, but it takes some extra care to cut around the line evenly with curved aviation snips. To bring the edge to final flat and square, use a fine belt on a belt sander, or place a piece of abrasive paper on a flat surface such as a bench-saw top or glass and work the edge on the abrasive in a figure-8 pattern. After squaring, soften the edge with very fine abrasive.

Forming metal over a hornlike stake permits development of many shapes. Always work from the inside towards the edge. Practice, with frequent annealing as you go, until you establish an inner feel for the way the metal will move. The hazards— thin spots, splits, wrinkles, and lack of symmetrical form.

Tighter Curves

Often a shaped vessel requires a sharper and tighter curve, or almost a corner, at the juncture of the flat surface of the bottom and the upward sweeping sides. In fact, at least one side of such a curve may be quite sharp to form a "reveal" or distinct break in planes. This type of curve may be formed by repeated tapping with a suitable peining hammer while the metal is slowly turned along a shaped forming block. Commercially made metal-forming stakes with a variety of radii and edge configurations are available, but it's educational and satisfying to make your own blocks from hardwood. Remember, when you are hammering the metal into a grooved pattern, each blow must stretch the metal slightly. The trick is to keep the stretching effect going evenly all around the work so that no section becomes too thin and so you don't build in metal tensions which distort the basic shape. When in doubt, stop and anneal.

Flattening Metal

In the metalsmith's language, the final operation to remove minor hammer marks, bulges, wrinkles, and ripples, is called "planishing." Planishing hammers are flattening hammers with a broad, almost flat face suited to large flat areas. They do not work well on a surface blending

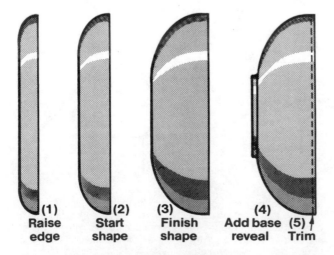

(1) Raise edge   **(2)** Start shape   **(3)** Finish shape   **(4)** Add base reveal   **(5)** Trim

Working art metal is a sequential operation. You don't do it all at once. The sequence shown is basic to most concave shapes.

into a curve. Thus, they must be chosen for the correct shape for what you want to do. One mis-strike in which the edge of the hammer head impacts a curved surface can be quite disastrous. There are times when prudence suggests forming a hardwood block to fit the work area and striking it rather than striking the metal directly. Flat blocks also do a good job of flatten-

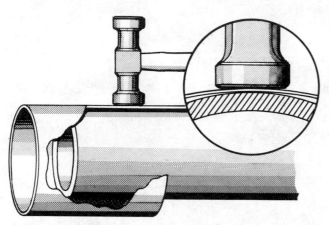

Planishing is a finishing process used to work out the visible hammer marks and small inequities left from forming. Highly polished hammers with faces suited to the work contour are used; the stake, too, must be polished and free of nicks if the interior of the work is to be seen. The cylinder shown here illustrates the process. Note that the stake curvature is slightly tighter than the work, and a flat hammer face is in use. For a flat surface a slightly curved face would be used. Here's a hint—place a light off to one side so it shines across the face of the metal. This relief lighting will make it easier to see the spots that need striking.

ing lightly rippled flat surfaces if you have a smooth, flat support surface for the opposite side.

Cheating or Technique?

Among some purists in metalworking the use of abrasives or files to clean up a finished piece of work is a complete negation of the creative art. They feel that the minor hammer and tool marks and visible flaws in shape are testimony to the act of handcrafting the piece.

Other metalworkers couldn't care less about such niceties and will work diligently to remove all tool marks. Few of the latter group would feel proud if you could spot hammer marks on the panel of a restored car or similar part expected to be smooth.

The views of the two groups may be unreconcilable, but the following techniques are routine and work well if what you're after is a slick finish rather than art. If you have ever watched the steps in straightening out a damaged car fender or body panel, you may have felt that the operation was hopeless to start with. Yet, in a short while, after a few initial pushes and pulls with a hydraulic jack to bring things back to approximate shape, the body man goes to work with hammers and backup blocks, called "dollies," and by judicious hammering reshapes the metal very much as the craft worker shapes a vessel. Pictures of a part of this process are shown in the section on pullers in Chapter 4. But the body man will never spend hours tapping away each minute hammer mark once he has reached a point where most of the surface is close to what it should be. At this stage he will skim over the surface with a power sander, either a disc or one with a long, flat pad to show up the high spots. Once again, he will try to bring up the low spots and reduce the high spots by hammering and again sand the metal to check results.

If there are areas where the surface is nearly smooth, he may elect to use the power sander to clean up any remaining minor high spots. Admittedly, this leaves thick and thin areas in the metal, but the final surface to be painted looks fine.

In the case of deep dents and grooves or puller damage, the body man will use a filler, probably of the epoxy type, and later sand that down to fill out the contour. I'm not recommending body filler for art-metal work, but abrasives can do wonders.

Obviously, some metal may be too thin for aggressive cleanup with abrasives. If you want to use this method, you should start with fairly thick stock. That was the way handcrafted aircraft-wheel pants and cowlings were made. Often the shapes and contours exceeded the potential for stretching or compaction and it was necessary to cut out vee-shaped openings to remove or add metal as you went. These joints were welded and the weld beads ground down to leave an unblemished surface.

The same techniques can be used to clean up crafted copper, brass, and aluminum projects. Strips of cloth-backed abrasive, orbital sanders, and belt sanders all can be used to surface the metal for a final polishing or buffing. If this be cheating, so be it.

PART IV
ADVANCED
TOOLS AND
TECHNIQUES

17. BENCH GRINDERS

As I pointed out when discussing sharpening twist drills, the single indispensable tool for metalworking is the bench grinder. I feel that this is also true for woodworking—how else could you sharpen chisels and plane irons efficiently? But in metalworking, you use the grinder not only for sharpening, but also as a prime shaping and forming tool. In this respect, of course, it is analogous to the various sanders used in woodworking.

If you have a choice I'd certainly recommend buying the best 6″ bench grinder you can afford. Your best source is an industrial tool supply shop. If you inspect the modestly priced grinders usually offered by hardware stores you'll see that although they may be suited to sharpening knives and lawnmower blades now and then they do not have the solid bearings and rigid housings really needed when you have a piece of ⅜″ steel and want to shape it extensively.

Many of these bargain grinders, in fact, have only sleeve bearings and plastic housings and bases. Some have only small snap rings set into annular grooves in the shaft to support the end thrust of the wheels. This can be dangerous, since any loosening or imbalance of the wheel can fling a piece of the abrasive stone into your face. Anyone with common sense will always wear eye protection while grinding and will develop the habit of standing out of line with the wheel at all times, but it's impossible to grind safely with an unsafe machine.

Most good grinders have a double-ended armature shaft so you can mount two stones of different grits, or maybe a wire brush or buffing wheel in combination with the abrasive wheel. Before buying a grinder, insist upon seeing the parts list and exploded view that should come with it. This will tell you what's inside the nicely painted housing. Look for a motor housing that's sealed or protected against the entrance of metallic grindings. Each end housing should contain sealed ball bearings, and on the shaft, outboard of these bearings, should be a husky collar on the shaft to back up the wheel washer when you tighten the wheel-retaining nut. Take special note of the washers that support the wheel on each side. These washers are very critical, since they locate, drive, and support what is essentially a rather fragile ceramic wheel. Note, also, that one of the threaded shaft ends will have right-hand threads and the other left-hand threads so that the force of the work against the wheel will tend to tighten, rather than loosen, the nuts.

A good grinder will have a smooth, rigid, adjustable tool rest on each side to permit adjustment of grinding angles when sharpening tools. Directly above the expected grinding contact point a better-grade grinder will have a heavy

Bench grinder is basic to all metalworking. Without it you can't even sharpen tools. This double-end shaft model takes 6" wheels, has safety eye shields, and a light

grinders are needed only for cleaning up heavy castings or weldments, in which hogging away a lot of metal in a hurry is helpful. Fractional-hp grinders will normally turn about 3,450 rpm. If you examine the label glued to an abrasive wheel you'll see that each wheel is rated for operation at a definite maximum speed. These labels are usually made of a paper resembling blotting paper; this paper helps seat the wheel firmly all around, supporting it evenly in spite of minor blemishes on the wheel washers. In a sense, the labels have a cushioning effect. Never remove such labels unless they become dam-

Typical grinding wheel for home shop use is 6" in diameter, ¾" thick, and has a ½" bore. Aluminum oxide is a good general-purpose abrasive, but for tool sharpening this stone is a bit too coarse. Blotter-paper label shows rotational speed limits, but it's more than just a label. Padding action is important to safe and secure mounting of the wheel.

transparent shield, and the wheel will be enclosed all around except for a small area at the front. A light, although handy, is not an essential feature.

Matching the Wheel to the Grinder

For practical home-shop use, your bench grinder seldom needs more than a ⅓-hp motor, although a ½-hp motor is not too much if you work with large, heavy stock. Heavier, more powerful

GRINDING WHEEL MARKINGS
32A46–H8VBE

Abrasive	Grit Size				Grade			Structure	Bond Type	Norton Symbol
Alundum = A				**Very**				The structure	V = Vitrified	Letter of numeral
19 Alundum = 19A	**Coarse**	**Medium**	**Fine**	**Fine**	**Soft**	**Medium**	**Hard**	number of a wheel	S = Silicate	or both to desig-
23 Alundum = 23A	10	30	70	220	A E	I M	Q V	refers to the rela-	B = Resinoid	nate a variation
32 Alundum = 32A	12	36	80	240	B F	J N	R W	tive spacing of	R = Rubber	or modification of
38 Alundum = 38A	14		90	280	C G	K O	S X	the grains of	E = Shellac	bond or other
44 Alundum = 44A	16	46	100	320	D H	L P	T Y	abrasive; the larger		characteristic of
57 Alundum = 57A	20	54	120	400			U Z	the number, the		the wheel. Typi-
75 Alundum = 75A	24	60	150	500				wider the grain		cal symbols are
37 Crystolon = 37C			180	600				spacing.		"P," "G," "BE."
39 Crystolon = 39C										

Grinding wheels almost always show their nominal diameter and maximum operating speed. Most also carry a code indicating the abrasive, grit size, and bond, but it's often difficult to be certain of the meaning because of the differences in maker's codes. If in doubt you'll have to obtain the details of the code from the wheel maker.

aged. If you must replace them always use circular blotting-paper cutouts made for this purpose.

The wheel, its cutting characteristics, and the motor should all be matched for a given wheel diameter and surface speed. It is not uncommon for beginning metalworkers to home-build a grinder with a salvaged motor, often 1,725-rpm, and use a vee-belt to drive a shaft mounted in a bearing pedestal. Such units are better than nothing, but be sure your pulley ratio is right to produce the proper rotational speed for the wheel.

Wheel Supports

Some grinding wheels are built with lead cores that are bored accurately to fit on the grinder shaft. Others have oversize bores and must be bushed to center them on the shaft. You can buy plastic bushings or shouldered discs to seat them. Certain hazards exist with these shouldered plastic bushings. Note that approved-type retaining washers are recessed near the hub to provide a clamping action on the wheel at some distance from the center. If the bushings are a little worn and the washers do not hold them in place, the bushings could escape from their centering location. This is most likely to happen if

the washers are of the shallow, dish-shaped, stamped-metal type.

Grinder Safety

I've tried to emphasize the inherent hazards of the apparently simple bench grinder. You need to experience only one wheel "blowup" to appreciate my cautions. Each element of the grinder—bearings, shaft, stones, bushings, supporting washers, housing, and tool rests—must be of good quality and properly assembled and mounted.

One important rule is to observe the operation of the grinder every time you turn it on. *Never* stand directly in front when you start the motor. Ideally, the motor and stones will come up to speed and rotate smoothly. Some grinders, perhaps because of their mounting or the combination of stones, will shudder or vibrate briefly as they come up to speed and again when they slow down after they are shut off. This type of harmonic vibration is often difficult to cure, and if it is only brief and transitory, and if the machine runs smoothly at operating speed, it can be tolerated. Any vibration that lasts over a second or that is detectable while grinding is cause for immediate shutdown. Don't even try to finish the job. Flip off the switch and stand clear. The

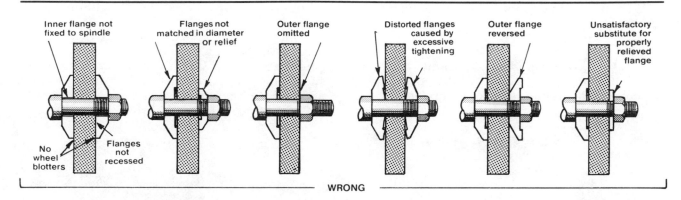

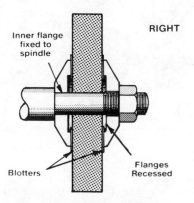

Mounting a grinding wheel properly is essential to its safe use. Proper side support from washers is very important. Here are right and wrong ways to do it.

condition must be corrected. Sometimes you'll find a chipped or unbalanced wheel. In other cases the bushings are damaged or loose; perhaps the paper discs are scarred, peeled, or wadded; or the motor may be losing a bearing.

Supporting work safely. It's easy to flip on the grinder for a casual job and not bother to adjust the tool rest. For nearly all jobs the tool rest or work support should be close and almost touching the wheel. Leaving a gap between the rest and the wheel is an invitation to disaster, since the work may be dragged down into the gap. This will damage the work, and it can also break the wheel and possibly drag your fingers in between the wheel and the tool rest.

Other snatching or grabbing actions can occur, not only on the grinding stone, but also with the wire brush and particularly with the buffing wheel. This happens so fast that there's no time to react; the work will be flung violently to the floor or at you. The usual cause is attempting to hold the work freehand. A freehand grip may be fine for a large workpiece like a casting or a bowl that can be gripped solidly in both hands. It is not so good for smaller items. These can sometimes be locked in Vise-Grips or some other holding fixture. The best protection, though admittedly it is not always possible, is to rest the work firmly on the tool rest and introduce it gradually to the wheel. Even so, protect yourself at all times and be prepared for an accident.

Wheel Dressing
Inevitably, grinding wheels become rounded, grooved, loaded, and glazed so they cut poorly. Wheel dressing removes the outer grains of abrasive and presents a fresh, true, sharp cutting surface.

The best abrasive wheel dressers use industrial diamonds, but most home shops settle for a dresser with a series of toothed wheels that work almost as well. Since it is quite possible for a wheel to become slightly out of round, the ideal truing procedure requires that the dressing tool be braced firmly against the tool rest and guided by a straightedge that lets you move the dresser across the wheel face evenly. Use a gentle approach so if there are high spots you'll clean them off first and gradually bring the wheel back to round. At other times a simple cleaning up of the wheel is adequate and resting the tool on the tool rest serves the purpose.

Portable Grinders
Many metalworking jobs are just too heavy, awkward, or unhandy to permit holding them to a grinding wheel safely. There are a number of practical solutions.

For light work you can use an arbor and a small stone in an electric drill. Or you can use a flexible shaft and suitable wheel. Once again, the characteristics of metal make these tactics unpleasant and possibly dangerous. The hard grinding wheel wants to bounce and jump on the work, and you cannot hold the relationship of the wheel to the work constant. For this kind of job a semiflexible abrasive disc, backed up with a rubber or other stiff but yielding pad, is much better.

If larger metal projects are your bent, try to acquire a Milwaukee portable grinder or its equivalent. Although this is heavy equipment, such tools are extremely rugged and powerful and will do a fast job of cutting down an edge,

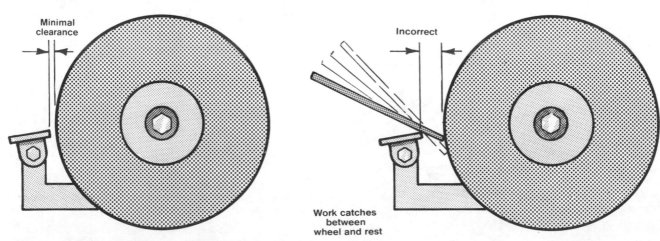

Adjusting the rest is the first step in safe grinding. In addition to adjusting the angle for the job involved, be sure to bring the rest in close to the wheel.

Too much space between the wheel and the rest can cause a very serious accident. Take time to adjust the rest safely.

Wheel dresser of this type can be purchased at any hardware store. For routine, quick cleanups, it may be used as shown, but if wheel is out of round a steadying guide is needed.

Milwaukee grinder is a powerful tool for all types of grinding where grinder must be brought to work. In this picture an abrasive disc is being used to straighten the edge of a roughly cut sheet of metal prior to layout.

removing rust or weld metal, and surfacing large areas. Be cautious with them. Their very powerful motors will coast for some time after you release the trigger, and the abrasive disc keeps on spinning. If you lower the tool to the bench top or floor while the disc is spinning, it can whirl around and strike you with the edge of the disc. The effect is about the same as being hit by a buzz saw. And if you are holding it in your hands and let it swing down against your leg it will bite deeply and produce a nasty wound.

Abrasive discs. Since portable grinders are so widely used in industry for everything from cleaning rough castings to finishing auto body work, there is an enormously wide selection of abrasive discs to choose from. You will seldom find such discs in hardware stores, but any store that sells auto-body tools or industrial tools will have a fine choice. Typically, these discs are intended for mounting on a pad with a recessed center so there is no protruding nut to strike the work. Try to stick to discs and pads that are made for your brand of grinder.

18. DRILL PRESSES

Certainly the first heavier power tool you should consider, after a bench grinder, is a drill press. The chuck should be a Jacobs key type or the equivalent. The table should be solid cast iron, not pressed metal or aluminum, because rigidity is important. A light pressed-steel or die-cast table will spring enough under drilling pressure to make accurate drilling in metal impossible, although this type of machine may serve for wood.

A drill press is essentially a means of rotating a cutting tool mounted to a firm, but movable, vertical axis with the work supported in an accurate plane relative to the tool. It is about as basic as you can get in metalworking. The immediate uses of this versatile machine are drilling, starting taps (turning the chuck by hand), reaming, surface grinding, drum or spindle grinding, and similar jobs.

Milling with a drill press. With the addition of a wonderful device called a universal compound vise you can perform a number of operations that would otherwise require a milling machine or at least a metal-cutting lathe. This novel vise bolts securely to the drill-press table and not only holds the work but also allows you to crank it along slowly to feed the work into a cutter. This means you can use your drill press to cut slots, dovetails, keyways, flats, and tee-slots in

metal. The results will seldom be as perfect as in a milling machine or a lathe, but they will probably be adequate. The reason they won't be quite perfect is that old bugaboo of metalworking—rigidity and the pressure required. A drill-press column is designed to exert vertical pressure on a drill. It's not really intended to take the heavy side thrust of milling. Lathe and milling-machine bearings are intended to resist side thrust, and for this reason they handle such jobs better. Even so, milling can be done very successfully in a drill press as long as you keep the cuts light.

Surface grinding with cup wheels, work with rotary grinders and rotary files, and many other jobs can be done on this remarkable and simple machine as long as you keep everything mounted and secured firmly.

Drill-press chucks. In the above discussion I mentioned the side pressure involved in milling. Over the years there have been several ways used to secure the chuck of the drill press to the rotating shaft. In some light drill presses the chuck is threaded on the shaft in the same manner as the chuck on a small electric drill. More commonly, however, chucks have been attached by the use of a Morse taper. Morse tapers are standard tapers widely used in machine tools. The tapered male shaft fits precisely into a matching taper in the female part to provide an efficient, highly accurate, and firm grip on the tool. Yet it releases instantly when the parts are tapped or wedged apart.

This works fine for holding chucks used only for drilling, since the force on the drill is directly in line with the rotating shaft. Trying to use the same chuck for a tool receiving side thrust such as a sanding drum, rotary file, or milling cutter spells trouble and danger. Sooner or later the chuck and tool will come off the shaft and prob-

After you've acquired a grinder to sharpen your twist drills, the next tool of choice should be a drill press to align, rotate, and provide pressure for the drill. Look for one with cast-iron parts and massive construction for rigidity.

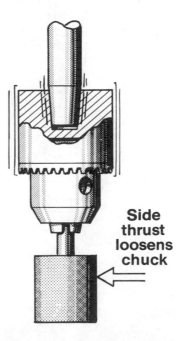

Side thrust loosens chuck

Tapered shank and chuck socket work fine for straight-on end loads but may release instantly and dangerously when subjected to side thrust.

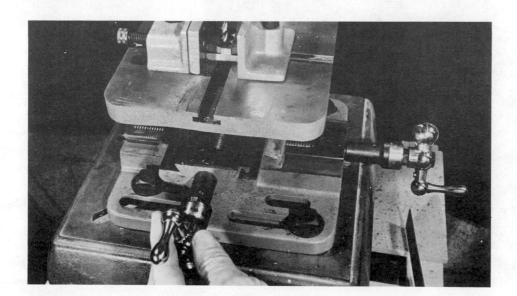

By adding a movable work table, called a compound vise, work can be shifted precisely, and your drill press can perform light milling accurate to one-thousandth of an inch.

ably bounce wildly about your shop. They may very well strike you, or your hand may be hit by the spinning cutting tool.

Some drill chucks have a threaded boss at the top and a collar on the shaft that can be tightened down to pull and hold the chuck on the

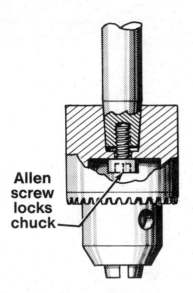

Allen screw locks chuck —

If your drill press lacks a means of locking the chuck in place, you may want to drill and tap for a retaining screw.

taper. This arrangement is safe and satisfactory. There are also collet chucks that thread on in this manner and have selective collets in fractional sizes to receive the arbors or shanks of tools. This arrangement is also safe but a bother because you're constantly changing from one type of chuck to another.

If your drill press has none of these means to secure the chuck, there's an old-timer's trick that solves the problem. First, use a spare chuck, or even a drill-press vise with a vee-block, to mount a ¼"-20 tap drill, ¹³⁄₆₄" in an inverted position under the drill-press chuck. Carefully close the chuck jaws until they are a free-running fit on the drill. Start the drill press at low speed and slowly lower the chuck with the feed handle so the drill penetrates the inner wall of the chuck and enters the end of the shaft. Drill about 1¼" or 1½" deep into the shaft. After drilling, remove the chuck, mount a ¼"-20 tap vertically so it feeds into the hole in the shaft, and gently turn the shaft by hand to cut threads. Follow with a bottoming tap.

There's another trick to make this easier if the drill-press shaft is hard. Go in first with a #14-20 tap that is slightly smaller than a ¼"-20 but is the right pitch to get the threads established. Follow with the ¼"-20. Finally, drill out the hole in the chuck to ¼", carefully remove all chips from the chuck and shaft, and install the chuck. Now you can install a ¼"-20 Allen screw inside

Collet chuck, rather than Jacobs-type chuck, is safer for heavy side loading.

the chuck to secure it firmly in place. Your drill press is now much safer.

Drill-Press Controls

If a drill press is your first venture into "machine" power tools, you'll find that unlike hand-held tools they have at least a few controls and adjustments to make your work easier and more accurate. First, of course, you can adjust the rotating speed by a series of step pulleys, or, on some recently introduced presses, by dial-in electronic controls.

Spindle return.   Most drill presses will also have some type of spring-loaded spindle-return device. When you release or ease up on the handle after drilling, this returns the chuck to the full-up position. If you experiment a little and release the return spring totally, you'll find that the weight of the chuck and the spindle makes the feed handle feel heavy and the whole action is uncomfortable. Tighten the retraction spring until the tension just balances the weight, and it feels better. Add a little more retraction so the chuck rises freely when you release the handle and you'll have it about right. Once set, it's seldom necessary to readjust and you'll become accustomed to the feel of the pressure needed for different jobs.

Depth stop.   The depth stop is an extremely useful and necessary feature. With it you can preset the depth to which you want to drill, establish the cutting level of a milling cutter or grinder, and avoid damaging or dangerous plunges into the stock. It is very important that the depth stop be of the type you can set accurately and lock securely. The normal vibration of cutting can cause creeping and errors if the stop is not secure.

Column lock.   It is also important to be able to lock the column anywhere in its travel if you do milling, routing, or surface grinding. The lock should flip on and off positively, and the control handle should be near your hand, not up behind the feed lever or elsewhere. There is seldom a way to control the vertical feed depth of a drill press with real accuracy. If, for example, you are using an end mill and you want to drop the depth to feed into the metal .003″ deeper, you can leave the lock engaged and bump the feed lever down with your hand. This may approximate what you want, but it may also cause an accident by overfeeding. If you want to be truly accurate you can mount a dial indicator and measure the increased feed depth. Still another way is to make a cut, slide a piece of paper, or several pieces, all of known thickness, under the work, and build up, so to speak, an increase in feed depth. As an example, this works fine when cup-grinding jointer blades.

Drill-Press Tables

Drill-press tables are normally adjustable for height on the column to accommodate varying

Step pulley is the usual way of adjusting drill press spindle speed, but lowest speed is generally adequate for most metalworking.

Adjust the spindle-return spring so the chuck floats freely and rises gently from the work when you release the feed handle.

Here, the drill press is being used as a grinder to sharpen a woodworking jointer blade. By adding one layer of thin paper under blade holder on each pass, feed is increased about .002".

Tilting table is a vaulable feature found on only a few drill presses. Here it's holding work to angle-mill a counterbore.

Although experienced metalworkers will recognize that this piece could have been hand-held for drilling, it was important to locate the drill on an accurate center. Clamps are always better.

work size and varying drill and tool lengths, and to position your work. Many such tables are quite heavy and something of a struggle to lift by brute force, especially if you have a milling vise mounted. If you find the table adjustment too hard, see if you can get an accessory with a counterbalance and a ratchet-and-winch action that attaches to the table and the column head.

Until recently, nearly all drill-press tables not only could be raised and lowered but also could be tilted through any angle up to 90° off the vertical axis of the drill. Although for precision it is necessary to make this adjustment with a bevel protractor against the drill or other tool, the tilt table is extremely useful. It is claimed that the same results can be obtained from a drill-press vise with an angle feature, but this is not quite true, since many larger pieces that cannot be gripped in the vise can be clamped to the tilting table.

Slots for clamps and bolts are also standard on most drill presses. Use them. For most jobs it is adequate to slip a C-clamp through a slot and grip the workpiece. Always use at least two clamps to avoid canting the work. In other cases you may have to resort to bolts and homemade clamps, since quite often C-clamps just don't have the reach or fail to seat securely.

Drilling large pieces.   Although the size of your drill-press table may suit most jobs, there will be times when you wish it were larger because the workpiece overhangs and is difficult to hold. Most metalworkers soon work out a solution by fitting a thick piece of hardboard or countertop material so it will go back around the column and clamp to the table from underneath. If this is still inadequate, as when drilling a long rail or other extended work, take the time to arrange an outboard support. Sometimes another machine such as a band saw can be pulled into place and the end of the work blocked up on it for support. Sometimes a stepladder can be used. The important point to remember is that if you try to support and balance an oversize workpiece by hand you are almost certain to break drills and do inaccurate work.

19. BAND SAWS

As explained in Chapter 6, hand hacksaws, jeweler's saws, and even carbide-tipped table saws can often be used to cut metal. Very often a saber saw is handy for roughing out stock from large sheets. These tools, however, become tedious, inaccurate, and plain hard work if you have a thick piece of metal or bar stock to cut or shape before, for example, mounting it in your lathe.

Suppose, for instance, you want to turn a narrow spacer ring from a 4"-diameter piece of brass stock. First you have to trim off ½" of material from a larger billet. This would be a formidable task by hand, although once the cut is made it may take only a few minutes to turn the ring to size. The answer is power sawing equipment.

Ideally, we'd all have an industrial metal-cutting band saw in our shop. Few of us do, since they cost thousands of dollars. No matter; by simply mounting a speed reducer on a woodworking band saw of the home-shop variety and installing a metal-cutting blade you can cut metal with amazing ease and speed. Since your speed reducer will probably have only one speed, much slower than for cutting wood, you will not be able to select the optimum blade

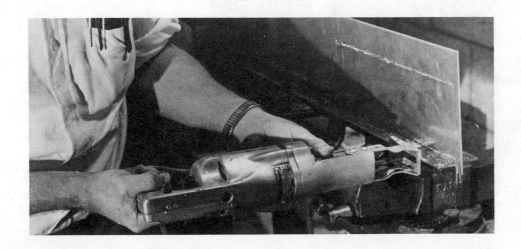

Heavy-duty Milwaukee Sawzall used with an angle-iron guide permits accurate sawing on this ⅛" metal. Small holes were drilled to provide initial entrance for blade.

travel in feet per minute, but you'll get by just fine. You'll learn that some metals, such as aluminum, clog the blade, and that a wax-type lube such as Johnson's stick wax, made for this purpose, helps. And you'll learn to secure the work in a drill-press vise or clamp to keep from burning your fingers on long, heavy cuts. But with a narrow, ¼" blade you'll be able to follow fairly complex curves and shape your metal fairly close to finished form on your band saw.

For those who want to go a step further, there are modestly priced band saws made especially for metal cut-off. These saws are often mounted so they are horizontal, or almost so, and the work is clamped to a table so the saw can be lowered into the work rather than the work pushed into the saw. The Rigid Portable band saw shown is a small but practical size; it will work efficiently to hew out workpieces from rough bar and angle stock up to 4" on a side. By clamping the work in successive positions you can work larger pieces from both sides. Just as for hacksaws, the rule for band saws is to use a blade that will place at least two, and preferably three, teeth on the metal.

Joining Blades

Metal-cutting band-saw blades may be purchased to size, welded in a continuous loop, ready to use. Or you can buy bulk blade material and join your own. A third choice is to buy bulk and have the dealer weld the ends electrically. The welding process is quick and neat; indus-

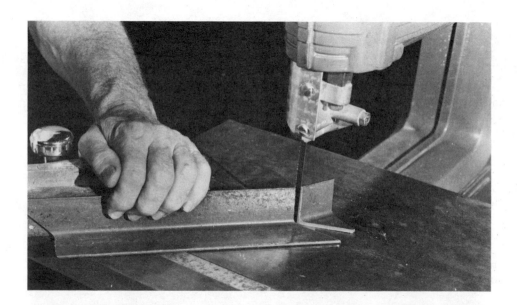

Home-shop woodworking band saw, fitted with a speed reducer and metal-cutting blade, is probably the greatest labor saver you'll find for metalworking. It certainly beats hacksawing.

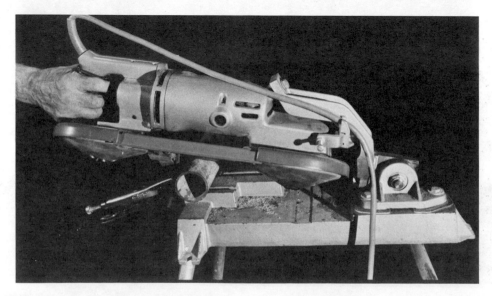

Although this Rigid band saw is portable and may be removed from stand for metal cutting somewhat in the manner of a chainsaw, its greatest use is for cutting off sections of heavy stock.

trial band saws usually have the welding devices built in. The outfit consists of two clamps that position the blade ends together and an electrical resistance circuit that quickly brings them to welding heat. At this moment the two ends are forced together to make a weld. A lower level of heat is used as a follow-up to anneal the joint. The slight bulge at the weld line is ground away to make an invisible joint.

This is fine, but there are times when you'll break a blade and want to repair it on the spot. Band-saw blades were brazed or silver-soldered together long before they were electrically welded, and the process is perfectly practical in the home shop. To go about it, square off the ends by grinding, and then with a file or grinder scarf or taper back for about ⅜" on each end so the tapered faces will overlap without creating a hump. Use a steel block to assure a flat surface and place a piece of asbestos paper on it. Place and clamp the blade ends so the bright, tapered faces are up but not touching. This requires twisting the blade temporarily, since one end will be "up" and, ultimately, the other "down."

Use a suitable gas torch to bring the metal to brazing or silver-soldering heat, apply flux, and tin or coat each tapered face with a thin layer of silver solder or brazing rod. Do not heat any more than needed to get a quick, even flow. Allow the ends to cool.

Now, bring the two faces together, without any twist in the blade, of course, and clamp them so they are in perfect alignment. The previous deposit of joining metal will hold them apart slightly. Heat the joint until the metal in it flows, then quickly press down firmly on the joint with the top of a spike or something similar to force out excess metal. Hold the faces solidly together until the metal cools.

All that remains is to dress off any excess metal with a file so that the back edge is straight and there is no excess thickness at the joint. In my experience such joints are as good as welded ones.

Blade Guides

One reason that the blade joint must be dressed to the same thickness as the rest of the blade is obviously that it must pass through the same saw kerf, and excess thickness would cause binding. But since the saw teeth have a set, the kerf is slightly wider than the saw thickness anyway, and the really critical point is the blade-guide clearance. Band saws have different types of blade guides. Some are bars of soft, low-friction material; some are one or another form of rollers. They all serve the same purpose. Those on the sides keep the blade aligned and hold it fairly true without twisting when you turn the work to follow a line. The back guides stiffen and back up the blade as you apply cutting pressure. They

When you've done it a few times you'll find that joining a band-saw blade is easy. The secrets—an evenly tapered scarf on each end; a thin, even, tinning coat without lumps; and a guide to keep the back of the blade aligned and straight.

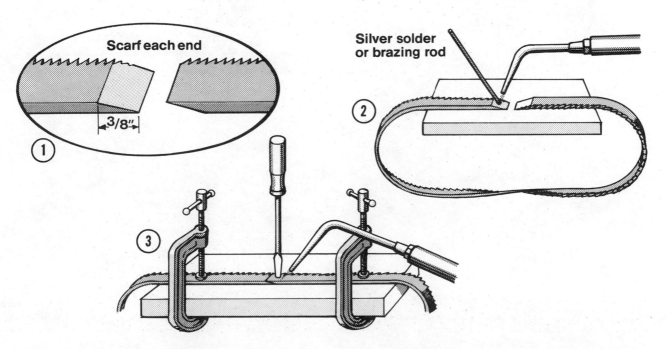

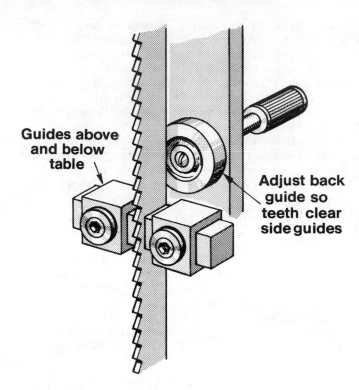

Guides above and below table

Adjust back guide so teeth clear side guides

Sawing metal is no problem with a band saw, but following the line requires that the blade guides be closely spaced to the saw blade to prevent twisting.

should be adjusted so the saw teeth are held forward and just clear of the side guides. The side guides or rollers must be adjusted, top and bottom, with the blade snug and straight. The usual technique is simply to bring them in until they just touch the blade without forcing it in any direction. After adjusting, check the back guides again by pulling the blade around a few inches by hand and gently forcing the blade back against the guides to see that both top and bottom guides help support the blade and that the teeth just clear the side guides.

If your saw has friction-type guides that are worn or uneven, replace them before sawing metal. The guides hold the blade in its proper cutting plane, and guiding the saw in metal demands that the blade be held quite solidly to avoid twisting.

20. METAL LATHES

The metal-cutting lathe is the grandfather of all metalworking tools. In woodworking, most lathe turning is decorative, but in metalworking, it is basic. In part, this stems from the fact that so many metal parts such as shafts and bearings are round. Nearly every piece of machinery has parts that turn in bearings, pivot, or slide in cylinders.

Thus, the principle of mounting a piece of metal between two centers and rotating it against a pointed tool, or holding the metal fixed and rotating the tool inside it, allows even a primitive shop in the most remote corner of the earth to create or repair a round surface. This is one of the objections to the Wankel engine and other engines that use cams rather than crankshafts. The most rudimentary equipment can return a crankshaft or rebore a cylinder, because the finished form is circular. But the oddly shaped interior of the Wankel engine requires computer-controlled cutting operations to generate the mathematically calculated contours. There's no way to bore it oversize in the field.

As you may gather from the above, if you're more familiar with wood lathes, boring out internal cavities and cylinders to precise dimensions impossible with a drill is an important function of a metal lathe. It ranks equally with outside turning. To that, add the function of

holding tools such as drills, reamers, and taps and the lathe has entirely new dimensions.

But that's not all. Mount a cutter in the headstock and provide a suitable vise where the cutting tool usually goes, and you can now feed the work into and across the cutter to produce flat surfaces, slots, keyways, and complex internal cavities and external shapes. This is called milling. Truly, the metal-cutting lathe is a tool of all uses.

Screw-Cutting Lathes

Here, one must distinguish between lathes that can cut threads and those that cannot. In my earlier discussion of hand tools and taps and dies I pointed out that once you reach a certain size, about ½", it becomes difficult to cut threads by hand. Although much larger taps and dies, driven by powerful machines, are used in industrial shops, they're not really practical in the home shop.

This problem inspired a man named Henry Maudslay to invent the screw-cutting lathe back in 1800. The principle seems simple enough: Rotate a piece of round stock and move a pointed tool along it to produce vee-shaped threads at an accurate, fixed spacing. The concept is as clear as winding a kite string around a broom-

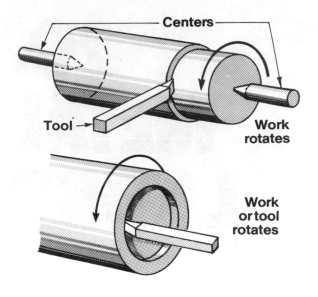

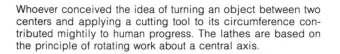

Whoever conceived the idea of turning an object between two centers and applying a cutting tool to its circumference contributed mightily to human progress. The lathes are based on the principle of rotating work about a central axis.

Roughing cut in a metal lathe shows the action of the cutting tool as it moves from right to left. Different metals machine in different ways. This particular alloy steel produces a stringy cut and leaves a slightly rough surface.

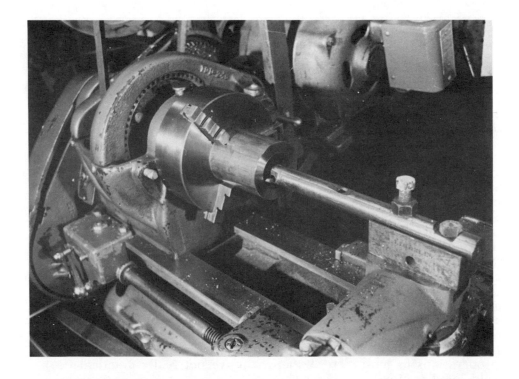

The metal lathe can produce true internal cylindrical surfaces as well as external. This brass bushing is being bored to fit the driveshaft to a garden tractor snowblower. The boring bar is homemade.

stick in spiral fashion with each wrap exactly spaced from the next. The secret was to maintain a fixed relationship between the rotation of the metal and the movement of the tool along the work. Maudslay did it by putting a gear on the headstock spindle that rotated the metal and using that gear to drive other gears to turn a long, threaded shaft, called a lead screw, which then moved the tool along the lathe bed at a fixed rate for each turn of the work metal. Actual history is clouded. Others appear to have used this idea, but Maudslay apparently added the

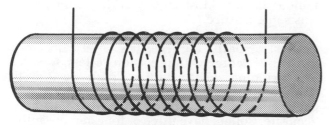

Evenly spaced spiral

If you wind a string evenly around a stick, you can demonstrate the principle of a thread-cutting lathe. Turn the stick between centers and move the string along at a fixed rate. Varying either the rate at which you turn the stick or move the string will expand or contract the distance between spirals.

feature of providing a selection of gears that could be altered in various combinations to produce nearly any thread pitch.

The same principle is still used, not only to cut threads but to deliver power to feed the cutting tool along or across the metal at a fixed speed. This is quite different from the manually controlled woodworker's chisel. At the same time, all lathes do have hand cranks to feed and position the tool manually. And some lathes, such as the miniature type I'll discuss first, have no power feeds at all. Let's look at miniature lathes first, since understanding them will make understanding larger lathes easier.

Miniature Lathes

Perhaps the earliest miniature lathes were used by jewelers, clockmakers, and makers of navigation instruments. These crude tools were called "the turns" and consisted of two pointed centers mounted on a metal bar so they could be adjusted for spacing. The workpiece was pressed or forced onto a tapered mandrel. The mandrel had a small grooved pulley at one end. Power came from a small bow with leather or horsehair strings. The strings were wrapped around the pulley and sawed back and forth to rotate the work. Obviously, one movement from the bow turned the work against the tool for

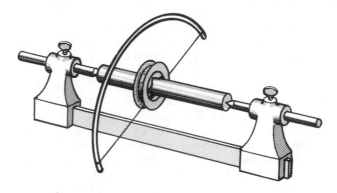

Early makers of clocks and navigation instruments turned shafts and pivots in a form of minature lathe they called "the turns." For power they used a horsehair bow sawed back and forth with a wrap around the drive pulley.

Typical jeweler's lathe, not so common in modern jewelery shops, is heavily constructed for rigidity. The tool rest, however, is similar to a woodworker's lathe and is suited only to hand-held tools and very light cuts.

cutting and the backstroke reversed it. The operator simply eased the cutting pressure for the backstroke. Obviously such a metalworker was no ball of fire in terms of high production. The finished work, however, remains to be marveled at.

Somewhere, later, the watchmakers developed the true "jeweler's" lathe. This little lathe clamped to the workbench and had a pulley with a series of steps at the headstock. The headstock bearings were very snug and smooth-working, and the tailstock could be moved along a massive, rigid base to the desired spacing. Power was often supplied by a treadle like that of an old-fashioned sewing machine.

One lack on such jeweler's lathes was a movable tool holder or "post." Instead, the tool rest, or tee-rest, resembled the tool rest used for wood lathes. The tools were pointed chisels or gravers, used much like wood chisels with a very light scraping or cutting action. Remember, though, fine small-diameter parts such as clock and watch staffs did not require heavy cuts and would have bent under heavy pressure.

Since jewelers were concerned with spacing gear teeth and little pin drives accurately, a jeweler's lathe had an indexing head. This consisted of a series of closely and evenly spaced holes in the face of a small disc on the headstock live center. Since the angular spacing of the holes was known, the work could be rotated by hand and an indexing pin inserted into selected holes to space gear teeth or cogs accurately without

tedious layout. Most metalworking lathes have this same feature.

Collets.   Finally, the jeweler's lathe held work in the live center with precision collets. A collet is a gripping device with a single accurately sized and centered hole to fit an adjustable chuck and is generally considered to be more accurate. Collets have three or four narrow splits cut lengthwise to the center hole. The outside of the collet is tapered to fit a matching taper in the live-center spindle bore. After the workpiece is inserted, the collet is drawn or forced into the internal taper and the splits are pressed together slightly to grip the work, without marring the finish.

Collets, or collet chucks, are still the most accurate way to center fine work in a lathe. Their disadvantage is that they fit only more or less standard-diameter material with a good finished gripping surface, and you need a large number of them for even a small range of work sizes. This makes collets fine in production work where pieces of the same size are gripped repeatedly. They are not useful for gripping roughly finished or odd-size material.

Modern miniature lathes.   Today, there are miniature lathes of extremely high quality and precision made especially for laboratory, optical, and industrial model-shop work. They cost many thousands of dollars and are unlikely to grace many home shops. Fortunately, there are

Collets are a superior gripping method for stock of accurate size. These, in fractional sizes, provide precise centering for this miniature table-top lathe.

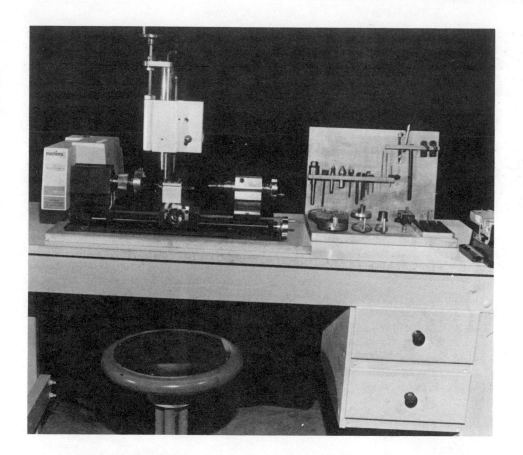

Workbench for small models is shown here with a miniature lathe and tool board, plus a vise for light work. The lathe can be lifted aside and bench used for jewelery or precision work. Top is a thick slab of hard, plastic-faced counter-top material. Drawers hold small tools and special parts. Note that the construction allows you to get your lap close in under bench and support your wrists on top.

By removing the head from the lathe bed and mounting on a column, miniature lathe becomes a vertical mill or drill press. Table feed is manual.

also quite capable, but much less expensive, machines that most home metalworkers will find adequate, if, at times, annoying. One type that uses two parallel bars for a bed is not rigid enough for more than the lightest metalwork. Another, larger variety, with a cast-iron bed, is an enormous jump ahead. First, the good points of such miniature lathes:

● The headstock spindle accepts collets, a three- or four-jaw chuck, a Jacobs-type chuck, or a faceplate. It also accepts a 60° dead center and a grinding arbor.

● The stepped drive pulleys permit a wide speed selection.

● The entire headstock may be removed and mounted on a vertical column to provide a precision drill press, vertical mill, or vertical grinder.

The greatest feature of these machines is versatility, since with the proper accessories, tables, and clamps, they permit a wide number of metal-cutting operations. There are other characteristics that are less endearing:

● All feeds are manual, and there is no way to disengage the lead screw, so each relocation of the carriage requires tedious cranking on rather tiny handles.

● The carriage or apron lacks sufficient front overhang to draw the tool back to fully accept the full potential work diameter.

● The vertical column assembly lacks rigidity, especially for milling cuts.

● There is no provision for screw-thread cutting and no power cross feed or longitudinal feed.

It may be that the above faults or lacks are more apparent to a person accustomed to running a conventional bench or tool-room lathe. Actually, the miniature lathe, in price, weight, and versatility, is a boon to the metalworker who may have no more space than the kitchen table or countertop in an apartment or mobile home. Moreover, using such a lathe introduces all the principles of metal-cutting tools, centering, and tool setups common to larger equipment, and it is a fine learning device.

Bench Lathes

The type of lathe commonly seen in the home metalworking shop is called a bench lathe be-

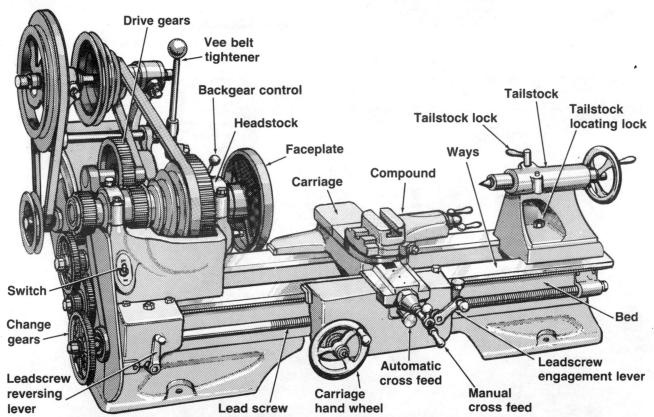

Different makes of lathes vary in the exact location and form of their controls, but they all have same basic features—a drive and feed system, and controls to move the tool and engage the feeds. Typical home-shop lathe shown here with safety covers removed has change gears. A quick-change would have a control box where the leadscrew reversing lever is shown. Vee-belt steps are easily understood and back-gear control reduces speed of headstock spindle to very low rotational speed for heavy drilling.

cause it is usually mounted as a unit on a bench or similar support. The size of a bench lathe is termed its "swing"—the maximum diameter of a workpiece that can be turned when the work is centered and rotated without striking the bed. For example, the center of the headstock on a 10″ lathe is slightly more than 5″ from the inside corner of the bed ways. Such a lathe can just accept a disc or plate 10″ in diameter. In practice, you'll seldom use the full swing of your lathe.

Common sizes of bench lathes are 9″, 10″, and 12″. The length of the bed may vary, but few are shorter than 36″ and few are longer than 48″. There are practical reasons for this. Bench lathes were also made, at one time, in a 6″ swing, primarily for hobby work. One of the bothersome limitations in this size was the small bore through the center of the headstock spindle. It is often very necessary with long workpieces to extend them all the way through the spindle, and a small bore is a definite handicap. If room in your shop is very limited, however, picking up one of these lathes used is probably a much better choice than buying a miniature, since you can cut threads on them and they have most of the conventional details except power cross feed.

Bench lathes are also graded according to the degree of precision offered and the frequency of use. Clearly, a lathe that is operated eight hours a day places greater demands on its working parts than one used for a few hours occasionally. And if the lathe is used in a tool room where common tolerances are .0001″ or .0002″, the

Nominal "swing" of a lathe is measured by diameter of the workpiece which can be centered and rotated without striking the bed. This is a 10-inch lathe.

bearings and bed must be more precise than for jobs where .001″ is close enough. Most home metalworkers will find a so-called utility lathe more than accurate enough. Even these lathes have beds ground to an accuracy of .001″. The bed is a massive piece of cast iron and very rigid, though it can nevertheless flex and cause puz-

Six-inch metal lathe has most of the features of larger models except power crossfeed. Biggest limitation is not necessarily its swing, but instead the small bore of the headstock spindle which limits the diameter of long stock it can accept.

zling problems if it is not mounted on a very firm and level surface. You can buy cast-iron bases for your lathe, but a sturdy wooden or metal bench will do as well if you mount the lathe carefully.

Homemade lathe mounting.   Many years ago I bought a used gas stove with lower ovens and drawers. I stripped away the stove parts and fitted the top with two layers of ¾″ marine plywood covered with ¼″ hardboard. This bench has served well, and the onetime oven and utensil drawers store all of the myriad chucks, bits, and gadgets that latheworkers accumulate. I mounted some industrial casters on the bottom, so I can move the lathe out from the wall for jobs needing more rear clearance, and for an occasional sweeping up of the inevitable accumulations of chips and cuttings.

Bare wood, or even nicely finished wood, is not a good top for a lathe bench. Many jobs require liberal applications of cutting oil or flushing down with solvent. Sharp and oily chips will pile up, and you'll want to wash down the entire machine with kerosene and a brush. A surface that can be brushed off and wiped clean is best. The main thing is to mount your lathe on a very solid, rigid surface that will not introduce twists and bends. Remember, although .001″ is only about ⅓ the thickness of this page, that much twist over the length of your lathe bed can give you fits.

Change-Gear Lathes

As discussed, the first real progress in lathes was the addition of a lead (or feed) screw to move the cutting tool along at a fixed speed relative to the rotating work. When cutting threads a very definite relationship is needed to produce a specific pitch or thread count per inch. Maudslay worked out a way to set up this relationship by changing gears in the gear train.

Nothing has really changed. That's the way the majority of home-shop lathes are built, even today. When you buy a screw-cutting lathe, new or used, expect to get a collection of mysterious-looking gears with it. If you don't get them, either you are getting a "quick-change" lathe, identifiable by a number of knobs, handles, and detents at the left front, or someone is leaving something out of the deal. Be certain the gear set is complete. Nothing is more frustrating than to find you lack the one gear size you need.

Assuming you acquire a change-gear lathe, your instruction book, a vital item, will provide tables of gear combinations and their exact positions for cutting a very large range of threads. It will also tell you the right gear combinations for moving the carriage along the bed a certain number of thousandths of an inch for each rotation of the workpiece. On my lathe, for example, I can change gears to provide carriage feeds from .0087″ to .00187″ per revolution. The quick-change lathe lets you do the same job just by positioning the handles. There are jobs for

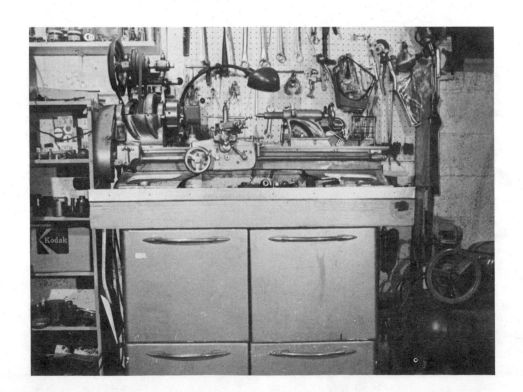

Ten-inch bench lathe is a heavy piece of equipment and must be very solidly supported. This lathe bench and tool cabinet is made from a discarded gas stove mounted on industrial casters. The top is two thicknesses of ¾″ plywood faced with hardboard.

Change-gear lathe uses a selected gear train for various feed speeds and thread pitches. Stack of gears, left, when installed according to table, far left, inside gear cover, offers an extremely wide range of cutting performance.

Such cuts are made to square up the ends of stock, produce a flat face on odd-shaped blocks and pieces, and open up bores in shallow pieces. Here, the lead-screw drive lever and the cross-feed are engaged. This moves the tool crossways of the bed at the speed equivalent to the longitudinal feed. By flipping a lever the operator can make the tool move in or out under power.

This is one of the times when a slow feed can be helpful while you're learning. If the tool moves too fast, things can happen more rapidly than you're prepared to deal with them. A nice, slow feed gives you more time for control and also produces a smoother finish. Remember, as the lathe tool moves along it's actually peeling out a chip which, in effect, is cutting a groove

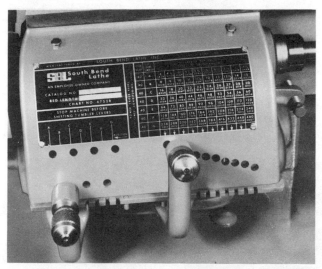

Quick-change lathe gives you much faster changes in feed and screw-threading cut by merely shifting controls at front.

Although you may think of a lathe as producing round surfaces, it can also produce true, flat surfaces with a facing cut using the crossfeed. When this facing cut is completed, work can be reversed against chuck face and the opposite side faced in an accurate, parallel plane. Note that this aluminum cuts to leave an almost polished surface.

which these maximum and minimum feeds are important, such as winding springs or electrical coils. But most metalworkers seldom need them. My choice for an especially fine finish would be .00187, but most of the time I leave the gears set at .0035″ for general use.

The Cross Feed

Although many lathe cuts are made along the long axis of the work, parallel to the ways, an equal number of so-called "facing" cuts are made by moving the tool directly across the face of the work at 90° to the bed ways.

in the metal. To produce a flat surface it's necessary that the grooves average out flat. The slow feed does this.

Lathe Chucks

As in all metalwork, holding the work firmly is very important in lathework. Several different methods are available, including the collet chucks described in the discussion of miniature lathes.

By far the most common method is the three-jaw chuck on the headstock spindle and the 60° center in the tailstock. Although the three-jaw chuck can be used to hold fairly rough stock, it is common to mount the workpiece temporarily so that it extends a short distance from the chuck, allowing a clean-up cut to be made. The stock is then reversed and the cleaned and trued area is clamped in the chuck.

The chuck jaws have two interesting features. For one thing, they can be closed inwardly to grip bar stock, or expanded outward to grip the inside of a ring or tubular piece. The second feature is a set of three extra jaws made for griping larger pieces externally. Opening the set of jaws most commonly used to grip a large-diameter piece leaves the ends of the jaws protruding dangerously and reduces the number of threads used for clamping. The second set of jaws is stepped just the opposite way so they can grip large stock without being opened wide.

To change jaws, the tightening screw is backed out until the jaws cease to move outward. They can then be lifted free for cleaning or exchange with the other set. Each jaw is numbered and each jaw slot is numbered. Number-one jaw must go into number-one slot, and it must go in before number-two. Number-two, of course, must precede number-three. To replace the jaws, look into number-one slot and turn the chuck key until you see the tip of the spiral just about to enter the slot area. Back off a fraction in the opening direction, push the jaw into the slot as far as it will go, and turn the key in the closing direction. A light tug on the jaw will tell you if the spiral has engaged. Now turn the key in the tightening direction until the tip of the spiral just shows up in number-two slot, and repeat the engaging process. Number-three goes in the same way.

The jaws described above are finish-ground to center in a given chuck. Jaws from another chuck cannot, or should not, be interchanged. On some chucks the jaws are left unfinished on the clamp face and the buyer is advised to mount the jaws and finish them in his own lathe. This is more feasible in a commercial tool room than in a home shop.

Three-jaw chucks require only very light lubrication. The most important point is to remove the jaws now and then and thoroughly clean all chips and dirt from the spiral and jaw threads. Use a solvent such as kerosene and a stiff brush.

Four-jaw chucks. Less used, but often needed, the four-jaw chuck with individually adjustable jaws permits gripping and centering pieces that

Three-jaw chuck is often used to grip external surface of work as shown. It would be very dangerous, however, to try to make a cut with no more support than this. A center must be drilled at the right end for the tailstock so the metal will be firmly supported between centers.

By expanding the jaws of a three-jaw chuck you can grip tubular or hollow-center work-pieces like this. Grip is adequate for facing operation and turning circumference of work.

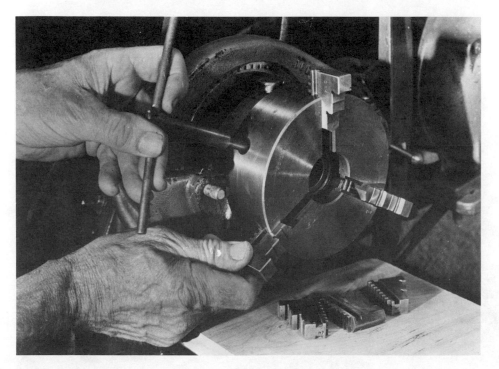

When it's apparent that work size would require running the previously shown chuck jaws out too far, you can exchange them for jaws which grip from the outer sides. Jaws are numbered and must be installed in order.

are not round. If most of your work is with round bar or hex stock you will seldom use a four-jaw. But if you want to machine oddly shaped castings and parts such as might, for example, be used on model engines, the four-jaw is a boon.

The difference involves both gripping and centering the work. With a three-jaw you have no choice, and if the work is shaped so that one jaw has no contact the metal will not stay in the chuck. Or even though you can grip the work, you may find that the area you want to machine is way off center. With the four-jaw you can shift

When chips and cuttings interfere with smooth chuck operation it's time to clean them out. A tray of kerosene and a brush worked into the spiral grooves as you rotate the chuck key should do the job. Compressed air helps, too.

A three-jaw chuck can center (approximately) only round stock. To mount nonsymmetrical work or center-off-center, as for example, a crankpin, a four-jaw chuck is needed. By shifting individual jaws, stock can be aligned as desired.

the work around and adjust each jaw individually to center where you want. For very precise work you can set up a dial indicator, rotate the work slowly by hand, and adjust the jaws to bring the work dead on center. When doing this you must give some thought to balance. Oddly shaped parts might wind up located with considerable weight far off center. As a precaution, set the rotating speed at several steps lower than you might for normal work and flip the power on briefly. If the work appears jumpy and the unbalance is severe, try bolting a suitable weight opposite the off-balance mass if possible. Otherwise, run at low speed and carefully.

Jacobs lathe chucks. Jacobs-type chucks are made for both the headstocks and tailstocks of bench lathes. They resemble drill-press chucks but are, or course, threaded to fit different-size spindles.

To understand the rationale for these chucks, a look at drill shanks and drilling practices in the lathe is necessary. If your past experience has been confined to woodworking it's likely that your twist drills have straight shanks. In contrast, many metalworking drill bits, reamers, and other tools have tapered shanks that simply slide—or, more accurately, jam—into tapered sockets and lock by taper action. Thus, a typical bench lathe will have a #3 Morse taper in the headstock spindle and a #2 in the tailstock. This works fine with taper-shank tools, and if you want to use a smaller drill or tool you use a reducing taper sleeve to hold the smaller taper.

But there are many times when you want to rotate the work in the headstock three-jaw or

Taper adapters slip into the headstock or tailstock to reduce the size to match the taper on the shank of the tool.

Adapter shown permits direct installation of a taper-shank drill in the headstock spindle. Wedging action of the taper grips the tool firmly. To remove drill and taper a drift rod through tailstock is needed.

This tailstock chuck and adapter is an extremely important lathe accessory since it allows you to drill critical center holes as well as other holes. The Jacobs ball-bearing chuck shown is expensive but worth getting.

Jacobs headstock chuck fits threads of spindle. One use is drilling with stock held in a vee-center in tailstock. This chuck is better than the big three-jaw for small work and lets you get the lathe tool in tight without interference you encounter with larger chuck.

four-jaw chuck and use a small straight-shank drill in the tailstock. One good reason for this is that taper-shank drills are primarily sold only industrially, and they're expensive. A full-range set of such drills is very costly compared to hardware-store twist drills. It is also true that some sort of chuck is needed to hold short, stubby center drills. Operations of this type are so common that the tailstock Jacobs chuck with a taper adapter is almost a must. You simply plunk the tapered adapter into the tailstock, install the twist drill or center drill in the usual manner, and go to work. So the first extra chuck you should buy will be a Jacobs type with an adapter to fit your lathe's tailstock.

The Jacobs chuck for the headstock is not used as often, but it does let you drill from the head end, and it is very good for holding small rod-type stock, which is unhandy to work in a big three-jaw chuck. In some instances, when you're machining small parts, the smaller diameter of the Jacobs chuck lets you crowd in closer with the tool without the danger that the chuck jaws will strike the tool mounting or the cross slide.

Milling Collets

The milling collet is a special holding device just for driving milling cutters in the headstock spindle. Milling cutters are heavily loaded and subjected to repeated shock impacts as each tooth bites into the metal. They are also very hard, and attempting to hold and drive them with a three-jaw or Jacobs chuck will sooner or later damage the chuck jaws. The milling collet is not split, but it does fit the headstock spindle taper

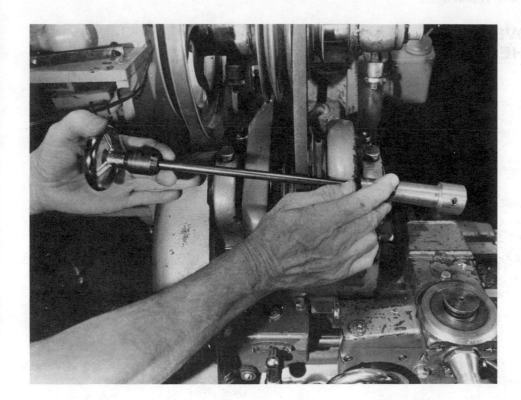

This holder for milling cutters extends through the spindle and draws the collet holder firmly into the headstock taper. It is poor practice to attempt to drive milling cutters by gripping them in a standard jaw chuck.

and is drawn in by a threaded rod that extends through the headstock spindle. The collet accepts milling cutter shanks, which are secured by a socket-head screw bearing against a flat on the shank. Bushings are used to size the collet for different-size cutter shanks.

LATHE TOOLS AND MOUNTINGS

Just as the workpiece must be solidly mounted, the tool that cuts the metal must be equally firm. Unlike woodturning tools, which can be graced across the wood by hand, metal-cutting tools must be set to a specific cut depth and moved along evenly without wandering or vibrating. At the same time, you must be able to move the tool freely along the bed, across the lathe bed, and often at an angle to the bed.

In a way the need for extreme rigidity is not totally compatible with freedom of movement. The method of accomplishing this in the bench lathe is typical of nearly all metal-cutting machinery. If you are not familiar with such machinery, picture the cutter bit as held firmly in the tool post by a lock screw. The bit can only be moved, swung, or adjusted in the tool post by releasing the lock screw.

The secret of the movement of this solidly anchored bit is the three movable members on which it rests. First, at the base, and riding on the precision-finished ways of the bed, the car-

riage moves longitudinally and may travel the full distance between the tailstock and the headstock either by manual cranking or by feedscrew drive. The top of the carriage has dovetail ways that run at 90° to the main lathe bed ways, and on these the cross slide can be moved in or out from the center axis for facing cutting and for adjusting the depth of cut.

The two directions of travel described above account for the majority of tool movements, but they do not provide for cuts made at angles other than 90°. For this reason, still another small slide or carriage, called the compound, is mounted on a short postlike projection on the top of the cross slide. This unit can be swung around 360° by loosening its locks. It also has dovetail ways and a manual feed screw. There is no power feed to the compound. The compound does, however, have a heavy tee-slot that receives the retaining member for the tool post, which holds the tool.

Gibs and Ways

Obviously, if the three sliding members, carriage, cross slide, and compound, are to have the freedom to slide on an oil film, a definite but minute clearance must exist between them and the ways that guide them. At the same time, any excess clearance would cause erratic action, chattering of the tool, and very poor accuracy.

THREE MOVEMENTS
OF LATHE TOOL

(1) Longitudinal

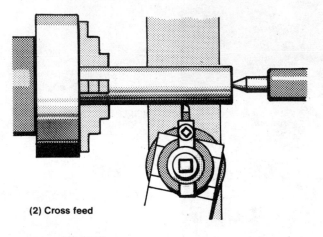

(2) Cross feed

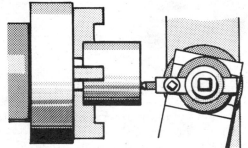

(3) Compound

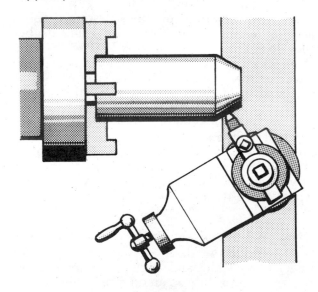

The basic metal-cutting lathe permits three movements—lengthwise of the bed; at right angles to the bed (facing cut); and for a short distance at a preset angle to the bed. It does not offer the freedom of tool movement of a wood lathe.

This problem is solved by "gibs" or thin strips of metal placed inside one side of the sliding-member dovetails. The gibs are individually adjustable at several places along their length by small screws that extend into the dovetail area from the outside. Slight tightening of the screws increases the friction and reduces clearance as desired. Some jobs—milling, for example—go best if the gibs are quite snug and the carriage and cross slide are actually somewhat hard to move manually. Most ordinary turning operations can be conducted with the gibs set to slide slickly and easily. One factor that should be kept in mind, and it also applies to the backlash or working clearances in the feed gears, is that the pressure is almost always in one direction. Once the cutting load has forced out the accumulated clearances between all the moving parts the

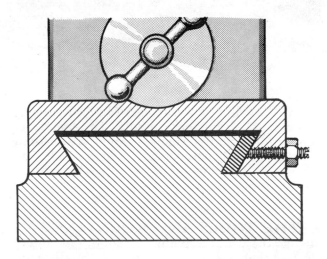

Lathe gibs provide a means of adjusting the sliding freedom and friction of the moving portions of the lathe. The gibs bear against one side of the dovetail and are adjusted with small screws and locknuts. Adjust so they're all evenly snugged.

clearance will not greatly affect the cutting operation. Too much sloppiness, however, makes adjusting for a precision depth of cut difficult.

Tool Post

The tool post mounts vertically on the compound and may be pivoted for the best placement of the tool for a given cut. The center of the post is slotted to receive the tool or tool holder. A clamp screw through the top of the post secures both the tool and the post. A slightly dish-shaped pad at the base of the post, together with a small, halfmoon-shaped "rocker," support the tool and make possible the necessary

Adjusting the gibs on your lathe is a delicate job. These are crossfeed gibs, and if they're too loose you lose rigidity between tool and carriage. Get them too tight and the crossfeed adjustment becomes tedious. For milling, however, they should always be on the snug side.

adjustment of the cutting tool's edge height. For most metal cutting on the lathe, the tip of the tool is set exactly on the longitudinal center of the workpiece.

Tool holders. It has long been customary to insert a sturdy member called a "tool holder" in the tool-post slot and place the actual cutting bit in a square hole in the tip of the holder, where it is locked by a setscrew. Holders are made for angling the tool right, left, or straight ahead. The only real justification for such holders is that on larger industrial lathes the costly, high-alloy tool would be even more costly if it were made large enough to extend all the way back and clamp in the tool post. For smaller lathes in the home shop this advantage is trivial. Admittedly, the tool holder will take small, ¼" bits, but it also extends the tool out some distance from the tool post and impairs rigidity. Such holders contribute to a very definite spring and vibration in the tool, and I've always found them undesirable.

My own experience is that it's definitely better to use a ⁵⁄₁₆" or ⅜" bit, or even a ⅜" × 1" bit, mounted firmly in the tool post with no intervening holder. Since most home metalworkers will take years to wear out a tool bit, and since many such tools are scraps and rejects liberated from industrial sources, the more solidly the tool can be mounted the more pleasant the work.

Conventional tool holder and tool are mounted in the tool post and adjusted to center on the central axis of the workpiece. In writer's experience, the arrangement tends to introduce chatter and is less rigid than it should be for most work.

By eliminating the tool holder, a more rigid tool mounting is gained. Spare tool bit is used as a spacer. This tool bit is sharpened for cutting aluminum. Note sharp rake angle.

Lathe Tools

Although in the past some lathe-tool bits were made from high-carbon steel and later from high-speed steel, most such tools today are made from complex alloy steels of the high-speed type. For many jobs, tungsten-carbide tools are ideal, but they are expensive and impossible to shape and sharpen on the home-shop bench grinder. The best source for lathe tools, unless you work in a machine shop, is an industrial supply house or the scrap bin of a small local machine shop. Tool stubs too short to regrind for larger ma-

Every metal-lathe worker soon accumulates an assortment of bits and not-very-pretty tools. These range from boring bars roughly, often hastily, ground from scrap reamers to tools ground to get into unusual corners. These are random pick-ups from my lathe bench. Tool at far left is for wood turning in a metal lathe.

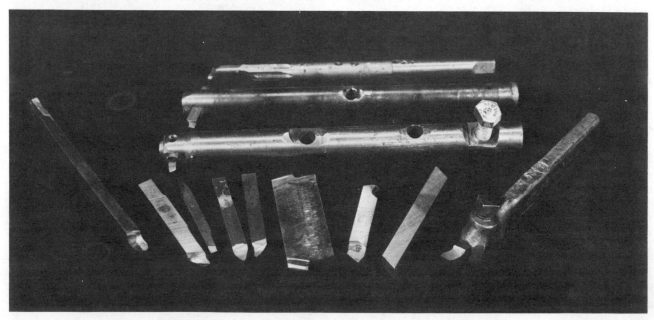

chines are often available. Big milling cutters, for example, use replaceable teeth that are useless when chipped or broken. These same pieces of alloy tool steel can be sharpened in your shop to work just fine in your lathe. In the same way, worn-out reamers can be ground into good boring bars.

Sharpening lathe-tool bits is an art and a science. We'll talk about it later, but for now simply remember that a lathe tool must be properly mounted on center just as firmly and just as close to the work as you can make it.

LATHE ACCESSORIES

No lathe you ever buy will be complete. For one thing, its very versatility and the variety of its uses have made it customary for manufacturers to sell the basic machine and let the customer choose even such items as chucks. Secondly, because of this same versatility there's always just one more attachment or accessory that it would be "nice to have."

When you've learned the fundamentals of external turning, you will certainly find that you now need boring bars and tools to cut internal surfaces. Or you'll want a milling vise and milling cutters. That's what makes metalworking on

the lathe so fascinating. The challenges are almost endless.

Faceplates

Even though I've discussed a number of devices for holding work in the lathe, they are by no means the only way. Suppose, for example, that you wish to machine a large, flat plate. None of the chucks discussed will grip a plate. You need a faceplate. A faceplate is simply a circular, flat metal plate with a hub threaded to fit the headstock spindle. Usually the plate will have a number of spokelike cutout slots. To machine the plate previously mentioned, you'd mount it, perhaps with short screws from behind, perhaps with clamps and bolts through the slots, so that it rotates on the faceplate.

Another common use for a faceplate gets into a lathe technique known as "working between centers." As I mentioned, even the best of three-jaw chucks will not center the work perfectly. This doesn't make much difference in many jobs, since as soon as you make a cut you establish a centered workpiece except for the waste stub in the chuck. But it's a different story if the nature of successive cuts requires that you remove the work from the chuck, to reverse it end for end,

Here are a few of the lathe accessories you'll want to get. They include a milling vise, top, collet-type milling cutter holder and a few milling cutters, a faceplate and a drive dog, head and tailstock chucks, a threading tool, and spurs for wood.

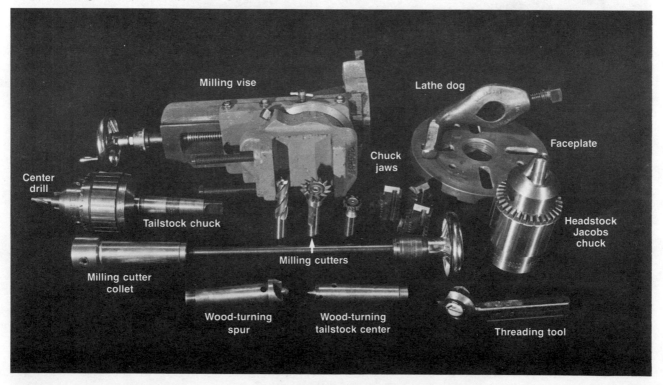

Faceplate threads onto the headstock spindle. As you can see, this one has been drilled and tapped here and there to hold special work. Once in a while a light facing cut should be made to true the face of the plate.

Work can be removed for checking and replaced on center with this faceplate, center, and drive-dog arrangement. Note the fine finish produced on brass stock with a properly ground tool.

for example. You'll never get it back on the original center in a three-jaw chuck.

With a faceplate, a lathe dog, and a 60° center in the headstock spindle, however, you can solve this problem. The trick is to drill both ends for centers initially. Now you mount the work between the two pointed centers and use the face plate and a lathe dog to rotate the work. Centering is automatic.

Milling Vises

The milling vise converts the lathe to a milling machine. Milling vises mount on the cross slide after removing the compound. This makes it possible to traverse along the lathe bed or at 90°. The 90° travel is the most common. The milling vise is mounted on a support casting with its own set of dovetails and gibs. The vise is also pivoted so angle cuts can be set up.

There are two limits to the work you can do with a milling vise in the lathe. The first limit is the distance the cross slide can be traversed without running off the dovetails or off the feed screw. This is seldom more than 4″ or 5″, often less. Secondly, rugged as the lathe is, you'll find that the heavy impact of the milling cutter will cause definite springing of the vise structure, and there will be inevitable movement because of the clearances in the ways, the cross slide, and the vise. In most cases this is not a serious limitation and you quickly learn just how heavy a cut is too heavy. Finish with light cuts and you'll do fine.

Taper Attachments

There are two ways to cut tapers on a bench lathe without a taper attachment. One is with the compound slide set at an angle. This works

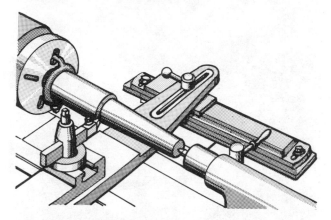

Taper attachment on the back of the lathe controls the cross travel of the tool as the carriage moves lengthwise. By setting the angle of the guide you can adjust the taper to suit.

well, but the limited travel, about 2″ as a rule, means that it is useful only for short tapers. It's the common way to chamfer the end of a workpiece.

The second method requires moving the tailstock off center by a calculated amount. This has two disadvantages. First, it's necessary to perform some fairly complex and difficult calculations involving the desired taper angle and the length of the stock, and then move the tailstock exactly the right amount. When the job is done you must recenter the tailstock, not the easiest of tasks.

For the above reasons, if turning tapers is important to you, a taper attachment is recommended, since it eliminates the above problems.

Tool-Post Grinder

Many metalworkers who enjoy working with high-precision workpieces of hardened steel, or making and sharpening tools, feel the need for a cutting tool able to do work impossible with ordinary bit-type cutters. The answer is abrasives. A device known as a tool-post grinder mounts on the lathe cross slide, together with its own multispeed motor. With this grinder mounted on the cross slide you can position the high-speed abrasive wheel for very accurate grinding. External and internal surfaces can be

Short, limited-length tapers are easily cut using the compound slide on your lathe. Longer tapers, however, require setting the tailstock off center or the use of a taper attachment. For most metalworkers, this need is limited.

ground to a high finish even though they are extremely hard.

There are pros and cons to the tool-post grinder. The pros, as stated, are simply that it lets you do work that is otherwise impossible. The negative side is that, as with all abrasive tools, there is a throwoff of grinding swarf and abrasive particles. The lathe bed and dovetail ways are closely finished, and if this abrasive waste gets trapped between the sliding surfaces, wear is inevitable. Moreover, the same material has a way of getting into the feed screw and other working parts. The instructions that will come with a tool-post grinder will advise that

Tool-post grinder is handy and can do extremely fine work almost impossible without it. But beware of the abrasive waste material which can severely damage your lathe.

these parts be masked off with cloth, paper, or the like, but it is almost impossible to maintain perfect cleanliness. Tool-post grinders are nice, but . . .

Reversing Switch

Motors made for lathe operation, and many other motors, can be reversed simply by switching one or two wires in the junction box. For most lathework it is necessary to rotate the work so it turns toward the top, cutting edge of the tool. There are times, however, as in backing a tool out of a thread, or removing a tap or die, when it is extremely handy to be able to reverse the motor and the spindle direction. This is easily done with a reversing switch mounted on or near the motor. A word of warning—don't mount

You can get by without a reversing switch for your lathe motor but it's handy for backing out of threads, especially when power threading with a die.

the switch where it is too convenient and can accidentally be brushed into reverse position. You can live without a switch, but it's one of those nice-to-have things.

Other Attachments

As you study your lathe's instruction manual you'll see other useful attachments. Among these are follower rests, steady rests, and turret attachments. The first two serve to steady long work and reduce spring. The turret lets you mount several different cutting tools so they can be swung into action without taking time to mount them individually. The turret is primarily for production jobs.

21.
OPERATING A METAL LATHE

It is impossible in a book such as this to detail the procedures for all of the operations possible on a metal-cutting lathe. Each lathe manufacturer has an instruction book, and such books are extremely comprehensive; they are also totally necessary, because lathes differ somewhat. Also, there are hundreds of books used for machine-shop training courses expanding on these techniques. You'd think that that would be enough, but my review of forty years of *Popular Science* and other magazines shows that home-shop metalworkers have always been able to come up with fresh and novel ways to put this wonderful machine to work. One result of the plethora of information has been an obscuring of the more elementary basics. They tend to get buried in the chatter of experts.

After we've covered the rock-bottom basics—safety, tool settings, and cutting fluids—we'll consider some of the arts of lathework. The first art the beginner must master is how to sharpen and shape a lathe bit. The second is how to maintain the first cut and all succeeding cuts on the same centers even though the finished work may require several steps. Once you learn to think in terms of how the tool must be presented to the work metal and how you can best proceed in a sequence of cuts, you're on your way. The rest—working to close tolerances, cutting threads, milling, metal spinning—is easy.

SAFETY TIPS

It used to be said that you could always tell when you shook hands with a machinist because one or more of his fingers would be missing. If your friendship reached a point where you felt comfortable asking how he'd lost his finger, you'd almost always hear the same story: He'd just reached in to flick away a chip or cutting while the work was turning. You, too, will experience this natural urge. Resist it. Start right from the beginning to keep a softwood stick, perhaps 5/16" square with a pointed tip, handy on the lathe bench. Use it to flick chips and guide long curling chips free of the spindle. Sooner or later, in a twinkling, the stick will get shortened. It could have been your finger.

Many metals, when cutting freely, will turn off endless strips of curling metal that tend to coil around the chuck, the spindle, and your arms. If you can arrange a trash bucket on the floor in front of the lathe you may be able to use your stick to guide these stringers into it without the mess of handling them. It's a good trick, but do it with leather gloves on. The stringy cuttings are usually razor-sharp and can coil around your hand and backward around the work, where they suddenly start to wind up and pull in your hand. The natural reaction to break away will probably break the chip but at the expense of a deep and nasty gash in your hand.

Beware the strong temptation to flick chips away with your finger. A scrap of wood is better and won't hurt when it inevitably gets pulled in between the work and the tool.

Other metals discharge short, crisp, broken, and often very hot chips. Eye protection is absolutely necessary.

HOME-SHOP TOOL SETTINGS

As mentioned in the preceding chapter, for reasons of tool economy it is customary to mount tools in holders in industry. But in the home shop you can usually get a better job if you clamp the bit directly in the tool post. This introduces a whole different aspect when grinding the rake angle at the nose. The tool holder normally slopes upward at a 16½° angle. Thus, a tool ground flat on top will automatically have about a 16½° rake, depending on how it seats on the rocker to align on center. But if you mounted this tool in the tool post it will have 0° rake unless you cant it up with the rocker.

In practice, you'll find that a short, 5/16″-square tool, for example, placed directly on the rocker would have to be cocked up outrageously to center, and then the front clearance would be lost. The solution is to stack two cutting tools, the bottom one as a spacer, and raise the working tool to a reasonable height. In due course you learn to judge the rake for such setups by eye.

Kinks and Tricks

You will also find that you have cutting tools too narrow to fill the slot in the tool post and that they cant or fail to clamp securely. The answer is to pad the clearance on each side with shims. I keep little tabs of scrap aluminum of various

thicknesses handy for such use. I also put a piece of soft, 1/8″-thick aluminum on top of narrow tool bits so the clamp screw exerts a very firm pressure without being damaged by the hard metal of the bit. Another use for these little shims is centering a piece of work in a three-jaw chuck. Often, with a little experimenting, you can shim one jaw, sometimes two, to move an unsymmetrical workpiece on center.

Such shimming may not be entirely orthodox, but it sometimes serves to make the impossible possible, and that's part of the fun of metalworking. The immortal cartoon series "Out Our Way," with its famous bull-of-the-woods foreman, occasionally portrayed the old-time machine operator who had his machine shimmed and wedged with pieces of tobacco tins, which baffled a stand-in when the old boy took a va-

Wedging and shimming tool bits is common metalworking practice. This bit of aluminum angle stock pads the screw against the slanted top of a make-do tool and shims it against side movement. Most important, be certain the tool can't shift in use.

cation. All machine tools, except, of course, today's computer-controlled marvels, respond to careful, personal adjustments.

CUTTING FLUIDS

Let it be said here and now that the most important fluid you'll use with your home-shop lathe is the oil to lubricate it. Most lathe makers recommend light engine oil. Be sure to keep an oil can handy, or several if necessary, with snouts to fit the little oil cups and points on the carriage slides and apron gears. Oil the headstock frequently, and keep the ways and slides wiped clean and well oiled.

That said, there is a world of difference between high-production cutting in industry and light cutting in the home shop. For industrial production a constant flow of carefully selected cutting fluid is a must to carry away heat and lubricate the tool. Lubricants are selected for a variety of reasons—for example, whether or not they discolor a given metal alloy.

Most home-shop lathework can be done dry. The exception is thread-cutting and tapping operations. Aluminum, too, often finishes better with a light lubricant. Use common sulphurized cutting and threading oil for thread cutting. If you're making a heavy cut in steel it may help to brush or squirt cutting oil on and along the path of the tool bit. Dense smoke at this point suggests you'd be wise to back off on the feed or the depth of cut.

Lathe bearings carry heavy loads and need lubrication, sometimes at points not immediately evident. A small screw concealed in this pulley groove must be removed to flow oil into vital internal bearings. Study your lathe manual for lube details.

Cutting oil cools and lubricates the tool and can improve the finish on final cuts, especially on threads. It is less important, however, in most home-shop work than in high-production machining in a factory.

SHARPENING THE LATHE BIT

The following remarks on how a lathe tool works are summarized from the *Atlas Manual of Lathe Operation.*

Unlike the keen, sharp edge of a wood chisel, which either severs the wood fibers in cross-cutting or combines a severing and splitting action when cutting with the grain, the cutting edge of a lathe tool is relatively blunt—between 60° and 90°. This reflects the tremendous heat and pressure involved. Atlas speaks of pressures on the tool as high as 250,000 lbs. per square inch. The cutting action is very different from that of a hand-held woodturning chisel. It is part shearing and part wedging. The metal chip must not only be sheared away but also curled or deformed, and all of the force is ultimately expended in heat.

The cutting action of a metal lathe involves a powerful wedge-like bite into the metal plus the necessary curling away of the chip. The forces needed are heavy and the entire tool and machine must be rigid enough to resist them. Surprisingly, a powerful motor is not needed; ⅓ or ½ hp is plenty for most home-shop lathes.

Woodworkers are always concerned with honing extremely fine edges on their cutting tools. In metal-lathe work, however, although a fine, even keen, edge contributes to a high-quality finish on light finishing cuts, such an edge cannot be maintained during heavier, normal cutting. In fact, a very hard, ridgelike false cutting edge of work-hardened metal commonly builds up right at the cutting edge of the tool and helps in the cutting action on heavy cuts. For practical purposes, then, rather than spending too much time trying to sharpen a lathe tool to great keenness, it is far more important to provide the rake and clearance angles needed for various metals.

Clearance Angles

When discussing the sharpening of twist drills I pointed out that once the basic 59° angle was established it was necessary to provide a clearance angle. In short, the tip edges have to contact the metal and everything behind the tip has to slope away so the entire end of the drill does not bear on the work. The same clearance angles are vital to the operation of a lathe bit.

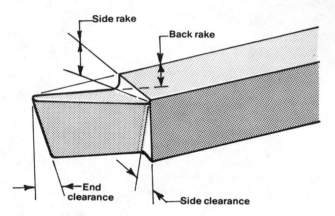

Like the twist drill, the lathe tool must present the cutting edges to the metal without having a noncutting face bearing on the surface. Clearance angles permit this action.

As a rule of thumb, remember that the common clearance angle for a twist drill is 12°. This same 12° is about right for the side clearance of a lathe bit. But a lathe tool cuts on both the nose, or front, and the side. This requires a second clearance angle at the front. Here, a common angle is 8°. Once the tool bit has been shaped to the desired contour, like the 59° on a drill, the front and side clearances can be ground in.

Back Rake

Note that both of the above clearances, front and side, are *only* clearances to keep the tool from riding flat against the workpiece. They do not relate to the cutting action as such. Two other angles must now be ground into the tool. The first is called "back rake," the angle at which the front cutting edge of the tool thrusts upward and into the metal. The back rake is the most critical angle you must grind in. If you consult the usual tables in your lathe manual, you'll find that 8° to 16° angles are specified for cutting various types of steel depending upon the alloy. Since most home shop work is done on mild steel and since you are not stretching for maximum

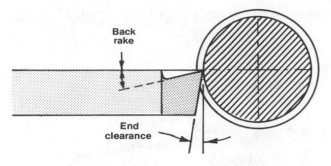

Angle of cutting tip relative to work metal is called back rake and varies according to the metal characteristics.

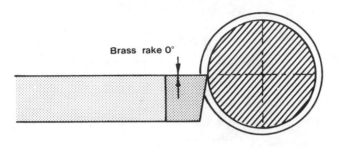

Although soft, brass has a peculiar response to cutting. For a smooth cut without snagging, no back rake, 0°, is used.

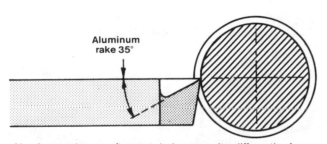

Aluminum, also a soft metal, behaves quite differently. A very steep back-rake angle generally works best.

production rates, 12° to 16° will usually do very well. Moreover, it is seldom necessary to check this angle precisely. With a little practice you'll soon learn to judge "about right" by eye.

When you start machining metals other than steel, things can change dramatically. There is often a temptation, for example, to make a quick and casual cut on brass without changing tool bits. The results are almost always bad gouge in the work and a broken bit. Or the workpiece may snag so badly as to be torn from the chuck. Brass simply cannot tolerate any rake angle. The standard rake for brass is 0°, but many experienced metalworkers prefer a slight negative or minus rake, which gives a nicer finish.

The peculiarities of different metals are apparent when comparing brass and aluminum. Logic indicates that since both are soft metals both ought to require the same back rake. But it's not so. A back rake of about 35°, quite an uphook, is needed for aluminum. Such a tool will usually produce an almost mirror finish on aluminum, whereas on brass it would spell instant disaster.

Side Rake

We have still another rake angle to consider, and that's side rake. Again, remember that a lathe tool moving along with the carriage cuts on both the nose and the side. As a matter of good practice it's common to try to cut from right to left. This places the cutting pressure on the headstock and chuck rather than on the smaller bearing area of the tailstock center. Obviously, this is not always possible, and you'll find yourself grinding both right-hand and left-hand tools. For a tool to move and cut toward the left, the

LATHE TOOL ANGELS

Material	Top Rake	Side Rake	Front Clearance	Side Clearance
Cast iron	5	12	8	10
Stainless steel	16-1/2	10	10	12
Copper	16-1/2	20	12	14
Brass and softer copper alloys	0	0	8	10
Harder copper alloys	10	0-2	12	10
Hard bronze	0	0-2	8	10
Aluminum	35	15	8	12
Monel metal & nickel	8	14	13	15
Phenol plastics	0	0	8	12
Various base plastics	0-5	0	10	14
Formica gear plastic	16-1/2	10	10	15
Fiber	0	0	12	15
Hard rubber	0 or –5	0	15	20

Rake and clearance angles shown here are good working practice but you'll probably deviate from them somewhat when you align the tool on center. If adjusting the tool-post rocker causes a major change in angle, you should shim the tool as needed to approximate these angles.

left edge should be higher than the right. This angle is called "side rake," and generally 10° to 15° is suitable for most metals except brass. The latter likes a 0° side rake. For tools that move and cut toward the right, of course, the side rake should slope down to the left.

The above information covers only the rudiments of lathe-bit grinding. A lathe manual will show you a wide array of tool profiles for various types of cutting operations and an equal range

THREE STEPS FOR MANDREL CENTERING

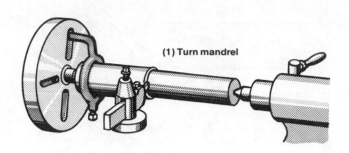

(1) Turn mandrel

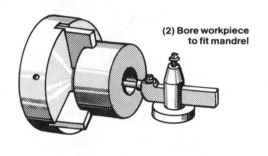

(2) Bore workpiece to fit mandrel

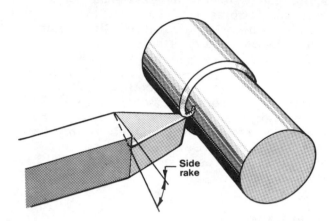

Since the cutting tool moves along the metal sideways, the cutting action is actually a combination of back rake and another angle called side rake. It can be ground for right- or left-hand travel.

of angles for special metals, plastics, etc. All of this is useful, but there are some practical aspects for the home shop that never get into the formal manuals.

HOLDING CENTERS

In Chapter 5, when talking about laying out sheet metal, I recommended establishing a center line and making all measurements from it. This avoids adding up errors that can creep in when you work progressively from point to point. Something of the same logic applies, but even more critically, with lathework. Here, a shift of even a few thousandths from the original work center results, usually, in a misshapen and useless workpiece. Indeed, the ability to think or plan through a series of progressive cuts without ever losing the original center is a secret, seldom emphasized enough, of successful lathework.

As an example, assume that you want to replace a bushing or a bearing in an electric motor or a garden-tractor transmission. Clearly, all that's needed is to take a piece of rough stock, turn the outside to a snug, press fit in the bore

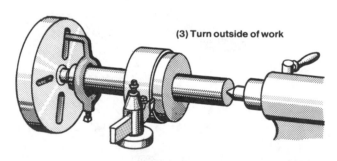

(3) Turn outside of work

Turning on a mandrel is one way to retain a center even though you must use two sequences in turning. Bore the central hole first; press the bushing on a mandrel with centers at each end; then turn the outside.

where it will eventually fit, and bore out the center to fit the shaft. The trick is to have the inner and outer diameters of the bushing on exactly the same center, and, of course, not angled.

If you start by first turning the outside and then withdrawing the tailstock center to permit drilling and boring the center hole, you will almost certainly get into trouble. Once the tailstock center is removed, the workpiece will be gripped at only one end. The force of the drilling and boring operation can easily cant the piece a few thousandths in the chuck.

There's a better way. Use a 60° center in both the headstock and the tailstock and turn a mandrel a few thousandths smaller in diameter than the shaft that will run in the bushing. Face off one end of your rough bushing stock to bear against the chuck face, leave the outside rough for the time being, and drill and bore the center hole.

The unfinished (outside) bushing may now be pressed over the mandrel, the mandrel centered, and the outside of the bushing turned. If sufficient extra stock is provided it's best to drive the bushing with a lathe dog and a faceplate. Note that it is possible, even probable, that the first outside cuts will show unevenness, but this doesn't matter because the final sizing will relate only to the center of the bore, which is centered by the mandrel. It is also true that the mandrel may mar the inside of the bushing slightly, but if you kept it a few thousandths undersize it will clean up when you ream the bushing after pressing it in.

There are literally hundreds of different situations in which it is important to hold center through several operations. There are two rules:
● Never expect a three-jaw chuck to retain center if the metal is removed and rechucked; it won't.
● Whenever possible, establish a center at both ends with well-seated center bearings in whatever you can provide, such as a mandrel or excess metal.

Drilling Center Holes

The beginner is likely to be casual about drilling his lathe center holes and assume that almost any sort of hole made with a twist drill will do if it's deep enough so the work doesn't slip off the center. This is an error. The center hole is actually a heavily loaded bearing.

The first step, of course, is to use a rule and center finder or other means to establish a point for a center punch. It's also important, after chucking the work, to locate the tailstock center dead on the mark. You may have to loosen the chuck slightly and tap the work into line. In fact, with soft metals, once the stock is chucked and approximately centered, it is often practical to

loosen the tailstock on the bed and slide it forward sharply so as to indent the work metal with the center itself. Follow with a center punch.

From here on the drilling should be done with a center drill in the tailstock chuck. Such drills cut rather slowly, and the small tip is easily broken off. Use plenty of lubricant and advance the tailstock feed screw slowly. Withdraw it frequently to clear the chips. After the tip has fully entered, the 60° edges will start to cut. Again, proceed slowly and inspect the hole until it is apparent that a nice bearing surface has been produced. Never drill so deeply that the drill shank starts to move into the metal. This leaves a sharp edge instead of a 60°-taper bearing surface. On the other hand, it is better to have a little extra bearing area than too little.

If you are using a conventional 60° dead cen-

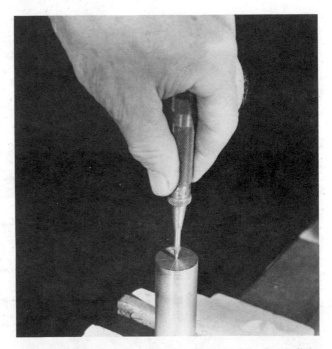

A good center is important to start any lathe job. Face off the end of the stock so you can scribe neat center lines. Use magnification to locate the tip of the prick punch. Automatic punch shown will drive the point into the metal as downward pressure is increased.

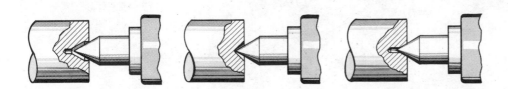

Neither too shallow nor too deep is the rule for center holes. You don't want the center to run on a shoulder after drilling too deep, left; but running on the tip, center, is equally bad. A good center hole is drilled just to the point where the taper angle on the drill stops.

ter, a lubricant must be applied to the center. This is unnecessary with a live center, which is another one of those lathe accessories it's nice to have. My own experience is that a good molybdenum-base grease works well. Before starting the cut, bring the tailstock center in snugly and lock it. Make an initial cut and then readjust the tailstock to take up for any slight wear-in of the center. Later, as successive passes are made, recheck the tailstock setting. The wear-in may have increased, or, more likely, because of heat and expansion the tailstock is excessively tight and needs tweaking back slightly.

WORKING TO ONE-THOUSANDTH

Although random turning of candlesticks and ornaments on a lathe may require little more than a good eye and an occasional check with calipers, more often than not a lathe project must fit some other piece or part accurately. Persons unacquainted with mechanical things find the concept of working to one-thousandth (.001″) difficult. One way to look at it is that the difference between a brand-new car and a worn-out clunker is about .002″ to .003″ at a few points. If, for example, the crankshaft bearings had a running clearance of .001″ to .0015″ when new, the engine will sound like a threshing machine when the bearings are worn by .002″ to .003″. If the piston clearance was .0025″ when new, at .005″ you'll hear the pistons rattle and blue smoke will roll out. Such fits and clearances are normal in all mechanical equipment. To learn this phase of metalworking you must learn to stay within them.

Center drills do not cut as fast as twist drills and should be entered and fed gently with plenty of lubrication. Continue until a good tapered center for the tailstock is apparent.

Good lubrication for the tailstock center is a must unless you use a live center with its own bearing. I use a general purpose "moly" grease and it stands up well. Even so, on prolonged operations, relube from time to time.

MACHINE FIT CLEARANCES

Nominal Diameter Inches		Allowances for Different Fits				
	Hole Tolerance	Running Fit	Push Fit	Drive Fit	Forced Fit
Up to 1/2″	+.0005 −.0005	−.001 −.002	−.0003 −.0008	+.0005 +.0003	+.001 +.0005
1/2″ to 1″	+.001 −.0005	−.0015 −.003	−.0003 −.0008	+.001 +.0008	+.002 +.0015
1″ to 2″	+.001 −.0005	−.002 −.004	−.0003 −.0008	+.0015 +.001	+.004 +.003
2″ to 3″	+.0015 −.001	−.0025 −.0045	−.0005 −.001	+.0025 +.0015	+.006 +.0045
3″ to 4″	+.0015 −.001	−.003 −.005	−.0005 −.001	+.003 +.002	+.008 +.006

Machined metal parts are normally fitted to provide a running clearance with a lubricant film, or, a nonrunning fit to secure the parts under operating loads. Size the bore of the hole to an accurate dimension and adapt the shaft diameter to suit the desired fit. Unlike in woodworking, even a few tenths of a thousandth of an inch can make a substantial difference in fit.

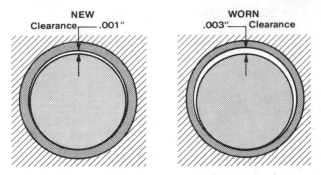

If you think you can't feel the difference a few thousandths of an inch makes, try a bearing and shaft with a nice, snug .001″ clearance and then one with about .003″ clearance. The difference will be very apparent. It's also the difference between "new" and "worn-out" in many machines including your car.

The feed screws on your lathe have collars calibrated in thousandths of an inch. These collars are secured by a small setscrew, and by loosening the screw you can turn them to zero or any desired reading. You might, for example, have turned a piece of stock that you want to finish at 2.000″ and it is now 2.005″. You are sure of the present dimension because you measured it with your micrometers. The obvious trap is to think of cranking in .005″ for a finish cut. But remember, as the work turns you're cutting from all sides, and hence you want to feed in only .0025″, half of the present oversize. In a perfect world you might do exactly that and wind up on the nose. In the real world this will almost certainly produce the wrong results. With luck, you'll wind up too fat—the work will still be slightly oversize, and you can correct it. But

Murphy's Law is more likely to prevail and your work will measure 1.999″ or worse, and it will be scrap.

There are a number of unpredictable variables involved. For one thing, the workpiece may be hot and expanded from your cutting. If the final dimension must be close, allow it to cool before measuring and making the final cut. Secondly, there is probably a certain amount of wear and backlash in the cross-feed screw and associated parts that make the little dial less than absolute. Thirdly, every lathe cut introduces a slight amount of spring or flex into the work and the machine. To prove this, make a cut in one direc-

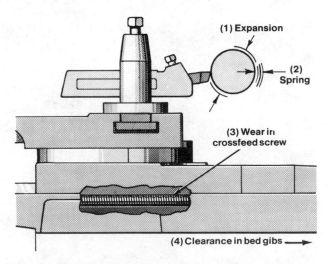

Nothing's perfect, particularly in home-shop lathes. Expansion from heat, wear, oil clearance in the gibs, and the spring of work and machine make that last half-thousandth touchy.

Calibrated crossfeed collar is divided in one-thousandths of an inch from zero to one hundred. The small setscrew allows you to rotate it to the desired zero setting. Don't take exact feeds for granted—there are too many variables which can slip in between the dial readings and the tool.

Nearly all lathe feed screws will have some backlash or slack where a slight turn of the feed handle does nothing. When feeding in, be sure this looseness has been removed before turning feed a measured amount. A delicate touch helps.

tion and then, without touching the cross-slide feed, reverse the carriage and run the tool back the other way. You'll see that the tool is taking a light cut. Reverse the direction once more for a third cut at the same setting and you'll still see the tool scraping up a fuzzy cut. This is simply the spring and the elasticity of the machine and the work bouncing back, so to speak.

The Final Cuts

Going back to our original example, to reach the final dimension of 2.000" from 2.005" you would probably tweak in .001" on the feed and make a pass to the left and back to the right. Better still, if you have left a little surplus stock at the tailstock end you can make some light trial cuts on a section just wide enough to measure with the micrometers. This will tell you if you're getting into trouble before you ruin the entire piece. If you're now within .0005", one-half thousandth, you should consider the level of finish you want. Usually, this will be a high polish. The remain-

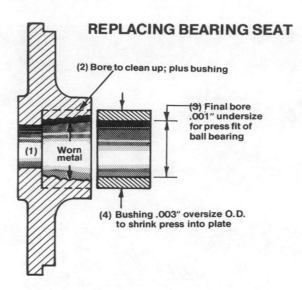

REPLACING BEARING SEAT

(2) Bore to clean up; plus bushing

(3) Final bore .001" undersize for press fit of ball bearing

(1) Worn metal

(4) Bushing .003" oversize O.D. to shrink press into plate

A typical metalworking repair might be a motor end plate in which a ball bearing had locked up and turned. With the bearing seat destroyed, the only hope of repair is to turn an oversize cavity and install a bushing or sleeve to reestablish the proper center and push fit for a new bearing.

To make a bushing to restore the damaged motor end plate, so it would again accept and center an armature ball bearing, an aluminum billet was sawed off and faced on both ends. One end was center drilled and the outside was turned to 2⁵⁄₁₆" (2.3125"), a dimension chosen to provide adequate wall thickness without removing too much metal from the motor end plate.

Without removing work from chuck, a small pilot drill, followed by a convenient size larger drill, was used to open working space for boring bar.

The boring operation was quickly done with a tool made from a discarded reamer. As the final bore was approached, the amount of metal removed was almost microscopic until a new ball bearing could just be pressed into the bushing with firm hand pressure. The bushing was then sawed free of waste chucking stock and the sawed surface cleaned up with a facing cut.

Establishing a center for the worn and corroded end plate was difficult. By bringing the lathe tool just to bear on the outer seating surface of the plate and adjusting the work in the chuck until contact was even all around, a close approximation was possible. Note the shim stock under the chuck jaw at the upper left. The shim was needed because the outer edge of the plate was too rough for accurate centering. The boring tool was used cautiously to clean up the damaged metal gradually until the new bushing would almost enter the bore with light tapping.

Meanwhile, the bushing had been chilled below zero in the family freezer to shrink it. When placed in the bore and quickly rammed home by the tailstock it seated and expanded to a very tight fit.

Pressing might have reduced bushing inner diameter so the assembly was left in the chuck in case further machining was needed. When armature bearing was tried in the bore, however, it was just right and later the motor ran fine.

ing extra metal may be cleaned up and polished with very fine abrasive cloth or paper and kerosene. Or it may work better, depending upon the metal, to use a well-lubricated flat hone and sweep the hone freely across the surface while the metal is turning. This is slower, but much safer, than attempting to make a final lathe cut of one-half thousandth or less.

Quite often what is important is not working to an exact dimension but achieving a suitable fit between the part you're making and another part. You may want a running fit where one part slides over or into another with a firm but easy twist; or you may want a tap fit, or even a press or a shrink fit. This is usually accomplished by retracting the tailstock and actually trying the mating pieces. Be sure all surfaces are wiped clean when doing this. If the final fit is to be a tap or a press fit, the entering part should have a slight chamfer or break-edge to ease the entrance. A slight tap will tell you just how snug it is.

Lapping.   If you want a very fine running fit with a small oil clearance—a piston in a cylinder, for example—you may have to lap the two surfaces together. This is done by finish-turning the parts so they won't quite go together without a considerable push and a twist. Now coat the surfaces with a fine abrasive such as aluminum oxide and oil. Put the lathe in back-gear so it

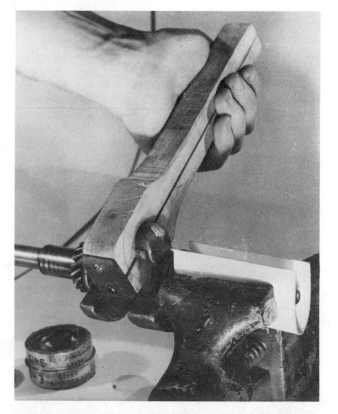

Lapping was one way to clean up and resize a worn crankpin for an antique engine. A maple block was bored to slightly less than the pin diameter and then sawed apart and hinged with leather. Valve-grinding compound was used for lapping.

turns very slowly and work one part into the other slowly and gently. The lapping abrasive will have to be flushed away and replenished frequently. Do not allow the work to become hot. A final polish may be given the parts with a mix of Bon Ami and a cooking grease such as Crisco. This makes an excellent lapping compound.

CUTTING THREADS

The screw-cutting, or thread-cutting, lathe gets its name, of course, from its ability to produce almost any kind of thread form and pitch. Most home-shop thread cutting will be confined to standard 60° U.S. threads, although you can also cut Acme threads, square threads, metric threads, and other threads. You should become familiar with the basic terms used when discussing threads, but if you understand that "pitch" refers to the number of threads per inch, the "major diameter" is the full diameter of the finished thread, and the "minor diameter" is the diameter at the bottom of the thread cut, you're on your way.

Thread cutting starts with turning the stock to its major, or finished, diameter in the area to be threaded. In most cases, beginners and occasional thread cutters should carry this diameter a little past the point where the thread is to terminate. I'll explain why in a minute. At the tailstock end you should also provide an extra ¼" or so of waste stock.

With the major diameter turned, use the extra stock at the tailstock end to turn a short section to the minor diameter. This will be your gage later, and when the threading tool just touches it your thread has been cut deep enough.

If you picture the tool moving along under power feed and cutting a thread until it suddenly comes to a point where you want to end the thread instantly, you'll realize that this is somewhat like repeatedly driving a car at a brick wall and suddenly applying the brakes with the bumper just touching the wall. Maybe some experienced machinists can do it consistently, but I can't recommend it. That's why I suggested leaving a little extra stock where the thread will end. The prudent practice is to cut a narrow groove in the stock at the end of the thread opposite the tailstock. This gives you a chance to run the tool tip out of the thread and into the open space of the groove and allows time to flip out the feed lever and stop the carriage travel.

There is a second sound engineering reason for this groove. Any metal section with a sharp notch in it is inherently weakened and subject to fatigue failure. The abrupt termination of a thread is such a notch. The bottom of the clear-

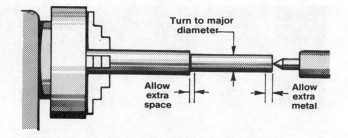

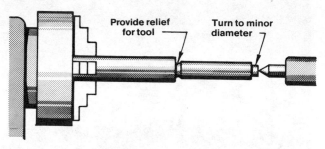

The unexpected can happen fast when you're cutting threads. A little extra metal at the tailstock end tips you when something's wrong. And the groove at the end of the cut lets you get out safely. Turn the tailstock end to the thread minor diameter; the left end groove a trifle deeper.

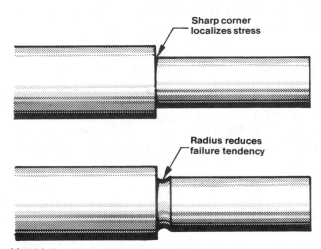

Metal-fatigue failure lurks in sharp corners just as a nick in a piece of wire makes it easy to break. Always provide a generous, smooth fillet in grooves and corners.

ance space should have a generous radius, or fillet, that blends into the metal and eliminates the sharp corner that would localize stress at that point.

The above cuts were made with the lathe set at normal feeds, but you must now change the gear setup to cut the thread pitch you want. If you have a change-gear lathe, prepare for some

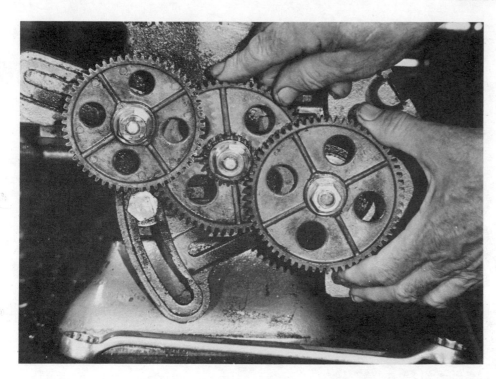

Nearly all gears require a few thousandths backlash or running clearance and these lathe gears are no exception. Hold one gear and rattle the other against it. You should set them so there is a barely perceptible, but audible, looseness between them.

close concentration on the tables in your lathe manual. They will call for gears with a specific number of teeth in a specific location. If at first this seems complex, don't let it bother you. After a few such changes it gets much easier. One thing that helps is to keep the spare gears clean, dry, and free of lubricant. Clean the other gears as you remove them and lube the spindles with oil as you install them. Hold off lubing the gears until the complete setup is made. Many beginners try to engage the gear teeth too tightly. Each gear needs a little tooth clearance, called "backlash," to run freely. Be sure that you can grasp each one and rattle it slightly against its mating gear. This will have no effect on accuracy.

Threading Tools

It is perfectly possible to grind a thread-cutting tool from any standard lathe bit, and your lathe manual will tell you how. It is infinitely better to purchase a threading tool that is precision-ground, will cut any 60° thread, and will last a lifetime. Note that although the point of the tool will have a 60° profile, there are interferences when working down in the vee of a thread that are not present in conventional turning. All of this concern is eliminated with the threading tool.

A second tool, called a "center gage" or "thread gage," is needed to align the tip of the threading tool with the stock. It has a 60° notch into which you insert the tool tip. You can examine it against the light or a white background to see if you have the tool properly aligned. The exact steps for threading may vary a little with different lathes, and the maker's directions must be followed exactly. Do not attempt to cut your first threads on a workpiece you would not want to scrap. Almost certainly you'll make a mistake. Thread cutting is a series of procedures that must be done by the numbers.

The numbered cross-feed dial should be set to zero with the tip of the threading tool conveniently close to but not touching the work. You

Although you can grind your own threading tool, one like this is much better. Resharpening requires only a light grinding touch on top of the cutter. Tool will last a lifetime.

Thread gage with its 60° notch is held against the work and the tool tip adjusted until it touches evenly on both sides. This aligns the tool tip at 90° to the axis of the work.

Once thread cutting is started, the moving cutting tool must reenter the partially cut and rotating thread at exactly the same point. The threading dial is divided into quarters, engages the lead screw, and turns slowly. At the instant the proper mark passes the index, you must quickly engage the carriage drive. Engaging at the wrong mark will tear up partially cut threads.

Here, the threading tool is moving towards the head-stock and cutting a heavier than usual chip.

will back the tool out to this point each time you complete a cutting pass. This is necessary to clear the work and allow you to bring the carriage back for the next cut. The addition of cutting depth for each pass is done with the compound.

If you stop to think about it, you'll see that it's important that the tool tip engage the metal at exactly the same point on each pass or else it wouldn't enter the threads. This is managed by watching a rotating dial on the carriage that is driven by the lead screw. When the proper mark on the dial lines up, you drop the feed lever in and the tool again moves into and along the thread. A slip-up results in watching your nicely cut threads torn to shreds. Concentration is vital.

Margins for Error

There are a few steps you can take to reduce the chance of a thread-cutting disaster. The first is to run your lathe in back-gear and at the lowest speed ratio of the drive belt. This slows things down and gives you time to react. Secondly, if at all possible, leave some extra stock at the tailstock end turned to the major diameter. This gives you a little time to react if you do something wrong. The damaged or extra threads can be cut off later. Never flip the carriage-feed lever

out with the tool in the thread. This will simply result in cutting a groove and destroying the threads. If you must react to an emergency, back out the cross-slide crank as fast as you can and retract the tool. This may misform some threads, but if you haven't progressed too far they may clean up fairly well on later cuts.

Finally, never remove the work from the chuck before completing the thread. It is almost impossible to replace it so the work is centered and the tool engaged properly in the partially cut threads.

Finishing Up Threads

Progress toward the final thread may be checked with a thread gage, but in the end the most important thing is to have a thread that works smoothly on its mating thread. In many cases, commercially threaded nuts tend to run slightly tight on what appear to be perfect vee threads that you've cut. Therefore, before removing the work from the chuck, back out the tailstock and try the nut on the new thread. In some cases you'll find that the nut thread is a trifle shallow at the bottom and the crest of the vee thread binds. If you've cut a few extra threads as recommended, try dressing off the crest of the threads. If the nut now goes on nicely, repeat

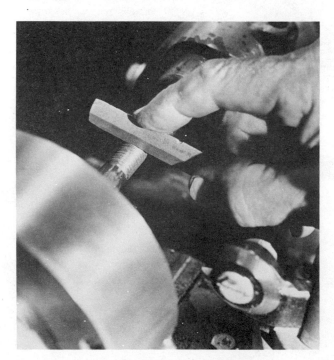

For a final finish on the new thread, a kerosene lubricated hone is held in the thread and allowed to move along as the lathe turns.

Although you've brought a new thread down to a previously turned root diameter and it appears finished, back off the tailstock and, if at all possible, try it with the nut or other part into which it threads. Once removed from the chuck it is very difficult to rechuck a thread for more cutting.

over the rest of the thread. Another good practice to produce a cleanly finished and smooth-running thread is to use a small 60° vee-shaped hone and plenty of kerosene to polish the threads as they run in the lathe. This removes small burrs and rough spots.

The above is only a partial coverage of threading operations, and I offer it to guide you past some of the more common pitfalls. Your lathe manual should be the final guide on detailed procedures.

MILLING

Although milling is not really a lathe operation, it is so useful that few lathe owners can resist acquiring or making a milling-vise attachment. Again, the topic is too complex to detail here, but you should understand milling as a basic part of metalworking even if you have to farm out such jobs to a local machine shop. One way for the woodworker to think of milling is to compare it with joining, routing, or spindle shaping. Some forms of milling cutters used industrially are mounted horizontally on an arbor or cross shaft and the work is passed under them on a moving table. The cutters, of course, are much heavier and somewhat differently shaped than planer or jointer blades for wood, but the principle is the same.

In lathe milling, however, the cutter bit is mounted in the headstock spindle using a collet as described in Chapter 20. The work is secured in the milling vise and moved across the cutter horizontally or vertically in a succession of fairly light cuts. The cuts must be light, because the

Milling cutters come in many shapes and forms but all work by rotating sharp edges while the work is fed past them. Milling vise to hold the work mounts on the lathe cross feed where the compound normally mounts. Vise may be raised, lowered, canted, or swung.

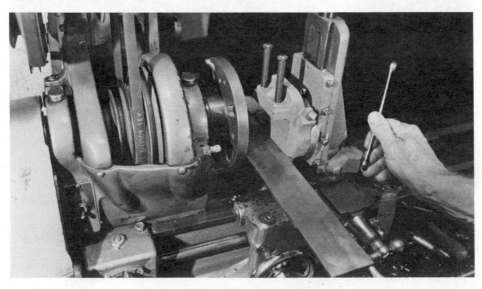

As a quick, preliminary squaring operation, insert a steel rule or straightedge between chuck face or faceplate and the jaw of the milling vise.

lathe and milling vise are not as strong and massive as milling machine parts.

Milling Procedures

Once you have determined the nature of the cut you need and selected and mounted a cutter, consult your lathe manual for the appropriate spindle speed for the metal involved. If you plan to use power feed it will be necessary to set the feed speed as well. Many small milling operations, however, are done with manual feed.

If you will want the path of the work to be at exactly 90° to the cutter axis, the vise must be turned and oriented at 90° to the headstock. Experienced metalworkers often make this the first operation and use either the faceplate or the face of a three-jaw chuck as a surface against which

to swing the face for squaring. It's important to make this setting against the inner face of the vise against which the stock will be backed or shimmed.

Since the travel of the cross slide is limited, you must locate the work so the desired milling area can be fully traversed without coming up against either limit to travel. Backing the feed screw totally out of the cross slide while milling is somewhat startling, to say the least.

The vertical positioning of the jaws must also be checked. Often you will have to block the work up with steel blocks. The downward travel of the milling vise is also limited, and again you must locate the work so it stays within the range of movement.

Even though you have clamped the work firmly against the back of the vise, or spaced it

The milling cutter is then locked firmly into the collet.

For final alignment between the feed travel and the tool, a dial indicator mounted on the tool should show zero movement when the feed is moved across the cutter axis. Make the same check with the vertical travel of the milling vise's jaws. Adjust the vise or shim the work as needed.

out with spacer blocks or shims, a final check should be made, preferably with a dial indicator, to be sure the work is truly at 90° to the spindle and not running at an angle. The same indicator can be used to be certain the work is running horizontally.

Milling Cuts

There are two ways to move the work relative to the cutter. One is called, for reasons lost to history, "conventional milling." Presume that the cut will be made on the bottom of the milling cutter. For conventional milling the metal is fed into the cutter in a direction *opposite* the direction of cutter rotation. This means that the cut starts at the bottom at the thinnest part of the chip and the chip thickness gradually increases until the cutter flute edge emerges from the metal. The other way is to move the work into the cutter in the *same* direction as cutter rotation. Here, the cutter takes the largest bite and produces the thickest part of the chip at the top and the chip thickness tapers out at the bottom. This is called "climb milling," since, in a sense, the cutter is trying to climb out of the cut.

Conventional milling, it is claimed, doesn't produce quite as smooth a finish as climb milling, since the cutter tends to slide along the metal a short distance before biting in. On the other hand, with light milling equipment on a home-shop lathe, the impact of each cutter edge striking the metal at full chip thickness is rather heavy. Conventional milling greatly reduces this jolting effect. Each job is different, and it pays to take a few light cuts both ways. Use the method that works best for you under the circumstances.

METAL SPINNING

Forming the softer metals such as aluminum, pewter, copper, and other art metals by the spinning process is a fascinating operation. You actually make the metal flow under your hands. It is a true handcraft in the sense that the feel of

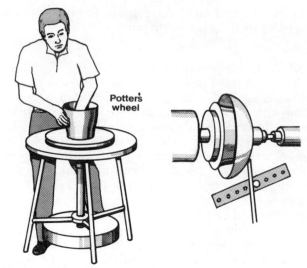

Potter's wheel

When rotated at fairly high speed, metal can be shaped and formed almost as a potter's hands and tools shape soft clay on a potter's wheel. The forces required are greater, but many of the same principles, including being wary of thick and thin spots, still apply.

the metal and visual judgment of progress is essential. Skill comes only with practice, but the beginner can enjoy the spinning technique as well as the artisan.

Spinning depends upon the fact that when metal is rotated at relatively high speed, 1,000 to 1,500 rpm, it can be forced, manually, to assume the shape supporting it. This means that a flat disc can be formed into a bowl, cone, or even a complex shape such as a necked vessel. A metal-turning lathe, or even a heavy-duty wood lathe with a ball or roller-bearing headstock, can be used.

Spinning Forms

The form over which the metal is spun is called the chuck, and its shape conforms to the shape desired for the interior wall of the project. Since we're working with sheet metal, the exterior form will be almost identical. Chucks are easily turned from any durable wood such as maple, cherry, birch, or even pine for a one-time project.

Conventional milling resembles scooping earth from underneath and lifting it up. The cutter teeth bite in under the metal as the work moves against cutter rotation.

Climb milling starts with a big bite from the top and pushes the metal out the bottom. Try both ways to see which works best on a given job.

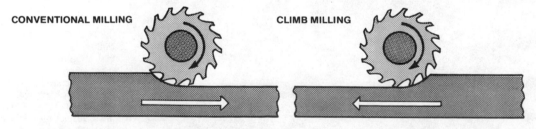

CONVENTIONAL MILLING

CLIMB MILLING

They must take considerable pressure, and since they are fitted with a member that can be screwed onto the lathe spindle or chucked, softwoods are not recommended. Many amateur metal spinners simply screw or bolt the wooden chuck to the lathe faceplate. The chuck should be dressed with a beeswax finish and polished smooth.

The workpiece, a flat metal disc, is clamped between the chuck and another turned wooden block called a "follow block." The follow block is supported by the tailstock, which applies the

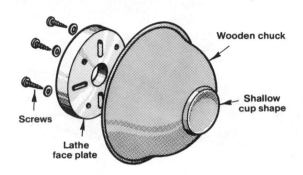

The spinning chuck conforms to the inner shape of the form you want to spin. It needs a means of driving from the headstock and benefits from a slight concavity on the tailstock end. Hard wood, polished and coated with wax, works fine.

clamping pressure. For this reason, the tailstock should be of the ball-bearing, live-center type, or a ball bearing can be positioned between the usual 60° tailstock center and the follow block.

Spinning Tools

The pressure to bring the spinning metal into conformity with the chuck is applied by one or two tools that are levered against fulcrum pins set in a tool rest. The tool rest somewhat resembles the usual wood-lathe rest except it has a flat top with spaced holes for fulcrum pins. The latter are shouldered and should fit the holes securely. The tools may be either wood or metal, but wooden tools are common for home-shop operations.

The best material for the spinning tool, which has a rounded end, and the follow tool or backstick, which has a wedge-shaped end, is probably hickory from a garden-tool, ax, or sledge handle. Anything about 1″ in diameter will do, and the two tools should be about 2½′ to 3′ long to provide the needed leverage.

Spinning Operations

To start, the disc of annealed metal is clamped between the chuck and the follow block and centered as closely as possible by turning the lathe

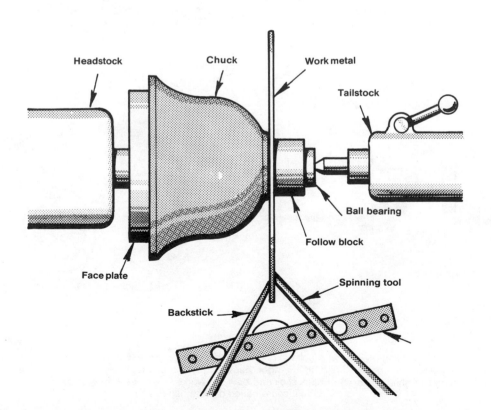

The spinning assembly of chuck, metal, and follow block, the latter with a ball bearing for free turning, are clamped together under tailstock pressure.

by hand and watching the edge of the metal move relative to the tool rest or other fixed object. After starting the lathe at low speed you can use the backstick, levered lightly between the tool rest and the edge of the disc, to readjust the centering by loosening the tailstock slightly so the adjustment can take place. Snug up the tailstock. In all of these operations stand *well away* from the area in front of the disc. It may fly out violently, and this is the reason for centering at low speed. Once the initial forming, called "hooking on," is done at the bottom of the work, the chances of the work's flying out are less.

When the metal is securely centered, coat it with tallow, very heavy grease, beeswax, or even laundry soap. Excess lubricant will be thrown off. Hold the spinning tool under your right arm so it can lever against a fulcrum pin and apply a sliding and rolling pressure right at the base of the chuck to produce the initial hook-on.

From here on you will learn more by experience than by reading. Each pressure stroke should be made in a continuous motion and eased right out to the edge of the work disc. When wrinkling or buckling start to appear, pressure from the back side between the backstick and the spinning tool should be used to straighten it out. Some metal spinners seem to work almost entirely with the spinning tool.

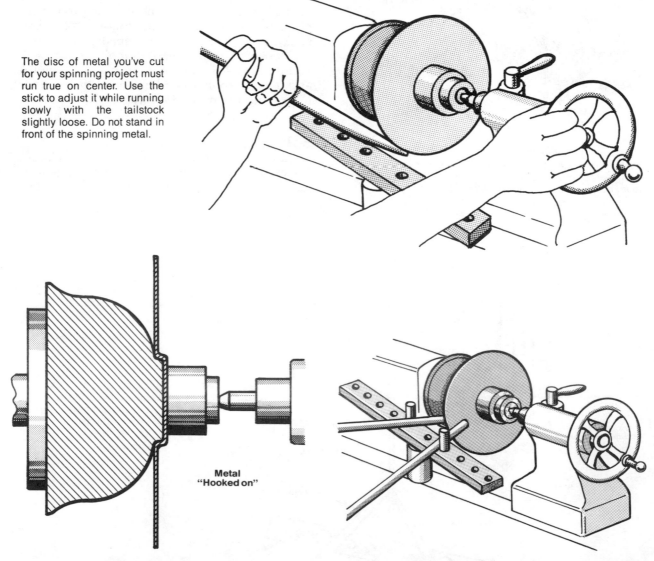

The disc of metal you've cut for your spinning project must run true on center. Use the stick to adjust it while running slowly with the tailstock slightly loose. Do not stand in front of the spinning metal.

Metal
"Hooked on"

"Hooking on" is the metalspinner's term for the initial tool pressure which shapes the metal to the tailstock end of the chuck and fairly well secures it against slipping out or shifting between the chuck and the follower.

Much of your spinning can be done with a single stick worked from the right, but wrinkles and other problems often call for a back stick and both are worked together. This is an exercise in skillful coordination of both hands and arms.

After final trimming, many spun pieces are finished off with a rolled, or partially rolled, edge. You can roll the edge with the stick or a grooved beading tool.

Others seem to use both tools almost constantly.

When the final shape of the metal has been worked solidly against the forming chuck, the edge of the material must be trimmed with a sharp steel cutting tool. You can make such a tool by grinding a diamond point on a file and using it much like a woodturning tool to trim the edge. Be certain to provide a long enough handle for a firm grip and to get your hands well clear of the waste metal.

After trimming, many metal spinners prefer to finish the project with a rolled edge. There are several ways of doing this, the simplest being pressure from the backstick to gradually raise, turn, and invert the edge in. If you get into spinning as a hobby, however, you will probably acquire a beading tool for this job.

Making Deep Forms

Although shallow vessels are easily spun on a single chuck, deeper pieces may require several chucks used in succession. The number of steps will depend, of course, on the complexity of the finished shape, but three or four, starting with a shallow cone and gradually stepping down, are common.

Other shapes with large bases, narrow waists, and flared-out tops can be spun, but there is the obvious problem of removing the chuck if the base end is larger than the waist. You can solve this either by making the project in two pieces and later joining them, or, more elegantly, by making up a chuck somewhat like an interlocking block puzzle. The outer faces must be keyed or dovetailed to an inner core. When the workpiece is completed, the core is withdrawn and the side forms removed individually through the narrow part of the vessel.

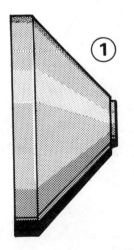 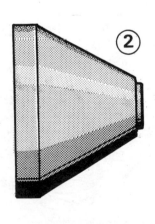 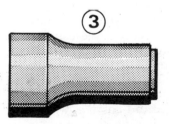

Some spinning projects involve more severe and agressive shaping than can be done on a single chuck. Chucks shaped for progressively deeper contours must be used.

22. SAND CASTING

The ability of metal to be melted and poured into a form is one of the significant differences between metal and wood. It makes complex shapes possible with a minimum of shaping.

The form or mold may be a permanent material and cooled so it is not destroyed by the hot metal. This process, usually called die casting or permanent-mold casting, is beyond the capabilities of the home shop. Lost-wax casting, which was discussed in Chapter 15, can be done in the home shop but is best suited to producing small, fine parts. However, sand casting, which was probably the first casting process used to form useful tools, weapons, and household and agricultural implements, can be done easily in the home shop using metals with low melting points. Often casting provides a way to form a basic shape, which can then be machined, drilled, tapped, or otherwise worked to make the finished part. This is common, for example, in model-engine work.

A Hole in the Sand

A casting starts as a hole or a hollow area the shape of the desired item in a bed of tightly packed sand. The sand must be of a nature and consistency to accept the shape into which it's been packed and to retain that shape without

If foundry work and casting are mysteries to you, think in terms of cake or gelatin molds. When the liquid hardens it will assume the shape of the cavity into which it was poured.

collapsing before and during the pouring of the metal. There are literally thousands of brands and formulations of sand used in commercial foundries. Some have highly specialized properties for use with certain metals and alloys. Many incorporate special binders, and some are baked to form a hard mold before pouring. These

Castings range from intricate to fairly simple, such as this lathe faceplate. To use this piece as a pattern, the central hole and two small holes must be filled.

MELTING POINTS OF METALS

Metal	Melting Temp. Deg. F.
Aluminum	1215
Brass (yellow)	.1640
Bronze (cast)	1650
Copper	1920
Iron, Gray cast	2200
Lead	620
Steel (.20%) SAE 1020	2800
Solder (50–50)	420
Tin	450
Zinc	785

Choose your home casting projects to suit your metal melting capabilities. Aluminum is popular because of its ready availability and relatively low melting temperature.

have little real application for the home metal-worker.

All that is really needed is a relatively fine-grained foundry sand, which when mixed with water, will pack together and retain the image of the pattern. Typically, this is called green sand, although the color may vary widely from black to brown to tan. The process of mixing it with water and working out the lumps is called "mulling" and essentially resembles mixing flour with water to make dough. In the home shop, the mixture can be simply shoveled and turned on the floor or a board until it is smooth and lump-free.

The Flask

For simple castings the metalworker can easily construct a two-part wooden box to contain the sand for molding and pouring. The only important concern is that the box be sturdy enough to resist the ramming action of packing the sand. Two flat supports for the flask, called molding boards, are also needed.

You can even use a one-part flask for the simplest form of molding by pouring molten metal into an open-face mold. This is exactly like pouring batter in a cake tin. Unfortunately, "cakes" made this way will not rise but will "fall," because the cooling metal will slump somewhat. Open-face molding, however, is perfectly practical for pouring weights or crude forms such as boat anchors.

The lower half of the two-part flask is called the "drag." The upper, usually identical half is called the "cope." Neither has a top or bottom; the molding boards serve as top and bottom. The

Foundry sand is messy. Use a sheet of plywood to keep it clean and off the floor while you mix in water. When properly moistened you should be able to squeeze a handful of sand and have it retain its shape without showing excess water. The small shovel is used for mixing sand and the next step, filling the flask.

cope has two guides or extension legs that extend down and engage matching guides on the drag. When the cope is placed over the drag the two parts of the flask are aligned by the legs so they cannot slide about.

Starting the Mold

I'll talk about patterns and their requirements later, but for the moment assume that you have a pattern, or an object that you want to reproduce, that is flat on one side and of complex shape on the other. It might be, for example, a bookend, a doorstop, or a metal faceplate for a lathe. The pattern must be free of any areas that would engage the sand and tear it apart when the pattern is withdrawn. Quite often when you are using an existing part it will have bolt holes or other openings that are added to the finished casting but cannot be cast. The faceplate shown, for example, had two tapped holes. Problem areas such as this should be filled with some substance such as wax, modeling clay, or even auto-body putty before attempting a mold. You can also change or modify the contours this way if you want.

A molding board is now cleaned of foreign material and the drag placed on it in an *inverted* position. Place the pattern, flat side down, pretty much in the center of the open drag. The first step, since the moist sand tends to stick to the pattern, is to sprinkle the pattern and the surface of the molding board with a very fine special sand called parting sand. Parting sand is kept in a cloth bag, and simply shaking the bag will let

enough parting sand through the cloth to coat the pattern lightly. You might liken the process to sprinkling dry flour on a breadboard to keep the dough from sticking.

Now the green sand that will pack the pattern and mold must be sprinkled over the pattern completely free of lumps. This is done by placing a shovelful of loose sand in a screen-bottom container called a "riddle" and shaking the riddle from side to side so the sifted sand falls onto and covers the pattern.

When the pattern is well covered, put a shovelful or two of sand in the flask and pack it firmly over the pattern with your hands. Add more sand to level out the partially filled flask and work it well into the corners. The packing or "ramming" of the mold is now started. Conventional, although old-fashioned, foundry rams are made of hardwood with a blunt, wedge-shaped end and a flat, malletlike end. The wedge end is best for working in the corners and around the walls of the flask, and the mallet end is used on more open areas. Ram and pack the sand to remove voids and produce a uniformly dense pack. Continue to add sand and tamp until the packed drag overflows slightly. Use a straightedge or board worked across the top of the flask to strike off the sand evenly.

Filling the Cope

The bottom half of the mold is now ready to invert so the cope may be added. To do this, place the second molding board on top of the filled drag and clamp or grip it tightly while gently inverting the entire drag. Removing the original molding board will now reveal the pattern firmly bedded in the sand.

Install the still-empty cope so the legs are solidly aligned in the guides in the drag and again sprinkle parting sand to prevent the two halves of the mold from sticking together. At this stage, several decisions are necessary. The first is where

Off center 1/8" each end

4-1/4"

2"

3/4" hardwood

1-1/8"

Cope

10"

8"

3/4" plywood

#10 x 1-1/4" flathead screws

#10 x 2" flathead screws

2-1/2"

Drag

Molding board 3/4" plywood

SMALL HOME-MADE FLASK

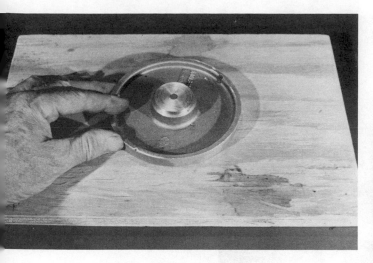

To prevent damp molding sand from sticking to pattern and board, it must be sprinkled with a dustlike parting sand. Use only enough for a light coating.

The pattern, in this case an existing part, is placed in the approximate center of the molding board. Note that the center hole has been filled with an aluminum plug turned to fit. The smaller holes have been plugged with wax so they won't fill with sand and tear the sand mold later.

Lumpy sand would impair detail contact. The first sand into the flask should be screened through a riddle. This riddle is an old food tin with screen wire riveted to the edges. Cover the pattern completely with riddled sand.

The remaining sand is now added, a layer at a time, and thoroughly tamped or "rammed" over mold and along edges and into corners of the drag. Here a piece of scrap wood has been bluntly tapered and is used for a make-do ram.

After ramming the sand in solidly and striking the top level with the edge of a board, the upper molding board is placed on the drag and the drag is carefully inverted.

you want the molten metal to enter the cavity when pouring. Your decision will have a major impact on your success. If you direct the metal into a thin part of the casting it may chill and block the flow to a heavier part. In some cases only trial and error will produce a good casting, but for a start try to direct the metal to the heaviest part first.

Sprues and vents. The actual entry of the hot metal will be through a hole, called a "sprue," from the open face of the cope to a trough, called a "gate," in the sand leading into the mold cavity. The sprue is formed by placing a "sprue pin" a short distance—about ¾" to 1" will do—from the edge of the pattern. Make the sprue pin from a length of broomstick or dowel; drive a nail into one end, cut off the head, and sharpen the point. The nail will help to keep the sprue pin from wandering when you ram the sand.

The second decision you must make is where you want to place a riser or risers. Risers are passages much like sprues except they generally come directly off a strategically chosen place on the pattern, and, rather than being an entrance for molten metal, they are exits. As the metal is poured it will fill the mold and seek a level with the sprue by coming up the risers. This is a venting action but also provides a mass or supply of metal to force, by gravity, a more complete filling of the cavity.

Vents allow the cavity to void itself of steam, gases, and air as the hot metal pours in. Failure to vent properly will inevitably produce bubble-shaped cavities in the casting. You can poke in

vents with lengths of steel rod after completing the mold, or you can position lengths of wire or small wooden sticks before you fill the cope with sand. Vents form small projections of the finished casting and must later be cut away, like gates and risers. This means you must be careful where you locate them, but it's better to put in

With cope in place, a sprue pin with a short nail in the bottom end is placed a short distance from the pattern. Other, smaller pins are placed on opposite side and at the center to provide risers for excess metal and to ensure casting cavity is filled with metal. Drawing below shows flask in cross section.

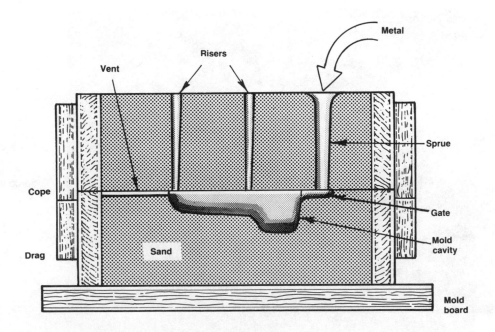

a little extra work trimming a vent residual than have no metal at all at that point.

With sprues, risers, and vents placed, proceed to dust the cope with parting sand and fill and ram it with molding sand exactly like the drag. After filling to the top, use a "slick"—a spatula-like tool for shaping molding sand—to form a small depression around the top of the sprue to make it easy to pour in the metal. Wiggle the sprue and risers slightly to loosen them, then withdraw them from the cope.

Removing the Pattern

Removing the pattern and finishing up the mold cavity is one of those jobs where you hold your breath and hope that you don't sneeze. Before lifting the sand-filled cope from the drag, some molders gently tap the cope along the sides at the parting line to encourage separation of the two bodies of sand. This may help, or it may cause bits to drop off the cope as you lift and tip the cope from the drag.

Lift the cope free of the drag ever so carefully and tip it to rest on the bench on its side. Inspect the bottom for defects and remove any vents. They were left in until now to be certain that they actually came all the way through right to the surface of the metal. Repair any minor damage by delicately wetting the surface locally and using the slick. You may have to press a small dollop of sand in here and there and smooth it down.

The professional molder will have a number of slicks or trowels to smooth and shape the sand. Maybe he'll also have a small syringe or dropper bottle and a small brush to apply water as he works the sand. For the occasional mold in the home shop an old table knife heated and bent to a dogleg or jog at the handle and filed or ground to a bluntly tapered tip will do fine for a slick.

Now, direct your attention to the drag and its embedded pattern. Apply a small amount of water all around the junction of the pattern and the sand. Look this edge over carefully, and if it appears that the sand has overlapped the pattern slightly at a few points, use the slick to press and smooth it back so the sand won't be broken when you lift the pattern. Use your slick to dig a vee-shaped channel from the sprue base directly to the edge of the pattern. Smooth away all crumbs and bits of sand. If any are left in the gate they will be washed into the casting by the metal.

Most patterns have two or more locations with screw threads for inserting lifting screws. Depending upon whether the pattern is wood or metal, use wood or machine screws. Anything you can grip with your fingers will do. The pattern must be loosened slightly so it will lift free of the sand. Use any piece of metal, even an old screwdriver. Place the tool against the lifting screw where it enters the pattern and tap sideways very gently. Do this in all directions until you see the pattern shift a bit in the sand. Repeat on the opposite lifting screw. If small areas around the edge of the pattern lift or flake away, repair them with the slick before lifting.

To lift the pattern, position yourself solidly,

Lift the cope off very carefully and straight up after using parting sand, riddle, and ram to fill and pack it exactly like the drag. Use a spatula or like tool to dig a vee-shaped gate for metal to flow from the sprue to the mold cavity.

With gate cut and soft wax plugs removed from the screw holes, a touch of water is added around the edges of the pattern and these edges are slicked down slightly to firm them up for lifting.

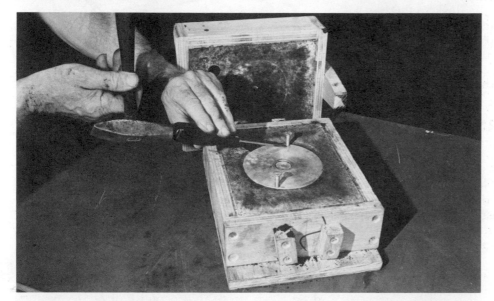

To loosen the pattern, tap gently on the lifting screws until you can see that the pattern shifts slightly in the sand. Repair any crumbled edges with the slick.

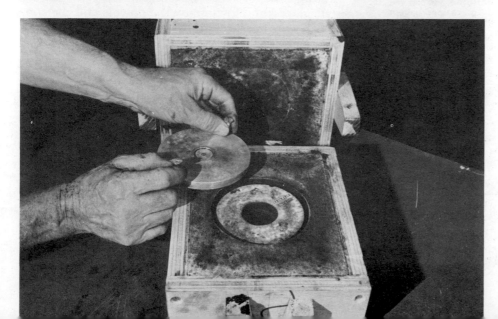

Take a deep breath and gently lift the pattern straight up. This one came free with only one or two minor tears, which could easily be patched with sand.

try to brace your arms or wrists on the edge of the flask, and lift the pattern straight up slowly. Remember, you do not want to bump the pattern against the edges of the fresh sand mold.

Preparing for Pouring

Unless you're extremely lucky you'll find a few crumbs of broken sand or other damage that must be patched up with a little water and your slick. Finally, pick up stray bits of sand by wetting a pencil or stick and lifting them out one by one. A can of compressed gas such as is used for cleaning film negatives can be used for a final dusting if you're careful.

Make a final inspection to be sure the sprue, risers, and vents are clear. Carefully lift the cope and slowly lower it into position on the drag after being certain that the guides are well aligned. A caution for beginners: It's wise to paint or mark the ends of the flask so there is a positive check that the cope is not being lowered in reverse, right to left. After making an apparently perfect mold it is quite disturbing to have the sprue fill instantly because the supposedly matching gate is on the other side of the flask.

TWO-PIECE PATTERNS

All of the above discussion applies to a pattern that has one surface flat and can be placed on the molding board flat side down. If there is even a little curvature or turn-in where the pattern joins the molding board, the sand will pack in under it and make it impossible to withdraw the pattern. Nevertheless, many round and otherwise complex shapes are made by sand casting.

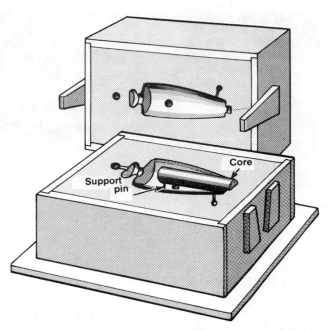

With the cannon-shaped cavity in the mold, you might want to provide a bore. A core of hard sand will provide this. After casting, the sand core is dug out.

The solution is a pattern made of two or more pieces. If you examine many cast articles you'll spot the split line.

As an example, suppose you want to cast a round model cannon. The pattern is easily made by putting two location dowels between two blocks of wood, lightly gluing or clamping the blocks together, and turning them to the finished shape in a lathe. You now have a pattern that may be divided into two halves. To make the mold, one half, without the dowels, is placed flat on the molding board as before. After the drag is inverted, the second half of the pattern is placed and located by the dowels and the cope is filled. Presto—you have a cavity for a round cannon.

Cores

If you have ever looked closely at your car's engine block you may have noticed round holes about 1½" to 2" in diameter that have been closed with pressed-in sheet-metal cups. Most people think these are "freeze plugs" provided to yield to ice pressure if the engine accidentally freezes up in cold weather. While it may be that these plugs would pop out, their real reason for being is to permit the removal of core sand after the casting is poured.

All water-cooled engines and other parts such as intake and exhaust manifolds have internal

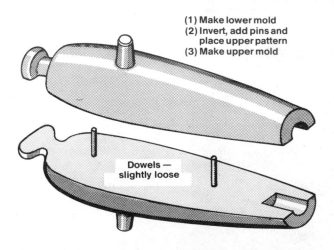

(1) Make lower mold
(2) Invert, add pins and place upper pattern
(3) Make upper mold

Dowels — slightly loose

Unless your pattern is flat on the bottom, it can't be readily placed on the molding board. The solution is a split pattern such as this one used for a round model cannon.

cavities and passages. Obviously, there is no way to remove metal and create these passages after making the casting, so there must be a way to produce a void inside a casting during the pouring process.

Cores do this. The complex passages in an engine block are duplicated, in reverse, in a device called a core box. When a special core sand is packed in, a sand image of the passages is formed. This is called a core, and it is baked to harden the binding agents with which the sand is mixed. The molder now has a hard, firm, and usually oddly shaped section of sand to place in his mold. In this type of molding, supports are provided to locate the core precisely.

After the metal cools and the main mold is broken up, the cores, with the binder now burned out by the molten metal, are dug or washed out of the internal cavities through the openings provided.

It is not likely that the home metalworker will become extensively involved with cored molds. The details of the technique can take a lifetime to learn. But with a project such as the model cannon I discussed, there's no reason not to have a try. The bore in the cannon barrel might be formed, roughly at least, by coring. One method might be no more complex than mixing some sand with a resin glue and packing it into a plastic or cardboard tube until it hardens. The result will be a hard, dowellike rod of sand that can be positioned in the center of the mold to produce a bore.

MAKING PATTERNS

Traditionally, patterns for castings have been made of easily worked woods such as mahogany or pattern pine. If you are a reasonably good woodworker you can certainly make your own simple patterns.

At the industrial level, the patternmaker's art is one of the most difficult. It requires many years to learn. For example, the patternmaker may be presented with a set of blueprints detailing the shapes, internal and external, of a car engine block. The patternmaker must translate the engineer's lines on the drawing to solid shapes and decide just how the pattern and cores can be placed and supported in the mold.

All of this requires knowledge of how the metal will flow and an understanding of the "shrink" of the metal as it cools. A patternmaker's rule is called a shrink rule, not because he is practicing psychology but because each graduation is slightly larger than a standard rule so that the pattern will ultimately be slightly oversize. When the metal cools it will be very close to the right dimensions.

Draft. Since any patterns you may make in the home shop will probably be quite small and fairly simple, you may overlook many of the above problems of the industrial patternmaker. The one thing you cannot overlook is something called "draft." Draft might be compared to the tapered cork in a bottle. It means that the sides of the pattern slope slightly, usually about ⅛" per foot, so that after the initial loosening of the pattern in the sand the pattern will lift free without dragging the sand sides of the mold. If you examine a sand casting, often recognizable by its slightly rough surface, you'll find that it has a taper. This applies to all surfaces, and the tapers will all run the same way. If the pattern was a single-piece type, the side surfaces will all expand toward the surface that would be down on the drag molding board. With a two-piece mold, the top and bottom side surfaces will expand toward the parting line.

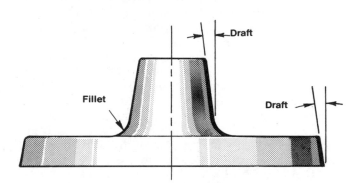

Unless a pattern has a taper or "draft" it will not withdraw easily from the molding sand. Sharp corners are also problems. Use generous fillets wherever two planes join.

Fillets. One other factor is important in your home patternmaking. There are seldom any really sharp corners in a sand casting. First, such corners do not relieve well from the sand and are hard to mold. Secondly, as the metal cools the square corners tend to cool at a different rate and develop cracks and porous areas. And, a third factor, in nearly all metalwork, but especially in cast material, square corners localize stress. The analogy is that of nicking a piece of wire and flexing it. The wire will break where the nick localizes the stress.

For these reasons, cast parts, and machined parts as well, will almost always have a blended curve at the juncture of two planes. If you make your own patterns, heed this practice. Patternmakers working in wood have long used leather strips, sold for this purpose in various widths and sizes, to form fillets. Sometimes wax or other material is used. If you are making such a pattern, try visiting a local pattern shop. Tell the patternmakers there your needs and they will likely offer good advice and a handful of material for your fillets.

MELTING METAL
The melting points of metals commonly cast in the home shop range from about 450° F. for tin to a high of over 1,800° for brass. Aluminum and its common alloys melt at about 1,200° to 1,250°. Bracketed within these extremes are other metals such as antimony and lead. Zinc melts at about 790°. Iron, on the other hand, requires 2,300° or higher. Thus, for most of us, there are limitations on the metals we can conveniently and safely use for castings.

The two most common heat sources for melting metal in the home shop are natural gas, available as a home heating fuel, and propane in bottled, liquid form. Charcoal is also used successfully and is probably less costly. All require some form of supplemental air supply, usually from a small blower. For melting a small ladleful of the lower-melting metals, an ordinary 1,200-watt hot plate will serve very well. So will a gas burner on a stove. It is worth noting that in times past, pewter, often used for drinking and food vessels, contained a dangerous amount of lead. Avoid any metal containing lead if there is any chance your project might be used in this way—now, or a century from now.

Do not melt brass or aluminum in a cast-iron ladle unless you first line the ladle with a fireclay made for this purpose. Ceramic crucibles are readily available from hobby and jeweler's supply houses. Purchase crucibles no larger than you need, and be sure to buy a set of tongs or a holder for handling the hot crucible. Spilling hot metal or dropping a crucible is extremely dangerous, and you must be very certain of your grip when lifting and pouring from a crucible.

A common mistake of inexperienced metalworkers is overheating the metal. Allow the metal to become completely melted, of course, but do not melt it beyond the temperature necessary for it to pour freely into the mold. Overheating destroys the metal's characteristics and often results in poorly textured castings.

Heating Furnaces
Many home-shop metalworkers make up their own heating furnaces from inexpensive firebrick. Never use ordinary brick or concrete block, since both will explode violently when heated. If you want a little furnace you can move about, you

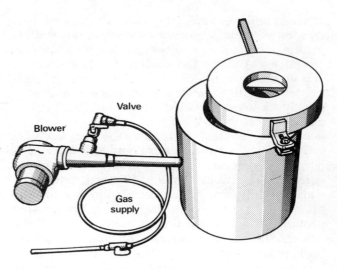

A sturdy, fairly large container such as an old refrigerant or propane tank, lined with fireclay and fired by gas and a salvaged, motorized blower, will melt most shop metals. A certain amount of experimenting and ingenuity are needed to make it work well. An outside location is by far the best.

can make one from almost any heavy steel container such as a scrapped refrigerant tank or propane tank, or even from large well casing. Here, you must line the inside with refractory clay.

The trick in building such a furnace is to lead the flame into the crucible area and direct it in a circular pattern as much as possible to expose the walls of the crucible evenly to the heat. Most workers use a vacuum-cleaner blower or similar small motor-powered fan to provide combustion air and circulate the flame. This is also necessary with charcoal, except that the air flow comes in underneath the grate that supports the fire. Cover the top partially, but leave a way for the gases to escape. If you are working indoors, an exhaust hood or other system is vital.

POURING METAL
There are a few cardinal rules for working with molten metal. First, always keep in mind that contact with hot metal is worse than direct contact with flame. The globules penetrate clothing, shoes, and flesh and continue to burn. Wear clothing resistant to burning, such as heavy woolen trousers and a woolen shirt. Wear heavy shoes and lace or tie the trousers around the top. Do not tuck your trouser cuffs into your boots, since this would provide a channel for metal to run down into them. Do not wear gauntlet-type gloves but heavy leather gloves over which your shirt cuffs can be buttoned. A plastic face shield is not enough eye protection. Buy a pair of in-

dustrial foundryman's goggles with safety lenses and snug-fitting side covers. A small drop of molten metal in your eye can be very destructive.

Molten metal can be handled safely, but it has two peculiarities. One is that it bounces and spatters skittishly when spilled. This means that you should not do your pouring where a stray spatter is likely to find its way into a pile of shavings, sawdust, wiping rags, or paper, or into a crack in a wooden floor. Obviously, all containers of solvents should be removed.

The second characteristic is metal's explosive reaction to even small amounts of water. Sometimes adding cold metal to a ladle of molten metal will carry in water. This can happen if you store metal in the corner of a basement or other place where it gets wet occasionally. Other sources of water are tongs or other tools dipped in water to cool them. Whatever the source, avoid mixing even drops of water with molten metal, since the instantaneous steam can cause a violent explosion.

When pouring into a mold, remember that the sand was damp, and even if you allow the mold

After returning the cope to its position above the drag ever so gently, pour the molten metal directly into the sprue hole in a steady stream until it exits freely from the risers.

When the metal has cooled completely, break apart the mold and remove your casting. Don't be surprised if your first efforts show the need for more vents or risers. Your casting can now be cleaned and machined as necessary.

to stand overnight there will be steam generated. Position yourself firmly, well away from the mold, and direct the hot metal into the sprue with no hesitation. Erratic pouring causes steam and air bubbles to be trapped in the metal. Pour continuously until the metal exits from the risers and the sprue fills and runs over. Deposit excess metal in a pocket in the sand or other safe place. Afterward, allow the mold and casting to cool with no effort to speed the process. When the casting is ready to break out you should be able to dig the sand away from the casting area with no sign of steam and the sand should feel comfortable to your hand. Then, and only then, is it safe to dump out the cope and drag and admire your casting.

FINISHED CASTINGS

Most sand castings come from the mold looking somewhat rough. They have sprues, risers, vents, and flashes where the metal slipped between the cope and the drag. With experience you'll soon learn to locate these dangling appendages where they can be trimmed away easily, although not at the expense of the pouring process. From here on, finishing a casting depends on how important it is that the surface finish be attractive and whether the finished surface is to be raw metal or painted or otherwise covered.

Obviously, a rough casting to serve as a boat anchor needs little, if any, clean-up other than hacking off the sprue and risers. However, a bronze casting to be placed on the mantel as an art object may require cleaning, polishing, and even filling and repair. Or you may want to strike a presentation mode between a finish which reveals the handcraft work and a fine, burnished area as a highlight. A casting for a model steam engine's cylinder block may be quite adequate with the fine sand texture showing. But an equivalent casting for an air-cooled model aircraft engine's cylinder block may require extensive machining that will obliterate all signs of sand casting.

Many castings, especially for model parts and even for decorative objects, will be painted or coated with epoxy or other finishes. As long as the coating does not require heating, as it would with ceramics, the procedure is easy and resembles auto-body repair. After the initial trimming, a tool with a variety of burrs or grinders, such as the Dremel tool, will neatly clean away blemishes and cut out small sand pockets or other pits. An auto-body filler can then be pressed into these areas and smoothed, much as Plastic Wood might be used on a wooden project. Sanded down, primed, and painted, the casting will show no evidence of your repairs. Some workers may prefer to fill and shape with solder on some metals, but there is little to be gained except the pleasure of doing it the hard way.

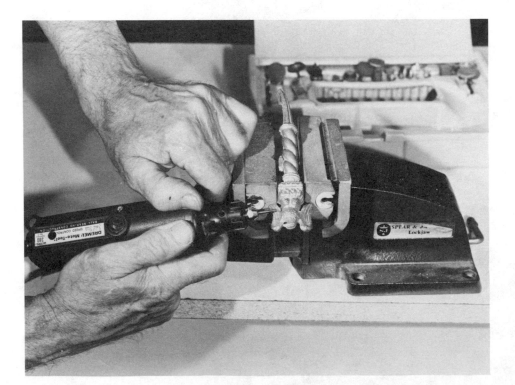

Small, detailed castings often need extensive cleanup work. A metal-cutting burr in a high-speed rotary tool is ideal.

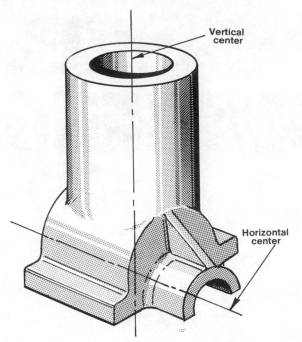

Vertical
center

Horizontal
center

Planning your sequence is always important in machining, but when faced with machining a casting such as this one for a model engine you must decide on a starting point and how you are going to hold the axial centers.

Machining Castings

If you have extensive machining to do on your casting, as, for example, might be needed on a cylinder block or crankcase, you should have left enough metal (pattern oversize) to cut away the outer surface and get to clean metal.

At this point you must decide which main center line or axis to work from and plan your machining sequence from there. For example, a simple small-engine cylinder and crankcase upper half has two possible reference centers. One is the center line of the cylinder bore, and the other, at right angles, is the center line of the crankshaft. The end result, after choosing either, would be the same in the finished part, but the machining order would be different.

In this case, the flat surface at the split line of the upper and lower crankcase halves might be a good starting point, since it would give you a flat mounting surface for securing and aligning future steps. All such planning is part of metalworking, and it often takes a bit of thinking and picturing before you go to sleep at night to come up with just the proper procedure.

BLACKSMITHING

A great many metalworking arts, including lost-wax casting, fine-art sheet-metal work, and even machining, preceded and followed the ancient art of blacksmithing. But the blacksmith's place is unchallenged in making tools and useful objects from iron and steel. Of course, all blacksmithing was not for strictly utilitarian items. The delicate work of old-time gates and rails was a vastly higher order of art than much of today's so-called metal sculpture.

Regardless of the end product, the blacksmith worked with "black" iron and steel. His basic tool was his hammer, his workbench was his anvil, and his work center was his glowing forge. Actually, of course, real smiths had many hammers, often shop-made and each with a purpose. The anvil served not only as a surface on which to hammer and form metal but also as a holding fixture for many shaping and cutting tools.

If one looks back over the old blacksmith trade publications of the 1800s it's apparent that most smiths were highly individualistic. They argued at length about metals, coal, forge fires, methods of hardening and welding, how to secure a wagon tire, and the proper form for a plowshare. Each devised and made his own tools and looked down on everyone else's tools and methods. Many of these old blacksmithing books are still available, and they offer a valuable insight into the highly personal world of early craftsmen.

One result of all this individuality was that unlike other skills and trades, such as carpentry, blacksmithing didn't really develop what today would be called "standard procedures." This is understandable, and there were many reasons. In our developing nation the New England smiths had access to imported iron but Western smiths did not, since it was too heavy to haul all the way from the East Coast. The forge coal available in one area differed significantly from that of another. Just these two factors explain some of the greatly diverse views on forges and fires and on the methods of welding and hardening. Different smiths were working with different materials.

Moreover, the Eastern smith, called upon to produce hinges, latches, kitchen hardware, knickknacks, and fancy sleigh parts, knew little of the problems of a smith serving a logging camp or a mine. The latter often became experts in saw-mill maintenance or excavating gear. Their jobs were as different as those of a wooden-ship builder and a furniture maker.

It is also true that many smiths had little to do with horseshoeing or carriage repair; others specialized in these trades. Perhaps a skilled farrier, extremely experienced with horses and

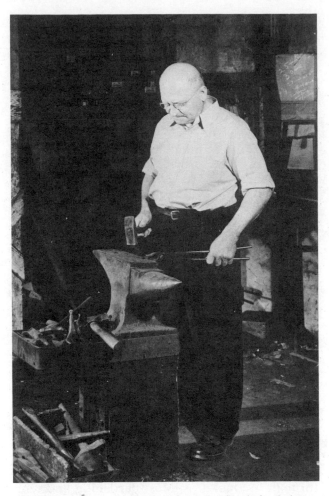

Nearly all smiths were inventors, not only of tools for their own trade and shops, but often of new tools for the farm, home, and other trades. Here, Bill Petersen revisits the blacksmith shop where he invented the world-famous Vise-Grip pliers.

horseshoes, would have felt lost if asked to design and build a New Orleans–style balcony rail, and the man who built heavy fittings for waterwheels and grain mills might have been dismayed if brought into a woolen mill to fabricate machine parts.

Thus, a review of the old smiths' writings shows only that they made an enormous variety of products, some of which we can scarcely recognize today. All that remains is the concept of making iron and mild steel malleable by heating and shaping it to suit our needs or fancies.

The Old and the New

Even if an ancient smith could be brought back from his reward and asked to fabricate a complex part for a horse-drawn cutter, for example a shifting bar for side or center draft (has to do

with the position of the horse and the sled), it is doubtful if he'd long cling to his former techniques. There would be little point in picking over bar stock for an approximate size when the desired diameter could be taken off the shelf. And there would be no reason to heat and sever the metal on a chisel held in an anvil hardy hole when it's faster and easier to cut it to size on an electric band saw. He might elect to hot-punch holes for bolts and fittings, but not for long after he discovered the electric drill press. The point is that there was nothing superior, or even especially craftsmanlike, about many of those old methods. They were simply the only practical ways of doing the jobs at that time.

On the other hand, the old-timer would very likely have found no better way to shape and form the toggle-end bars and the hardware to engage the wooden parts of the hitch-up than to heat the metal red and hammer it. That's still the only way to make a one-of-its-kind piece without first making forging dies or welding it together from pieces.

For the home-shop metalworker the only logical conclusion is that you are wasting your time hacking and hammering on a chisel if a power

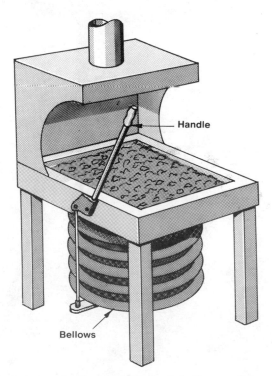

Many of the early blacksmith tools needed two persons, one to hold the tool or piece, the other to strike. But the helper was needed anyway to operate the bellow, tend the forge coal, and remove ashes. Old-time bellows yielded to the hand crank, later to electric blowers.

Handle

Bellows

cut-off tool will do the same thing. If a modern drill press, grinder, or abrasive tool will do the job, use it. The real art of the smith was in creating a useful shape and form by hand forging, and for the purposes of this book that's what smithing is about.

The Forge

Forges used in the old smith's shops were often hand-built of firebrick plus some purchased grates and other parts. While at work, the smith kept the actual fire quite small most of the time. In fact, it was seldom larger than needed to heat the size of work in hand. He might also have had a larger forge of a size to accommodate a wagon-wheel rim or like part, but this forge was usually cold.

All forges used an air blast from some source to raise the coal fire to useful temperature. Sometimes it was a foot-operated bellows, although more often a helper provided the power. Eventually, the smiths discovered that a centrifugal blower, even hand-cranked, gave a steadier and better-regulated air flow. Most forges had such blowers.

The rest of the art of forge building again drifted off into opinion and theory. A forge with a chimney that "drew well" was a real prize. Few of them did, as evidenced by the smoke-blackened walls of the old shops. Another huge debate related to the hearth or the grates and the tuyers. The tuyer is the passage through which the air is delivered. Basically, there had to be an air box or chamber to bring in the air from below, but there also had to be a means of dropping the ashes down and out, and of breaking up the slag formed in the fire.

If you like, you can study these old forges, build one, and then try to locate a suitable coal to fuel it. But if you want to get on with forging, I also suggest that you investigate a modern natural-gas or propane forge with an electric blower, draft control, and exhaust hood. Many of the purposes served by the old forges are handled as well or better with a propane torch or acetylene torch played directly on the metal or with the metal partially enclosed in a small shelter of loosely stacked firebrick. The important thing is to heat the metal thoroughly and evenly through its thickness. Most hardening and tempering can be done this way.

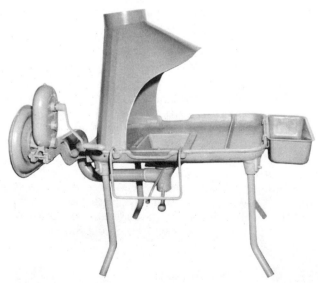

Two "modern" forges are actually pretty much unchanged from those of years ago. The smaller one limits the size of your work and requires a well ventilated area. The larger one can handle large wrought-iron pieces and needs a flue or chimney. Both have hand-crank blowers but could be motorized.

For better and more consistent temperature control for hardening and tempering you might even want to take a look at both gas and electric ovens. Such ovens are sold in small sizes equipped with thermostats and temperature gages. If your metalworking runs to making cutting tools, knives, and other objects made of high-carbon or alloy steels, such equipment is worthwhile. If all you want to do is bend up wrought iron or hand-forge decorative hardware, almost any form of heating, including a charcoal grill, will serve.

The Anvil

The old-timers were just as fussy and opinionated about their anvils as about their other tools. Some swore by imported British or German anvils. Others favored specific brands of U.S.-made anvils. The modern metalworker can either acquire an anvil from the past at a sale, buy a modern anvil (which looks just like the old ones), or use a makeshift made up from a section of heavy railroad rail or the like.

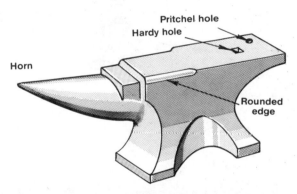

So far, no one has improved very much on the anvil. The pritchel hole is handy for bending and breaking off a notched bar. The hardy hole serves as a receptacle for the lower member of many two-part tools such as swages. Most important—a good solid base.

If I seem a bit casual about the choice of an anvil, here's why. Basically, the anvil, whatever its source and type, should provide a solid, flat upper surface on which to hammer, a surface that won't chip or spall off dangerous flying pieces. The familiar tapered horn at the front of the anvil is handy for bending curves, but an equivalent surface can be obtained by clamping a bar or heavy pipe in a vise.

The other features of an anvil, namely the pritchel hole used for bending and the hardy hole used to hold a wide variety of cutting tools, are less important in the home shop. One point

that's often overlooked when recalling the old smith is that he almost always had a helper. The helper lugged coal, tended the forge and cranked the blower, and hauled out ashes. But, more importantly, he was the one who swung the hammer.

The smith would draw the metal from the fire and hold it in place with his tongs on a chisel, swedge, or other tool mounted in the hardy hole of the anvil. On a nod of the smith's head, or a grunted command, the helper swung the hammer. If he was well trained the blow was true and neither too hard nor too light.

This team combination performed a great many shaping and forming operations, and the tools in the hardy hole were often, in modern terms, dies, which formed the reverse side of the metal. In your shop you can just as easily clamp the hardy tools in a vise, but you'll probably have to learn to grip the tongs and hold the metal with one hand and strike the metal with a hammer held in the other. This, as you will see, becomes pretty much impossible when you also need another forming tool placed above the metal.

The blacksmith considered his anvil not only a support surface but also a forming surface for the reverse side of the metal. He struck along

Working over the edge of his anvil, a modern craftsman in wrought iron develops the curl at the beginning of a scroll. *Kreissle Forge, Sarasota, Florida.*

the edge, for example, to "set down" metal and form a square shoulder. In such cases the railroad rail is unsatisfactory, because its top and sides are curved. Serious home smiths can solve this by having the top of the rail dressed flat at a local machine shop. A few milling or grinding cuts along the top and along part of the edges will do the trick. A part of the original curved edge should be left, however, because you'll have many occasions to bend metal over the curve.

In any case, you can work without an authentic anvil, but you must have a very firm, non-springy surface upon which to hammer. The anvil mounting was considered as important as the anvil itself. Maybe the reason that the legendary smith worked "under the spreading chestnut tree" was that that particular location had a very solid stump on which to mount his anvil. You're unlikely to have a handy stump firmly rooted in the middle of your shop, but the next best is a section of stump or tree trunk of husky dimensions and the right height. This will form a good anvil base and at the same time allow you to drag the anvil out of the way for storage or swing it around for clearance if you're working on a long strip.

Forming Tools

If you looked at the typical blacksmith's tool rack, you'd probably comment that he had a great many "hammers." Undoubtedly he did have quite a few ball-pen, cross-pen, and straight-pen hammers and sledges in various weights, but many of the tools that resemble hammers at first glance were actually forming tools.

As noted, the usual practice was for the smith to hold the handle of this type of tool and, after placing the working portion the way he wanted it, signal his helper to strike. Today, these tools would probably be called forging dies. They had a hammerlike handle so the smith could hold and position them. Enumerating all of these tools would be tedious, but there are some broad general classes you should recognize if you want to try your hand at smith work.

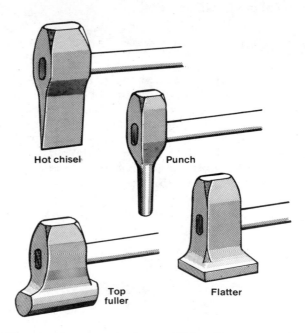

Hot chisel   Punch

Top fuller   Flatter

When is a hammer not a hammer? When it's a swage, chisel, punch, or other tool to be held in position by its handle and struck by a hammer. The old smithy shops had many such "hammers" and special tools.

Wide view of a modern blacksmith shop shows several forges at the rear. Gas furnace is in operation, heating several small pieces at a time. Along the wall the smith has numerous forming and striking tools, tongs, and special patterns. Quenching barrel is at right.

The "hammers" that appear to have one blunt, headlike face and an opposite sharp-edged face are actually chisels. The chisel for cutting hot metal is narrower, more acutely angled, than the chisel for cutting cold metal. Either could be used singly, or with another chisel in the hardy hole of the anvil. For a rough cut, the smith might notch the metal deeply on both sides with the chisel and then insert one end in the pritchel hole and flex it back and forth to achieve a break. He almost certainly would not drive the chisel completely through the metal and into the face of the anvil.

Other tools that also looked like heavy hammers on one face but had round, or square, tapered opposite sides were punches for opening holes in hot metal. One method was to place the area to be punched over the pritchel hole, hold the punch on top, and have the helper strike the punch upper face smartly.

Swages.   Still another group of tools, called "swages," were used to produce or improve a rounded portion of the work, perhaps an axle extension on which a wheel ran. The swage was definitely a two-piece tool and was normally used with the mating, lower portion in the hardy hole. The working face of each part was curved much like a piece of pipe that has been split lengthwise.

To picture the swaging operation, visualize a piece of round or square stock that has been heated and hammered to reduce its dimensions in cross section by "drawing" it with a hammer. Drawing, in smith's terms, meant extending the length of the metal by reducing the cross section. The hammering, of course, would leave a number of flats from the hammer blows. To make it round, the drawn part was inserted in the lower half of the swage, the upper half was placed over it, and the latter was struck with a hammer. By turning and striking successive blows the metal could be rounded nicely.

Fullers and flatters.   Two other more or less standard tools, although they were made in a wide variety of sizes and shapes, are fullers and flatters. The fuller has the appearance of a rounded or blunt wedge opposite the striking force. A fuller could be used independently to develop recessed areas, corners, and similar contours. Or it could be worked against another fuller in the hardy hole. Books on smithwork discuss at length using the fuller to stretch metal, take out ripples and bulges, and flatten saw blades. These operations were, indeed, an art, since the angle and placement of the fuller and its successive positions could move metal around remarkably in the hands of a skilled smith.

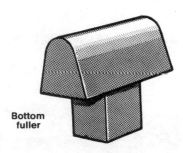

Bottom fuller

Fullers were the basic shaping tools and were used for forming bends, channels, and grooves. They also served for flattening and distributing metal, even developing tension in the metal of a lumber-mill saw.

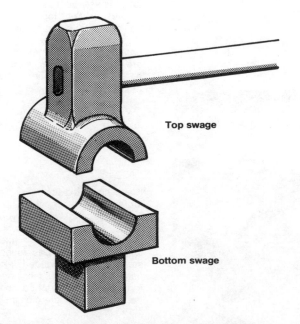

Top swage

Bottom swage

Swaging is a form of die shaping using an upper and lower die to squeeze hot metal into round or other shapes, such as hexagons for nuts and bolts. Since swaging is also a sizing operation, you needed swages of many sizes.

The flatter, as might be guessed, was a finishing tool in most cases, since its broad, flat face, sometimes with square edges and sometimes with rounded edges, could remove tool marks and true up work.

A discussion of these tools could be almost endless, because the working smith forged bolt heads with swages, formed a huge variety of special parts for horse-drawn vehicles and farm equipment, and often made hardware ranging from hinges to relatively intricate latches and locks. He inevitably found that by altering a conventional forging tool for a special job he could improve production. Today, we call it "tooling up."

Tongs and Holders

Obviously, handling bright, hot metal requires a sure grip both when removing the metal from the forge and when holding it for striking. The smith's tongs were often shop-made and, again, tended to be specialized. There are, however, some general standards.

Typical tongs for gripping flat and bar stock resemble large duck-bill pliers except that they have a definite spacing between the jaws when the jaws are closed to parallel position. To work properly and hold the metal firmly it was important that this spacing closely match the thickness of the metal being gripped. If the jaw spacing was too narrow, the tongs would grip at the rear and the metal would be poorly held and swivel in the jaws; too wide a spacing would place the grip at the tip and again the hold would be poor. Therefore the smith needed a wide array of tongs, each matched to a different metal thickness. It was not by accident that the modern Vise-Grip pliers, adjustable for a wide

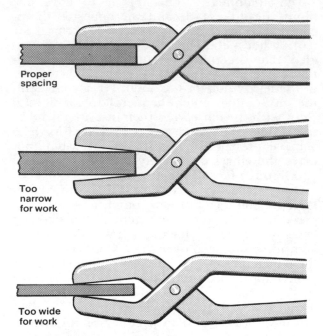

Tong jaw spacings come in three sizes—too large, too small, and just right. The gripping surfaces must close to a gap approximating the size of the work metal. Otherwise, you're trying to hold on the corners only; dangerous with red-hot metal.

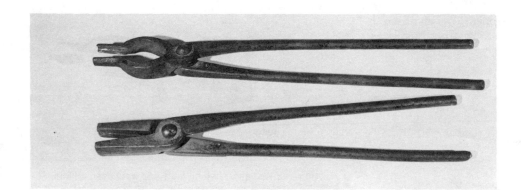

Specialized nature of smith's tongs is seen in these two examples. Jaws of top pair are contoured to grip round stock; those of lower tongs to grip corners of square stock. Both are for light material, as can be judged from closure angle of jaws.

If you have a discerning eye for smith work, these hand-forged ice tongs will give you pause. Was basic stock round and flattened for joint and tong section? Or was round stock for handles welded onto flat stock? In any case, note forge weld where round and flat merge at handle closure.

spread in gripping dimensions, were invented by a blacksmith.

Still another assortment of tongs was needed for gripping round and square stock, and still others for horseshoes, small parts, and hardware. In many cases, not only did the jaws have to be fashioned to fit the work but the position in which the work was held also had to be special to allow the correct relationship to the anvil or the anvil tool.

Legend has it that after a smith's apprentice had gained some experience, his first real project was to forge a set of tongs for his own use. I have a set of cutting tongs with forge-welded cutting edges, made by my father as a youth. Surprisingly, eighty years later, they outcut the best of modern cutting tools. If you would like to try smithwork you might start by making yourself a few sets of tongs.

GETTING STARTED IN SMITHING
No book such as this is going to provide the equivalent of long days and years of apprenticing to a working smith. Nor are there many opportunities for such a thankless approach to a career these days. There are, however, excellent classes in metalsmithing at various trade schools and even in the fine-arts departments of universities. In most cases the instruction is directed toward craft and hobby work more than serious smithwork.

Nevertheless, there is great satisfaction in producing hand-wrought works in iron, even though you confine your efforts to pothooks, fireplace tools, railings, antique hinges, and the like. Remember, the old-time smith did many things the hard way simply because he had no better tools. There is, as mentioned before, absolutely nothing gained, except fatigue, in hand-chiseling a rough form from a piece of ¼"-thick mild steel when you can cut it with a hacksaw or band saw quicker and better. Nor is there a lot of reason to try to punch holes that can be drilled with an electric drill.

Forge or Modern Welding?
Feelings are mixed among craftsmen on using modern welding equipment instead of forge welding. At the risk of offending the purist set, I advocate gas or electric welding in nearly all cases. While it is true that the smith could heat two pieces of metal in a forge, judge the heat by eye, and hammer the faces together to merge them into a joint, modern X-ray or other forms of inspection would show many stuck-together joints rather than true welds.

The choice is yours, of course, but if you want to enjoy working with iron, there seems little reason to be blocked by the difficulties of forge welding when a modern plug-in transformer welder will make all the joints you want. Both gas and electric welding are sufficiently challenging skills in themselves. Moreover, without casting any disrespect on the old methods, it must be noted that the first shops to adopt both gas and electric welding were blacksmith shops. The old boys knew a good thing when they saw it.

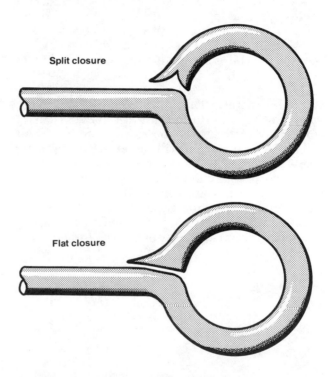

Split closure

Flat closure

Smiths didn't necessarily agree on how to shape up and join a forge weld. Sometimes it depended on the end use, such as an eye-bolt or a link-bolt. Modern gas or electric welding techniques are so different from forge welding that you'd start with entirely different workpiece shapes to arrive at the same point.

That said, both forms of welding are skills that must be learned, and the techniques exceed the range of this book. Suffice it to say that 100-amp transformer welders are available for about $100 and will handle most home shop jobs. Good oxyacetylene equipment is more expensive, and for the type of work ordinarily considered forging and smithwork, gas welding has little advantage. It does, however, offer extremely useful heat for forming, bending, heat-treating, and hardening. For a much more extensive treatment of the subject, I suggest the Popular Science Skill Book *Electric and Gas Welding*.

Hot-Forming Iron

Although some may consider an object hammered into more or less random shape to be a form of art or expression, this is not the way to learn smithwork. Assuming that you've equipped yourself with a heat source—coal forge, gas furnace or torches, or even a vacuum-cleaner blower and a charcoal hibachi—the important thing is to set out to make a specific form with controlled dimensions.

Just for getting the feel of working red-hot metal you might take a square bar about 1" on each side and try to produce a round shank about 3" long on each end. Picture yourself, if it helps, as making the axle ends for a pioneer wagon or a stagecoach. Your first concern is to be sure that the metal is thoroughly and evenly heated to the core in the section you plan to work.

Drawing metal. The next step, using your hammer and anvil, and holding the metal securely in a pair of tongs, is to "draw" the end. This means that since you will be reducing the metal section from 1" to ¾" and also rounding it from the square, you will have excess metal. Note that the machinist would make the same part in a lathe by chucking the bar and turning the round end to size. The excess metal would be removed as cuttings. But this is smithwork, and here you

will start back at about 2" from the end and reduce the square section to approximately ¾" by hammering on each side and working or drawing the metal out longer. You'll have to reheat as needed.

The second step is to start rounding the shank by placing a corner on the anvil and hammering the upper corner. Again, by starting near the square portion and working outward you will be making the bar longer, since the metal must go somewhere.

If you proceed properly you will produce an octagon shape and on the next go-around a 16-sided figure. This is not as easy as it sounds. You may find that you have produced some areas less than ¾" in diameter and other fat areas. Perhaps you drifted off center and came up with a shank that isn't straight and aligned with the original center.

At this point you will appreciate why the old smith used swages for such jobs. Even if he used his hammer to get to the same stage you did, and maybe didn't do a lot better job, he knew he could mount a swage in the hardy hole, place another swage on top, and have the helper whack the top swage while he turned the work and let the swages even things up to an approximately round shape.

I say "approximate" because the difference between the lathe-turned shaft, which might be accurate to .001" or less, and the swaged shaft, which might be accurate to ¹⁄₃₂", is enormous for a machined part onto which a precision ball bearing must be pressed, but it's inconsequential for a wagon-wheel bearing. In the latter case, a file would clean things up fairly well, and the turning of the wheel with a little road dust in the axle grease would finish the job. In fact, if someone wanted to pay the smith for really fine work, he could make up a lap from two hardwood blocks and a leather strap and use a little oil and emery to lap the axle practically perfect.

Round to square. Your next practice step might be a reversal of the above. Start with a round bar and forge a portion square. Here, you're going to encounter a shortage of metal. You'll have to "upset" the end to force enough metal back into the stock to provide corner material.

If some of this seems obscure and hard to visualize, I suggest modeling clay to experiment with. Take a square bar of clay, as in the first project, and using a solid block of wood for an anvil and another block or wooden mallet, go through the steps outlined. Do the same for the second procedure. The drawing and upsetting requirements will be clearer.

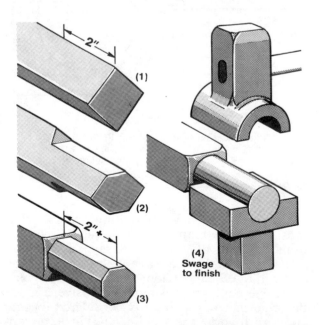

Drawing square stock into round and changing its dimensions was routine for forming axle ends, pivots, and threaded ends on larger pieces. Unlike a turning operation which removes metal at the corners to make a round section, drawing successively flattens and reflattens until square becomes round—almost. Final shaping might be done with swages and a file.

Bending hot iron.   Earlier in this book I discussed several ways to bend scrolls, curled ends, and twists. In general, if there is a way to use a forming piece to bend the metal around, and especially if you can anchor one end and apply pressure to the other, that's the way to do it. This applies to hot or cold bending. In some cases, such as freehand bent pothooks, L-shaped hooks for latches, and the like, even this is not necessary. They can be bent in a vise. But short, tight bends are another matter.

Picture, for example, two hinge halves cut from ³⁄₁₆″ flat stock. Perhaps you've shaped them handsomely with fleur-de-lis and the like. Now the problem is to roll in the hinge-pin areas. Again, you come to the reason for the old smith's tools. He would place a small female swage in the anvil, put a fuller or like male tool on top, and with a stroke or two from the helper produce a half-closed section on each half. Now, by placing a pin in these halves and using a swage, larger by the thickness of the stock, on the outside, he could close the metal over the pin.

If you want to do this type of bending and smithwork you'll probably have to make, or buy, some swage forms and other tools. The old smith was really less of a hammer shaper than is commonly thought. He actually used dies just as are used today. The difference, of course, was that he used his helper's muscles and hammer rather than a modern die-stamping machine.

Heat and Hardness

Although some metalworkers may spend a lifetime without finding a need to harden a piece of steel, or even to work with hardenable steel, others take great pleasure in making workshop tools, knives, and parts for guns or models that require more than mild-steel qualities.

If you refer to Chapter 1 on steelmaking and grades of steel you'll find that modern steels are enormously varied. Merely scanning a list of the highly specialized steels available to industry boggles the mind. No matter; unless you have a friend in an industrial stockroom who can borrow a piece of steel of known alloy and specification you will have no way of knowing the exact alloy that you're working with. All you need to know is whether it's high-carbon steel or mild

Curled iron workpiece in this picture was red hot as smith gripped it in his tongs and tapped gently to flatten spiral. If you look at his grip on both hammer and tongs you can see that his touch is delicate in spite of hammer weight and tong size.

steel. Only high-carbon steels can be hardened. Mild steels can be given a very thin coating of hardness by adding carbon to the outer surface. This process is called case hardening, and I'll talk about it later. But for now we're going to look at the processes that will allow you to soften, harden, and temper a piece of hardenable steel.

In most cases your only source for such steel is scrap metal from salvaged equipment—rotary-mower blades, for example, or old car and truck springs, torsion bars, saws, and garage-

door springs. And unless you have a forge, your source of heat will be a gas flame from a stove, propane torch, or oxyacetylene torch. This rules out the complex, temperature-precise, industrial heat-treating processes. Fortunately, rule-of-thumb heating and quenching procedures work well enough most of the time.

Testing steel. A scrap of steel may be rusted and ugly but have wonderful qualities for the tool or other project you have in mind. There are two quick checks you can make to get some

STEEL USES VS. CARBON CONTENT

Carbon Class	Carbon Range %	Typical Uses
Low	0.05–0.15	Chain, nails, pipe, rivets, screws, sheets for pressing and stamping, wire.
	0.15–0.30	Bars, plates, structural shapes.
Medium	0.30–0.45	Axles, connecting rods, shafting.
High	0.45–0.60	Crankshafts, scraper blades.
	0.60–0.75	Automobile springs, anvils, bandsaws, drop hammer dies.
Very High	0.75–0.90	Chisels, punches, sand tools.
	0.90–1.00	Knives, shear blades, springs.
	1.00–1.10	Milling cutters, dies, taps.
	1.10–1.20	Lathe tools, woodworking tools.
	1.20–1.30	Files, reamers.
	1.30–1.40	Dies for wire drawing.
	1.40–1.50	Metal cutting saws.

Courtesy The James F. Lincoln Arc Welding Foundation

If you salvage steel for your projects you can often guess its approximate carbon content from its original use. It's still nec-

essary to make a trial hardening and see how your unknown steel performs.

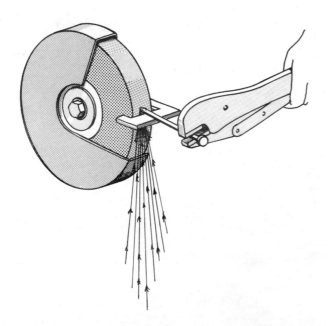

Touch an ordinary nail or spike to an abrasive wheel and you can be fairly sure the sparks are typical of low-carbon steel.

A file subjected to the same spark test produces a much different spark from the nail. This is the characteristic spark of high-carbon steel. Now try the same test on random tools or pieces of steel and try to guess what you have.

idea of its quality. The first check worked better fifty years ago than it does today. It consists of touching a corner of your sample to a spinning abrasive wheel and observing the spark pattern. This is the classic spark test shown religiously in metalworking texts. To try it, take an ordinary nail, perhaps 16d or 20d, and touch it lightly to the wheel. The sparks produced will be fairly plentiful but not particularly brilliant. The individual sparks will appear to fork and die out. Now repeat the test with the corner of a file. The difference in brilliance and profusion of sparks will be apparent, and the individual sparks will appear to burst and burst again. Here, unless you are working with an exotic file, you have two known extremes. The nail is mild steel and cannot be hardened. The file is carbon steel and is clearly very hard.

The confusion arises when you attempt to test with unknown metals. To prove this, try random samples of tools such as drills, taps, and the like from your shop. Try other samples such as springs, old engine valves, and whatever else is handy. Before writing this I reassured myself of the accuracy of what I'm saying by doing the above tests on a large number of bits and pieces in my own shop. Some very hard pieces, undoubtedly of a special alloy, produced almost no spark; others gave off red sparks with no flaring or branching; and some, actually hard tools, gave the appearance of sparks from a nail. Thus, with the multitude of alloys used today the old spark tests are more or less meaningless.

The second, and more useful, test is to actually try hardening the sample. If it is hard to file before the test, you may be fairly sure it is some form of carbon steel. But some of your acquired scrap may have been used in a less than fully hardened state. To test it, heat an inch or so in a flame or forge to a light cherry red as seen in a dim light. Quench it by immersing in a bucket of water and moving it up and down slightly. Remove the sample from the water when it has cooled *completely* through its entire length and thickness to room temperature. If you remove it from the quench too soon the residual inner heat will draw the hardness, a process we'll discuss later. The heated area should now have a gray color. Try filing it or scratching it with the corner of a file. If the file slides over the metal as though it were glass, your sample is hardenable.

You will also probably want to find out if the sample is capable of being softened or annealed enough to work if you plan to saw, mill, drill, or lathe-turn it. This is less important, of course, if you plan to forge it hot. Annealing is a slower process than hardening. Prepare some sort of fireproof box—a metal can will do—and make a bed of fine ashes, powdered dry lime, or even fine dry sand. Heat the sample as before, bury it in the bed, and cover it deeply so the heat can escape only very slowly. Allow the sample to cool to room temperature. Overnight or all day is about right for larger pieces.

When it's fully cooled, repeat the file test. An ordinary carbon steel should be soft enough after annealing to be filed quite easily. For a further check, center-punch the piece and try drilling it. With these tests you can assure yourself that you can anneal the material, work and shape it, and later harden and temper it.

How Steel Hardens

The following discussion, although a highly simplified presentation of steel's behavior when heated, may be disregarded. If you follow the procedures given you will still be successful at hardening and tempering your projects. It is certainly true that prior to the modern technology of metallurgy, microscopic examination of steel samples, and all the rest, the old-time smiths hardened and tempered without having the least notion of what took place in the steel when they did it.

Nevertheless, it helps to know why you're doing certain things in almost any technique, and having a mental picture of the changes that occur as you heat or cool steel is no exception. If you were to examine a polished sample of fully soft carbon steel under a metallurgist's microscope, you'd probably be struck by its mother-of-pearl appearance. Actually, such soft carbon steel is called "pearlite." What you are looking at is striations or mechanically mixed portions of iron in its ferrite form and iron carbide, the latter called "cementite." The proportions will vary depending upon the carbon content of the steel.

This steel, when heated, will reach a stage at slightly over 1,300°F. called the critical point. The cementite now starts to merge or go into solution with the ferrite, and if you could again examine it you'd see the pearlite layers start to disappear. Continued heating will cause the process to carry on to a second, upper critical point, where the cementite is totally in solution and a new product called "austenite" is formed.

If you now allow the heated steel to cool slowly it will again pass through the critical points, although somewhat lower ones, and resume its original, soft pearlite characteristics. If, however, the cooling is done abruptly by quenching the hot metal in a water or oil bath, another remarkable transformation occurs and an extremely hard, crystallike material, called

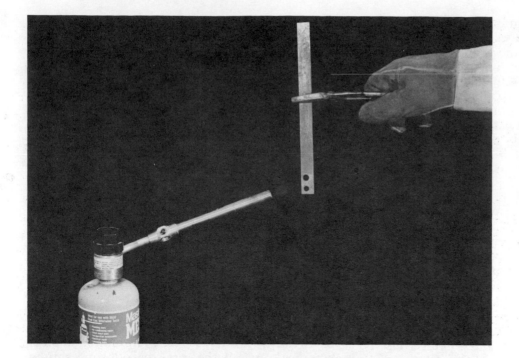

Any convenient heat source, such as a propane torch, may be used to bring your steel sample to cherry-red heat.

Protect your hands when quenching hot metal. The instant steam can burn your skin

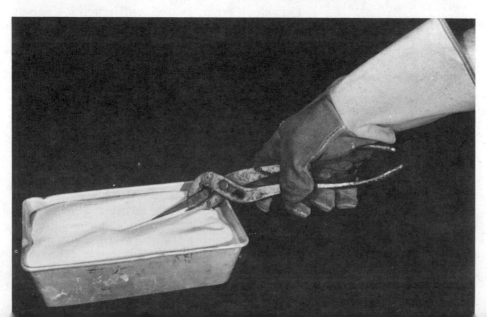

To determine if your steel sample will anneal, again heat it to cherry red and instead of quenching bury it in a box of dry insulating material such as fine sand where it will cool slowly.

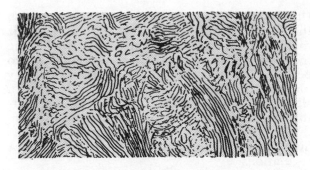

When the metallurgist etches and polishes a tiny sample of steel and photographs it through the microscope, the actual structure of the metal becomes visible, although it takes an expert to interpret it. This is a pearlite structure with iron carbide and ferrite arranged to have a pearl-like appearance.

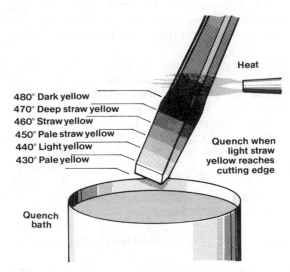

A rainbow of sorts forms on brightened steel as it is heated for tempering. Surprisingly, each color band is quite accurately representative of a definite temperature range.

you have to judge temperature is by color. Surprisingly, however, if you practice a little in dim light you'll soon learn to evaluate temperature quite accurately.

The table shows the rule-of-thumb colors. Note that steel has a barely visible, dark-red glow as it is heated above 1,000°F. From here the red brightens and intensifies up to about 1,450°, the hardening range for carbon steel. At this point the color starts to become orange and then yellow. At white heat the metal is almost

STEEL TEMPERATURE BY COLOR

Degrees Centigrade	Degrees Fahrenheit	Color
400	752	Red heat—Visible in the dark
474	885	Red heat in twilight
525	975	Red heat in daylight
581	1077	Red heat in sunlight
700	1292	Dark Red
800	1472	Dull Cherry Red
900	1652	Cherry Red
1000	1832	Bright Cherry Red
1100	2012	Orange Red
1200	2192	Orange Yellow
1300	2372	Yellow White
1400	2552	White Welding Heat
1500	2732	Brilliant White
1600	2912	Dazzling Bluish White

Courtesy Machinery's Handbook

When heating steel for hardening and annealing, try to do it where the light is consistent and not too bright. Most steels are hardened between dark red and dull cherry red.

"martensite," is formed. In practice, these transformations are very often incomplete and mixed structures may result. In addition, the percentage of carbon will have a strong influence on the exact temperature needed for a given result both when heating and cooling.

In general, hardening requires that the steel be brought to temperatures ranging from just under 1,400° to 1,550°. Very-high-carbon steels are normally hardened at 1,380° to 1,420°. For lower-carbon steels, 1,450° to 1,550° is recommended.

COLORS FOR TEMPERING

Degrees Centigrade	Degrees Fahrenheit	Color
221.1	430	Very Pale Yellow
226.7	440	Light Yellow
232.2	450	Pale Straw Yellow
237.8	460	Straw Yellow
243.3	470	Deep Straw Yellow
248.9	480	Dark Yellow
254.4	490	Yellow Brown
260.0	500	Brown Yellow
265.6	510	Spotted Red-Brown
271.1	520	Brown Purple
276.7	530	Light Purple
282.2	540	Full Purple
287.8	550	Dark Purple
293.3	560	Full Blue
298.9	570	Dark Blue

Home-Shop Hardening

Obviously, the above temperatures tend to be academic if you don't really know the carbon content of your workpiece and if the only way

Progressive changes in color as steel is tempered is fascinating to watch. It is also quite accurate and properly used will produce the desired hardness in the finished project. Quench at pale yellow for maximum hardness. As you approach purple and blue most hardness is gone.

molten. An important part of using this visual temperature scale is to do your heating and observing at some point in the shop where lighting is consistently fairly dim and is not influenced by time of day.

Quench baths.   Since the actual hardening takes place in the quench bath and since this involves the very rapid removal of heat, it follows that the heat-conduction characteristics of the bath will influence the final result. The bath will also effect the surface appearance of the steel. In some projects a layer of scale is of no importance; in other jobs you'd like a clean appearance. Even the way you handle the metal in the bath will have an effect. A red-hot piece of steel plunged into a water bath will naturally produce instant steam bubbles. If these bubbles coat the metal surface they act as an insulator and slow the cooling process. If you agitate the metal slowly to keep bringing it into contact with fresh water and free it of bubbles the rate of cooling will be faster.

On the other hand, a liquid with a slightly higher boiling point than plain water may cool the work more slowly, and this can be desirable for some projects if you want toughness inside and hardness outside. Extreme hardness is usually marked by brittleness or the inability to flex without fracture. A tough steel will be slightly less hard but able to take practical use as a tool.

If you read extensively about quenching and hardening techniques you will probably become more confused than ever. Some metalworkers say that plain water is perfectly adequate.

Others recommend adding enough rock salt to the water to make a saturated solution. This raises the boiling point about 15°F. Probably the most exotic brine quench bath was that said to be used by the ancient swordmakers. They plunged the red-hot blade into the body of a slave. The blood (brine) and slightly-higher-than-air-temperature quench supposedly produced an extremely fine blade. Today, this quench would probably be opposed by OSHA regulations.

But many metalworkers do not like water or brine at all. They swear that used crankcase oil is best, and some suggest cutting the crankcase oil by half with diesel fuel. Older books and smith's guides favor fats, especially rendered lamb fat. A few modern workers feel vegetable oils such as olive oil are best. Each may be right in his own way for his own shop and type of projects. The general rule is that plain water cools faster, brine next, and the various oil baths more slowly.

From a practical standpoint, a relatively thin knifeblade or small working part for a model engine will probably come out cleaner and with less scale, as well as being tougher and less brittle, if oil-quenched. Thicker parts are well suited to brine, and heavier pieces are handled as well or better in water. Common sense tells you that when all of the variables, including the fact that you don't really know the steel's carbon content, are added up, a little experimenting is worth more than endless advice.

Tempering.   To add to the mysterious ways of

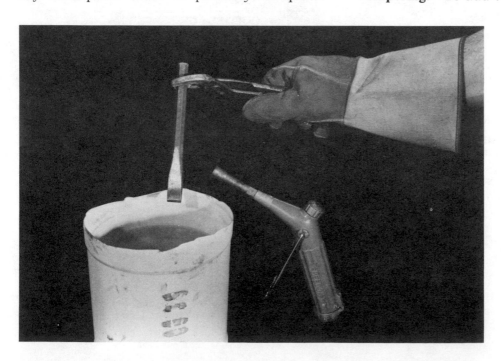

After heating and quenching your cold chisel, it should be glass hard when tried with a file. Now polish the cutting end brightly and heat well above the end. Quench instantly as the light-straw color band reaches the tip. Don't withdraw from the quench until tool is completely cool all the way through.

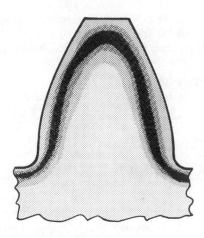

Hard on the outside, soft or tough on the inside, is best for some parts such as this gear tooth. By adding carbon through the case-hardening process, you can convert the outer layer of soft metal to hardened, high-carbon steel.

needlelike crystals of martensite to a more useful form called "troostite." And, once again, you will be called upon to make a color judgment, since this is the only way you have of knowing when your metal has reached the right temperature. Tempering not only alters the hardness but also relieves the internal strains from the original quenching bath.

STEEL TEMPERATURE, CRITICAL	
Percent Carbon	Critical Temperature for Hardening and Full Annealing
.10	1675–1760
.20	1625–1700
.30	1560–1650
.40	1500–1600
.50	1450–1560
.60	1440–1520
.70	1400–1490
.80	1370–1450
.90	1350–1440
1.00	1350–1440
1.10	1350–1440
1.30	1350–1440
1.50	1350–1440
1.70	1350–1440
1.90	1350–1440
2.00	1350–1440
3.00	1350–1440
4.00	1350–1440

Carbon steels have basic, critical temperatures for hardening and annealing. It's difficult to hold these accurately in the home shop, but note that the low-carbon steels require a higher (brighter) temperature than those with a high carbon content.

heat and steel, the truth is that you will seldom use your workpiece in its fully hardened state. After the initial hardening you will normally draw, or temper, the working surface to a degree of hardness best suited for its end use. For example, a cold chisel, with its rather massive, sturdy shape, is normally harder than a thinner blade on a wood chisel, a small punch, or a delicate tool where toughness is more important than brittle hardness.

Once again, you are going to use heat in the tempering process, but this time it will be only about 300° to 750°F. You want to transform the

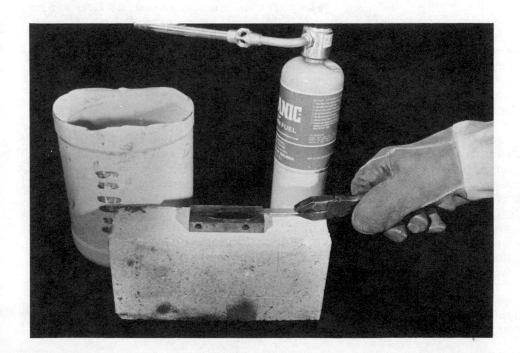

Thin steel, such as a small tool or knife blade, is easily tempered by using a larger piece as a heat source.

To practice tempering before trying it on a project, harden a piece of carbon steel as outlined. Or if you have a cold chisel that needs sharpening, use it for practice. If you use a chiscl, sharpen it first. Heat the metal to a bright cherry red for about 2″ from the cutting end and quench it. Your practice piece should now be almost glass-hard.

Use a sanding belt or other fairly fine abrasive to clean the surface to a polished brightness. The colors you will be watching for will appear on the bright surface. Now hold the piece in tongs at the end opposite the polished surface and apply heat well above the polished area. *Do not* heat the polished area directly. The heat must move to it through the metal. Apply the heat slowly so the metal is heated through rather than just on the surface. Remember, this time you are not going for a red heat.

In a short time you will see a very pale yellow color appear on the polished surface, and this color will start to move downward toward the cutting edge. As it moves you'll note that a succession of other colors will form near the hot area and also start to move toward the cutting edge. Each color band, as shown in the table, represents a rather narrow temperature range.

The trick is to quench the metal at the exact instant the desired color (temperature) reaches the critical portion. In the case of a cold chisel this would be the cutting edge and you'd want to quench at a light straw color. For a wood-cutting tool you'd let the color band progress until a darker straw appeared. As each color appears it represents a higher temperature and a softening of the original metal hardness.

Experiment with the above process and colors until you are fairly sure of the end results. But note that the above technique works best when you have something such as a chisel or a screwdriver with a limited portion devoted to the working area or edge and a substantial amount of metal available for gripping and heating with a torch.

Obviously, this would be less handy if you were tempering a small knifeblade or model part. To temper such parts, indirect heating works better. The simplest way is to heat a block of steel until it approaches or just reaches a dull-red heat. Let it cool until it loses color. Now lay or hold the work flat against the heated block until the desired color shows on the workpiece.

Other, more sophisticated methods for tempering use hot lead baths, hot salt baths, and precisely controlled electric furnaces beyond the capability of most home shops.

A final caution: Although the color scale given is representative of temperature, it is not representative of hardness. A piece of mild steel, which cannot be hardened, will color when polished and heated, but it will not harden.

Case Hardening

In all of the discussion above of hardening and tempering it was presumed that the steel had about .65% to 1.0% carbon content. Steels lacking carbon cannot be hardened totally, but a process called "case hardening" can produce an extremely hard skin a few thousandths of an inch thick on otherwise mild steel.

Case hardening leaves a surface that may be polished and fitted to high precision for wearing parts without inducing brittleness in the main mass of metal. Gunsmiths, modelmakers, and others who fabricate small working parts find it extremely useful.

The basic principle of case hardening is to add carbon to the surface of a steel lacking carbon. There are two ways to go about such carburizing; one is very old and the other newer and faster. The original process consisted of packing the part tightly in such materials as powdered charcoal, hoof shavings, horn shavings, various beans or nuts, or even leather scraps. The technique somewhat resembles roasting a pig at a Hawaiian luau. The carbonaceous material and the work were packed several inches thick with fire clay or the like and wrapped with wire screening and cloth and thoroughly dried. A more advanced method used a box or pot of fairly heavy metal with a lid that could be sealed. The object, in both cases, was to exclude air.

The pack then must be placed in a heat source of 1,600° to 1,700° for an extended period, such as overnight. The entrance of the carbon is a slow process, and time controls the depth of the action. After the heating period the pack is removed and the work quickly quenched while still at yellow heat. When cool, the outer surface will be glass-hard and in most cases must be tempered, like any carbon steel.

Although the above method produces good results, it is hard to come up with a sustained heat source around the modern house. More modern carburizing agents are available through machine-shop supply houses, and these require no more than heating the steel to a red heat and immersing the part in the powder or crystals. Reheating, with the crystals adhering to the metal, and a subsequent quenching produce an excellent case-hardened surface. These materials are beyond the scope of this book, but extreme caution is urged, since both the materials and the fumes may contain some form of cyanide, a deadly poison.

PART V
PROJECTS

BRASS LOG BASKET

Basket and base of this handsome fireplace accessory are formed from .035" sheet brass, or heavier. Hand-form the curve in the basket. Wrap-bend the scroll-shaped base using a vise and a 1¾" pipe or bar for a mandrel (see Chapter 8). Handle may be brass or iron. Note that the edges of the handle are bent by squeezing them between vise jaws to stiffen them.

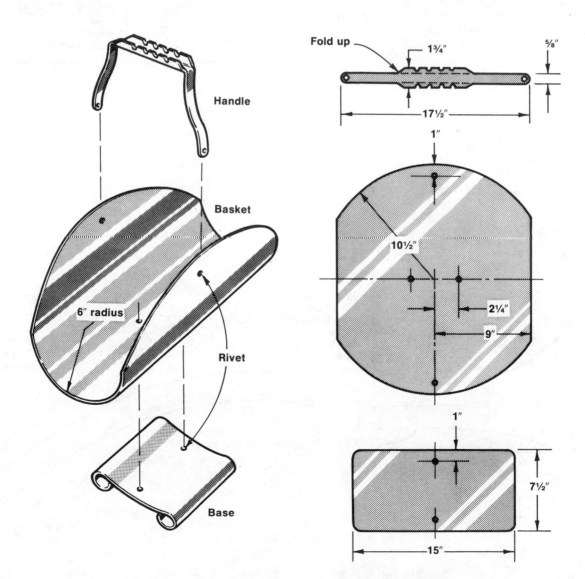

BRASS WATERING CAN

This watering can will challenge your metal-working skills in shaping and soldering. After soldering the top, lap, and handle joints, wipe away and polish clean any excess solder. Note that the top is laid out oversize, for shaping by art-metal hammering and planishing techniques, and fitted and soldered in place before trimming to the dotted outline. The decorative panels for each side of the can may be floral, initials, or a design of your choice. Saw them out with a jeweler's saw, file smooth, and solder to the sides by the sweat method of precoating the panel packs with solder. Secure them for soldering by binding with a few wraps of wire. Buff the completed project to a bright finish, clean, and spray with clear lacquer.

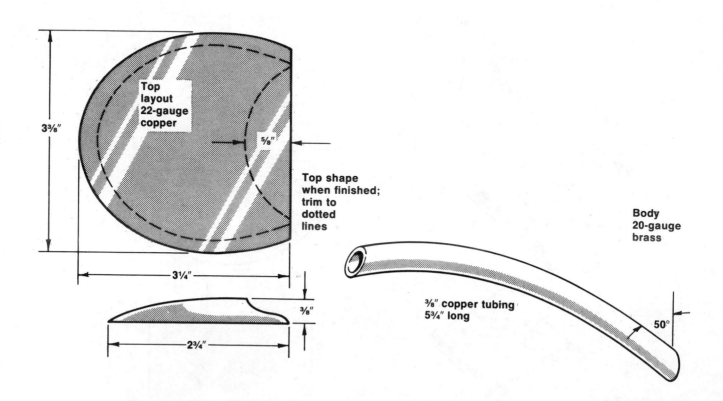

Top layout 22-gauge copper

3⅜"

5⅝"

Top shape when finished; trim to dotted lines

3¼"

⅜"

2¾"

Body 20-gauge brass

⅜" copper tubing 5¾" long

50°

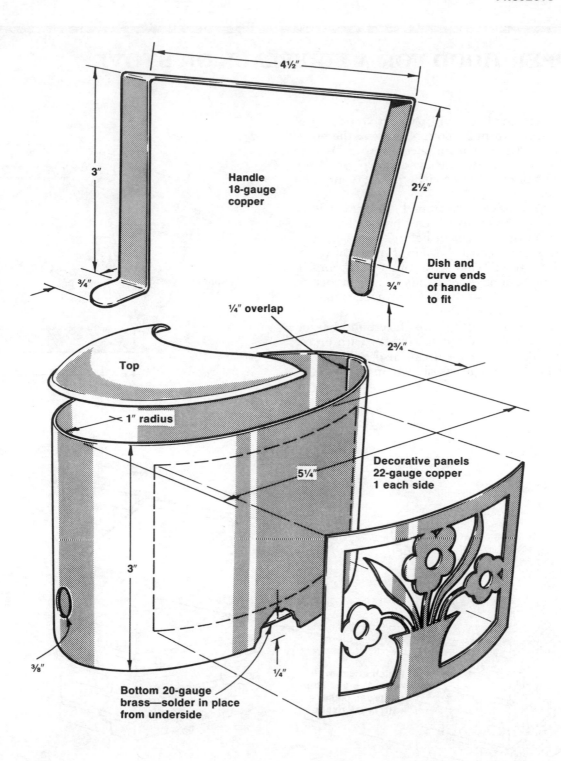

4½"

3"

Handle
18-gauge
copper

2½"

¾"

Dish and
curve ends
of handle
to fit

¾"

¼" overlap

Top

2¾"

1" radius

5¼"

Decorative panels
22-gauge copper
1 each side

3"

3"

¼"

⅜"

Bottom 20-gauge
brass—solder in place
from underside

COPPER HOOD FOR A FIREPLACE OR STOVE

A bright copper hood will prevent smudging of your fireplace front and often improve the burning action. Make it from sheet copper .045″ to .062″ thick. The dimensions shown are only starters; adapt as you wish to suit your own fireplace.

Once you have determined all dimensions, mock up the hood in stiff cardboard. This way, you can be sure it will fit before you begin cutting the metal. The 11½″ flap dimension is approximate; it will vary with minor variations in other dimensions and bends. The important thing is to size it so the hood projects squarely from the face of the fireplace.

Fill the corners with scraps fitted and brazed in place. Or glue scraps in corners with epoxy after installing. The hood can also be installed over a kitchen range, as shown in drawing.

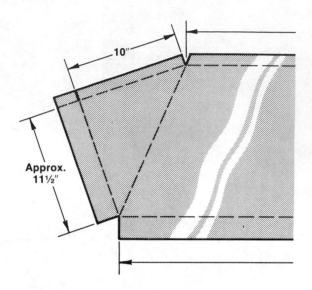

10″

Approx. 11½″

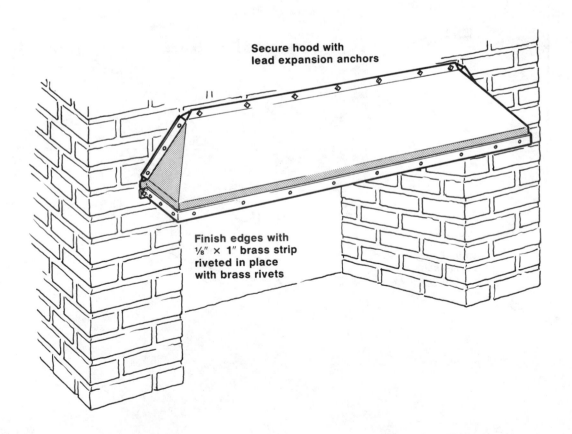

Secure hood with lead expansion anchors

Finish edges with ⅛″ × 1″ brass strip riveted in place with brass rivets

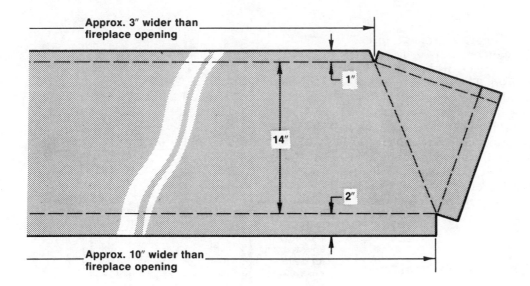

Approx. 3″ wider than
fireplace opening

1″

14″

2″

Approx. 10″ wider than
fireplace opening

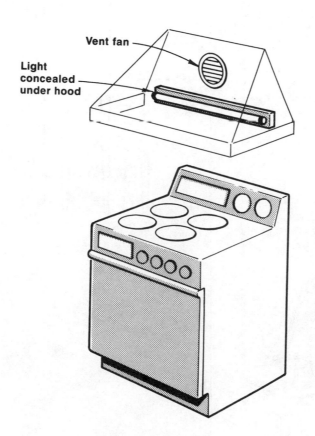

Vent fan

Light
concealed
under hood

FIREPLACE SET

Any source of adequate heat, a propane torch, or charcoal in a grill can be used to heat the mild steel used for this project. Either ⅝" or ½" square stock may be used. The dimensions and shapes shown may be altered to choice.

The fork and poker side prongs are preferably attached by welding or brazing. However, the fork could be made by cross-lap joint and rivets, and the hook could be eliminated. Shape the shovel handle end to match the shovel and rivet in place. For a decorative effect, the shanks of the fork, poker, and shovel may be cold twisted with a vise and wrench.

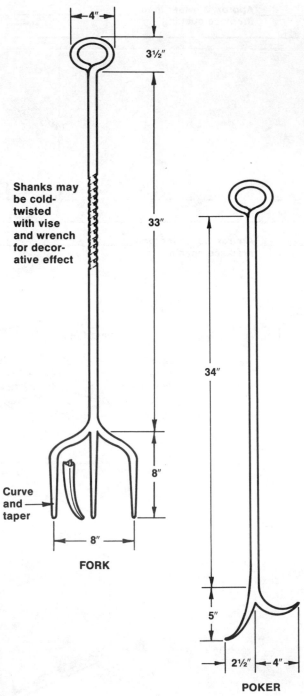

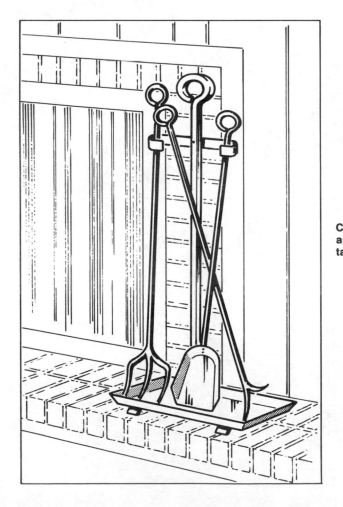

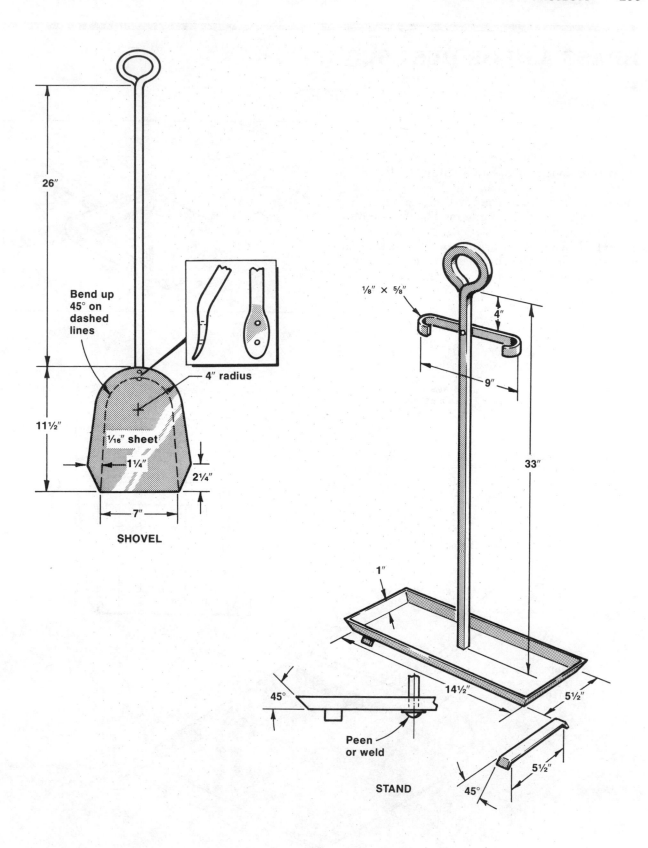

Bend up
45° on
dashed
lines

4" radius

26"

11½"

¹⁄₁₆" sheet

1¼"

2¼"

7"

SHOVEL

⅛" × ⅝"

4"

9"

33"

1"

45°

14½"

5½"

Peen
or weld

5½"

45°

STAND

BRASS ASH OR DUST SCOOP

This attractive scoop is bent from .035″ or slightly heavier sheet brass. Start with the approximate layout shown but leave some extra metal for final fit of rounded ears after rolling back of scoop to 1⅜″ diameter. The handle must be tapered and a brass socket bent and fitted. Socket is inserted in a hole in the back of the pan and held with a brass screw. Buff all brass parts to a bright finish.

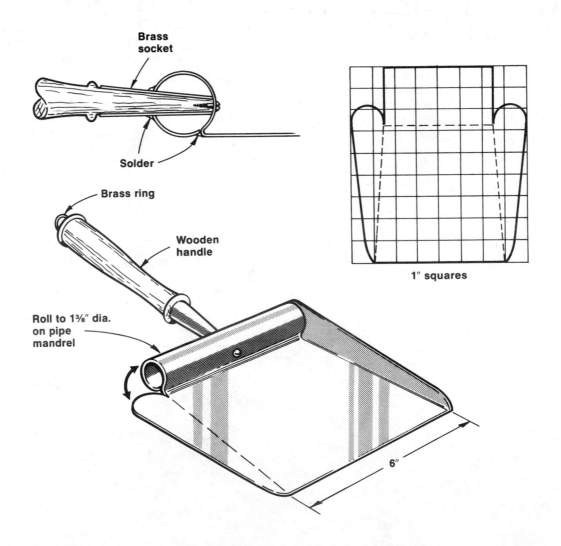

Brass socket

Solder

Brass ring

Wooden handle

Roll to 1⅜″ dia. on pipe mandrel

6″

1″ squares

WEATHERCOCK

This handsome weathercock always heads into the wind. Make it of ¹⁄₁₆″ mild steel sheet, brass or copper. With a coat of rust-inhibiting paint the steel will last many years. The body of the arrow is made by bending down flanges on a long, narrow diamond-shaped layout. The arrow head is double thickness. The pivot parts should be fitted to a loose, free-running fit. After assembly, be sure your weathercock balances on the pivot. If necessary, trim or add solder to balance. Brazing is the best assembly method since high winds impose violent loads especially on the rooster's feet.

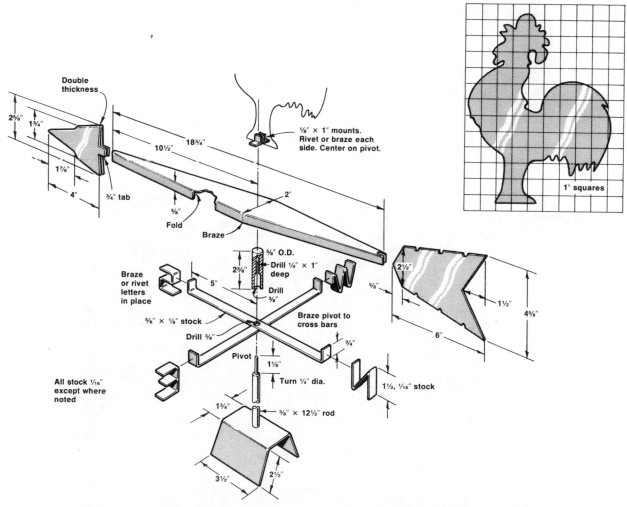

WROUGHT-IRON PORCH RAILING

This porch railing is made of standard steel straps, bars, or tubing. If you decide to use flat stock for the spindles, you can achieve a decorative wrought-iron effect by twisting the ends. To do this, lock the spindle in a vise 4″ from the end, grip the spindle with a wrench 2″ from the end, and twist. Heating is unnecessary. Alternate methods of building the railing are shown in the insets.

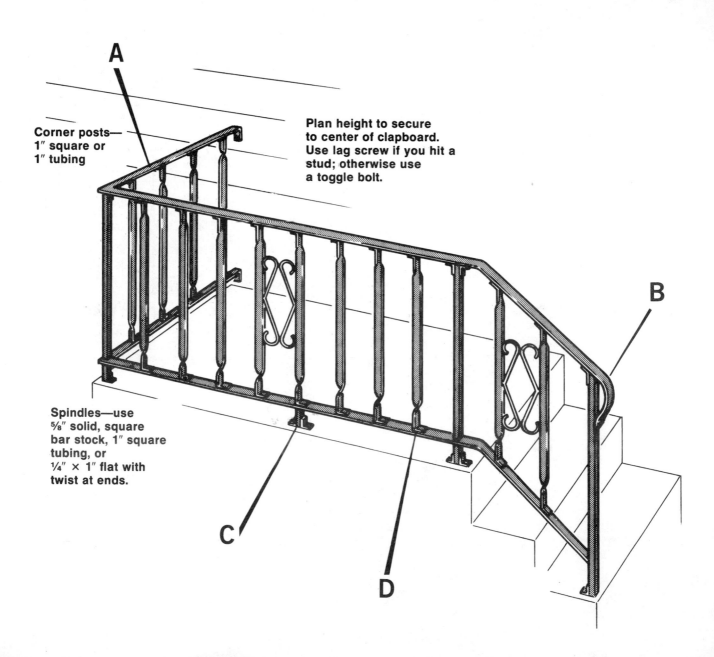

A

Corner posts—
1″ square or
1″ tubing

Plan height to secure
to center of clapboard.
Use lag screw if you hit a
stud; otherwise use
a toggle bolt.

B

Spindles—use
⅝″ solid, square
bar stock, 1″ square
tubing, or
¼″ × 1″ flat with
twist at ends.

C

D

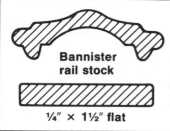

Bannister
rail stock

¼″ × 1½″ flat

For top rail
use either shaped
bannister stock or
flat stock. Rail
stock requires
welding or
brazing spindles.

A

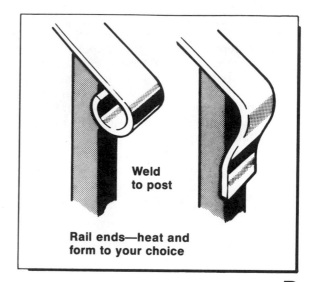

Weld
to post

Rail ends—heat and
form to your choice

B

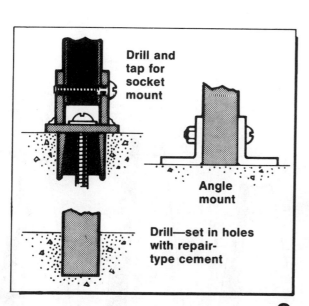

Drill and
tap for
socket
mount

Angle
mount

Drill—set in holes
with repair-
type cement

C

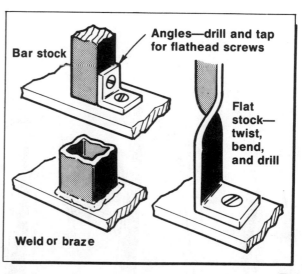

Bar stock

Angles—drill and tap
for flathead screws

Weld or braze

Flat
stock—
twist,
bend,
and drill

D

METAL CHESSMEN

Turn these chessmen on a lathe from brass and aluminum or other contrasting metals. When you've made one set you can use them for patterns for lost-wax casting or sand-casting other sets.

Turn all pieces using headstock chuck and tailstock center. Finish the upper tapers and balls last, as a cut-off. Bore the castle end of the rooks first; before turning the taper, add a small center inside and proceed with remaining cuts. Remember, if you use brass and aluminum, the lathe tool must have a very different rake angle. Adhere felt pads to bases when finished.

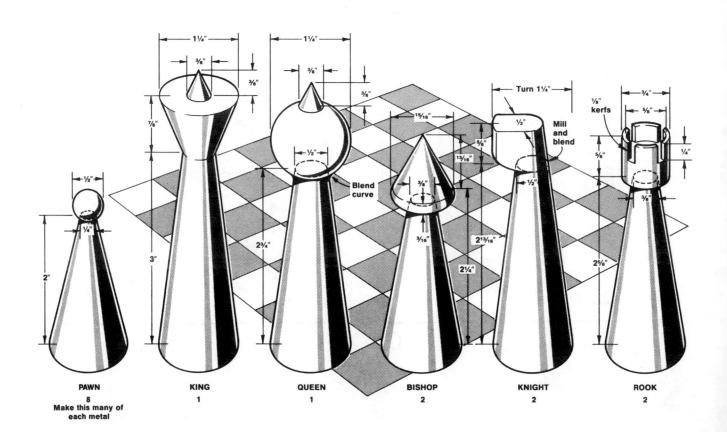

PAWN
8
Make this many of
each metal

KING
1

QUEEN
1

BISHOP
2

KNIGHT
2

ROOK
2

INDEX

INDEX